FROM LEARNING PROCESSES TO COGNITIVE PROCESSES:

Essays in Honor of William K. Estes

Volume 2

Participants at Harvard symposium honoring W. K. Estes (September, 1989). (1) R. D. Luce, (2) C. Krumhansl, (3) R. Falmagne, (4) M. Gluck, (5) J. Kagan, (6) P. Holzman, (7) E. Hilgard, (8) D. LaBerge, (9) G. Bower, (10) D. Medin, (11) J. Young, (12) G. Wolford, (13) G. McKoon, (14) J. Townsend, (15) C. Lee, (16) C. Izawa, (17) P. Suppes, (18) D. Noreen, (19) E. Smith, (20) S. W. Link, (21) R. Day, (22) S. Kosslyn, (23) W. K. Estes, (24) V. Reyna, (25) A. Healy, (26) R. Shiffrin, (27) R. Ratcliff (photograph courtesy of S. W. Link).

FROM
LEARNING PROCESSES
TO
COGNITIVE PROCESSES:

Essays in Honor of
William K. Estes

Volume 2

Edited by
ALICE F. HEALY
University of Colorado
STEPHEN M. KOSSLYN
Harvard University
RICHARD M. SHIFFRIN
Indiana University

LEA LAWRENCE ERLBAUM ASSOCIATES, PUBLISHERS
1992   Hillsdale, New Jersey   Hove and London

Lawrence Erlbaum Associates, Inc., Publishers
365 Broadway
Hillsdale, New Jersey 07642

Library of Congress Cataloging-in-Publication Data

Essays in honor of William K. Estes / edited by Alice F. Healy,
    Stephen M. Kosslyn, Richard M. Shiffrin.
        p.   cm.
    Includes bibliographical references and indexes.
    Contents: v. 1. From learning theory to connectionist theory — v.
    2. From learning processes to cognitive processes.
        ISBN 0-8058-1097-8 (hard : v. 1). — ISBN 0-8058-0759-4 (hard : v.
    2). — ISBN 0-8058-1098-6 (pbk. : v. 1). — ISBN 0-8058-0760-8 (pbk.
    : v. 2)
        1. Learning, Psychology of—Mathematical models.   2. Cognition.
    I. Estes, William Kaye.   II. Healy, Alice F.   III. Kosslyn, Stephen
    Michael, 1948–   .   IV. Shiffrin, Richard M.
    BF318.E86   1992
    153.1'5—dc20

                                                                    91-39697
                                                                         CIP

Printed in the United States of America
10 9 8 7 6 5 4 3 2 1

Contents

Preface

These two volumes are dedicated to the distinguished research career of William K. Estes. The first volume is entitled, "From learning theory to connectionist theory" and emphasizes mathematical psychology; the second volume is entitled, "From learning processes to cognitive processes" and emphasizes cognitive psychology. We will not attempt to recount here the details of Bill Estes' illustrious and productive career, which included training at the University of Minnesota followed by faculty positions at Indiana, Stanford, The Rockefeller, and finally Harvard University. Much information about Bill's career is included in two illuminating autobiographical chapters (Estes, 1982, 1989). The chapters in the present volumes are written by many of Bill's students and colleagues who mark different stages of his career. Undoubtedly, there are many other of his friends, colleagues, "children," "grandchildren," and "step children" who would desire to add their contributions, but space limitations did not make this possible. Bill has admitted that the number of students who have worked with him is so great that "even a list would be formidable" (Estes, 1989, p. 122). Despite the large number of his friends and students, it is clear that Bill has had a profound and lasting impact on each one of us, and we all hold Bill in a special place in our hearts. This deep and sincere affection should be evident from the brief reminiscences or personal comments included in many of the chapters in the present volumes. In addition, to convey a more intimate view of Bill's interactions with his students and friends, we present next some particularly appropriate comments made by one of his students, Robert A. Bjork; these comments were given at a banquet honoring Bill at Harvard University on September 16, 1989.

REFERENCES

Estes, W. K. (1982). *Models of learning, memory, and choice: Selected papers* (pp. 337–364). New York: Praeger.
Estes, W. K. (1989). In G. Lindzey (Ed.), *A history of psychology in autobiography* (Vol. VIII, pp. 94–124). Stanford, CA: Stanford University Press.

A.F.H.
S.M.K.
R.M.S.

William Kaye Estes as
Mentor, Colleague, and Friend

Robert A. Bjork
University of California, Los Angeles

In 1975, at a dinner held at the Meetings of the Psychonomic Society in honor of the 25th anniversary of the publication of Bill Estes's "Towards a statistical theory of learning," I described Bill as a pure accumulator of research interests. He has been able, somehow, to move his research focus over the years from mechanisms of reinforcement and punishment in animals, to human verbal learning and memory, to visual information processing, and to problems of choice and categorization without really abandoning any of those interests along the way. Other speakers at the 1975 dinner stressed his equally remarkable ability to anticipate new developments in a given field.

How are we to understand how one person could be so flexible and innovative while also maintaining a striking continuity in the style and standards that characterize his research? Part of the answer, I think, was provided by Bill himself at that 1975 dinner. David LaBerge had entertained those present with a story about Bill's famous long pauses in one-on-one conversations, saying that he had once got up the courage to ask Bill to explain those long response latencies. He said he outlined what seemed to be the reasonable hypotheses—methodical central processing, rapid processing coupled with excessive editing, rapid processing leading to a conclusion that a given comment or question did not merit a timely reply, and so forth—and asked Bill which was correct. David reported that Bill's response latency to that question had yet to be recorded.

When it was Bill's turn to speak that evening, he commented on the fact that a number of people had referred to his long pauses and that people had also wondered how he had been so able to anticipate important new directions in the field. He said he was prepared to answer both questions, which he did in a singularly clever and gracious fashion. Looking out over the collection of his students, colleagues, and friends in attendance, he said that there was one answer to both questions, "During those pauses, I have been listening to you."

In a very real sense, I *do* think Bill Estes has been listening to us. We, his students, colleagues, and postdocs, have brought our interests to Bill. Those interests have sometimes been triggered by Bill's own work, but sometimes not. He has been willing to listen to us in either case, and he has helped to shape the quality, rigor, and direction of our work. We, in turn, have had the chance to influence Bill Estes. Did Bill, for example, trigger the interest of Doug Medin and Ed Smith in categorization, or was it the other way around? I think the latter was the primary direction of influence. He has done us all the honor of thinking that we may have a good idea—that our new problem may be important and interesting, or that we may have seen a new way to approach an old problem.

Bill has been able to work effectively with all of us, males and females, younger and older, those of us who won't shut up and those of us who are painfully shy, the modelers and the empiricists. He has put his stamp on all of us, but that stamp has nothing to do with telling us what to study. He has never pressured his students to adopt his interests or theories. Saying that one is an Estes student does not have much value as a predictor of one's research domain. His stamp has to do with a commitment to the experimental method, a commitment to rigorous theorizing, and a commitment to scholarship.

Bill's flexibility and ability to listen have kept him young in spirit and in tune with current events. People of his age tend, I have observed, to get together with their cronies at meetings like Psychonomics. No doubt we, too, not that many years from now, will be eating dinner together and grumbling that graduate students are not like they used to be, and that in one way or another the field has gone to hell. Not Bill. He and Kay are surrounded by younger people at such meetings. The "Estes Dinner," which has become a tradition at Psychonomics, has nearly gotten out of hand; getting reservations for a group of that size has become difficult.

In the interests of providing a completely veridical picture, it should be emphasized that Bill is not always the easiest person in the world with whom to work. A serious problem for many of us is that Bill is an impossible model. There is such a thing as having *too* much respect for a person—in the sense that it can impede the natural give and take in the collaborative process. On any of a number of dimensions, it seems hopeless to set one's sights on matching Bill's accomplishments—as a scientist, as a writer, and as a human being. I remember as a graduate student feeling depressed at the ease with which Bill seemed able to improve my laboriously-generated scientific prose. I despaired of ever becoming a good writer. One particularly devastating instance took place when Bill was working over a draft of my dissertation. On one page, where I had labored to clarify a complex point, Bill drew one of his faint pencil lines from the middle of a sentence in the first paragraph—through the entire second paragraph—to the middle of a sentence in the third paragraph, and he replaced everything in between with the single word "provide."

Bill's contributions as an editor, of course, would stand by themselves as an impressive career achievement for most people. In addition to editing books such as the *Handbook of Learning and Cognitive Processes* series, he has edited the *Journal of Comparative and Physiological Psychology, The Psychological Review,* and—at the present time—*Psychological Science.* At the 1975 dinner, David Grant read a series of devastatingly funny excerpts from some of Bill's reviews of manuscripts submitted to the *Journal of Experimental Psychology* while Grant was Editor. They were devastating and funny because such damning comments were stated in such a charitable and gentle fashion (e.g., "In work submitted to this journal, it is customary for there to be an independent variable . . ."). John Swets and myself were recipients of a more recent example of Bill's gentle phrasing: "In the paragraphs following the first one we certainly run into a stretch of rather dry reading." Note that, as stated, Bill does not blame us for that deadly stretch of prose; rather, it is as though he is saying that we have this common problem—that we are all in the same boat. Given that John Swets had drafted that particular section, I, of course, thought Bill's comment was more humorous than John did.

A final unusual aspect of working with Bill that merits mention is that he is impossible to interrupt. Some of his response latencies may set records, but once he is launched on a point or comment he wants to make he has unusual inertia. Even Pat Suppes, in their joint seminars at Stanford, was typically unable to break in once Bill got going. In a famous incident in the Friday-afternoon research talks at Ventura Hall, Karl Pribram did manage to break in, but, as it turned out, at his own peril. A student working with Karl had presented some results that seemed to defy interpretation. Bill started to put forth a possible interpretation by saying, "suppose there are a series of little drawers in the brain . . . ," at which point Karl interjected, "I have never seen any drawers in there." Without missing a beat, Bill said, "They're very small" and continued with his argument.

It is my goal in these remarks to speak not only for myself but for all of us who have been privileged to be Bill's students and, later, his colleagues and friends. I would be remiss if I did not add some final comments about Bill as a person and about his relationship with Kay. Bill has always been there for us, whether that meant never missing a Friday-afternoon seminar, being in his office at Indiana/Stanford/Rockefeller/Harvard when we needed to see him, or when we dropped by from out of town to visit, or being out there in the audience when our paper was scheduled for an early Saturday morning at Psychonomics. He has worried about us, written letters for us, and opened his home for us. Except to Kay, possibly, he may never have uttered an uncharitable word about any of us. In small ways and, sometimes, in very big ways, he has been there when different ones of us needed him.

We have been doubly enriched by being Bill's students, colleagues, and friends because that has meant that we have fallen under Kay's wing as well. It is impossible to reflect on Bill Estes as a person and as a scientist without thinking of Bill and Kay as an inseparable and mutually complementary team. Their warmth, their humor, and their mutual respect have been a joy for all of us. They each in different ways act as though the other is a profound treasure. They are both right.

1

Test Trials Contributions to Optimization of Learning Processes: Study/Test Trials Interactions

Chizuko Izawa
Tulane University

In fall, 1962, I designed my first experiment to unveil the effects of unreinforced test (T) trials. The occasion was a seminar chaired by a newly arrived professor at Stanford, William K. Estes. From said experiment evolved the fundamental idea for my 1965 doctoral dissertation, which, it turned out, was the first one of many he supervised during his productive tenure at Stanford. That initial involvement has consistently underpinned my subsequent long-term projects (e.g., Izawa, 1989b); many of these were inspired by the theoretical framework of Estes' (1955) stimulation fluctuation model. It deserves to be viewed as his most elegant and powerful contribution *so far*—a remarkable pinnacle of creativity! But despite the attention it commanded (e.g., Bower, 1967; Izawa, 1966; Peterson & Peterson, 1959), many more potential opportunities were unexplored. Given its enormous significance, the model's theoretical foundations deserved fuller exploitation. This was one of the reasons for its incorporation into the test trial potentiating model (Izawa, 1971b), which evolved into the retention interval model (Izawa, 1981c), and later still into the identity model (Izawa, 1985a, 1985b). There can be no better tribute by a student to her mentor than elaborating and enhancing his teachings; a highly valued virtue in the Japanese tradition (see Appendix). I was his first PhD from Japan.

Although Gates (1917) noted that retrieval practice of recitation is an important positive factor in memory, the majority of theoretical and empirical investigations in learning and memory since Ebbinghaus (1885) have primarily concentrated on study (S) or reinforced (R) trials. For example, in cued-recall (paired-associate) learning situations, T and S phases for each item come alternately within the cycle as T-S, T-S, . . . under the anticipation method. But under the study-test method, S and T are administered on separate cycles. However, since S and T cycles come alternately as $S_1T_1S_2T_2$ . . . , it is impossible to isolate T effects. (A cycle is defined as one run-through of the n-item list, one item at a time.)

In order to examine the functions of T trials per se, it is necessary to administer T trials (cycles) i (≥ 2) successive times after j-th S cycle (cf. Izawa, 1966) under the modified study-test method as:

$$S_jT_1T_2T_3 \ldots T_i \tag{1}$$

where T_i shows the effects on all i-1 T trials following S_j.

Program 1 may be compared with:

$$S_1S_2S_3S_4 \ldots S_{i+1} \tag{2}$$

Comparisons of Programs 1 and 2 are also often used in short-term memory (STM) design with individual items. For instance, by letting $j = 1$, $i = 3$ (STTT vs. SSSS), Hogan and Kintsch (1971) found S trials to be more effective than T trials for immediate recall, but the opposite held for the delayed recall Ts. If measured via recognition, however, S trials were better than T trials for delayed Ts as well. Although the same results were replicated in Experiments 1 and 2 by Thompson, Wenger, and Bartling (1978) and in Experiment 1 by Wenger, Thompson, and Bartling (1980), the two conditions (Programs 1 and 2) resulted in the same levels of performances on immediate or short retention intervals. However, in line with Slamecka and Graf (1978), the STTT condition excelled over the SSSS condition with 48-hour delayed tests in Experiment 3 by Thompson et al. (1978) and in Experiments 2, 3, and 4 by Wenger et al. (1980). Using STST versus STTT comparisons, Birnbaum and Eichner (1971) also obtained similar outcomes from S and T trials, but they attributed their results to different processes.

On the one hand, Mandler, Worden, and Graesser (1974) found the number of prior T presentations to have no effect on subsequent recall, and Bregman and Wiener (1970) contended that T effects were not as large as those of S trials. On the other hand, empirical effects of T trials were reported to be as large as that of S trials (e.g., Lachman & Laughery, 1968; Rosner, 1970; Tulving, 1967). By far the most extreme position was advanced by Whitten and Bjork (1977) and Whitten and Leonard (1980); it assumed the virtual identity of S and T trials.

Varied findings and interpretations can in part be attributed to different types of memory measures (e.g., free versus cued recall, recall versus recognition—although the same processes are often assumed by Wenger et al., 1980, and Lockhart, Craik, & Jacoby, 1976); these include different stages of acquisition or memory states, and single versus multiple S conditions, among others.

Studies utilizing a single S trial followed by multiple T trials, with a very small number of items (STM design as shown) suffer serious limitations. Observations are restricted to only one S opportunity, that is, a very early stage of acquisition, where accumulated and/or interactive effects of S and T trials (with a large number of items under the list design) cannot be demonstrated. Equally unsatisfactory are the studies that provide successive T trials at the end of acquisition only; for example, a block of 5 to 16 T trials after criteria of 87.5–100% correct performance were attained (Goss, Morgan, & Golin, 1959; Richardson, 1958). Similarly, those administering successive Ts only at the intermediate learning stages are inappropriate.

In order to build a viable theory as well as for empirical and applicational purposes, a systematic investigation must address all stages of acquisition. Ample evidence indicates S and T trials do interact and are memory-state (acquisition stage) dependent (e.g., Bregman & Wiener, 1970; Izawa, 1966–1988; Lachman & Laughery, 1968). Therefore, we propose to employ the basic replication unit (pattern) in Program 1 many times during the experiment.

Let us call it *Replication Program;* by letting $j = 1$, we obtain:

$$S \ T_1 T_2 T_3 \ldots T_i. \tag{1'}$$

In several scores of studies, acquisition under Replication Program 1′ progressed as $S_1 T_1 T_2 \ldots T_i$, $S_2 T_1 T_2 \ldots T_i$, $S_3 T_1 T_2 \ldots T_i$, $\ldots$ until a given criterion was met. Data are discussed in terms of (a) *within replication,* that is, performance over successive T trials (T_1 vs. T_2, T_2 vs. T_3, $\ldots$, T_{i-1} vs. T_i, etc.) following S_j (a given S); and (b) *between replication,* that is, comparisons of the effects of S_1 vs. S_2, S_2 vs. S_3, $\ldots$, S_{j-1} vs. S_j, etc. The distinction between these two aspects of the data is essential.

By varying i up to 19, Izawa (1966–1988) consistently demonstrated a striking invariability[1] of performance over successive T trials at all phases of acquisition. These results were reinforced via findings at one or more acquisition phases by Allen, Mahler, and Estes (1969), Birnbaum and Eichner (1971), Hogan and Kintsch (1971), Landauer and Bjork (1978), Rosner (1970), and Wenger et al. (1980). No evidence from the acquisition phase supports either performance increment (learning) or decrement (forgetting) on T trials per se following each S trial (for striking examples, see Izawa, 1970a); this phenomenon is referred to as the *forgetting-prevention effect.*

Another salient empirical function of T trials uncovered via the repetitive program was that the greater the i, the better the performance: The learning curves plotted as a function of preceding S trials neatly line up in accordance with the density of T trials up to $i = 7$ (Izawa 1966–1988), demonstrating the T trials' *potentiation effect* on subsequent S trials.

---

[1]Significant improvement observed over the successive Ts in long-term memory search such as the names of the 50 states or the names of the U.S. presidents (e.g., Roediger & Challis, 1989) may be attributed to quite different processes, because a longer retrieval time was a likely factor. Similarly, a large drop in performance in distance learning (e.g., Hagman, 1983; Izawa & Patterson, 1989) may be primarily based on the size of response deviations from the target (rather than on either "correct" or "incorrect" as in cued-recall learning with linguistic materials). Neither case seems to involve any *new* encoding on T trials per se.

Program 2 enables us to obtain S trial effects unadulterated by any T trials. However, without any T, we have no means to observe subjects' performances. To make possible the needed observation at varied acquisition phases, Replication Program 3 is proposed as:

$$S_1S_2S_3 \ldots S_u \, T \tag{3}$$

When we combine Replication Programs 3 and 1' we obtain:

$$S_1S_2S_3 \ldots S_u \, T_1T_2T_3 \ldots T_i \tag{4}$$

where $u \geq 1$, $i \geq 0$; their respective values used by Izawa during the last 25 years were $1 \leq u \leq 8$, $0 \leq i \leq 19$.

Replication Program 5 was developed to isolate the effects of T trials from that of time taken by the T trials by replacing all first $i-1$ Ts in Replication Program 1' by blank (B, nothing was presented) or neutral (N, naming colored geometrical figures, irrelevant to the learning task) trials (differences between B and N trials can be regarded as negligible; Izawa, 1988):

$$S \, B_1B_2B_3 \ldots B_{i-1} \, T, \text{ or } S \, N_1N_2N_3 \ldots N_{i-1} \, T \tag{5}$$

which also serves as spacing variations between S and T cycles. Most intriguingly, the performance on the T of Replication Program 5 was significantly inferior to T_i ($= T_{i-1} = T_{i-2} = \ldots = T_1$) of Replication Program 1': The greater the i, the worse the performance in Replication Program 5 (the complete opposite to Replication Program 1'). Two new graphic presentations of this state of affairs are based on data by Izawa (1971b, Experiments 3 and 4) in Fig. 1.1. Forgetting does occur on B trials.

Because no such forgetting resulted with T trials in Replication Program 1' conditions, T trials not only effectively prevent forgetting, but also potentiate subsequent S trials. Yet, in Replication Program 5, the varied retention interval between S and its subsequent T per replication may be contaminated. To remedy this, Replication Program 6 was devised to measure the effect of each S on the cycle immediately following every S:

$$S \, T \, B_1B_2B_3 \ldots B_{i-1}, \text{ or } S \, T \, N_1N_2N_3 \ldots N_{i-1}. \tag{6}$$

No significant differences were observed in Replication Program 6 conditions (Fig. 1.2), originally prepared from Izawa's data (1971b, Experiment 5 and 6, $1 \leq i \leq 5$). The amount of forgetting that may occur during Cycle 1 immediately following each S, till the last T per replication, may be expressed reliably as in Fig. 1.3. For example, let $i = 2$. When the two cycles following an S were T trials as in Condition ST_1T_2 (Program 1'), both T cycles produced about the same performance levels, that is, $T_1 = T_2$. However, by replacing T with a B (blank) trial, the result was substantial forgetting in Condition SBT_2 (Program 5). In order to assess the amount of forgetting incurred during a $i - 1$ (i being 2 in this example) B trial, we may compare the performance T_1 ($= T_2$) in Condition

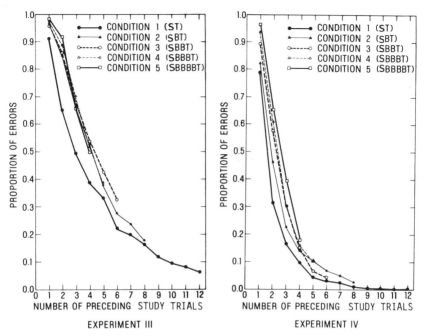

FIG. 1.1.   Performance for Replication Program 5, $SB_1B_2 \ldots B_{i-1}T$ with $1 \le i \le 5$ conducted by Izawa (1971b, Experiments 3 & 4, where the study [S] trial was referred to as the reinforcement [R] trial, i.e., $RB_1B_2 \ldots B_{i-1} T = SB_1B_2 \ldots B_{i-1}T$).

ST_1T_2 or in Condition ST_1B (Program 6) with that of T_2 in Condition SBT_2. In Fig. 1.3, the forgetting occurred between the first and the second (i-th, i being 2) T cycle, expressed as the distance between open and solid reverse-triangles. In general, the greater the number of B trials (i.e., the size of i) in Program 6 versus Program 5, the greater the forgetting. The most salient demonstration of this is seen in the right panel of Fig. 1.3.

What is striking in Replication Program 6 is the apparent absence of spaced practice effects produced by the number of B (N) trials, because Condition ST = STB = STBB = STBBB = STBBBB. Alternatively, there may be a special overriding effect on the T, given immediately after each S cycle, a T witnessed frequently; we may designate it as $T_{(1)}$ (Allen et al., 1969; Izawa, 1966–1988).

THE DISTRIBUTED (SPACED) PRACTICE EFFECT

Whereas the spacing effect of individual items can be easily demonstrated (Hintzman, 1974), the *spaced* or *distributed practice effect* under the list design

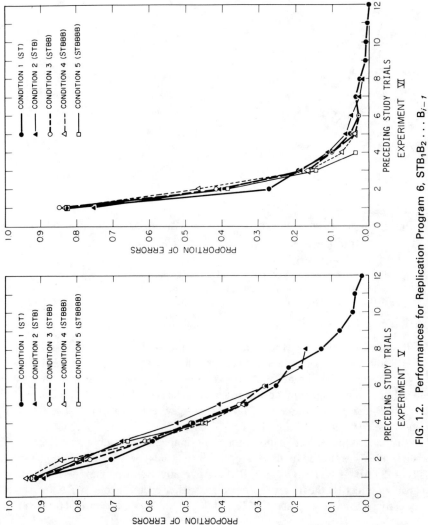

FIG. 1.2. Performances for Replication Program 6, $STB_1B_2 \ldots B_{i-1}$ with $1 \leq i \leq 5$ conducted by Izawa (1971b, Experiments 5 & 6, where the study [S] trial was referred to as the reinforcement [R] trial, i.e., $RTB_1B_2 \ldots B_{i-1} = STB_1B_2 \ldots B_{i-1}$).

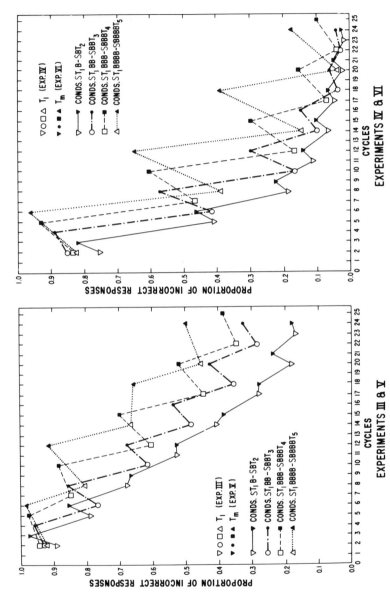

FIG. 1.3. Forgetting occurring on B (blank) trials, where nothing was presented, by comparing T_1 and T_i, with $2 \leq i \leq 5$, in Replication Programs 6 and 5 by holding i constant in Experiments 3 versus 5, and 4 versus 6 by Izawa (1971b).

eluded experienced investigators for several decades (see Underwood & Ekstrand, 1967). Via the novel approach as shown, however, Izawa (1971a) pinpointed the cause of this longstanding difficulty: (a) inadequate variations of spaced practice dimension by adherence to the traditional anticipation method, and (b) the complete disregard of the T trial as a "task."

From the current perspective, the traditional spaced practice of S trials may be expressed as in Replication Program 7:

$$S \; B_1B_2B_3 \ldots B_i, \text{ or } S \; N_1N_2N_3 \ldots N_i, \qquad (7)$$

which allows the manipulation of spaced practice (rest) effect by the size of i. However, we need at least one T at the end of the experiment after m replications:

$$S_1B_1 \ldots B_i \, S_2B_1 \ldots B_i \ldots S_mB_1 \ldots B_iT, \text{ or}$$
$$S_1N_1 \ldots N_i \, S_2N_1 \ldots N_i \ldots S_mN_1 \ldots N_iT \qquad (8)$$

Using Replication Program 8 ($0 \leq i \leq 5$ and $5 \leq m \leq 18$), spaced practice (rest) effects were indeed positive (e.g., Izawa, 1968, 1976, 1988) in addition to intercycle interval manipulations (Izawa, 1971a).[2]

Given the latter findings, why does Replication Program 6 not show any positive spaced practice effects attributable to N (rest) cycles? Note further, spacing of S trials was identical for both Replication Programs 6 and 7. The only difference between Programs 6 and 7 was $T_{(1)}$, a T trial given on the cycle immediately following each S. Is the $T_{(1)}$ work trial more powerful in generating the spaced practice effect than the (N) rest trial?

To view the issue from a different perspective, N (B, rest) trials seem to generate three different kinds of effects: positive effects with Replications Programs 7–8, negative effects with Replication Program 5, and no effect with Replication Program 6. Apparently, then, the empirical effects of the rest interval are controlled by the type of Replication Programs administered.

Notice, in particular, that *the key to the seemingly varied effects may lie in the programming of T trials.* When no T trial is given within replication (Replication Program 7), N (B) trials produce positive effects; but when a T trial is given at the beginning or end of the replication immediately following an S, the T trial produces either neutral (Replication Program 6) or negative (Replication Program 5) effects, respectively.

Furthermore, we introduce a novel variation of T trial spaced practice manipulations, under the list design, with new replication programs to investigate the target effects throughout the entire acquisition period. Landauer and Bjork

---

[2]In the current situations, intercycle intervals were kept to a minimum, 2 sec, and the spaced (distributed) practice dimension was manipulated by the number of B (blank) or N (neutral) cycles. In all studies viewed from the current perspective, a B cycle for an n-item list consisted of n exposures of blanks, and an N cycle consisted of naming n colored geometrical figures, which are regarded as neutral to the ongoing main learning task. B or N trials were presented at the same rate as S and T trials.

(1978) investigated spacing of T trials using people's names (relatively easy learning materials). However, because they only gave one S trial, their findings pose some limitations: Neither information regarding interactive processes nor cumulative effects of S and T throughout the acquisition phases were accessible. Under the list design, the only notable exception was Izawa (1971a), where spacing manipulations were achieved via the intercycle or interitem interval.

SPACED PRACTICE EFFECT OF TEST (T) TRIALS: A NOVEL EXPERIMENT

Under the modified study-test method all nine conditions of the present experiment had S trials on every eighth cycle, starting Cycle 1 as in Table 1.1. S trial spaced practice effects were held constant. Control, Condition 1 (STTTTTTT), is from Replication Program 1' with $i = 7$ where the T effect is likely to be optimal (Izawa, 1969). Conditions differ only as to how many and which of the 7 successive Ts are replaced by N (neutral) trials on which the learner named colored geometrical figures. Conditions STNTNTNT, STNNTNNT, and STNN-NNNT retained four, three, and two Ts per replication in spaced T trials, whereas Conditions STTTNNNN, SNNTTTNN, and SNNNNTTT all had three Ts in massed practice early, middle, and late in each replication. Conditions STNNN-NNN and SNNNNNNT had only one T each per replication at the beginning and at the end, respectively.

For explanatory convenience, let the subscript of a T (or N) be the number of Ts (Ns) experienced *per replication,* and the subscript in the parenthesis of a T (or N) be the respective trials occurring on the cycle after each S per replication. For example, Condition 1 can be expressed as $ST_1T_2 \ldots T_7$ or $ST_{(1)}T_{(2)} \ldots T_{(7)}$ because the seventh T, T_7, occurred on the seventh cycle, $T_{(7)}$, after each S. Similarly, Condition 6 can be expressed as $SNNNNNNT_1$ or $SNNNNNNT_{(7)}$ because the first T, T_1, comes on the seventh cycle after each S per replication. The distinction is important.

Method

The learning task consisted of 20 CVC-noun paired-associates: 20 Consonant-Vowel-Consonant (CVC) nonsense syllables and 20 concrete nouns were, respectively, selected from intermediate ranges of Noble (1961) and from Thorndike and Lorge (1944) in such a way that the initial consonants are unique. The vowels of the CVCs were equally distributed among five of them, and the final consonants were as different as was feasible. Apparent preexperimental associations between the cue and target were avoided to make the pairs as homogeneous as possible. Twenty colored geometrical figures for N trials came from five colors (red, blue, yellow, green, and orange) and four figures (circle, square,

TABLE 1.1
Experimental Design

	Cycle																										
Condition	1	2	3	4	5	6	7	8	9	10	11	12	13	14	15	16	⋯	57	58	59	60	61	62	63	64	65	66
1 STTTTTTT	S_1	T	T	T	T	T	T	T	S_2	T	T	T	T	T	T	T	⋯	S_8	T	T	T	T	T	T	T	S_9	T
2 STNTNTNT	S_1	T	N	T	N	T	N	T	S_2	T	N	T	N	T	N	T	⋯	S_8	T	N	T	N	T	N	T	S_9	T
3 STNNTNNT	S_1	T	N	N	T	N	N	T	S_2	T	N	N	T	N	N	T	⋯	S_8	T	N	N	T	N	N	T	S_9	T
4 STNNNNNT	S_1	T	N	N	N	N	N	T	S_2	T	N	N	N	N	N	T	⋯	S_8	T	N	N	N	N	N	T	S_9	T
5 STNNNNNN	S_1	T	N	N	N	N	N	N	S_2	T	N	N	N	N	N	N	⋯	S_8	T	N	N	N	N	N	N	S_9	T
6 SNNNNNNT	S_1	N	N	N	N	N	N	T	S_2	N	N	N	N	N	N	T	⋯	S_8	N	N	N	N	N	N	T	S_9	T
7 STTTNNNN	S_1	T	T	T	N	N	N	N	S_2	T	T	T	N	N	N	N	⋯	S_8	T	T	T	N	N	N	N	S_9	T
8 SNNTTTNN	S_1	N	N	T	T	T	N	N	S_2	N	N	T	T	T	N	N	⋯	S_8	N	N	T	T	T	N	N	S_9	T
9 SNNNNTTT	S_1	N	N	N	N	T	T	T	S_2	N	N	N	N	T	T	T	⋯	S_8	N	N	N	N	T	T	T	S_9	T

triangle, and diamond). The subject's oral response was recorded by the experimenter.

The item presentation orders for all cycles were randomized from cycle to cycle. The presentation rates on S, T, and N cycles were all 2 sec per item with 2 sec intercycle intervals (the minimum needed for cycle identification).

The 90 subjects were paid college students of both sexes, 10 in each condition. Three others participated but could not complete the experiment due to surprise fire drills. Assignments to conditions were random. A practice task with three additional pairs and three colored figures, identical for all subjects, preceded the main task. Performance on the practice task among the nine groups did not differ significantly, thus suggesting initial comparability.

The Spaced Practice Effect of Study (S) Trials

All conditions had the identical S trial spacing (Table 1.1). Thus, should the S trial spaced practice effect predominate, all present conditions were expected to show the same level of performance. See Figs. 1.4 and 1.5: Examining the last tests that demonstrated the total learning effect *without* differential short-term memory (STM) losses (Table 1.1, Cycle 66) revealed that the nine conditions differed significantly—$F(8, 81) = 2.61, MS_e = 10.61, p < 0.05$. Apparently, S trial spacing did not control performance to an appreciable degree.

These significant differences among the conditions also create doubts about the total time hypothesis (Bugelski, 1962). It predicts identical performance levels from the same total time, and conditions differ only with respect to the spacing and programming of T trials.

Performance on Successive Test (T) Trials
Within Replication—No New Learning Occurred

A replication here is defined by a basic unit of repetition pattern, starting with an S trial (Table 1.1; conditions are identified by their replication patterns). Consistent with earlier findings, performances over the seven successive Ts in Condition 1 ($ST_1T_2 \ldots T_7$) differed little following any S throughout the entire course of acquisition (Fig. 1.5), $ps > 0.25$. The lack of performance improvements over the successive Ts contrasts sharply with large improvements produced over successive S trials (e.g., Fig. 1.4), clearly indicating definitive differences between S and T trials.

Two new phenomena emerged. First, the lack of change over successive T trials within replication did not require that all cycles (other than S) be T trials. Conditions STTTNNNN, SNNTTTNN, and SNNNNTTT, involved only three successive T trials, each concentrating on the early, middle, or later phase in each replication. See Fig. 1.6: No replication produced any significant differences among the three consecutive Ts. This invariance could be observed at any phase

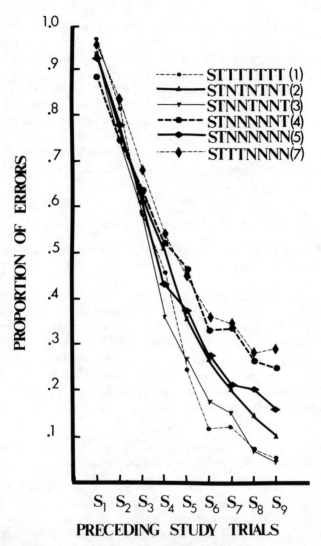

FIG. 1.4.   Learning curves of Conditions 1, 2, 3, 4, 5, and 7 on the test (T), given on the cycle immediately following each study (S) cycle, that is $T_{(1)}$, as a function of preceding S trials.

in replication, independent of the proximity to the S cycle, or the acquisition phase; it is not specific to either location or time.

Second and most fascinating is the stationary performance over successive Ts even when N trials were interspersed with the Ts, as in Conditions STNTNTNT, STNNTNNT, and STNNNNNT. As shown in Fig. 1.5, none of these T trial-spaced-conditions demonstrated any performance gains or losses over the spaced

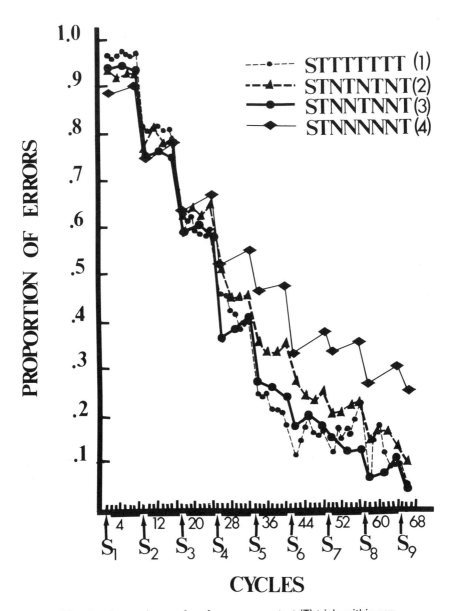

FIG. 1.5. Comparisons of performances on test (T) trials within replication following each study (S) cycle for Conditions 1, 2, 3, and 4
where the first and last cycles after each S were filled with T trials.

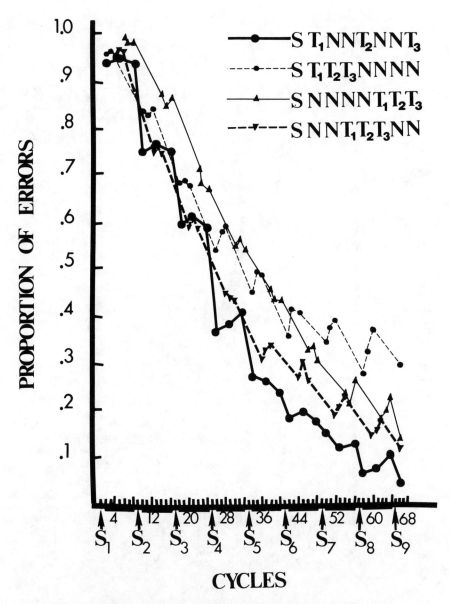

FIG. 1.6.   Performances for all conditions which had 3 test (T) cycles per replication with 7 possible cycle positions following each S cycle (massed vs. spaced practice of T trials); that is, Condition 3 (STNNTN-NT) versus Conditions 7 (STTTNNNN), 8 (SNNTTTNN), or 9 (SNNNNT-TT).

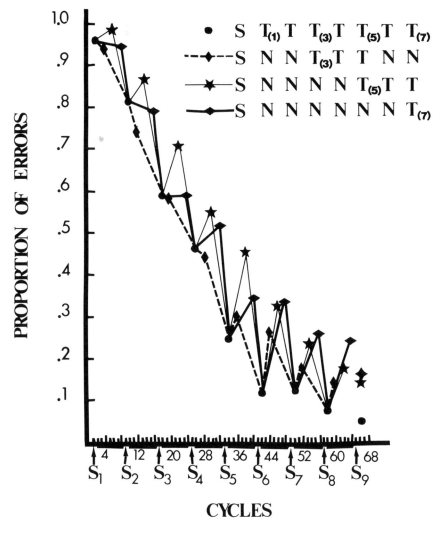

FIG. 1.7. Comparisons of T (test) trials and N (neutral task) trials at Test Positions 3, 5, and 7 per replication, as manifested in Conditions 7 (STTTNNNN), 8 (SNNTTTNN), 9 (SNNNNTTT), and 6 (SNNNNNNT), respectively.

T trials within any replication. The phenomenon was noted after one S trial by Landauer and Bjork (1978), and the present study extended the effect by demonstrating it at *all* stages of acquisition. The N trial that often produces forgetting (Replication Program 5) did not lead to reliable performance decrements for as many as five Ts within the STNNNNNT replication.

Recall that Replication Program 6 did not produce forgetting on N (B) trials.

The common characteristics found for current spaced T trial conditions and those of $STN_1N_2N_3 \ldots N_{i-1}$ are that (a) a T trial occurred in the cycle immediately after each S (the $T_{(1)}$ effect), and (b) the Ns did not produce any performance decrement when preceded by a T. These two characteristics were highly important, because it is the T trials that may control the presence or absence of forgetting during the N (B) interval, rather than the latter interval itself.

The effect of stationariness as noted (Conditions 1, 7, 8, and 9) can be identified as the *forgetting-prevention effect*. Although N (B) trials preceded by T trials do not produce forgetting, the same N (B) trial in Replication Program 5 (Fig. 1.3) generated large forgetting in Conditions $SNNT_{(3)}TTNN$, $SNNN-NT_{(5)}TT$, and $SNNNNNNT_{(7)}$, respectively, with two, four, and six N trials prior to their first T, T_1, following each S. To assess the extent of the forgetting that occurred between S and its T_1 in these conditions, we compared them with respective $T_{(1)} = T_1$ in the control condition ($ST_{(1)}T_{(2)}T_{(3)}T_{(4)}T_{(5)}T_{(6)}T_{(7)} = ST_1T_2T_3T_4T_5T_6T_7$) in Fig. 1.7.

The three comparison conditions produced reliable forgetting vis-à-vis the control: $F(1, 38) = 7.00$, $MS_e = 30.65$, $p < 0.02$. No such forgetting occurred on any successive T trials in the present (Conditions 1, 7, 8, and 9) or past (cited earlier in the chapter) conditions, thus the forgetting-prevention effect remains intact. Note that the conditions that produced substantial forgetting on N (B, rest) trials are preceded by S trials, and those preceded by T trials produced much less forgetting: another crucial difference between S and T trials.

The Potentiating Effect of Test (T) Trials—
Between Replication Phenomena

Although no explicit performance gain occurred over the successive Ts within replication, some latent incremental gains may develop over successive Ts within replication. To examine that possibility, all six current conditions were investigated on the T cycle immediately after each S trial: Conditions $ST_{(1)}TTTTT$, $ST_{(1)}NTNTNT$, $ST_{(1)}NNTNNT$, $ST_{(1)}NNNNNT$, $ST_{(1)}NNNNNN$, and $ST_{(1)}TTNNNN$. As in Fig. 1.4, differences among the conditions steadily grew larger, and toward the last half of the acquisition period, the differences became very obvious: $F(5, 54) = 2.96$, $MS_e = 47.81$, $p < 0.02$. In general, the more Ts per replication, the greater the advantage. Conditions with seven or four Ts per replication are therefore likely to advantage performance more than those with one or two Ts per replication.

MASSED AND SPACED PRACTICE OF THE
TEST (T) TRIALS

Earlier in this chapter we found that the S trial spaced practice effect was inconsequential as compared with T trial effects. What about the distributed (spaced) practice effect of the T trials?

The Forgetting-Prevention Effect of Spaced Test (T) Trials—Within Replication Phenomena

The T trial spacing was achieved by interspersed N (rest) trials as seen in Conditions STNTNTNT, STNNTNNT, and STNNNNNT. We now compare them with the control, STTTTTTT, filled with T trials (massed T condition). As seen in Fig. 1.5, none of these conditions produced significant differences among the T trials within any replication. T massed and spaced conditions had a common property in the sense that no difference was produced within replication. However, what is most fascinating is that the T spaced condition did not produce any forgetting over the N (rest) cycles (Fig. 1.5)! This contrasts sharply with the large forgetting occurring over N trials preceded by the S trial in Conditions SNNTTTNN, SNNNNTTT, and SNNNNNNT (Fig. 1.7: Replication Program 5, Fig. 1.3).

The findings suggest that N trials were empirically equivalent to T trials for the T trial spaced conditions in preventing forgetting within replication at all stages of acquisition! The phenomenon was reproducible, as shown by four experiments in Conditions ST_1BT_2 and ST_1NT_2, and was quantitatively accounted for by the test trial potentiating (TTP) model (Izawa, 1971b, 1988).

The Potentiating Effects of the Spaced Test (T) Trials—Between Replication Phenomena

The learning curves, as a function of preceding S trials, exhibited the T trial potentiating effect. That is, they presented large differences among the massed T condition (STTTTTTT) and three spaced-T-conditions (STNTNTNT, STNNTNNT, and STNNNNNT) in Fig. 1.5, particularly toward the second half of the acquisition period. Tested by $T_{(1)}$s, common to all relevant conditions, differences were reliable, $F(3, 36) = 3.18, MS_e = 95.90, p < 0.05$. On Cycle 66 the last Ts reflected the total accumulated effects of acquisition; therefore differences were more highly significant: $F(3, 36) = 4.95, MS_e = 7.41, p < 0.006$.

However, large differences among the four conditions may be in part attributable to the disproportionately inferior performance on Condition STNNNNNT. Finer-grained analyses confirmed no reliable differences among Conditions STTTTTTT, STNTNTNT, and STNNTNNT. Nonetheless, the latter three conditions with most T (seven, four, and three per replication) trials as a group showed a distinct superiority over Condition STNNNNNT with two T (least Ts, most spaced) trials per replication: $F(1, 36) = 8.03, MS_e = 94.89, p < 0.01$ during the last half of the acquisition period, and $F(1, 38) = 14.22, MS_e = 7.22, p < 0.001$ on the last T.

Particularly impressive were the virtually identical performances on Conditions STTTTTTT and STNNTNNT. Their near equivalence (Fig. 1.5) was especially pronounced from the middle to the end of acquisition; the final T performances were indistinguishable from each other! This amazing effectiveness of the T trial spacing effect was replicated elsewhere: Experiments 5, 6, 7, and 8 by Izawa (1988) produced nearly the same levels of performances for Conditions STTT and STBT (STNT).

Our current findings suggest that: (a) both spaced and massed T trials prevented forgetting over the successive T trials within replication to nearly the same extent; and (b) with respect to the T trial potentiating effect, demonstrable between replication, some complexity enters. The greater the density of the T trials, the greater the potentiating effect, but only up to a point. The optimal spacing of the T trials in the present situation seems to lie between all T trials (control) and the spaced T trials by two N cycles (Condition STNNTNNT); there were no differences among Conditions STTTTTTT, STNTNTNT, and STNNTN-NT. However, when T trials were too widely spaced (Condition STNNNNNT), the arrangement reduced the potentiating effect, thus poorer overall performance occurred.

Absolute Number of Test (T) Trials versus Spacing of the Test (T) Trials

The fact that the massed T condition (STTTTTTT) was as good as some of the best spaced T conditions (STNNTNNT and STNTNTNT) implies that on the one hand, massed versus spaced practice may not create decisive differential effects, but on the other hand, an optimal T trial spacing arrangement does exist. Findings also suggest an advantage for high T trial density conditions. Thus the absolute number of T trials per replication becomes a factor. In a sense, the massed versus spaced T trial comparisons of the four conditions mentioned may have invited undesirable contaminations because they had unequal numbers of T and N trials.

It may be worthwhile at this point to review the traditional variations of the massed versus distributed practice dimensions. For more than a century since Ebbinghaus (1885), the number of trials in the learning (S) task were kept constant among the relevant conditions, and these differed only in the quantity of rest (N, B) trials. Among many possibilities (see Izawa, 1971a, for details), the total time hypothesis modified can provide an elegant rationale for an advantage of the distributed condition; it allows for greater total time!

Ideally, then, we require an experiment where S (learning task), T (retrieval task; see Izawa, 1971a), and N (rest) trials are held constant respectively among the conditions under comparison. This was the precise motivation for the present study; in it four conditions had exactly one S, three T, and four N trials (Conditions STNNTNNT, STTTNNNN, SNNTTTNN, and SNNNNTTT). The first condition was the T trial spaced condition, whereas the remainder had massed T trials at early, middle, and late stages of each replication, respectively.

Figure 1.6 illustrates these highly controlled comparisons between massed and spaced T conditions. Here again, among the four conditions, no differences were found between massed and spaced T presentations with respect to their forgetting-prevention effect over all T trials (which followed each S trial per replication).

What is most intriguing in this new set of comparisons are the differences between massed and spaced T trial conditions with respect to the test trial potentiating effect. There were no tangible differences among the three massed T trial conditions, $p > 0.15$. However, it is very interesting that the three massed T trial conditions as a group were already inferior to the spaced T trial condition (STNNTNNT) early in acquisition, and that the difference steadily increased as acquisition advanced, becoming decisive during the second half period: $F(1, 38) = 5.02$, $MS_e = 14.97$, $p = 0.03$. Consequently, the *positive* T trial spaced practice effect was unveiled by a very stringent design that minimized external contaminations!

The Immediate Test ($T_{(1)}$) Trial Effect

A single test, given on the cycle immediately after an S trial, $T_{(1)}$, may generate an overwhelming effect to facilitate subsequent retrieval as well as to prevent subsequent forgetting (e.g., Allen et al., 1969; Estes, 1979; Izawa, 1970b, Replication Program 6). The present experimental design clearly provides more direct evidence on this issue than did earlier ones. Indeed, we already noted the possibility with respect to four massed and spaced T conditions (Fig. 1.5): Conditions STTTTTTT, STNTNTNT, STNNTNNT, and STNNNNNT, which all had $T_{(1)}$. However, significant differences among the conditions suggest: $T_{(1)}$s alone do not determine ultimate performance levels.

Also note please that there were two more conditions with $T_{(1)}$s: Conditions STNNNNNN and STTTNNNN in the present experiment. When all six of these conditions were considered, as seen earlier in Fig. 1.4, differences were also very large ($p < 0.02$). The immediate test, $T_{(1)}$, effect then is not as great as previously conjectured. The test trial potentiating effect that determined the overall performance level seems controlled predominantly by the arrangements of T trials that followed $T_{(1)}$s.

THE MODIFIED TEST TRIAL POTENTIATING (TTP) MODEL

The TTP model (Izawa, 1971b) underwent minor evolutionary changes via the retention interval and identity models (Izawa, 1981c, 1985a), which addressed differential retention interval and the identical acquisition processes for study-test and anticipation methods. However, the basic theoretical orientation, the incorporation of Estes' (1955) stimulus fluctuation model, and the intercycle interval, equivalent to N trial in our approach, all stay the same; their names simply reflect particular issues under consideration. The T trial effect being the primary concern, we henceforth refer to the latest version by Izawa (1985a, 1985b) as the *modified TTP model*.

The powerful effect of the rest (N, B) interval that cannot be paralleled by other theories comes from Estes' stimulus fluctuation construct, and may be expressed in the modified TTP model as in Equation 9:

$$
I_{N(B)} = \begin{array}{c} \\ EA_v \\ E\bar{A}_v \\ UA_v \\ U\bar{A}_v \end{array}
\begin{array}{cccc} EA_{v+1} & E\bar{A}_{v+1} & UA_{v+1} & U\bar{A}_{v+1} \end{array}
\left[\begin{array}{cccc}
1-g & g & 0 & 0 \\
g' & 1-g' & 0 & 0 \\
0 & 0 & 1-g & g \\
0 & 0 & g' & 1-g'
\end{array} \right], \tag{9}
$$

where EA, $E\bar{A}$, UA, and $U\bar{A}$ indicate elements (assumed for the item to be learned) are, respectively, encoded and available, encoded but unavailable, unencoded but available, unencoded and unavailable for sampling. Components g and g' are the elements' fluctuation rate from the available to the unavailable set, and the unavailable to the available set, respectively.

The stochastic processes in Equation 9, along with those of S and T processes summarized in Equations 10 and 11, plus the retention interval filled with S and T trials of *other* items within the list in Equations 12 and 13, make it possible to explain multifaceted and complex data obtained in the present study that uncovered the positive T trial spaced practice effect:

$$
S = \begin{array}{c} \\ EA_v \\ E\bar{A}_v \\ UA_v \\ U\bar{A}_v \end{array}
\begin{array}{cccc} EA_{v+1} & E\bar{A}_{v+1} & UA_{v+1} & U\bar{A}_{v+1} \end{array}
\left[\begin{array}{cccc}
1 & 0 & 0 & 0 \\
0 & 1 & 0 & 0 \\
c & 0 & 1-c & 0 \\
0 & 0 & 0 & 1
\end{array} \right], \tag{10}
$$

$$
T = \begin{array}{c} \\ EA_v \\ E\bar{A}_v \\ UA_v \\ U\bar{A}_v \end{array}
\begin{array}{cccc} EA_{v+1} & E\bar{A}_{v+1} & UA_{v+1} & U\bar{A}_{v+1} \end{array}
\left[\begin{array}{cccc}
1 & 0 & 0 & 0 \\
k' & 1-k' & 0 & 0 \\
0 & 0 & 1-k & k \\
0 & 0 & k' & 1-k'
\end{array} \right], \tag{11}
$$

$$
I_S = \begin{array}{c} \\ EA_v \\ E\bar{A}_v \\ UA_v \\ U\bar{A}_v \end{array}
\begin{array}{cccc} EA_{v+1} & E\bar{A}_{v+1} & UA_{v+1} & U\bar{A}_{v+1} \end{array}
\left[\begin{array}{cccc}
1-e & e & 0 & 0 \\
e' & 1-e' & 0 & 0 \\
0 & 0 & 1-e & e \\
0 & 0 & e' & 1-e'
\end{array} \right], \tag{12}
$$

and

$$
I_T =
\begin{array}{c}
 \\
EA_v \\
E\bar{A}_v \\
UA_v \\
U\bar{A}_v
\end{array}
\begin{array}{cccc}
EA_{v+1} & E\bar{A}_{v+1} & UA_{v+1} & U\bar{A}_{v+1} \\
\left[\begin{array}{cccc}
1\text{-}f & f & 0 & 0 \\
f' & 1\text{-}f' & 0 & 0 \\
0 & 0 & 1\text{-}f & f \\
0 & 0 & f' & 1\text{-}f'
\end{array}\right]
\end{array} .
\tag{13}
$$

For Equation 10, Component c is the encoding or conditioning probability on the S trial. In Equations 11, 12, and 13, Components k, e, and f represent the probabilities of the elements moving from the available set to the unavailable set on the T trial, intervening other S, and other T events, respectively, whereas Components k', e', and f' stand for those of the elements moving from the unavailable to the available set, respectively, in Matrices T, I_S, and I_T. For other details, see Izawa (1989b).

The modified TTP model has ample support from a large number of stringent quantitative examinations (e.g., Izawa, 1971b, 1981a, 1981b, 1981c, 1982a, 1982b, 1985, 1988, 1989a) inclusive of N (B) trial effects. In the limited space following, therefore, we present a qualitative account of the present data from the modified TTP model.

Perhaps the most difficult aspect of the present and past data from other theoretical positions is to account for multifaceted, seemingly contradictory effects of N (B) trials. First, Replication Program 8 with S trials alone, given with or without interspersed N (B) trials (tested only once at the end of the experiment), produced the positive S spacing effect. The spaced conditions are advantaged, because the fluctuations of the encoded elements entering the available set (in order to be newly encoded) are greater in number, compared to the massed condition. That is, the encoding power of each S trial is greater for spaced S conditions than massed ones.

The element fluctuations during N (B) trials (Equation 9), if measured during each replication, appear as performance decrements, because encoded elements in the available set become fewer and fewer as the length of N (B) trials increases until an equilibrium is reached, a fact precisely verified by this and earlier studies (Figs. 1.3, 1.7; Replication Program 5).

However, much of the forgetting over N (B) trials can be prevented if a T trial follows immediately after each S (as in Replication Program 6) by virtue of the forgetting-prevention and potentiating effects of T trials (postulated in Matrix T). Apparently the duration of the forgetting-prevention effect of T may exceed 5 consecutive N trials (STNNNNNT) per replication (Fig. 1.5).

Naturally, within-replication forgetting-prevention effects should be more salient if such N trials were interspersed with more Ts, as in spaced T trial arrangements, for example, in Conditions STNTNTNT and STNNTNNT; this turned out to be the case. Thus, the modified TTP model can account for within-replication spaced T trial conditions via Matrix T, when applied to the cycle immediately following each S, while at the same time preceding N trials (with or without further T, N, or both trials).

As for the test trial potentiating effects of spaced T trials: Due to active participation by the subject in producing overt responses, element fluctuations producing subsequent S trials were much more effective on T trials than on any other trials, for example, N (B) or even S trials. For that reason, it is still true that the greater the number of T trials, the greater the potentiating effects. In the present experiment where the total time and S trial spacing were tightly controlled among all conditions, those with the greatest number of T trials were among the best (i.e., Conditions STTTTTTT and STNTNTNT).

Among the conditions that had three T trials, the spaced T trial condition (STNNTNNT) was significantly better than all massed conditions. Interspersing T trials among the rest (N) trials was the most effective means for maintaining performance supremacy, as good as that in Condition STTTTTTT!

RELATIVE CONTRIBUTIONS OF STUDY (S) AND TEST (T) TRIALS: INTERACTIVE DYNAMISM

We have here obtained compelling evidence for the *positive* spaced practice effects of unreinforced T trials, effects that are hard to explain via alternative positions (e.g., Izawa, 1988); most are not equipped to handle the data presented here. We discuss in the remaining space a few hard-to-maintain theoretical assumptions of other models; for example, an assumption that S and T trials are essentially identical (e.g., Whitten & Bjork, 1977; Whitten & Leonard, 1980). From the data analyses already set forth, S and T trials are clearly so different that it would appear any observed identity may be either phenomenally coincidental (stemming from very different basic processes) or at best limited to a very few special cases. Certainly, it can no longer be assumed that such identity exists as a general rule!

For the reason that the relative role of S and T trials may differ depending on the memory state (Izawa, 1966, 1967a, 1967b, 1968, 1969, 1970a, 1970b, 1971a, 1971b, 1976, 1988; Izawa & Patterson, 1989; Lachman & Laughery, 1968; Thompson et al., 1978), we consider them according to the acquisition stages.

Transition from the Unlearned to the Learned State

Prior to the first study trial, S_1, no encoding (conditioning) is possible, and therefore, administering any number of T trials should produce no correct response except for a rare lucky guess.[3] However, the presentation of S_1 or any S is likely to produce some encoding (in the case of the modified TTP model, with a probability c), and others will stay unencoded (with probability $1 - c$). For the encoded items, on a subsequent T trial, they are likely to be correct. A strong argument has been made that a T trial can be equivalent to an S trial for those items that are correct on a T (e.g., Whitten & Bjork, 1977; Whitten & Leonard, 1980; Wilkinson & Koestler, 1984, who base their assumptions on Raaijmakers & Shiffrin, 1981).

There are indeed some common properties between S and T trials after encoding has taken place: T trials prevent forgetting, as do S trials (Izawa, 1969). For those theories that distinguish between short- and long-term memory stores (STMS and LTMS), both S and T trials may assist the items in STMS to enter the LTMS; for those that do not distinguish the two memory states, S and T assist the encoded items to move from the temporary to the permanent phase of the memory state.

But then, how about the items that were *not* encoded on S_1 and were incorrect on the subsequent T (they may be particularly numerous early in the acquisition period, especially when learning is difficult)? It is the modified TTP model that propounds a powerful positive effect that other theories neglect. See the model's postulates in Matrix T in Equation 11, and its Components k and k'.

The salient characteristic of the modified TTP is that the items that are incorrect on a given T will enhance the encoding power of the subsequent S trials. This positive effect may be attributable to the large or heightened interchange rate of element fluctuation after the T trial so that a greater number of unencoded elements enter the available set to be sampled and encoded on the subsequent S trials. The interspersed T and N combinations (T trial spaced conditions) are particularly effective in this regard (if there are not too many Ns in a row).

This aspect of the model may have implications for such processes as selective attention to yet-unlearned items, cue-learning/differentiation to facilitate subsequent cue-target hook-ups, and discriminations of encoded versus unencoded items, among others. The processes involved with applying T trials together enhances encoding ability during the S trials (cf. Izawa, 1966–1988; LaPorte & Voss, 1974). However, this facilitation by the T trials is indirect in the sense that it does not include the capability for new encoding. That latter capacity, to be examined next, is limited to the S trial.

---

[3]There may be a very small possibility (probability d) that items that were unlearned but guessed correctly may have been encoded by virtue of being guessed correctly. However, such a possibility is expected to be infinitesimal, precisely because of the "unlearned" context. In nearly all cases (with probability $1-d$), such "accidents" were unlikely. Items in the unlearned state, if tested again without intervening S trials, were likely to score "incorrect."

TABLE 1.2

Encoding Probability on Test (T) Trials Estimated From the Second (T_2) or Subsequent T Trials Following Each Study (S) Trial: Proportions Correct for the First Time, Given Incorrect on All Previous Trials, in All Conditions With Two or More Ts per Replication

			Preceding Study Trials								$P(T)$ Weighted Mean	$P(S)$
Condition	T_i	S_1	S_2	S_3	S_4	S_5	S_6	S_7	S_8		
1 $ST*_1T_2T_3T_4T_5T_6T_7$:	T_2 N	.015 193	.037 161	.028 109	.091 77	.167 36	.000 14	.111 9	.000 4	.043	.189
	T_3 N	.000 190	.013 155	.000 106	.071 70	.033 30	.000 14	.125 8	.000 4	.016	
	T_4 N	.000 190	.007 153	.038 106	.031 65	.103 29	.071 14	.000 7	.250 4	.021	
	T_5 N	.000 190	.007 152	.000 102	.000 63	.038 26	.000 13	.143 7	.000 3	.005	
	T_6 N	.000 190	.013 151	.010 102	.016 63	.000 25	.077 13	.000 6	.000 3	.009	
	T_7 N	.000 190	.000 149	.000 101	.032 62	.000 25	.000 12	.000 6	.000 3	.004	
2 $ST*_1NT_2NT_3NT_4$:	T_2 N	.027 187	.020 152	.035 115	.165 85	.122 49	.133 30	.059 17	.091 11	.059	.169
	T_3 N	.011 182	.020 149	.045 111	.042 71	.023 43	.000 26	.000 16	.000 10	.023	
	T_4 N	.000 180	.014 146	.000 106	.029 68	.048 42	.000 26	.063 16	.100 10	.013	
3 $ST*_1NNT_2NNT_3$:	T_2 N	.011 187	.020 147	.063 112	.109 64	.049 41	.091 22	.071 14	.286 7	.044	.205

24

	T3 N	.011 185	.028 144	.019 105	.000 57	.128 39	.150 20	.000 13	.000 5	.028	
4 ST*₁NNNNT₂:	T2 N	.011 177	.027 147	.034 118	.074 94	.068 73	.057 53	.045 44	.081 37	.040	.153
7 ST*₁T₂T₃NNNN:	T2 N	.010 191	.036 165	.053 131	.020 99	.052 77	.036 55	.021 47	.081 37	.033	.131
	T3 N	.005 189	.006 159	.024 124	.031 97	.041 73	.038 53	.087 46	.029 34	.023	
8 SNNT*₁T₂T₃NN:	T2 N	.005 189	.034 149	.063 112	.114 79	.059 51	.050 40	.077 26	.056 18	.045	.171
	T3 N	.000 188	.021 144	.038 105	.043 70	.000 48	.158 38	.000 24	.000 17	.025	
9 SNNNNT*₁T₂T₃	T2 N	.005 197	.041 172	.067 135	.029 104	.089 79	.058 52	.156 32	.000 22	.044	.138
	T3 N	.000 196	.006 165	.032 126	.040 101	.042 72	.082 49	.000 27	.045 22	.023	

N = Number of cases.
*First test (T) trial within replication of each repetitive pattern or replication program.

No New Encoding Occurs on Unreinforced
Test (T) Trials

If the T trial could truly replace the S trial, learning (encoding) should occur on both trials. From the effect of fixedness over the successive T trials (Replication Programs 1−1′) observed in several scores of cued-recall (PAL) experiments over more than two decades by Izawa, as well as in the current experiment (Figs. 1.5 and 1.6), we may conclusively deny the possibility of new learning, as do Allen et al. (1969), Birnbaum and Eichner (1971), Hogan and Kintsch (1971), Landauer and Bjork (1978), Rosner (1970), Slamecka and Graf (1978), Thompson et al. (1978), and Wenger et al. (1980). (Also refer to footnote 1.)

Another way to examine whether new learning occurs on T trials per se is to estimate the new encoding probability per T trial in the condition that has two or more T trials per replication; we would do this from the probability of a first correct response, given incorrect responses on all previous trials. The statistics are entered in Table 1.2 for all relevant conditions for T_is, $i \geq 2$, for each S_j, $1 \leq j \leq 8$. No systematic pattern was detected from early S through late S trials. The weighted mean was entered in the second to last column of Table 1.2. The encoding probability thus estimated is virtually 0, varying from 0.059 to 0.004. Because guessing is possible with a probability of 0.05 when 20 target words were learned, we may conclude that no new encoding is likely on T trials.

When items are barely encoded and highly unstable, these items may not be recalled on T_1, requiring more time to search for the response, say until T_2. Those items even more unstable may require still longer time, until T_3, . . . , T_i; $i \leq 7$ here. We expect, however, the number of items of greater instability to decrease for the greater i's. This seems to be the case. The same phenomenon was observed in several scores of studies by Izawa (1988, recent examples); the current interpretation is also supported by reaction time data (Izawa, 1988, Experiment 3).

In sharp contrast to the negligible encoding probability of T trials, the probabilities for S trials estimated in the same manner via T_1s, are very large, as seen in the last column of Table 1.2. Furthermore, corresponding consistently with our earlier data analyses in Figs. 1.4–1.6, encoding probabilities directly related to the potentiating effect of the conditions with the greatest numbers of Ts (Conditions 1, 2, and 3-spaced T) had larger encoding probabilities. Moreover, massed T conditions (STTTNNNN, SNNTTTNN, and SNNNNTTT) as a group had distinctively less encoding powers than a spaced condition (STNNTNNT).

Table 1.2 then, clearly indicates that (a) no new encoding (learning) is likely on T trials per se, but that (b) encoding occurs exclusively on S trials, and that (c) the potentiating effects of T trials appear to stem from the larger encoding probability of S trials for conditions with relatively larger numbers of T trials and intermediately spaced T trial conditions (too narrowly or too widely spaced ones are not optimal).

Transition From the Short-Term (Temporary) Memory Store (STMS) to the Long-Term (Permanent) Memory Store (LTMS)

Both new encoding on S trials and the potentiating effect on T trials, which are unique to respective trials (e.g., Izawa, 1969), are expected to continue in all stages of the acquisition period until and possibly beyond the point where perfect performance was reached; this is also expected of processes that may overlap between both S and T trials phenomenally.

Whereas new learning (encoding) may not be possible on T trials, different kinds of learning may be possible:

1. Learning to retrieve or retrieval practice may occur. This is likely because the context of the S trial and that of the T trial differ: The target (correct) response is given on the former, but not for the latter.

2. Active production of overt responses is the core of both effective forgetting-prevention and the test trial potentiating effect. Izawa (1976) discovered that when some of the T trials of Condition STTTTT were replaced by covert, silent test (t) trials, both forgetting-prevention and potentiating effects lost substantial impact. This directly relates to subjective cognitive effort, or maximization processes (Izawa, 1971b). Indeed, the process summarized in Equation 11, Matrix *T,* presumes the subject's active production of overt responses and subjective and cognitive effort. The generation effect by Slamecka and Graf (1978), or the act of producing responses (retrievability, Thompson et al., 1978) bear some relevance here.

3. Retrieval practice acquired on T trials (including search strategies and identification of correct responses) may enhance long-term memory (LTM). Effectiveness of T trials in facilitating LTM retrieval has long been noted (e.g., Allen et al., 1969; Cooper & Monk, 1976; Estes, 1979; Hagman, 1983; Hogan & Kintsch, 1971; Izawa, 1966–1988; Izawa & Patterson, 1989).

Overlearning and Overtesting

When an item is firmly established in LTMS or permanent memory store, further S or T trials may have very little tangible effect. On the other hand, overlearning is known to enhance LTM (see Postman, 1962). This particular aspect too is well accounted for by the element fluctuation notion embedded in the modified TTP model: Perfect performance may occur probabilistically, when a great majority of elements in the available set are encoded, with some left unencoded. Overlearning with additional S trials will increase further encoded elements in the universe (both available and unavailable sets; element fluctuations between them do not lead to appreciable performance decrements over time here). In an extreme case, when *all* elements are encoded due to overlearning (far beyond perfect learning), forgetting from LTM is unlikely.

Similarly, the consequences of overtesting will also be better explained by the modified TTP model: Additional T trials beyond perfect performance will assist further element fluctuation between available and unavailable sets. This will lead to further encoding of still unencoded elements in the universe for the subsequent S trials, if any. Furthermore, overtesting should continue to enhance learning to retrieve, and enhance already strong LTM, by building resistance to forgetting and facilitating LTM retrieval. Thus, when overlearning and overtesting occur jointly, lack of forgetting over an extended period would not be surprising. Available data are strikingly consistent with the given interpretation from the modified TTP model.

These previously mentioned considerations lead one to conclude that salient features of S and T trials are fundamentally different (Allen et al., 1969; Birnbaum & Eichner, 1971; Darley & Murdock, 1971; Izawa, 1966–1988; Weinstock & Daly, 1971), and latency data seem to support differences between the two types of trials as well (cf. Allen et al., 1969; Izawa, 1966, 1988; Umilta, Snyder & Snyder, 1972).

SUMMARY

Early in acquisition, S trials' primary role of encoding predominates, transferring unlearned items to the learned state. Once an item becomes learned, both S and T trials participate in maintaining the newly acquired information in the learned state (the forgetting-prevention effect). The T trial participates in acquisition processes by making the subsequent S trials more effective (the potentiating effect), but without encoding capabilities of its own. By active production of overt responses, coupled with the subject's maximization of effort and the gener-ation of response processes, T trials enhance performance level, and help in learning-to-retrieve. In the end, T trials not only improve S trials' powers of acquisition, but also enhance performance levels in both STM and LTM re-trievals by conserving information during both the acquisition and retention periods. The T trials' role is especially powerful in facilitating resistance against forgetting LTM materials. All of this seems best accounted for by the modified TTP model. Its capacity for explaining current multifaceted and complex data from a single set of theoretical assumptions seems not only parsimonious and potent but owes a debt of gratitude to the clarity of vision characterizing Estes' (1955) stimulus fluctuation model.

ACKNOWLEDGMENTS

The author is indebted to Marcia Hataye and Elaine N. Blesi for the data collec-tion, to Nobumasa Watari and Kathy Koesterer for their data analyses and illustrations, and to Paul Watson for assisting with manuscript preparation. Their dedication and professionalism made this chapter's timely completion possible. This study was supported, in parts, by MH 12584-02 of the National Institute of Mental Health, and by a grant from the Flowerree Foundation. Parts of the results were reported at the Second Annual Meeting of the American Psychological Society in Dallas, Texas, in June 1990.

REFERENCES

Allen, G. A., Mahler, W. A., & Estes, W. K. (1969). Effects of recall tests on long-term retention of paired associates. *Journal of Verbal Learning and Verbal Behavior, 8,* 463–470.

Birnbaum, I. M., & Eichner, J. T. (1971). Study versus test trials and long-term retention in free-recall learning. *Journal of Verbal Learning and Verbal Behavior, 10,* 516–521.

Bower, G. H. (1967). A multicomponent theory of the memory trace. In K. W. Spence & J. T. Spence (Eds.), *The psychology of learning and motivation: Advances in research and theory* (pp. 229–325). New York: Academic Press.

Bregman, A. S., & Wiener, J. R. (1970). Effects of test trials in paired-associate and free-recall learning. *Journal of Verbal Learning and Verbal Behavior, 9,* 689–698.

Bugelski, B. R. (1962). Presentation time, total time, and mediation in paired-associate learning. *Journal of Experimental Psychology, 63,* 409–412.

Cooper, A. J. R., & Monk, A. (1976). Learning for recall and learning for recognition. In J. Brown (Ed.), *Recall and recognition* (pp. 131–156). New York: John Wiley & Sons.

Darley, C. F., & Murdock, B. B., Jr. (1971). Effects of prior free recall testing on final recall and recognition. *Journal of Experimental Psychology, 91,* 66–73.

Ebbinghaus, H. (1885). Über das Gedächtnis: Untersuchungen zur experimentellen Psychologie. Liepzig, Germany: Duncker & Humbolt.

Estes, W. K. (1955). Statistical theory of distributional phenomena in learning. *Psychological Review, 62,* 369–377.

Estes, W. K. (1979). Role of response availability in the effects of cued-recall tests on memory. *Journal of Experimental Psychology: Human Learning & Memory, 5,* 567–573.

Gates, A. I. (1917). Recitation as a factor in memorizing. *Archives of Psychology, 6,* No. 40.

Goss, A. E., Morgan, C. H., & Golin, S. J. (1959). Paired-associates learning as a function of percentage of occurrence of response members (reinforcement). *Journal of Experimental Psychology, 57,* 96–104.

Hagman, J. D. (1983). Presentation and test trial effects on acquisition and retention of distance and location. *Journal of Experimental Psychology: Learning, Memory, and Cognition, 9,* 334–345.

Hintzman, D. L. (1974). Theoretical implications of the spacing effect. In R. L. Solso (Ed.), *Theories in cognitive psychology: The Loyola symposium* (pp. 77–99). Potomac, MD: Lawrence Erlbaum Associates.

Hogan, R. M., & Kintsch, W. (1971). Differential effects of study and test trials on long-term recognition and recall. *Journal of Verbal Learning and Verbal Behavior, 10,* 562–567.

Izawa, C. (1966). Reinforcement-test sequences in paired-associate learning. *Psychological Reports, Monographs, 18,* 879–919.

Izawa, C. (1967a). Function of test trials in paired-associate learning. *Journal of Experimental Psychology, 75,* 194–209.

Izawa, C. (1967b). Mixed- versus unmixed-list designs in paired-associate learning. *Psychological Reports, 20,* 1191–1200.

Izawa, C. (1968). Effects of reinforcement, neutral and test trials upon paired-associate acquisition and retention. *Psychological Reports, 23,* 947–959.

Izawa, C. (1969). Comparison of reinforcement and test trials in paired-associate learning. *Journal of Experimental Psychology, 81*, 600–603.

Izawa, C. (1970a). Optimal potentiating effects and forgetting-prevention effects of tests in paired-associate learning. *Journal of Experimental Psychology, 83*, 340–344.

Izawa, C. (1970b). Reinforcement-test-blank acquisition programming under the unmixed-list design in paired-associate learning. *Psychonomic Science, 19*, 75–77.

Izawa, C. (1971a). Massed and spaced practice in paired-associate learning: List versus item distributions. *Journal of Experimental Psychology, 89*, 10–21.

Izawa, C. (1971b). The test trial potentiating model. *Journal of Mathematical Psychology, 8*, 200–224.

Izawa, C. (1976). Vocalized and silent tests in paired-associate learning. *American Journal of Psychology, 89*, 681–693.

Izawa, C. (1981a). Quantitative tests of the retention interval model. *Journal of General Psychology, 105*, 273–292.

Izawa, C. (1981b). The retention interval model: Qualitative and quantitative examinations. *Japanese Psychological Research, 23*, 101–112.

Izawa, C. (1981c). Toward a quantitative theory for performance differences between anticipation and study-test procedures: The retention interval model. *Scandinavian Journal of Psychology, 22*, 79–91.

Izawa, C. (1982a). Fundamental similarities and differences between study-test and anticipation item presentation procedures in the learning of linguistic items: Quantitative tests of the retention interval model via varied parameter estimation modes. *Psychologia, 25*, 1–17.

Izawa, C. (1982b). The retention interval model examined by delayed test performances. *Journal of General Psychology, 106*, 219–231.

Izawa, C. (1985a). A test of the differences between anticipation and study-test methods of paired-associate learning. *Journal of Experimental Psychology: Learning, Memory, and Cognition, 11*, 165–184.

Izawa, C. (1985b). The identity model and factors controlling the superiority of the study-test method over the anticipation method. *Journal of General Psychology, 112*, 65–78.

Izawa, C. (1988). A search for the control factors of the repetition effect. *Japanese Psychological Review, 31*(3), 367–403.

Izawa, C. (1989a). A test of the identity model: Encoding processes differ little between anticipation and study-test methods. In C. Izawa (Ed.), *Current issues in cognitive processes: The Tulane Flowerree symposium on cognition* (pp. 210–245). Hillsdale, NJ: Lawrence Erlbaum Associates.

Izawa, C. (1989b). Similarities and differences between anticipation and study-test item information presentation methods. In C. Izawa (Ed.), *Current issues in cognitive processes: The Tulane Flowerree symposium on cognition* (pp. 201–209). Hillsdale, NJ: Lawrence Erlbaum Associates.

Izawa, C., & Patterson, D. J. (1989). Effects of the item presentation methods and test trials on Euclidean distances and location learning via the tactile sense. In C. Izawa (Ed.), *Current issues in cognitive processes: The Tulane Flowerree symposium on cognition* (pp. 279–312). Hillsdale, NJ: Lawrence Erlbaum Associates.

Lachman, R., & Laughery, K. R. (1968). Is a test trial a training trial in free recall learning? *Journal of Experimental Psychology, 76*, 40–50.

Landauer, T. K., & Bjork, R. A. (1978). Optimum rehearsal patterns and name learning. In M. M. Gruneberg, P. E. Morris, & R. N. Sykes (Eds.), *Practical aspects of memory* (pp. 625–632). London: Academic Press.

LaPorte, R., & Voss, J. F. (1974). Paired-associate acquisition as a function of number of initial nontest trials. *Journal of Experimental Psychology, 103*, 117–123.

Lockhart, R. S., Craik, F. I. M., & Jacoby, L. (1976). Depth of processing, recognition and recall. In J. Brown (Ed.), *Recall and recognition* (pp. 75–102). New York: Wiley.

Mandler, G., Worden, P. E., & Graesser, A. C. II (1974). Subjective disorganization: Search for the locus of list organization. *Journal of Verbal Learning and Verbal Behavior, 13*, 220–235.

Noble, C. E. (1961). Measurements of association value (*a*), rated associations (*a'*), and scaled meaningfulness (*m'*) for the 2100 CVC combinations of the English alphabet. *Psychological Reports, 8*, 487–521.

Peterson, L. R., & Peterson, M. J. (1959). Short-term retention of individual verbal items. *Journal of Experimental Psychology, 58*, 193–198.

Postman, L. (1962). Retention as a function of degree of overlearning. *Science, 135*, 666–667.

Raaijmakers, J. G. W., & Shiffrin, R. M. (1981). Search of associative memory. *Psychological Review, 88*, 93–134.

Richardson, J. (1958). The relationship of stimulus similarity and number of responses. *Journal of Experimental Psychology, 56*, 478–484.

Roediger, H. L. III, & Challis, B. H. (1989). Hypermnesia: Improvements in recall with repeated testing. In C. Izawa (Ed.), *Current issues in cognitive processes: The Tulane Flowerree symposium on cognition* (pp. 175–199). Hillsdale, NJ: Lawrence Erlbaum Associates.

Rosner, S. R. (1970). The effects of presentation and recall trials on organization in multitrial free recall. *Journal of Verbal Learning and Verbal Behavior, 9*, 69–74.

Slamecka, N. J., & Graf, P. (1978). The generation effect: Delineation of a phenomenon. *Journal of Experimental Psychology: Human Learning and Memory, 4*, 592–604.

Thompson, C. P., Wenger, S. K., & Bartling, C. A. (1978). How recall facilitates subsequent recall: A reappraisal. *Journal of Experimental Psychology: Human Learning and Memory, 4*, 210–221.

Thorndike, E. L., & Lorge, I. (1944). *The teacher's wordbook of 30,000 words.* New York: Bureau of Publications, Teachers College, Columbia University.

Tulving, E. (1967). The effects of presentation and recall of material in free-recall learning. *Journal of Verbal Learning & Verbal Behavior, 6*, 175–184.

Umilta, C., Snyder, C., & Snyder, M. (1972). Repetition effect as a function of event uncertainty, response-stimulus interval, and rank order of the event. *Journal of Experimental Psychology, 93*, 320–326.

Underwood, B. J., & Ekstrand, B. R. (1967). Effect of distributed practice on paired-associate learning. *Journal of Experimental Psychology, 73*(4, Pt. 2), 1–21.

Weinstock, R. B., & Daly, H. B. (1971). Response learning, association formation, and repeated testing effects in a paired-associate task. *Journal of Experimental Psychology, 87*, 343–347.

Wenger, S. K., Thompson, C. P., & Bartling, C. A. (1980). Recall facilitates subsequent recognition. *Journal of Experimental Psychology: Human Learning and Memory, 6*, 135–144.

Whitten, W. B. II, & Bjork, R. A. (1977). Learning from tests: Effects of spacing. *Journal of Verbal Learning and Verbal Behavior, 16*, 465–478.

Whitten, W. B. II, & Leonard, J. M. (1980). Learning from tests: Facilitation of delayed recall by initial recognition alternatives. *Journal of Experimental Psychology: Human Learning and Memory, 6*, 127–134.

Wilkinson, A. C., & Koestler, D. (1984). Generality of a strength model for three conditions of repeated recall. *Journal of Mathematical Psychology, 28*, 43–72.

APPENDIX

THE WILLIAM K. ESTES SYMPOSIUM AT HARVARD: A SHORT AFTER DINNER APPRECIATION

Bill Estes has taught at four of the best universities in the world. But in my considered view, his best move of all was to the West Coast, still America's frontier, and separated from Japan by only a small body of water. He came to Stanford in 1962. Anticipating his move by occult means, I decided to welcome him at Stanford. For that reason, I arrived there from Tokyo one year before he did. This premeditated move led to my becoming Bill's first PhD at Stanford.

I considered it to be a signal honor that Bill was inclined toward involvement in my dissertation. That is one reason why I am wearing the purple Imperial robe *with fans,* actually reserved for the forthcoming enthronement of Japan's new Emperor. I assume what is good enough for the Emperor is adequate for William K. Estes.

According to an age-old Japanese belief, real life begins after 60. There are two scientific reasons for this: One, both the solar and lunar calendars coincide only once every 60 years, as does the 12-animal Buddhist zodiac, which gives each year its name. So, those of you who want to or must practice frugality, do save this year's calendar; it will be handy in the year 2049! Your 60th birthday, therefore, is the first anniversary of that 60-year-cycle since your birth. That is the reason why the Japanese reserve the biggest and best birthday celebration for age 60. It was also the official age for retirement.

Two, see, this means that the first 60 years of your life do not count, because you are too young to know better! Your real and truly meaningful life commences at 60, when adequate experience and preparation have been acquired. It was the Japanese, not the British empiricists such as Locke, Berkely, and Hume, who maintained that nothing can substitute for experience. Thus, for the Japanese, official retirement marks the commencement of life's really significant portion. Consequently, after 60, persons initiate various new careers, enterprises, and businesses, and often go into politics. The same philosophy and attitude continued to prevail in recent years even *after* the official retirement age was increased far beyond 60. Retirement thus initiates true independence.

Also symbolized by the fans on my kimono is the fact that Bill is finally launching an auspicious career of real research, free from conventional constraints such as committee work and teaching schedules. He is now at the starting point, or on the hinge of the fan, as is said in Japan. As time passes, the fan unfolds, and the area under the fan's curved portion expands. That is, from this day forward, the significance and magnitude of your endeavors will grow steadily!

So, Bill, all of us gathered here eagerly anticipate your new contributions, and all of us join you in these renewed efforts to advance science.

We all greatly appreciate the splendid efforts by the Harvard Psychology Department and by Steve Kosslyn and his committee, for arranging this occasion. It seems appropriate now for me, as Bill's first PhD at Stanford, to propose that this symposium in his honor be the first of many more William K. Estes Symposia at various other locations. Although it is premature to talk about dates, I would, however, like to set one date. I will now begin to organize an Estes Symposium for June 17th, in the year 2019. Why this particular date? Well, exactly 20 years ago, on June 17th, 1969, I planned an occasion for celebrating Bill's 50th birthday, but I had to change the nature of the celebration, because he did not acquiesce to any birthday-related festivities before the age of 100. How Japanese could he get? After all, he was merely 50 years of age, definitely too young! He had not in fact started real life!

I was greatly intrigued by his wish, and promised to postpone any birthday celebration for 50 years. Of the 50, 20 years has already elapsed. How fast time flies! So, in order not to be too late for that special occasion, I am starting preparation of the invitation list today by asking you to place your names and addresses on the yellow pad now circulating. Please notify me of address changes between today and April, 2019. I am also passing around a white pad. Please write down the names and addresses, if known, of other suitable persons. I would really appreciate your assistance.

Mark Bill's centennial on your calendar now before you leave, and let us look forward to it. I will see all of you there. Thank you, everyone!

Chizuko Izawa
Cambridge, MA; September 16, 1989

P. S. Readers of this volume wishing to be invited to the William K. Estes Centennial on June 17, 2019 should make their wishes known promptly (unless they did so already, September, 1989) by writing to Chizuko Izawa, Department of Psychology, Tulane University, New Orleans, LA 70118-5698.

2 A New Theory of Disuse and an Old Theory of Stimulus Fluctuation

Robert A. Bjork
Elizabeth Ligon Bjork
University of California, Los Angeles

Speakers at the William K. Estes Symposium at Harvard University were asked to pick, if possible, a research topic where they could trace the influence of W. K. Estes in the work to be reported at the symposium. In the first author's case, that did not narrow down the possible topics in any substantial way. The work that seemed most timely to report at the symposium, however—the collaborative effort we refer to herein as a "new theory of disuse"—seemed not to be a particularly good example of the various significant influences William K. Estes has had on the two of us. Upon reflection, however, certain formal aspects of our theory correspond to a version of Estes' stimulus sampling theory, a version that incorporates what we consider to be one of the great insights in the history of research on learning and memory. That insight, initially reported in two short papers in the 1955 volume of the *Psychological Review* (Estes, 1955a, 1955b), is implemented in the so-called stimulus fluctuation version of Estes' statistical theory of learning.

However delayed and unconscious the influences may have been, we feel that our new theory of disuse owes some of its features to Estes' theory of stimulus fluctuation. One goal of this chapter is to sketch the similarities and differences between our theory-of-disuse framework and Estes' fluctuation model. In the sections that follow, we first summarize the characteristics of human memory that we feel suggest the storage and retrieval properties we postulate in our theory of disuse. We then present that framework along with some of its predictions and some arguments why such a pattern of storage and retrieval characteristics might be, overall, adaptive. We conclude with a section in which we first describe and pay homage to Estes' stimulus fluctuation insight, and we then compare and contrast the fluctuation model and our theory of disuse.

SOME IMPORTANT PECULIARITIES
OF STORAGE AND RETRIEVAL PROCESSES
IN HUMANS AND ANIMALS

In some important respects, the storage and retrieval properties of the human memory system differ markedly from the storage and retrieval properties of man-made memory devices, such as a tape recorder or the memory in a computer. The particular properties of human memory we summarize in the following sections have some important implications, in our view, as to the overall functional organization of the memory system.

Our Differing Capacities for Storage and Retrieval

In the modal view of human long-term memory, new information is stored in memory—not by recording some literal copy of that information, but, rather, by interpreting that information in terms of what we already know. New items of information are "fit in" to memory, so to speak, in terms of their meaning; that is, in terms of their semantic relationship to items, schemas, and scripts already in long-term memory. The process appears to be one of virtually unlimited capacity. Rather than using up storage capacity, as would be the case if our long-term memories were some kind of box or tape, the act of storing new information in memory appears to create the opportunities for additional storage: The more knowledge we have in a given domain, the more ways there are to store additional information. It also appears, at least to a first approximation, that once "entrenched" in long-term memory, information remains in memory for an indefinitely long period of time. (See Landauer, 1986, for some impressive estimates of the functional capacities of human long-term memory in some separate domains of knowledge; see, also, Miller & Gildea, 1987, for an impressive example of knowledge accumulation in a given domain—vocabulary items—across the first 18 years or so of life.)

As impressive as we appear to be in terms of getting information into long-term memory, we are far less impressive at getting information out of the system. The retrieval process is erratic, highly fallible, and heavily cue dependent. Information (such as a name, phone number, or street address) that is recallable on one occasion without apparent effort can be impossible to recall on another occasion. Even the most highly-overlearned and frequently accessed information, such as a street address or phone number, eventually becomes nonretrievable over years of disuse, though it is a simple matter via tests of relearning or recognition to demonstrate that such items still exist in storage.

What we can and cannot recall at a given point in time appears to be governed by the cues that are available to us, where such "cues" may be environmental, interpersonal, emotional, or physical (body states) as well as ones that bear a direct associative relationship to the target item. Cues that were originally associated in storage with the target information need to be reinstated, physically or mentally, at the time of retrieval. The importance of such reinstatement is, of course, at the heart of Tulving and Thompson's (1973) encoding specificity principle. (For a discussion of the importance of mental rather than physical reinstatement, see Bjork and Richardson-Klavehn, 1989.)

Retrieval as a Memory Modifier

In contrast to a computer or a tape recorder, where retrieving stored information leaves the stored representation of that information—and other information—unchanged (except for some slight physical deterioration, if any, that may result), the act of retrieving information from human memory modifies the system. The information retrieved becomes more retrievable in the future, and other information can become less retrievable.

In terms of its positive consequences, the act of retrieval is itself a potent learning event. As an overall generalization, the act of retrieving an item of information is considerably more potent in terms of facilitating its subsequent successful recall than is an additional study trial on that item. The actual extent to which a *successful* retrieval facilitates later retrieval appears to depend on how difficult or involved that act of retrieval is, with the subsequent benefits being a positive function of retrieval difficulty.

The foregoing assertions about the positive consequences of retrieval are based on a huge body of empirical research dating back decades (an abbreviated list of references is Allen, Mahler, & Estes, 1969; Bartlett, 1977; Bjork, 1975; Gardiner, Craik, & Bleasdale, 1973; Hogan & Kintsch, 1971; Izawa, 1970; Landauer & Bjork, 1978; Modigliani, 1976; Thompson, Wenger, & Bartling, 1978; and Whitten & Bjork, 1977). The assertion that there may be negative consequences for other items in memory, however, is a more novel idea that requires some more explicit evidence. Experiments by Bjork and Geiselman (1978) and by Richardson-Klavehn (1988) have the nice property of demonstrating simultaneously the positive (retrieval practice) and negative (retrieval competition) effects of retrieval.

In the Bjork and Geiselman experiment (1978, Experiment 3), subjects were presented two lists, each of which consisted of 12 word pairs (i.e., there were 24 words in each list). Within each list, after a filled delay of 6 s or 12 s, subjects were cued, in unpredictable fashion, whether to continue to remember or to forget each word pair. The consequences of the forget/remember and delay manipulations were of primary interest to Bjork and Geiselman, but are not relevant to the present issue. What *is* relevant is that each list was followed either by an immediate test of free recall for the to-be-remembered pairs or by a comparable period of deductive reasoning problems, and there was a final (end of experiment) test of free recall for all the words in both lists.

In Fig. 2.1 the final free recall of List 1 (bottom pair of curves) and List 2 (top

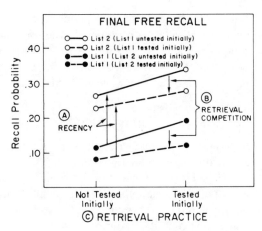

FINAL FREE RECALL

O——O List 2 (List I untested initially)
O——O List 2 (List I tested initially)
●——● List I (List 2 untested initially)
●——● List I (List 2 tested initially)

Ⓐ RECENCY

Ⓑ RETRIEVAL COMPETITION

Not Tested Initially   Tested Initially

Ⓒ RETRIEVAL PRACTICE

FIG. 2.1. Final free-recall probabilities as a function of list position and initial-test conditions. The influence of list recency (A), retrieval competition (B), and retrieval practice (C) is indicated. (After Bjork & Geiselman, 1978).

pair of curves) are shown as a function of the four possible combinations of whether List 1 and List 2 were tested or not tested. There was a recency effect (List 2 recalled better than List 1), but independent of that effect, each list was better recalled if it had been tested initially (the right hand points vs. the left hand points) and if the other list had not been tested initially (the top curve for each list vs. the bottom curve for each list). Thus, an initial free recall test on a given list not only facilitated its final free recall, but also impaired the final free recall of the other list.

Richardson-Klavehn (1988, Experiment 3) obtained analogous results with a different paradigm. Subjects were presented a list of 40 word-word paired associates to study. The stimulus and response words in each pair were low associates of each other, and the list of 40 pairs was presented three times in succession. At the end of the study phase, to give subjects a sense of closure, 10 of the 40 pairs were tested by presenting a given stimulus word as a cue for its associated response word. After a 5-min break, subjects were asked to learn a second list of 40 paired associates that consisted of the same 40 stimulus words paired with new response words, which were also low associates of the stimulus words (the lists, therefore, bore an AB-AC relationship to each other). List 2 was also presented three times for study and at the end of the study phase, 10 stimuli (a different 10 stimuli) were presented as a cued-recall test for their corresponding response words. Finally, 24 hours later, subjects' cued recall of List 1 response words was tested by presenting all 40 stimulus words one at a time.

Richardson-Klavehn was actually interested in the degree to which the retroactive interference owing to List 2 in the recall of List 1 items was a function of whether List 2 was learned in the same physical setting as List 1. His design, however, permits one to look at the 24-hr delayed recall of List 1 items for which neither the List 1 nor List 2 response was tested on Day 1 (20 pairs) versus the

List 1 items for which only the List 1 or the List 2 response was tested on Day 1 (10 pairs in each case). Collapsed across the same environmental manipulation, 63% of the List 1 responses were recalled when neither response had been tested on Day 1. When the List 1 response had been tested on Day 1, performance rose to 84%, and—of more interest—when the List 2 response had been tested on Day 1, performance *dropped* to 49%.

In both the Bjork and Geiselman and the Richardson-Klavehn experiments, then, an initial act of retrieval facilitated later retrieval of those items while impairing the recall of other items. In the former case, that pattern appeared on a whole-list basis in delayed free recall where the only obvious relationship between the lists was their common episodic context. In the latter case, that pattern appeared on a pair-specific basis where the List 1 and List 2 response words each bore a weak semantic relationship to a given stimulus word.

Relative or Absolute Accessibility to Items in Memory Regresses over Time

A final important peculiarity of human memory is that, over time, the accessibility of memory representations constructed earlier tends to increase relative to the accessibility of related memory representations constructed later. That is, a kind of regression process appears to be a fundamental factor in determining which items are and are not accessible (retrievable) from storage. When we update our memory representations (by learning to operate a new car, for example, or by learning a new golf swing, or a new word processing program, or the new married name of a friend, or a new list in a memory experiment), it is the new representation that is most accessible at the end of that learning process. With disuse of both representations, however, the pattern changes: There is loss of access to the more recent representation and a recovery in access (sometimes in absolute as well as relative terms) to the earlier representation.

The evidence for such memory regression in the real world is mostly observational and anecdotal. Coaches and skilled athletes tend to be aware that a long layoff leads to recovery of old habits. A layoff can even help a skilled athlete recover from a recent problem, whereas a layoff can lead to a major step backwards for an amateur who has been improving rapidly (the regression would be to good and not-so-good habits, respectively, in those two cases). People in the military tend also to be aware, in a general way, that regression is a problem. Personnel trained in new procedures and equipment can appear to be well-trained but nonetheless take inappropriate actions (that is, actions appropriate to the old equipment or procedures) at a later time, particularly under stress, as in the heat of battle.

Such regression processes no doubt generalize beyond the military and sports worlds. Bjork (1978) has argued that the common experience of being surprised "at how much a child has grown up, a friend has aged, or a town has changed since the last time one saw that child, friend, or town" (p. 250) may be interpretable in terms of the regression of memory representations.

> Children do grow up, of course, friends do age, and towns do change, but a subjective judgment of such changes based on the difference between a regressed memory representation and the current state of the child, friend, or town will overestimate the actual changes. One particularly compelling instance of such overestimation, in my view, occurs when one is away from one's small children for a week or two. The apparent growth can far exceed any actual growth that could have taken place in that time. The fact that a day or so later such phenomenal growth is no longer apparent argues against the reality of such apparent changes. (p. 250)

Beyond such real-world observations and anecdotes, there exists solid experimental evidence for such a regression process in humans and animals. In classic list-learning paradigms in the interference tradition (such as the AB-AC paired-associate paradigm), the pattern of proactive and retoractive effects changes markedly with the retention interval following List 2 learning. With the AB-AC paradigm, for example, retroactive interference (impaired recall of AB pairs owing to AC learning) tends to decrease with retention interval, whereas proactive interference (impaired recall of AC pairs owing to AB learning) tends to increase with retention interval (see, for example, Briggs, 1954; Ceraso & Henderson, 1965, 1966; Forrester, 1970; Koppenaal, 1963; Postman, Stark, & Fraser, 1968). In a number of those experiments employing MFR (give the first response that comes to mind) or MMFR (give all responses that you can remember) tests, there was an absolute increase in List 1 responses with an increasing retention interval following List 2 learning. Such "spontaneous recovery" is, of course, a common finding with extinction paradigms in animal research.

Another type of result that we feel demonstrates memory regression is the change from recency to primacy with delay. If subjects are asked—at the end of an experimental session during which a series of lists has been presented—to recall all the items they can remember from any of the lists, there is typically a strong list-recency effect: More items are recalled from the last list than from the next-to-last list, and so forth. After 24 hours (Bjork & Whitten, 1974) or a week (Bower & Reitman, 1972), however, if subjects are again asked to recall the lists, their recall exhibits primacy: The first list is recalled better than the second list, and so forth. Such a recency-to-primacy change with delay appears to occur across a broad range of time scales, types of tasks and materials, and species.

A particularly dramatic cross-species demonstration on a short time scale is provided by the work of Wright and his co-workers (Santiago & Wright, 1984; Wright, Santiago, & Sands, 1984; Wright, Santiago, Sands, Kendrick, & Cook, 1985; for a discussion see Wright, 1989). Pigeons, monkeys, and humans were given analogous memory-search tasks with visual materials. On each trial, four stimuli were shown one at a time (pictures in the experiments with pigeons and monkeys, kaleidoscope patterns in the experiments with humans). A probe item was then presented at various delays following the last item in a given memory set; the organism was required to make one response if the probe item had been in the memory set and another response if it was a new item. For "old" items (i.e., probes that matched a memory-set item), a plot of percent correct responding as a function of input serial position and probe delay exhibits a strikingly similar pattern for the pigeons, monkeys, and humans. At the shortest (zero s) delay, there is a monotonic recency effect for all three species; at the longest delay (10 s for pigeons, 30 s for monkeys, 100 s for humans), there is a monotonic primacy effect for all three species; and at intermediate delays, the functions are U-shaped for all three species. In addition to that change of pattern, there is an *absolute* increase in performance on the first memory-set item from the shortest to the longest probe delay.

A NEW THEORY OF DISUSE

In this section we sketch the assumptions, predictions, and adaptive features of a new theory of disuse. The assumptions of the theory emerge, in large part, from our analysis of the "peculiarities" of human memory summarized in the preceding section. We give those phenomena heavy weight because we feel (a) that they reflect an architecture of the memory system that differs from the architecture of man-made memory systems, and (b) that they imply storage and retrieval properties that are adaptive in the overall day-by-day functioning of human memory. In the latter respect, our approach corresponds in a general way to the approach advocated by Anderson (1989), who argues for "an alternative way of casting a theory of memory" based on his *Principle of Rationality* ("Human memory behaves as an optimal solution to the information-retrieval problems facing humans" [p. 195]). Baddeley (1988), too, has asked researchers to keep in mind that ". . . man is a biological and social animal, and like other animals is the product of evolution" (p. 15).

In formulating the theory, we take as a starting point the fact that items of information, no matter how accessible and overlearned they may be at some point in time, eventually become nonrecallable with disuse. In a symposium on autobiographical memory at a conference on practical aspects of memory held in Wales in the summer of 1987, we (Bjork & Bjork, 1988) argued that it is a mistake to view the frequent retrieval failures that characterize human memory as simply a weakness of the system. In terms of keeping the system current—in part *because* our storage capacity is so enormous—it is adaptive that we lose retrieval access to information with disuse. In attempting to recall our current home address, it is not useful to recall from our memories every home address we may have had in the past. That those prior addresses have, for the most part, become nonretrievable (though they remain stored) reduces confusion and speeds access to our current address.

A variety of such considerations led us to formulate a new theory of disuse. Thorndike's (1914) original law of disuse, of course, stands as one of the most thoroughly discredited of the various "laws" psychologists have put forward over the years—which is a considerable distinction. Thorndike argued that learned habits, without continued practice, fade or decay from memory with the passage of time. Interference theorists (e.g., McGeoch, 1932) presented compelling evidence against the notion that memory traces decay and that such decay takes place as a function of time alone. We, however, believe—the fate of the original law of disuse notwithstanding—that the "important peculiarities" of human memory that we have summarized suggest a modified theory of disuse. The following assumptions represent an attempt to specify in considerably more detail than we did initially the assumptions of such a theory.

Assumptions of the Theory

1. An item in memory can be characterized by two "strengths," a storage strength and a retrieval strength. The former measures, in a general way, how well learned an item is; the latter measures the current ease of access to the item in memory. The probability that an item can be recalled in response to a given cue is completely determined by its retrieval strength (and on the retrieval strength of other items in the set of items associated to that cue, as specified in Assumption 3) and is independent of its storage strength. That is, storage strength is a latent variable that has no direct effects on performance. Items with high storage strength can have low retrieval strength (e.g., a home phone number one had for 5 years 20 years ago), and items with low storage strength can have high retrieval strength (e.g., one's room number at a resort hotel on, say, the third day of one's stay at that hotel).

(Viewed historically, the distinction we make between storage strength and retrieval strength is analogous to distinctions made by learning theorists of another era. Hull [1943] distinguished between habit strength and momentary reaction potential; Estes [1955b], as we discuss in more detail later, distinguished between habit strength and response strength; even Skinner [1938], distinguished between reflex reserve and reflex strength.)

2. The storage strength of a given item grows as a pure accumulation process, that is, as a monotonic function of opportunities to study or recall that item. To at least a first approximation, therefore, it is assumed that storage strength once accumulated is never lost. One consequence of this assumption is that there is no limit on the amount of information that can be stored in long-term memory; that is, on the sum of storage strengths across items. The growth function for a given item is, however, assumed to be negatively accelerated: The increment in

storage strength for a given item owing to a study or test event is assumed to be a decreasing function of its current storage strength. We also assume that the increment in storage strength is a decreasing function of its current retrieval strength; that is, high retrieval strength is assumed to retard the accumulation of additional storage strength.

3. Whereas there is no limit on storage capacity, there is a limit on retrieval capacity; that is, on the total number of items that are retrievable at any one point in time in response to a retrieval cue or set of cues. In fact, we assume two kinds of limits on retrieval capacity. The first, an overall limit, simply reflects our assertion (Assumption 5) that retrieval strength, in contrast to storage strength, is lost as a function of subsequent study and test events on other items. Thus, at some point, a kind of dynamic equilibrium is reached where any gain in retrieval strength for items being studied or tested is offset by a corresponding loss in retrieval strength summed across other items in memory.

The second, and often more significant limitation, arises from how we characterize the cue-dependent nature of retrieval. For an item to be recalled in response to a given cue, we assume that its representation must be discriminated from the representations of other items in memory associated to that cue, and that it must be reconstructed or integrated from its representation. Discriminating an item is assumed to be a function of its retrieval strength relative to the strengths of other items in the cued set (its strength, e.g., normalized with respect to the sum of the item strengths in the cued set). Reconstructing the item for output, on the other hand, is presumed to be a straightforward function of its absolute retrieval strength. The net effect of these assumptions is to put a limit on the number of items that can be accessible in memory at a given time. As items are added to memory, or as the retrieval strengths of certain items are increased, other items become less recallable.

4. The act of retrieving an item from memory, and the act of studying an item, both result in increments to that item's retrieval strength as well as to its storage strength, but retrieval is the more potent event. That is, the act of retrieving an item (successfully) results in larger increments to storage strength and retrieval strength than does studying an item. Increments in retrieval strength, in either case, are assumed to be a decreasing function of an item's current retrieval strength and an increasing function of its current storage strength. One consequence of these assumptions is that the benefits of a successful retrieval, in terms of its influence on that item's subsequent retrieval strength, are larger the more difficult or involved the act of retrieval (low retrieval strength) and the better registered the item is in memory (high storage strength).

5. The decrement in an item's retrieval strength owing to the learning or retrieval of other items is, conversely, assumed to be greater the higher the item's current retrieval strength and the lower the item's current storage strength. An-

other way to characterize these assumptions is to say that the gain and loss of retrieval strength are both negatively accelerated, and that storage strength acts to enhance the gain and retard the loss of retrieval strength.

It follows from the foregoing assumptions that increasing the retrieval strengths of certain items (via study or test events) makes other items less retrievable. Such competitive effects will tend to be governed by similarity or category relationships defined semantically or episodically. That is, a given retrieval cue or combination of cues will define a set of associated items in memory—which, in general, will bear some type of similarity relationship to each other—and the dynamics of competition for retrieval capacity, as was spelled out in Assumption 3, take place across that set.

"Predictions" of the Theory

Although we stay at the qualitative level in this chapter, it is, of course, our goal to predict the kind of phenomena we summarize below quantitatively as well as qualitatively. As may be apparent from how the assumptions of our theory are stated, one straightforward, though surprisingly complex, mathematical implementation of the theory is in terms of a set of interdependent linear difference equations. That representation, judging from our preliminary efforts to derive certain predictions, appears quite promising.

The "important peculiarities" of human memory discussed earlier influenced heavily the assumptions of our new theory of disuse, so it is not surprising or impressive that the theory can accommodate those findings. Certain aspects of the theory's account of those and other properties of human memory, however, warrant comment.

Storage versus Retrieval.   The heroic storage capabilities and relatively frail retrieval capabilities of human memory emerge directly from the assumptions. The cue-dependent nature of retrieval processes is built into the theory as well. It should also be apparent that an item in memory, however well learned (that is, however high its storage strength), becomes inaccessible if not retrieved periodically. As other items are learned or strengthened via retrieval practice, the item in question becomes less and less accessible. It is not staying competitive, so to speak, for the limited retrieval capacities that characterize the system. The gradual (or, under some circumstances, not so gradual) loss of retrieval access is not a consequence of the mere passage of time, but, rather, is a consequence of the learning and practice of other items. It is worth noting that the memory-as-a-box analogy, which is so wrong on the storage side (as argued earlier) may have some truth on the retrieval side. As we make some items in memory more and more accessible, according to our theory of disuse, there is less and less remaining retrieval capacity for other items. This viewpoint, then, may exonerate the ichthyologist David Starr Jordon, who as President of Stanford University complained that every time he learned the name of a student, he forgot the name of a fish. He is often cited uncharitably as someone who had a fallacious idea of the capacity of human memory. Given the limit on retrieval capacity assumed in our theory, however, an ichthyologist suddenly spending considerable time learning and retrieving the names of a large number of students could well lose access to the names of certain fish.

Retrieval Practice and Retrieval Competition. That retrieving an item from memory facilitates the later retrieval of that item, and that such effects are greater the greater the difficulty of the initial retrieval, is simply assumed in the theory. The competitive effects of retrieval—that is, that certain other items in memory become *less* retrievable in the future—arise because of the cue-specific and global limitations on retrieval capacity. As some items in the set of items associated to a given cue gain in retrieval strength, other items in that set will suffer, in part because they become less discriminable or "findable" in memory owing to their lessened *relative* retrieval strengths, and in part because their *absolute* retrieval strength will decrease with their disuse and the "use" of the other items in the set.

Regression/Recovery Phenomena. The relative or absolute recovery of older memory representations with time emerges from the theory in a somewhat less obvious way. It may be easiest to explicate the basic mechanisms in the context of classic unlearning and spontaneous-recovery phenomena (e.g., Melton & Irwin, 1940; Postman et al., 1968). The unlearning of a first list as a consequence of learning a similar second list (say, e.g., in an AB-AC paired-associate paradigm) comes about in the theory because increasing the accessibility of second-list responses decreases the accessibility of first-list responses. With the passage of time, however, and the disuse of both List 1 and List 2, the loss of List 1 retrieval strength will be offset by a greater loss of List 2 retrieval strength (because the loss of retrieval strength is negatively accelerated).

Whether there is an absolute increase in the recall of List 1 responses as the retention interval increases, or only an increase relative to the recall of List 2 responses, depends in the theory on certain parameter values. In particular, if List 1 responses can be viewed as having achieved a higher level of storage strength than List 2 responses (which could happen, e.g., if List 1 responses are rehearsed during List 2 learning), then the recovery of List 1 responses could be substantial in absolute terms. In that case, as asserted in Assumption 5, the higher storage strength of List 1 responses will slow the rate of loss of their retrieval strengths; at some value of the delay since List 2 learning, the retrieval-strength curves for List 1 and List 2 responses will cross, with List 1 responses having higher absolute retrieval strength after that point.

The change from recency to primacy as a function of retention interval is predicted for similar reasons. Once again, the absolute increase in performance on initial lists or items with delay (as in the pigeon/monkey/human data discussed by Wright, 1989) is explicable in the theory by assuming that early items, via cumulative rehearsal or other factors, reach a higher level of storage strength than do later items. The kind of anecdotal regression phenomena cited earlier for skilled athletes and military personnel may constitute cases where it is particularly plausible to assume that early habits have a higher level of storage strength in memory than do later habits. One's new, improved tennis serve is not going to be as entrenched in memory as one's old tennis serve, for example; nor is it likely that the operator of a new piece of military hardware has had the same amount of experience with its controls as he or she had with the controls of the hardware it replaced.

Overlearning and Repeated Learning.   It is a time-honored result in both the human and animal literature that additional learning trials given after perfect performance is achieved (overlearning), or additional relearning sessions where performance is brought back to the original criterion (repeated learning) act to slow the rate of subsequent forgetting (e.g., Ebbinghaus, 1885/1964; Krueger, 1929). In the present theory, such effects have a straightforward interpretation in terms of the distinction between storage strength and retrieval strength. Performance is a function of retrieval strength, and performance cannot go beyond 100%. Storage strength can continue to accrue, however, as a function of overlearning or repeated learning, and increased storage strength acts (in the theory) to slow the loss of retrieval strength (and, hence, the observed forgetting).

This type of explanation of the effects of overlearning and repeated learning is not new or unique to our theory of disuse. In fact, Woodworth and Schlosberg's (1954) interpretation of the effects of repeated learning, as quoted below, corresponds quite closely to our interpretation (if one thinks of "trace strength" as storage strength and "readiness" as retrieval strength).

> On each successive day [the subject] learns to the same standard of one correct recitation. At the end of each day, he has reached the same degree of mastery. Why then should not forgetting proceed at the same rate? We are forced to conclude that the trace becomes stronger and stronger with each relearning. What is the same at the end of each day's learning is not the trace but the immediate recitability or recallability of the lesson, and recall obviously depends not alone upon the trace but also upon the momentary condition of readiness. Readiness depends very much on recency of impression. (p. 730)

Distribution of Practice.   Our theory of disuse can account for the benefits on long-term retention of spacing repeated study trials, and for the interaction of repetition spacing and retention interval. At a formal level, the explanation is much the same as that provided by Estes' fluctuation model, which is outlined later in this chapter. In general, spacing of repetitions results in higher storage strength than does massing of repetitions, which in turn slows the rate of loss of retrieval strength and, therefore, enhances long-term performance. Massing, however, can produce a higher initial level of retrieval strength, which, given a short enough retention interval, can result in a higher level of recall than that produced by spaced repetitions.

It is worth mentioning that the theory of disuse gives a natural interpretation of Jost's (1897) Law: If two associations are of equal strength but different ages, further study has greater value for the older one. In general, for two associations differing in age to be of equal retrieval strength, the older association must be at a higher level of storage strength. In that case, the increment in retrieval strength will be larger for the older association.

A Test of the Cue-Specific Nature of Retrieval Competition

The primary locus of retrieval competition, as specified earlier in Assumption 3, is within the set of items defined by a retrieval cue or combination of cues. Access to weaker items in the set is inhibited or obscured by the presence of stronger items in the set (see, e.g., the list strength experiments of Ratcliff, Clark, & Shiffrin, 1990). To ascertain whether such inhibitory or competitive effects are indeed cue (or category) specific, Anderson and Bjork (1990) have carried out several experiments using a new paradigm devised by Michael Anderson at UCLA. The basic procedure is as follows. Subjects are presented a list of pairs to study, each of which consists of a category name and an instance of the category (e.g., TREE Maple or DRINKS Scotch). Typically, six instances of eight different categories are presented in unblocked fashion producing a total of 48 pairs. There is then a retrieval-practice phase during which half the exemplars of half the categories (i.e., three members of each of four categories) are each tested three times. The retrieval of a given category member is induced by the category name and letter cues (e.g., TREE Ma_____), and the several retrievals of each of the 12 practiced items are interleaved with the tests on other items in such a fashion as to produce an expanding sequence of intertest intervals for each item (which appears to maximize the consequences of retrieval practice; see Landauer & Bjork, 1978). After an additional delay, subjects are given a final test in which they are cued with each category name and asked to free recall as many members of that category as they can remember having been presented in the original study list.

From the standpoint of the final test, a given category may have been accessed during the intervening retrieval-practice phase (an RP category) or it may not have been accessed (an NRP category). If it was a practiced category, then items within the category may have been practiced (RP+ items) or not practiced (RP− items).

This paradigm bears some relationship to part-list cuing procedures. At issue is the level of recall for RP+, RP−, and NRP items. Our theory predicts not only that RP+ items will be better recalled than NRP (and RP−) items, but also that NRP items will be recalled *better* than RP− items. The several intervening retrievals of RP+ items during the retrieval-practice phase will not only enhance their retrieval strength, but should also create problems for RP− items. The category name coupled with the instruction to recall members of that category presented during the study episode constitute a combined cue that designates a set of items in memory. For an NRP category, those items are on equal footing, so to speak, but for an RP category the RP− items are put at a competitive disadvantage by virtue of the presence of RP+ items in the cued set.

It is worth noting that the key prediction of the theory, that RP− items will be recalled more poorly than NRP items, runs counter to the effects of any episodic or semantic spread of activation to RP− items during the retrieval-practice phase. That is, the process of responding to TREE Ma_____ should, in semantic network models, spread some activation to other traces, particularly to other trees that were on the list and also bear some semantic relationship to *maple* (e.g., *oak*).

The basic pattern of results obtained by Anderson and Bjork (1990) is consistent with the theory of disuse. The size of the retrieval-practice effect (RP+ items vs. NRP items) and the retrieval inhibition effect (NRP items vs. RP− items) have varied as a function of category-to-exemplar associative strength and exemplar-to-category associative strength, but averaging across such manipulations the overall proportion of RP+, NRP, and RP− items recalled is .73, .49, and .37, respectively. Thus, the primary negative impact of the retrievals of RP+ items is on RP− items in the same category, not on NRP items in another category (although they, too, were in the original study list with RP+ items). To be able to say whether there are *any* inhibitory effects on NRP items requires a control condition (no retrieval practice phase at all) that has yet to be tested.

Adaptive Consequences
for Autobiographical/Real-World Memory

We stated earlier our belief that the storage and retrieval properties of human memory define a system that is, all things considered, adaptive. In terms of the demands the world places on our memories, there is much to be said for a system with the properties embedded in our new theory of disuse. In general, the theory says that the items in memory that are most readily accessible to us are those we have been using (retrieving) lately. The items that have been retrieved frequently in the recent past will tend to be items highly relevant to our current interests, problems, goals, and general station in life. Statistically, those items will be relevant to the near future as well.

What about the items (names, numbers, facts, . . .) that we stop using? The theory says that eventually, however high their storage strength, they become nonretrievable. But why would we stop, for example, using the maiden name of a female friend or the combination on our gym locker? There are a variety of reasons, but they break into two types: Either that name or number is replaced (our female friend assumes a new married name; we get a new locker with a different combination) or events conspire to make us lose contact with our friend or locker (we move, she moves; we abandon hope and stop using the gym, and so forth). In either case, there are adaptive consequences of our losing retrieval access to that name or number. In the replacement case, the reason is obvious: We do not want to intrude our friend's maiden name or our old combination when trying to recall the current name or number. Items that are nonretrievable are also noninterfering (we do not, for example, typically have much difficulty recalling our current home phone number, even though we may have had many phone numbers in the past, some for a number of years, and even though we could verify that those out-of-date numbers still reside in our memory).

The adaptive aspects of losing retrieval access to names and numbers that we stop using by virtue of moving or changing our lives in some other way are a bit less obvious. If we consider, however, that for reasons of retrieval speed as well as accuracy we do not *want* everything in memory to be accessible, the adaptive consequences are fairly clear. The changes that result in our not using certain names and numbers will tend to require that we start using new and different names and numbers. Consider a new graduate student moving across the country to begin his or her graduate work. A whole panoply of new names (of people, streets, restaurants, campus buildings, . . .) and numbers (phone numbers, addresses, office numbers, ATM numbers, course numbers, . . .) must be learned and used—in addition to the learning that is a formal part of that student's graduate education. Those new names and numbers will gradually gain in storage strength and retrieval strength, and corresponding names and numbers from that student's past life will gradually lose retrieval strength. That pattern, overall, is adaptive. Put another way, *because* the storage capacity of human memory is so enormous, we need something to filter or direct access to the subset of items most relevant to our current needs. In our theory of disuse, retrieval strength plays that role.

It is also adaptive that items lose retrieval strength rather than storage strength with disuse: Because they become nonretrievable, they are noninterfering, but they are relearnable at an accelerated rate should they become pertinent again. (In the theory, the largest increments in retrieval strength as a consequence of studying or recalling an item take place for items that are high in storage strength and low in retrieval strength.) Such items may be recognizable as well. We have yet to characterize the process of recognition in our theory, but, presumably, recognition is sensitive to storage strength and is less dependent on retrieval strength than is recall. As an updating mechanism, then, the loss of retrieval strength for out-of-date items has several advantages over decay or displacement processes that leave no representation of the item in memory (such as the kind of destructive updating or overwriting characteristic of a tape recorder or a computer memory; for more on this argument, see Bjork, 1989).

The cue-dependent nature of retrieval assumed by the theory (not that that assumption is by any means unique to our theory) also has an important adaptive aspect. Normally inaccessible information becomes retrievable if the original environmental or situational cues to which that information was associated are reinstated. When we return to a town where we grew up, or to a school we attended, the environmental and interpersonal cues that are reinstated enable us to access memories that without those cues are not retrievable. That information tied to earlier contextual cues in our lives becomes more accessible when we are back in that context is, of course, adaptive: By virtue of our very return to an old context or situation, our need for access to information associated with that setting becomes greater.

Finally, although the argument is somewhat tenuous, the relative or absolute recovery of older memory representations with time may frequently be adaptive. Suppose that some new name or number or procedure has replaced an old name or number or procedure. With use of a new procedure, for example, that procedure will become more accessible in memory and the old procedure will become less accessible. The procedure in question, for example, might be the steps one goes through in moving blocks of text in a new word processing program. Suppose now that we stop using the new procedure. Many of the circumstances that would lead us to do so would also involve the old procedure becoming relevant again (we were on leave at some location where the new program was the institutional standard, and now we are returning to our own computer and office, or maybe we simply decided we did not like the new procedure). In such cases, the recovery of access to the old procedure, with disuse of the new procedure, would be adaptive.

ESTES' THEORY OF STIMULUS FLUCTUATION

Our theory of disuse represents our attempt to formulate, in a relatively neutral and abstract way, a representation of human memory that captures some storage and retrieval characteristics that we deem to be fundamental. As it turns out, a number of those "fundamental" characteristics are derivable from Estes' stimulus fluctuation theory. In this section we sketch the assumptions and achievements of the fluctuation theory.

In two papers published in the 1955 volume of the *Psychological Review,* William K. Estes shifted the focus of his "statistical theory of learning," from acquisition and extinction processes taking place within an experimental session, to between-session phenomena such as spontaneous recovery, forgetting, and distribution-of-practice effects on learning. The key idea was to assume that the stimulus aspects of a given environmental situation that were actually available to (that is, could potentially have an influence on) the organism changed continuously over time. Such fluctuation processes could, then, result in a quite different functional stimulus situation when an organism returned to the same nominal experimental environment.

The initial assumptions of Estes' statistical learning theory, as put forward in his now classic 1950 paper, were summarized as follows by Estes (1955a) himself.

a. Any environmental situation, as constituted at a given time, determines for a given organism a population of stimulus events from which a sample affects the organism's behavior at any instant; in statistical learning theories the population is conceptualized as a set of stimulus elements from which a random sample is drawn on each trial.

b. Conditioning and extinction occur only with respect to the elements sampled on a trial.

c. The behaviors available to an organism in a given situation may be categorized into mutually exclusive and exhaustive response classes.

d. At any time, each stimulus element in the population is conditioned to exactly one of the response classes. (pp. 146–147)

Those initial assumptions presumed a perfectly constant physical environment in which the population of stimulus "elements" from which the organism sampled on any given trial was fixed. Such an idealized situation was unrealistic Estes argued, particularly if one wanted to understand recovery and forgetting across delays separating successive experimental sessions in the same or altered contexts. He assumed instead that at any moment only a subset of the possible stimulus elements in a given situation was available to the organism to sample, and that a random process over time governed whether a given stimulus element would be available or unavailable to the organism; that is, elements "fluctuated" between available and unavailable states. Such elements were presumed to correspond to "a large number of independently variable components or aspects of the environmental situation, all of which undergo constant random fluctuation" (1955a, p. 147). Bower and Hilgard (1981) summarized the possible reasons for such fluctuation as ". . . day to day fluctuation in the temperature or humidity of the experimental room, changes in the subject's internal milieu, postural set, or attitudes, sensitivity of various receptors, and so forth" (p. 227).

Achievements of the Stimulus Fluctuation Theory

The fluctuation idea implemented within the framework of stimulus sampling theory was able to account for a wide range of phenomena, in many cases quantitatively as well as qualitatively.

Spontaneous Recovery and Regression (Estes, 1955a).   One of the elegant outcomes of Estes' analysis is that spontaneous recovery and forgetting, from the standpoint of the fluctuation theory, became formally equivalent. Assume that in an experimental apparatus of some kind an animal is reinforced for a certain behavior. At the beginning of acquisition, none of the elements, available or unavailable, would be conditioned to the appropriate response. At the end of a training session (given typical values of the fluctuation parameters), most or all of the elements in the available set will be conditioned, so the animal may be responding at a high rate, but most of the unavailable elements will remain unconditioned to the target response. If the animal is now given a period away from the apparatus, there will be forgetting; that is, a reduced rate of responding when the animal is brought back to the apparatus. Such forgetting is the consequence of conditioned elements fluctuating from the available to the unavailable set and unconditioned elements fluctuating from the unavailable to the available set. With a long enough delay, the system will reach an equilibrium state where the ratio of conditioned to unconditioned elements in the available and unavailable sets will be the same; that ratio will determine the asymptote of the forgetting function.

Assume now that as a consequence of repeated training sessions the animal is fully trained, which would mean that all the elements in the available *and* the unavailable sets are conditioned to the target response. An extinction session carried out with such a fully trained animal would correspond to unconditioning most or all of the elements in the available set. Many elements in the unavailable set would remain conditioned, however, and the fluctuation of those elements into the available set as a consequence of the animal being given a period away from the apparatus will lead to spontaneous recovery. The same type of dynamics, then, leads to both forgetting and spontaneous recovery.

The effects of overlearning and repeated learning on the rate of forgetting, and the effects of repeated extinction sessions on spontaneous recovery were accounted for in a natural way by the theory. The intervals between repeated learning sessions permit unconditioned elements in the unavailable set to fluctuate into the available set where they can be conditioned during the next training session. In an analogous fashion, the intervals between repeated extinction sessions permit conditioned elements to fluctuate from the unavailable to the available set, where they can then be unconditioned. The consequence of repeated learning or extinction sessions, then, is to condition (learning) or uncondition (extinction) more of the total population of stimulus elements, available and unavailable, thereby slowing the subsequent rate of forgetting or spontaneous recovery. The asymptotes of the forgetting and spontaneous-recovery functions will, of course, also be influenced by repeated learning or extinction sessions. In the limit, if all the elements in the available and unavailable sets are conditioned or unconditioned, respectively, there can be no forgetting or spontaneous recovery at all.

Distributional Phenomena in Learning (Estes, 1955b).   In the second of his 1955 papers, Estes begins by saying "One aspect of distribution of practice that recent reviewers . . . seem agreed upon is its persistent refractoriness to any general theoretical interpretation" (p. 369). He then goes on, in our opinion, to provide such an interpretation—an interpretation that has been rediscovered in various guises periodically by subsequent researchers.

Within the framework of the fluctuation theory, Estes distinguished between *habit strength* and *response strength* (which correspond, as mentioned earlier, to storage strength and retrieval strength in our theory of disuse). Habit strength is determined by the total number of conditioned elements across the available and unavailable sets. Appropriate observable indices of habit strength are measures such as resistance to extinction and rate of forgetting. Response strength, on the other hand, is determined by the proportion of conditioned elements in the available set at any given point in time. It is reflected in terms of the momentary probability, rate, or latency of responding.

The importance of this distinction, with respect to the analysis of distribution (spacing) of practice, is that between-session stimulus fluctuation will have the opposite effect on the growth of habit strength and response strength. Increasing the spacing of trials or experimental sessions will increase stimulus fluctuation between trials or sessions, which will enhance the rate of growth of habit strength (because more new unconditioned elements will be available to condition during each trial or session) but will decrease the rate of growth of response strength, at least early in training, because more conditioned elements will fluctuate out of the available set from one trial or period to the next. Using the quantitative machinery of stimulus-sampling theory, Estes was able to account for a large variety of existing spacing effects in the conditioning and extinction literature. Among those phenomena are (a) that resistance to extinction is enhanced by spacing of conditioning periods; (b) that retention is increased by spacing learning periods with the advantage increasing with the length of the retention interval; and (c) that learning (or extinction) tends to be faster at the beginning of training with massed trials, but later in training the advantage shifts to spaced trials.

The observed interaction of spacing interval and retention interval (massing better for shorter retention intervals, spacing better for longer intervals) was later observed in experiments with humans as well (e.g., Glenberg, 1979; Glenberg & Lehmann, 1980; Peterson, Hillner, & Saltzman, 1962). That interaction, which emerges in a natural way from the fluctuation theory, has been particularly difficult for most other theories of the spacing effect to predict.

Finally, the fluctuation theory provides a staightforward interpretation for what seems to be a "paradoxical" aspect of the fact that long-term retention is enhanced by spaced repetitions. Melton (1967) pointed out that such an effect seems to suggest that forgetting helps memory, because more forgetting takes place prior to the second presentation the greater the interval from the first to the second presentation. Such "forgetting" in the fluctuation model corresponds to conditioned elements moving from the available to the unavailable set and unconditioned elements moving from the unavailable to the available set, which, of course, is exactly what is necessary to maximize the effectiveness of the second presentation.

Developments Since 1955.   It is not possible here to track fully the influence of the fluctuation theory in the years following the two 1955 papers. A few examples, however, may illustrate the explanatory range of the fluctuation idea. Probably the most impressive extension of the theory has been to interference phenomena, particularly interference and recovery phenomena as a function of temporal variables and degree of learning. Estes (1959) presented some initial examples of how the fluctuation idea could account for certain retroactive and proactive effects, and Bower (1967) gave a more thorough and explicit treatment of interference phenomena in terms of fluctuation mechanisms. Recently, in an effort to account for a variety of interference and forgetting phenomena, Mensink and Raaijmakers (1988) incorporated the contextual fluctuation mechanism of stimulus sampling theory within the SAM framework of Raaijmakers and Shiffrin (1981). As we read that impressive paper, the successful analysis of various classic interference phenomena are more a consequence of the contextual-fluctuation assumption than of the SAM framework itself.

The fluctuation idea also has been extended to account for tests as learning and forgetting-prevention events (Izawa, 1971; Whitten & Bjork, 1977), and to experiments on verbal short-term memory (Bower, 1972; Estes, 1971; Peterson, 1963). In a particularly systematic and thorough exercise, Bower (1972) showed how encoding variability ideas, implemented within the stimulus-fluctuation version of stimulus sampling theory, can account for characteristics of recognition, temporal-lag judgments, list-differentiation, and consolidation/retrograde-amnesia.

Beyond such explicit, quantitative, extrapolations of the fluctuation theory, there have been widespread conceptual influences of the fluctuation idea. The fluctuation-plus-sampling process is a forerunner of the various incarnations of the encoding-variability idea (e.g., Martin, 1968). Glenberg's (1979) ambitious theory of spacing phenomena in human memory, in particular, can be viewed as a generalization and extension of Estes' original stimulus-fluctuation idea. In some cases, researchers have apparently not been aware that their ideas were expressed earlier in stimulus-fluctuation terms. Cuddy and Jacoby's notion (1982; Jacoby, 1978), for example, that for a repetition to be effective there needs to be some forgetting of the initial presentation, is stated explicitly by Estes (as mentioned earlier) in the second of the 1955 papers. (In fairness to Cuddy and Jacoby, their argument as to *why* such forgetting is helpful differs from the fluctuation-theory argument.)

Fluctuation Theory as a Guide to Intuition: An Illustration

One informal measure of a theory's value is whether it can serve as a guide to one's intuition, in the sense that it is a better basis for prediction than one's "common sense." Put in a way that seems to be gaining popularity, does the theory pass the "grandmother test"; that is, does it tell us something more than our grandmother could have told us? On that measure, fluctuation theory holds up very well indeed.

To illustrate that unintuitive implications of the fluctuation theory often prove to be correct, we describe briefly the results of an unpublished experiment carried out by the first author some years ago.[1] In this study, 60 subjects each went through a deck of 88 cards at a 10-s rate. On a given card in the deck, a pair of 4-letter nouns was presented for study (e.g., FERN-WASP), or the left hand member of a prior pair was presented as a test of the subjects' memory for the right hand member of that pair (e.g., ROPE- ??). Thus, the experiment employed a continuous paired-associate paradigm, but there was an updating requirement: About half the time, the first study card involving a given stimulus (FERN-WASP) was followed, after a variable number of intervening cards involving other pairs, by a second study card on which that stimulus was paired with a new response word (e.g., FERN-PULP). On the later test of that pair in the deck (FERN- ??), subjects were to give only the current, most recent, response (PULP). Subjects could not ignore the first study card involving a given stimulus, however, because half the time, in unpredictable fashion, that first pairing was the only study card involving that stimulus (that is, there was no second response paired with that stimulus) in which case the correct response to the test (FERN-??) was WASP.

The pairs involving a repeated stimulus, then, corresponded to an AB-AC paradigm. The question motivating the experiment was a simple one: What would happen to the recall of the second response (C) as a function of the interval between the AB and AC pairings? And would the effects of the AB-AC interval interact with the retention interval from AC to the test? In the experimental design those two intervals were co-varied: 0, 3, or 9 cards intervened between the AB and AC cards, and 3 or 9 cards intervened between the AC pairing and the test. Across those six conditions, the interval from the AB pairing to the test, then, was 3, 6, 9, 12, and 18 events involving other pairs. For the purpose of providing a baseline against which to evaluate the intrusion rates of the B response in the different AB-AC conditions, a subset of the once-presented AB pairs was tested at those same AB-Test delays (where, now, B is the correct response).

---

[1]Lisa White and Brenda Hasson provided invaluable assistance in this research.

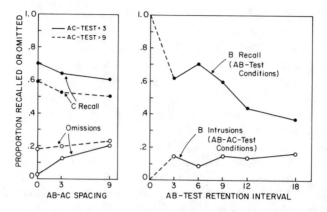

FIG. 2.2. Proportion of responses that were correct (C recall) or omissions as a function of the AB-AC spacing interval and the AC-Test retention interval (left panel); proportions of B responses correctly recalled and intruded, respectively, as a function of the AB-Test retention interval in the control (no AC presentation) and AB-AC conditions.

From a common-sense standpoint, there seems little doubt (for a fixed retention interval) that the recall of C should increase with the AB-AC interval. After all, not only should the AC event be more discriminable from the AB event the greater the spacing interval, but the B response should be weaker as well (because the interval from AB to the test increases with the AB-AC interval). About the only reason to expect otherwise—and the reason we bothered to do the experiment—is the spacing effect itself. If one views the repetition case (AB-AB-Test) as a positive-transfer paradigm, then it could be that the conditions that maximize positive transfer (increased AB-AB spacing) might also maximize negative transfer in the AB-AC paradigm.

The results of the experiment are shown in Fig. 2.2. In the left panel, proportion correct recall of C responses and omissions are plotted as a function of AB-AC spacing for each retention interval. In the right panel, recall of the B response from the AB once-presented control items, and intrusions of the B response in the AB-AC conditions, are plotted as a function of the AB-Test retention interval.

Common sense notwithstanding, the level of C recall in the left panel goes down (and omissions go up) as a function of the AB-AC spacing interval. Performance is also higher at the shorter AC-Test retention interval, which is no surprise. In the right panel, recall in the AB control condition goes down with retention interval, as it should, but the rate of intrusions of B in the AB-AC conditions does *not* show a corresponding decrease across the same AB-Test intervals.

The fluctuation theory has little difficulty in accounting for the general pattern of results in Fig. 2.2. The basic argument is that the longer the interval from AB to AC the more opportunity there is for elements "conditioned" to B to fluctuate to the unavailable state prior to the AC event. To the degree they are lurking in the unavailable set at the time the AC pairing is studied, they are protected from being "counterconditioned" to the C response, which means they may fluctuate back to the available set during the AC-Test interval. If they are in the available set at the time of test, they may cause intrusions of the B response (right panel) or they may contribute to omissions (left panel) by, for example, leading to a sample of elements that does not favor the B or the C response.

Some Metacomments on the 1955 Papers

We cannot resist sharing a few reactions we had in rereading the original 1955 papers. First of all, those papers are surprisingly short; they are nine and one-half and nine pages long, respectively, and those are the small pages of 1955, not the current large pages.

We were also surprised in going back over those papers how much the empirical phenomena Estes cited, and the terminology he used, were drawn from animal research. In virtually every case where results from the animal literature are cited, analogous human results could have been cited instead or in addition. Those relevant human results, in fact, were nicely summarized in the outstanding books on experimental psychology published by Osgood (1953) and Woodworth and Schlosberg (1954) just prior to the Estes 1955 papers.

The only basis for our surprise, of course, is that *we* think in terms of the more cognitive Bill Estes who emerged in the late 1950s, and blossomed in the early 1960s. According to Estes' (1989) autobiography, the influence of his graduate mentor, B. F. Skinner—who would not let him use the word "memory" in their coauthored papers—and an early philosophical commitment to operationism guided his empirical and theoretical work during the first 15 to 20 years of his professional career. His eventual shift toward a rigorous type of constructivism was a consequence, in part, of the influence of Patrick Suppes, Gordon Bower, Richard Atkinson, and other neomentalists at Stanford University. (The use of "neomentalists" is our, not Estes', characterization.)

From a philosophy-of-science standpoint, the 1955 papers seem to constitute a kind of balancing act. There seems to be an effort to defend such theorizing to the radical behaviorists while rejecting a certain type of untestable mentalism.

All such considerations aside, we were struck again at how beautifully written and elegantly argued those papers are. In both papers, the ideas are sketched in very understandable terms before being phrased, in separate sections, in mathematical terms (". . . to permit self-selection diets for readers of varying mathematical appetites" [p. 369]). Even abstract points are stated in ways that are lively (". . . but an unfilled interval never remains permanently satisfying as an explanatory variable" [p. 145]) and entertaining ("Few hypothetical entities are so ill-favored that once having secured a foothold they cannot face out each new turn of empirical events with the aid of a few ad hoc assumptions" [p. 145]).

A COMPARISON OF FLUCTUATION THEORY AND OUR NEW THEORY OF DISUSE

On several occasions in this chapter, we have referred to our new theory of disuse as a "framework." Because there is a general correspondence between Estes's response strength and habit strength concepts to our retrieval strength and storage strength concepts, respectively, and because the theories account for many of the same phenomena, the question arises as to what extent the fluctuation theory has the storage and retrieval properties that define our theory of disuse. That is, to what degree does the fluctuation theory fit our framework?

Before we address that question, it is important to clarify that it is the *formal* properties of the two theories that are at issue. The original stimulus-response phrasing of the stimulus fluctuation theory, and its focus on conditioning and extinction phenomena in animals, makes the theory seem different in kind than our more abstract and human-memory-oriented theory of disuse. The basic fluctuation idea, however, can be expressed in more modern-sounding and cognitive ways. In Bower's (1972) representation, for example, contextual influences of various kinds are presumed to influence what subset of the set of possible encoding operations are activated when a given nominal stimulus is presented, and each resulting stimulus encoding is presumed to be associated with one or more responses in memory. The strength of a given associated response in memory, then, is equal to the proportion of active encodings to which it is associated.

Bower's (1972) assumption that more than one response can be associated to a given stimulus encoding violates an original assumption of stimulus-sampling theory (that one and only one response is conditioned to a given stimulus element). Such a change was necessary, according to Bower, given the ". . . evidence showing that learning a second association to a stimulus need not cause unlearning of an earlier association but rather only edited differentiation or temporary suppression of the earlier response" (p. 91).

Going further in that direction, one could assume that as a consequence of environmental/social/physiological/cognitive/ and emotional aspects of context, a single functional encoding of the nominal cue configuration is extracted by the human subject, which then defines a set of items in memory associated to that functional cue. The "response strength" of a given item to that cue would then be defined in terms of the recency or frequency of the past co-occurrences of that cue and response (*apple* would have greater response strength than *pomegranate* to the cue *fruit* because of the prior history of the organism). Habit strength would then correspond to the strength of association summed across all possible functional encodings of a given nominal cue configuration. Available and un-available response items in memory would then correspond to the set associated to the currently active encoding of that cue configuration and the sets associated to the other possible encodings of that configuration, respectively. What would fluctuate across successive presentations of a given nominal cue is the particular encoding or interpretation the subject extracts from or gives to that nominal cue. Such fluctuation would be the consequence of changes in one or more of the dimensions of context listed above.

The foregoing rephrasing of fluctuation theory is intended to illustrate that the theory can be phrased in ways that increase its apparent compatibility with the human-memory domain that is the focus of our theory of disuse. Most, but not all, of the formal properties of the fluctuation theory are left unchanged by such a reformulation. Before we comment on what properties might change, we first want to compare the original version of fluctuation theory to our theory of disuse.

Response Strength Versus Retrieval Strength

Similarities. Response strength, defined as the proportion of elements in the available set conditioned to a given response, corresponds in spirit and function to our retrieval-strength concept. Some formal similarities are the following:

1. The probability that a given response is accessible in a given situation is solely a function of its current response strength.

2. The increment in the strength of a given response as a consequence of a study (reinforcement) trial is a negatively accelerated function of that response's prior strength.

3. Following a study (training) session during which a given response is reinforced, the loss of response strength over time (forgetting) proceeds more slowly the higher the level of habit strength at the end of training.

4. The decrement in the response strength of a given response as a conse-quence of the reinforcement of a competing response is greater the higher the response strength of the response in question.

5. In general, although the immediate size of such decrements in response strength will depend only on the response strength of the response in question, not on its habit strength, the observable decrement in response strength over time will be smaller the greater its habit strength. (In the fluctuation model, of course, there need not be any actual decrement at all, as in the case of spontaneous recovery.)

Differences. The response-strength properties of the original fluctuation the-ory differ from the corresponding retrieval-strength properties in the following ways.

1. Without there being a reinforcement or feedback event, response strengths are unchanged as a consequence of the organism making a given response. This difference between the fluctuation and disuse theories is basic, because the act of retrieval is assumed to be a potent event (in altering the strength of the retrieved response—and the strengths of competing responses) in the theory of disuse.

2. Another significant difference is that response strength declines over time not to an eventual asymptote of zero, as in the theory of disuse, but to an asymptote defined by habit strength. That is, response strength declines to an asymptote equal to the overall proportion of conditioned elements in the available and unavailable sets (habit strength).

3. The global limit on retrieval capacity assumed in the theory of disuse has no counterpart in the fluctuation theory. There is no effect on a given response's strength in one stimulus situation as a consequence of increasing a different response's strength (or even the same response's strength) in a different (non-overlapping) stimulus situation.

4. Finally, there are differences in the two theories as to how response/retrieval strength translates into response probability. In the fluctuation theory the translation is quite straightforward: Response strength is equal to the proportion of conditioned elements in the available set and response probability is equal to the proportion of conditioned elements in a given sample from the available set. The expected value of the latter proportion is, of course, equal to the former proportion; in virtually all applications of the model the variance in momentary response probability owing to the sampling process can be ignored. In the theory of disuse, at the level it is specified in this chapter, response probability depends on both relative and absolute retrieval strengths: A given item must be discriminated from the other items associated to a given cue configuration, which is a function of its strength relative to the strengths of the other cued items, and it must be reconstructed once it is discriminated, which is a function of its absolute retrieval strength. This two-step process, analogous to the sampling-plus-recovery process in Raaijmakers and Shiffrin's (1981) SAM model, attributes a level of complexity to the retrieval process that does not seem compatible with the stimulus-response roots of stimulus-sampling theory.

Habit Strength Versus Storage Strength

Similarities. Habit strength, defined as the overall proportion of elements in the available and unavailable sets conditioned to a given response, corresponds in a general way to storage strength in the theory of disuse. Some particular similarities are the following:

1. Habit strength, like storage strength, has no direct effects on performance. Its influences on performance are manifested through its effects on the gain or

loss of response strengths across study sessions or intervening intervals, respectively. Those effects on response strength, as cited earlier, are quite similar to the presumed influences of storage strength on the gain or loss of retrieval strength.

2. In the fluctuation model, as in the disuse model, there is no limit on learning (storage) as expressed by habit strength summed across all possible cue/stimulus configurations and associated responses.

3. The increment in habit strength as a consequence of a reinforcement or study trial is a negatively accelerated function of current response strength.

4. In general, the increment in habit strength is also a decreasing function of current habit strength. (In a given situation, however, the effect of a study trial on habit strength will depend on how elements already conditioned to the target response are partitioned between the available and unavailable sets: The fewer conditioned elements there are in the available set, the larger the increment in habit strength.)

Differences.   The following are the most significant differences in the properties assigned to habit strength and storage strength.

1. A major difference in the two theories is that storage strength, once accumulated, is never lost, whereas habit strength is reduced in the fluctuation model whenever elements conditioned to that target response are reconditioned to another response. Habit strength can go to zero in the fluctuation model, as would be the case after repeated spaced extinction sessions. (From such a point of "complete extinction," relearning the extinguished response should be as slow as the original learning of that response, whereas in the theory of disuse, relearning would be much more rapid than original learning, owing to the storage strength remaining from the original learning phase.) Another way to phrase this difference between the theories is to say that changes in response strength owing to conditioning or unconditioning of stimulus elements in the available set result in corresponding changes in habit strength, whereas there is no such correspondence in the theory of disuse. Changes in response strength that result from the fluctuation process, on the other hand, do leave habit strength unchanged.

2. Although there is no limit on habit strengths summed across situations and responses, there is a limit on the habit strengths summed across the responses associated to a given stimulus situation. Increasing the habit strength of one response decreases, in general, the habit strength of other responses (there are only so many stimulus elements corresponding to a given configuration of cues, and only one response can be conditioned to a given element). In the disuse theory, on the other hand, increasing the storage strength of one member in the set of items associated to a given cue configuration does not alter the storage strengths of the other items in that set.

Towards a Resolution of Certain Differences

Some of the differences between the formal properties of the original version of the fluctuation theory and the properties of our new theory of disuse do not seem fundamental to the fluctuation idea, per se, but to the initial phrasing of certain assumptions. We indicate in the following sections how changes in those assumptions might reduce or eliminate some of the differences outlined earlier.

Test Effects.   As originally formulated, the production of a response, without some kind of feedback, does not alter response strengths or habit strengths in the fluctuation model. The potent effects of a test event can, however, be accommodated in several ways in the fluctuation theory. Izawa (1971) was able to account quantitatively for the effects of unreinforced test cycles in paired-associate learning with a modified version of the fluctuation model. She was able to capture two distinct benefits of test trials (they retard forgetting and they potentiate subsequent study trials) by assuming that a test cycle perturbs the fluctuation process (conditioned elements in the available set remain available, unconditioned elements in the available set fluctuate to the unavailable set with probability k, and elements in the unavailable set fluctuate to the available set with probability k'). Whitten and Bjork (1977) were able to fit the quantitative consequences of tests in a modified Brown–Peterson distractor paradigm by assuming that a successful recall slowed the fluctuation rate of alternative "retrieval routes" to a given item in memory. Such an assumption has the effect of increasing the likelihood that a successful retrieval route will again be available in the future.

In the Izawa (1971) and Whitten and Bjork (1977) formulations, no learning is presumed to take place on test trials per se. One could assume that sampled elements conditioned to responses other than the one produced are reconditioned to the response given. Such an assumption, however, yields an increased rate of responding across a series of unreinforced test trials. Such "hypermnesia" (Erdelyi & Becker, 1974) does occur in well defined situations (see, e.g., Roediger & Challis, 1989), but such cases are the exception, not the rule.

The Asymptote of Forgetting.   In the fluctuation model, response strength does not decrease to an eventual asymptote of zero, as is assumed in our new theory of disuse, but to a level that corresponds to habit strength. Response strength cannot be driven to zero unless habit strength, via repeated extinction sessions, is driven to zero. To the extent, however, that (a) little or no fluctuation takes place during a training session, and (b) the size of the unavailable set is large with respect to the size of the available set, the asymptote of forgetting will be close to zero. (Researchers have typically made the former assumption, and best-fitting parameter estimates have typically implied the latter relationship.) Under those conditions, performance can reach a high level at the end of training, but the overall proportion of conditioned elements across the available and unavailable sets will remain small.

The Loss of Habit Strength.   In the fluctuation model, any loss of response strength (by virtue of elements in the available set being reconditioned to another response) results in a corresponding decrease in habit strength. In the theory of disuse, the storage strength of a given response is not altered by changes in the retrieval strength (or storage strength) of other items. Put another way, a response's habit strength in the fluctuation model is tied to its response strength, and to the response and habit strengths of other responses, in ways that storage strength is not in the theory of disuse. There is only so much habit strength and response strength to go around in the fluctuation model because the number of elements is assumed to be fixed and each element is assumed to be associated to one and only one response. One consequence of this property of the fluctuation theory, among others, is that the habit strength of a given response can be driven to zero via extensive training on another response (or responses), however high that response habit strength may have been at one point.

In Bower's (1972) formulation, in which more than one response can be associated to a given stimulus encoding, items can gain in response or habit strength without altering the response strength or habit strength of other items. In Bower's version of the theory, an item's response strength (defined as the proportion of active encodings to which it is associated), or its habit strength (defined as the proportion of all possible encodings to which it is associated), can be altered without necessarily changing the response or habit strengths of other items.

There is, however, a cost associated with the flexibility that is gained in Bower's (1972) reformulation of the theory: The translation of response strength into response probabilities becomes complicated. Using the simple proportionality rule in the original formulation of the fluctuation model (that is, setting the probability of a given response equal to the proportion of elements in the available set conditioned to that response), the sum of the probabilities of alternative responses can, in Bower's formulation, exceed one (in fact, in principle, the probability of every response could be unity). Assuming it is the case that a variety of responses (items in memory) are triggered (associated to) a given cue, rules must then be specified to designate which response is given (or in what order multiple responses are given)—which is what Bower does in his paper for each of a set of experimental paradigms.

Remaining Differences

In one sense, it is a mistake to overemphasize the formal properties that correspond, or could be made to correspond, in the fluctuation and disuse theories. There *are* some fundamental conceptual differences between the two theories. In particular, what is meant by retrieval strength in our theory and what is meant by response strength in Estes's fluctuation theory differ in a fundamental way. We think of retrieval strength as a property of an item's representation in memory:

how active or primed that representation is at a given point in time. That is, retrieval strength is a property of the item per se. Response strength, on the other hand, is defined in terms of the association of a given response to aspects of a stimulus situation that happens to be sampled by the organism. As long as the organism has no intervening experience in that situation, response strengths stay intact however long the intervening interval; whereas retrieval strength, as an activity attribute of an item in memory, decreases as a consequence of intervening activities whatever the setting of those activities.

One other difference seems significant from a conceptual, if not formal, standpoint. In the fluctuation theory, the sampling dynamics are formulated with respect to the stimulus constellation impinging on the organism. Retrieving a response once stimulus sampling has taken place is a relatively automatic (though probabilistic) process governed by stimulus-response association. In our theory of disuse, on the other hand, the "sampling" dynamics are on the contents of the memory system itself. The configuration of cues presented to the subject is assumed to restrict (relatively automatically) the search of memory to an associated set of items in memory. Retrieval of a particular item in that set requires that it be discriminated from the other items in the set (a function of its relative retrieval strength) and then reconstructed (a function of its absolute retrieval strength).

CONCLUDING COMMENTS

The new theory of disuse represents our conjecture as to the adaptive interplay of storage and retrieval processes in human memory. In formulating the theory, we have taken as an article of faith that what appear to be peculiarities of human memory, as exhibited in certain real-world and laboratory settings, are in fact reflections of storage and retrieval processes that are adaptive in the overall functioning of human memory.

The theory as formulated, in the distinction it makes between storage strength and retrieval strength, and in many of its formal properties, bears a close relationship to the stimulus-fluctuation theory published by William K. Estes (1955a, 1955b) 35 years ago. As we have tried to indicate, the fluctuation idea remains one of the major theoretical insights in the history of research on learning and memory. It is one—but only one—of the significant contributions to our field by the man in whose honor we write this chapter.

ACKNOWLEDGMENTS

The preparation of this report was supported in part by Grants 4-564040-RB-19900 and 4-564040-EB-19900 to the first and second authors, respectively, from the Committee on Research, University of California. We thank Steve Clark, Harold Gelfand, Todd Gross, Barbara Spellman, and, especially, Michael Anderson, for their criticisms of and contributions to our theory of disuse.

REFERENCES

Allen, G. A., Mahler, W. A., & Estes, W. K. (1969). Effects of recall tests on long-term retention of paired associates. *Journal of Verbal Learning and Verbal Behavior, 8,* 463–470.

Anderson, J. R. (1989). A rational analysis of human memory. In H. L. Roediger III & F. I. M. Craik (Eds.), *Varieties of memory and consciousness: Essays in honour of Endel Tulving* (pp. 195–210). Hillsdale, NJ: Lawrence Erlbaum Associates.

Anderson, M. C., & Bjork, R. A. (1990, November). *Category-based retrieval inhibition in human memory.* Paper presented at the meeting of the Psychonomic Society, New Orleans, LA.

Baddeley, A. (1988). But what the hell's it for? In M. M. Gruneberg, P. E. Morris, & R. N. Sykes (Eds.), *Practical aspects of memory: Current research and issues: Vol. 1. Memory in everyday life* (pp. 1–15). London: Wiley.

Bartlett, J. C. (1977). Effects of immediate testing on delayed retrieval: Search and recovery operations with four types of cue. *Journal of Experimental Psychology: Human Learning and Memory, 3,* 719–732.

Bjork, R. A. (1975). Retrieval as a memory modifier: An interpretation of negative recency and related phenomena. In R. L. Solso (Ed.), *Information processing and cognition* (pp. 123–144). New York: Wiley.

Bjork, R. A. (1978). The updating of human memory. In G. H. Bower (Ed.), *The psychology of learning and motivation* (Vol. 12, pp. 235–259). New York: Academic Press.

Bjork, R. A. (1989). Retrieval inhibition as an adaptive mechanism in human memory. In H. L. Roediger III & F. I. M. Craik (Eds.), *Varieties of memory and consciousness: Essays in honour of Endel Tulving* (pp. 195–210). Hillsdale, NJ: Lawrence Erlbaum Associates.

Bjork, E. L., & Bjork, R. A. (1988). On the adaptive aspects of retrieval failure in autobiographical memory. In M. M. Gruneberg, P. E. Morris, & R. N. Sykes (Eds.), *Practical aspects of memory: Current research and issues: Vol. 1. Memory in everyday life* (pp. 283–288). London: Wiley.

Bjork, R. A., & Geiselman, R. E. (1978). Constituent processes in the differentiation of items in memory. *Journal of Experimental Psychology: Human Learning and Memory, 4,* 344–361.

Bjork, R. A., & Richardson-Klavehn, A. (1989). On the puzzling relationship between environmental context and human memory. In C. Izawa (Ed.), *Current issues in cognitive processes: The Tulane Flowerree symposium on cognition* (pp. 313–344). Hillsdale, NJ: Lawrence Erlbaum Associates.

Bjork, R. A., & Whitten, W. B. (1974). Recency-sensitive retrieval processes in long-term free recall. *Cognitive Psychology, 6,* 173–189.

Bower, G. H. (1967). Verbal learning. In H. H. Helsen & W. Bevan (Eds.), *Contemporary approaches to psychology.* Princeton, NJ: Van Nostrand.

Bower, G. H. (1972). Stimulus-sampling theory of encoding variability. In A. W. Melton & E. Martin (Eds.), *Coding processes in human memory.* Washington, DC: W. H. Winston & Sons.

Bower, G. H., & Hilgard, E. R. (1981). *Theories of learning* (5th ed.). Englewood Cliffs, NJ: Prentice-Hall.

Bower, G. H., & Reitman, J. S. (1972). Mnemonic elaboration in multilist learning. *Journal of Verbal Learning and Verbal Behavior, 11,* 478–485.

Briggs, G. E. (1954). Acquisition, extinction and recovery functions in retroactive inhibition. *Journal of Experimental Psychology, 47,* 285–293.

Ceraso, J., & Henderson, A. (1965). Unavailability and associative loss in RI and PI. *Journal of Experimental Psychology, 70,* 300–303.

Ceraso, J., & Henderson, A. (1966). Unavailability and associative loss in RI and PI: Second try. *Journal of Experimental Psychology, 72,* 314–316.

Cuddy, L. J., & Jacoby, L. L. (1982). When forgetting helps. *Verbal Learning and Verbal Behavior, 21,* 451–467.

Ebbinghaus, H. (1964). *Memory: A contribution to experimental psychology.* (H. A. Ruger & C. E. Bussenius, translators) New York: Dover. (Original work published 1885).

Erdelyi, M. H., & Becker, J. (1974). Hypermnesia for pictures: Incremental memory for pictures but not for words in multiple recall trials. *Cognitive Psychology, 6,* 159–171.

Estes, W. K. (1950). Toward a statistical theory of learning. *Psychological Review, 57,* 94–107.

Estes, W. K. (1955a). Statistical theory of spontaneous recovery and regression. *Psychological Review, 62,* 145–154.

Estes, W. K. (1955b). Statistical theory of distributional phenomena in learning. *Psychological Review, 62,* 369–377.

Estes, W. K. (1959). The statistical approach to learning theory. In S. Koch (Ed.), *Psychology: A study of a science* (Vol. 2, pp. 380–491). New York: McGraw-Hill.

Estes, W. K. (1971). Learning and memory. In E. F. Beckenbach & C. B. Tomkins (Eds.), *Concepts of communication* (pp. 282–300). New York: Wiley.

Estes, W. K. (1989). William K. Estes. In G. Lindzey (Ed.), *A history of psychology in autobiography* (pp. 95–124). Stanford, CA: Stanford University Press.

Forrester, W. E. (1970). Retroactive inhibition and spontaneous recovery in the A-B, D-C paradigm. *Journal of Verbal Learning and Verbal Behavior, 9,* 525–528.

Gardiner, J. M., Craik, F. I. M., & Bleasdale, F. A. (1973). Retrieval difficulty and subsequent recall. *Memory & Cognition, 1,* 213–216.

Glenberg, A. M. (1979). Component-levels theory of the effects of spacing of repetitions on recall and recognition. *Memory & Cognition, 7,* 95–112.

Glenberg, A. M., & Lehmann, T. S. (1980). Spacing repetitions over 1 week. *Memory & Cognition, 8,* 528–538.

Hogan, R. M., & Kintsch, W. (1971). Differential effects of study and test trials on long-term recognition and recall. *Journal of Verbal Learning and Verbal Behavior, 10,* 562–567.

Hull, C. L. (1943). *The principles of behavior.* New York: Appleton-Century-Crofts.

Izawa, C. (1970). Optimal potentiating effects and forgetting-prevention effects of tests in paired-associate learning. *Journal of Experimental Psychology, 83,* 340–344.

Izawa, C. (1971). The test trial potentiating model. *Journal of Mathematical Psychology, 8,* 220–224.

Jacoby, L. L. (1978). On interpreting the effects of repetition: Solving a problem versus remembering a solution. *Journal of Verbal Learning and Verbal Behavior, 17,* 649–667.

Jost, A. (1897). Die Assoziationfestigkeit in Ihrer Abhangigheit von der Verteilung der Wiederholungen. *Zeitschrift fur Psychologie, 14,* 436–472.

Koppenaal, R. J. (1963). Time changes in strength of A-B, A-C lists: Spontaneous recovery? *Journal of Verbal Learning and Verbal Behavior, 2,* 310–319.

Krueger, W. C. F. (1929). The effects of overlearning on retention. *Journal of Experimental Psychology, 12,* 71–78.

Landauer, T. K. (1986). How much do people remember? *Cognitive Science, 10,* 477–493.

Landauer, T. K., & Bjork, R. A. (1978). Optimal rehearsal patterns and name learning. In M. M. Gruneberg, P. E. Morris, & R. N. Sykes (Eds.), *Practical aspects of memory* (pp. 625–632). London: Academic Press.

Martin, E. (1968). Stimulus meaningfulness and paired-associate transfer: An encoding variability hypothesis. *Psychological Review, 75,* 421–441.

McGeoch, J. A. (1932). Forgetting and the law of disuse. *Psychological Review, 39,* 352–370.

Melton, A. W. (1967). Repetition and retrieval from memory. *Science, 158,* 532.

Melton, A. W., & Irwin, J. M. (1940). The influence of degree of interpolated learning on retroactive inhibition and the overt transfer of specific responses. *American Journal of Psychology, 53,* 173–203.

Mensink, G. J., & Raaijmakers, J. G. W. (1988). A model for interference and forgetting. *Psychological Review, 93,* 434–455.

Miller, G. A., & Gildea, R. M. (1987, September). How children learn words. *Scientific American,* pp. 94–99.

Modigliani, V. (1976). Effects on a later recall by delaying initial recall. *Journal of Experimental Psychology: Human Learning and Memory, 2,* 609–622.

Osgood, C. E. (1953). *Method and theory in experimental psychology.* New York: Oxford University Press.

Peterson, L. R. (1963). Immediate memory: Data and theory. In C. N. Cofer & B. S. Musgrave (Eds.), *Verbal behavior and verbal learning* (pp. 336–353). New York: McGraw-Hill.

Peterson, L. R., Hillner, K., & Saltzman, D. (1962). Time between pairings and short-term retention. *Journal of Experimental Psychology, 64,* 550–551.

Postman, L., Stark, K., & Fraser, J. (1968). Temporal changes in interference. *Journal of Verbal Learning and Verbal Behavior, 7,* 672–694.

Raaijmakers, J. G. W., & Shiffrin, R. M. (1981). Search of associative memory. *Psychological Review, 88,* 93–134.

Ratcliff, R. C., Clark, S., & Shiffrin, R. M. (1990). The list-strength effect: I. Data and discussion. *Journal of Experimental Psychology: Learning, Memory, and Cognition, 16,* 163–178.

Richardson-Klavehn, A. (1988). *Effects of incidental environmental context on human memory: Elusive or nonexistent?* Unpublished doctoral dissertation, University of California, Los Angeles.

Roediger, H. L., & Challis, B. H. (1989). Hypermnesia: Improvements in recall with repeated testing. In H. L. Roediger III & F. I. M. Craik (Eds.), *Varieties of memory and consciousness: Essays in honour of Endel Tulving* (pp. 175–199). Hillsdale, NJ: Lawrence Erlbaum Associates.

Santiago, H. C., & Wright, A. A. (1984). Pigeon memory: Same/different concept learning, serial probe recognition acquisition and probe delay effects in the serial position function. *Journal of Experimental Psychology: Animal Behavior Processes, 10,* 498–512.

Skinner, B. F. (1938). *The behavior of organisms.* New York: Appleton-Century-Crofts.

Thompson, C. P., Wenger, S. K., & Bartling, C. A. (1978). How recall facilitates subsequent recall: A reappraisal. *Journal of Experimental Psychology: Human Learning and Memory, 4,* 210–221.

Thorndike, E. L. (1914). *The psychology of learning.* New York: Teachers College.

Tulving, E., & Thompson, D. M. (1973). Encoding specificity and retrieval processes in episodic memory. *Psychological Review, 80,* 352–373.

Whitten, W. B. II, & Bjork, R. A. (1977). Learning from tests: Effects of spacing. *Journal of Verbal Learning and Verbal Behavior, 16,* 465–478.

Woodworth, R. S., & Schlosberg, H. (1954). *Experimental psychology.* New York: Holt.

Wright, A. A. (1989). Memory processing by pigeons, monkeys, and people. In G. H. Bower (Ed.), *The psychology of learning and motivation* (Vol. 24, pp. 25–70). New York: Academic Press.

Wright, A. A., Santiago, H. C., & Sands, S. F. (1984). Monkey memory: Same/different concept learning, serial probe acquisition, and probe delay effects. *Journal of Experimental Psychology: Animal Behavior Processes, 10,* 513–529.

Wright, A. A., Santiago, H. C., Sands, S. F., Kendrick, D. F., & Cook, R. G. (1985). Memory processing of serial lists by pigeons, monkeys, and people. *Science, 229,* 287–289.

3 The SAM Retrieval Model: A Retrospective and Prospective

Richard M. Shiffrin
Indiana University

Jeroen Raaijmakers
TNO Soesterberg

A Brief Reminiscence from the First Author

My professional relationship with Bill Estes began as a graduate student at Stanford in the years 1964–1968. I spent my first year with Gordon Bower and the next 3 years with Dick Atkinson as research advisors, but nevertheless learned much from Bill in classes, research seminars, and discussions. Certainly a central impetus toward the development of the SAM retrieval model took place during a qualifications examination in which Bill asked me how I knew whether the memory effects I was describing arose during memory storage or memory retrieval. Much of the subsequent development of the SAM model and its attendant research has revolved around attempts to deal with this question. Subsequently I spent two different years on leave with Bill at Rockefeller University, and we developed a close friendship as well as a fruitful professional relationship. I have learned much from Bill, about research, science, humor, and life.

This chapter describes the evolution of the SAM model for memory, summarizing the model as described in Raaijmakers and Shiffrin (1980, 1981) and Gillund and Shiffrin (1984), and its precursors, but focusing primarily upon developments since 1984. It is particularly appropriate for this volume as the second author has recently utilized the idea of stimulus fluctuation theory (Estes, 1955a, 1955b) in an extension of SAM to deal with classical interference phenomena (Mensink & Raaijmakers, 1988, 1989).

PRECURSORS

Atkinson and Shiffrin (1968) discussed a search model for retrieval, but were most concerned with processes and control processes in short-term store. These short-term processes are still an important component of the model, but have not recently been a focus of empirical research or further theoretical development. Shiffrin and Atkinson (1969) discussed the structure of long-term store, and the way in which such a structure is used to facilitate retrieval. Both articles assumed unitized separate traces are stored in long-term store, and search to consist of random sampling of these traces. Applications of the search model were limited to free recall. Shiffrin (1970) quantified these notions more precisely, and proposed stages for the search of memory. The model was applied both to free recall studies and continuous paired associate memory studies. The idea of specifying retrieval cues, and their strengths, weights, and combination rules, appeared in the 1980 and 1981 articles by Raaijmakers and Shiffrin. These articles dealt mainly with recall, but pointed out that recognition could be carried out in two ways: (a) as a memory search (a model utilizing this component was adopted by Mensink and Raaijmakers, 1988, to deal with interference among lists when recognition tests are used); and (b) on the basis of the total activation of memory. This latter recognition process, in which the decision is based on a sum of activations across traces, was laid out in detail in the 1984 article by Gillund and Shiffrin. Admitting that both search and global summation could be used to recognize, Gillund and Shiffrin proposed that the global summation process is used predominantly.

THE *SAM* MODEL CIRCA 1984

Early formulations of SAM were designed to incorporate as few representational assumptions as possible, but two lay at the core of the theory: (a) experience is divided into relatively unitized events (partitioning occurring through the operation of control processes in short-term store); and (b) events are stored in memory as separate *images*. Both these assumptions are crucial to recent developments and are discussed later in the chapter.

Images (I_i) contain many kinds of information, consisting of some proportion of the information rehearsed and coded together in short-term store. For example, if a pair of words is presented, the information stored might contain sensory, lexical, semantic, and conceptual information about the two words, information linking, relating, or associating the words, and a wide variety of context information (e.g., the environment, the setting, the thoughts and feelings of the subject). The information is unitized in the sense that there is a tendency for it to be retrieved as a group during one stage of a memory search, in a recall task.

The information in long-term store (LTS) is always accessed with the use of retrieval cues (Q_j). These cues have properties similar to those of images: Each is relatively unitized and separate. Several cues can be used together to probe memory, each being assigned a *weight*, $w(j)$, representing that cue's relative salience. Retrieval is assumed to be (at least weakly) a limited capacity system;

that is, cues cannot be accumulated in the probe set in indefinite numbers without some cost. The Raaijmakers and Shiffrin 1980 and 1981 articles were concerned with situations involving just two cues, so capacity limitations were discussed but not incorporated explicitly in the fits of the model to data. However, Gillund and Shiffrin (1984) varied number and types of cues in recognition and collected evidence that the sum of all weights should add to a constant (a constant that was set to 1.0 in their article for convenience; the limitation on retrieval capacity was needed also in subsequent research such as that by Gronlund & Shiffrin, 1986, Clark & Shiffrin, 1987, and Shiffrin, Murnane, Gronlund, & Roth, 1989). Examples of cues are a *word,* and *context.* We assume that a context cue is always one of the cues used in any episodic memory task; its role is the focusing of retrieval upon the recently presented information that is being tested.

Each cue has a tendency to activate each memory image, represented by a weighted strength,

$$S(Q_j, I_i)^{w(j)} = A(j,i).$$

The strengths are determined by rehearsal and coding processes carried out in short-term store during study, and by preexisting relationships between cues and items. Total activation of image I_i is determined by the product of the weighted strengths across all cues:

$$A(i) = \prod_j A(j, i).$$

In a free or cued recall task, a search of memory is carried out. The search consists of a series of search cycles. On each cycle cues and weights are selected, a sample of one of the memory images is made, information is recovered from that image and assessed, a recall may be emitted, new information may be added to memory, and a decision is made whether or not to continue the search.

The probability of sampling image I_i given a set of cues and weights $\{Q_k;$ $w(k); k = 1, \ldots, m\}$ is just the ratio of the activation strength of I_i divided by the sum of the activations of all the images:

$$P_s(I_i) = \frac{A(i)}{\sum\limits_j A(j)}. \tag{1}$$

Once an image has been sampled, the information in it must be recovered and used to generate an appropriate decision and response. The simplest case occurs when the sampled image contains just one word, and has not previously been sampled using any of the present cues. In this case the probability of being able to recover the correct name is assumed to be:

$$P_R(I_i) = 1 - \exp\left\{-\sum_j w(j)S(Q_j, I_i)\right\}$$ (2)

where the sum is taken over the m cues. Special assumptions are used when an image has previously been sampled using one or more of the present cues and the previous recovery did not succeed. In this case the components of the sum in Equation 2 corresponding to the previously unsuccessful cues are removed (in effect, only one recovery chance per cue is allowed for a given image).

When a successful recovery does occur, it is assumed that the strengths between each of the cues used and the image in question are increased (a process called *incrementing* in previous work; e.g., in Raaijmakers & Shiffrin, 1981, the value added depended on the cue but not the initial level of strength). This process tends to produce an increased sampling probability for previously re-called or recovered items. This in turn means that recall of as yet unrecovered items from memory decreases as recall proceeds, at least if new cues are not utilized (an hypothesis well supported by data; see Bjork, 1988).

To model memory processes in laboratory tasks that utilize presentations of lists of items, particular assumptions are made concerning the rehearsal and coding processes occurring during list presentation; these assumptions determine the strengths between cues and images (except when no coding or rehearsal took place between cue and image; in this case a constant residual strength reflecting preexperimental factors was assumed). For example, when lists of single words are presented, a rehearsal buffer of r items is commonly assumed; the mean strengths between context cue and item image, and between item cue and its own image, are assumed to be monotonically related to the total time that item stays in the rehearsal buffer. Similarly, the strength between an item cue and the image of some other item is assumed to be monotonically related to the total time both items are in the rehearsal buffer together. As another example, if pairs of items are presented, it is generally assumed that only the current pair of items is rehearsed; thus the mean strengths are monotonically related to the presentation time. The monotonic relationship would quite possibly be the same in each of these cases. In most applications to date we have assumed that the relationship is linear. For simplicity, a linear relation is also assumed in the following descriptions.

To be specific, suppose that words are studied (denoted by i, j, . . .), and that the images stored in memory (denoted by I_i, I_j, . . .) encode words, but not more than one word per image. Suppose word i has been rehearsed for t_i seconds, and has been rehearsed for t_{ij} seconds with word j. Then there are retrieval strengths, $S(Q,I_i)$, to image I_i from various cues. The most important cues and their strengths are: (a) word i—ct_i (the self-strength); (b) word j—bt_{ji} (the interitem strength); (c) word x (not rehearsed with word i)—d (the residual strength); and (d) the context cue—at_i (the context strength).

Finally, the retrieval strengths are assumed to have a distribution (due to item variability and many other factors). The variance of the strength distribution does not much affect the recall predictions because the large variance associated with sampling washes out the effect of strength variability. However, strength variability is essential to obtain sensible predictions for recognition, as distributional variance is often the only source of variability in this paradigm. For various technical reasons we have assumed that the standard deviation of the distribution is a constant times the mean (in many cases a symmetrical three-point distribution was utilized; the details are not crucial because the summation of independent activations across images produces a near-normal distribution).

To model retrieval during recall tasks, a strategy is assumed by which the subject generates cues at each stage of the search, and by which the search is terminated. In free recall the subject is assumed to start with the context cue only. Whenever a new item is recalled it is used in combination with context as joint cues. If I_{max} consecutive unsuccessful search cycles occur, then the context cue only is used; if K_{max} total failures occur the search ceases (actually in many instantiations an additional search phase then occurs, termed "rechecking": Each recalled word is used along with context as cues, each until L_{max} samples occur). In cued recall, the subject is assumed to use both context and the provided cue on each cycle of the search, stopping when some fixed number of unsuccessful cycles has occurred.

In the Gillund and Shiffrin (1984) version of SAM, recognition is not assumed to proceed as a memory search (though there is nothing to prevent a subject from searching during recognition if he or she desires; in fact Mensink & Raaijmakers, 1988, have modeled recognition as a search process). Rather it is assumed that global activation determines the decision. In particular, context and the test item(s) are used as cues. The sum of all the image activations (i.e., the denominator of Equation 1) is termed *familiarity* (F). A criterion, C, is chosen. If F > C, the subject gives an "old" response; else "new." New storage can also occur during recognition testing; Gillund and Shiffrin (1984) assumed that each item tested resulted in a new image being added to memory with some fixed strengths.

The model in this form has been used to predict numerous findings in free recall, cued recall, and recognition. Raaijmakers and Shiffrin (1980, 1981) demonstrated SAM predicted the following effects: (a) in free recall, the effects of serial position, list-length, presentation time, recall time, repeated recall attempts, picture or word stimuli, ordinal output position on interresponse times, and providing some list words as retrieval cues; (b) in categorized free recall (category cues, strengths, and weights are added to the basic model) the effects of category cuing, cuing with studied and nonstudied category members, number of items per category, recall of one category member upon recall of the others, noncued testing upon subsequent cued testing, and order and ordinal position of testing of categories; and (c) in cued paired-associate paradigms the effects of list length, presentation time, relative proportion of paired versus single items on a list, and ordinal test position.

Gillund and Shiffrin (1984) showed that SAM predicted the effects of most of these variables in recognition paradigms. They also showed for both recall and recognition paradigms that SAM predicted the effects of time available for test, orienting task at study, type of distractor used, type of coding and rehearsal, test expectancy, match of study and test encodings, context shifts between study and test, test delay, serial test position, natural language word frequency (high frequency words are assumed to have higher retrieval strengths than low frequency words), and type of recognition test (cued, single, or paired).

DEVELOPMENTS SINCE 1984

Contextual Fluctuation:
Interference and Estes' Stimulus Fluctuation Theory

The original SAM model (Raaijmakers & Shiffrin, 1980, 1981) used context cues primarily to allow the memory search to be focused on the target list of items. The possibility of changes in context between study and text and the implications of such changes were also discussed in these articles and in Gillund and Shiffrin (1984).

Context and changes in context play an important role in the prediction of forgetting phenomena, due to the operation of two basic factors: First, the context cue used after a shorter delay may be more strongly associated to an image than the context cue used after a longer delay. Second, the strength and number of other images associated to the context cue may be greater after a longer delay. Both factors are based on the assumption that the strength of the context cue to an image is related to the similarity of the context at retrieval to the context at storage. When the current context is used as a cue to probe memory, context changes between study and test will lower the strength of activation of the target image and increase the activation strength of images that are more similar to the test context (typically the intervening items). These factors lead to a reduction in the proportion of activation due to the target image, lowering sampling probability in recall and lowering the signal to noise ratio in recognition.

In addition to the type of discrete, discontinuous changes typical for studies that explicitly manipulate the test context (e.g., Godden & Baddeley, 1975; Smith, 1979), there may also be a more gradual type of context change, more typical for the changes occurring within an experimental session. If the experimental paradigm is quite homogeneous in character (as may occur in a continuous paired associate paradigm; see Shiffrin, 1970) then the similarity of study and test contexts might decrease smoothly as the study test interval increases. In most other situations the context changes might well be fairly discontinuous in nature, occurring, for example, at boundaries between lists, at breaks between study and test periods, and at switches between distinct classes of study items. State-dependent learning studies (e.g., Bjork & Richardson-Klavehn, 1989) often include conditions in which attempts are made to reinstate the study context after a delay interval, and performance is shown to improve. In most other studies, however, context similarity will be a nonincreasing function of delay.

Mensink and Raaijmakers (1988, 1989) presented an extension of the SAM model that was designed to handle time-dependent changes in context. In particular, it was assumed that changes in context could be modeled by adopting the notion of fluctuation, as used in Estes' Stimulus Sampling Theory (Estes, 1955a, 1955b). As in the original fluctuation model, the basic idea is that there is a random fluctuation of elements between two sets, a set of available elements and a set of (temporarily) unavailable elements. Performance is a function of the relationship between sets of available elements at different points in time (viz., study and test trials).

In this version of the SAM model, the experimental context is represented as a set of contextual elements. At any given time only a part of this set is perceived by the subject and this subset is denoted the current context. Elements in this set are said to be in the active state. All other elements are inactive. With the passage of time, the current context changes due to a fluctuation process: Some inactive elements become active and some active ones will become inactive. At storage, only active elements are encoded in the memory image. If there are multiple study trials, each study trial gives a new opportunity for encoding a particular element in the image. As in Estes (1955a), the encoding of an element is all-or-none, that is: Each contextual element is either encoded or not in a given image; once an element is encoded in an image, further opportunities for encoding that element have no effect. The context strength at test is proportional to the overlap between the set of context elements encoded in the image and the set of context elements that are active at the time of testing.

Mensink and Raaijmakers (1989) gave general equations similar to those of Estes (1955a) that may be used to compute the probability that any given element is present both at the time of storage and at the time of retrieval, and hence compute the overlap between encoding and test context. Although the general idea is similar to that of Estes, there are a number of important differences. First, in the SAM model, context elements may be "conditioned" to (i.e., stored in) many memory images, not just to one. Second, these elements do not directly determine recall or recognition probabilities, and only contribute toward the activation value for an image. That is, the overlap measures determines the strength of the contextual association to a particular image; this strength combines with the strengths of any other cues in the probe set (using the weights) to determine activation. The activations are then used to determine retrieval (via sampling and recovery functions).

Mensink and Raaijmakers (1988) showed that this elaborated SAM model can handle a number of important interference and forgetting phenomena. Not all of these predictions are specifically due to the contextual fluctuation assumption, however. A number of interference phenomena are due to the increase in the number of images associated to the retrieval cues and not primarily to the strength of these associations.

For example, suppose two lists of pairs are learned in succession, both with the same stimulus terms, but with different response terms (an A-B A-C paradigm). The model predicts both retroactive and proactive inhibition, even when the subject is asked to try to produce the responses associated with each of the two lists (termed *MMFR testing*). The reason for this prediction is simple: retroactive and proactive inhibition in a two-list design occur because the probe cues at test (say A and context) are associated to more images in the interference conditions (say B and C) than in the control conditions (after learning A-B and D-C, say, B will be the strong response to A and context). Increasing the number of trials on the interfering list increases the strength of both the item and the context cues to the "other" response, and hence the interference effect. (This description is conceptually straightforward, although the quantitative fitting of the model to the results of various conditions from a number of studies is far from trivial).

Traditional interference theory (e.g., Postman & Underwood, 1973) always has had great difficulty in explaining the occurrence of retroactive and especially proactive interference on a MMFR test because it assumed that such a test was not affected by response competition. To explain the retroactive interference, it had to be assumed that second list learning led to unlearning of the first list associations. This however could not explain the observation of proactive interference on a MMFR test. The SAM model does not have this problem because it predicts that "competition" (in this model due to the fact that sampling is influenced by other images) will not be eliminated by MMFR testing.

Of the predictions that do depend on the contextual fluctuation model, two are especially interesting. The first has to do with the phenomenon of spontaneous recovery and the dependence of proactive inhibition on the length of the retention interval. In the SAM model, the probability of recalling (sampling) a particular List-1 image is a function of its relative strength. Let s1 and s2 be the contextual strengths for a List-1 and a List-2 image, respectively. The probability that a List-1 image is sampled depends (among other things) on the ratio s1/s2. Mensink and Raaijmakers (1989) show that the fluctuation model predicts that this ratio increases as a function of the retention interval. This implies a relative and possibly an absolute increase in the probability of recalling List-1 responses as the retention interval increases. That is, the model predicts spontaneous recovery of List-1 responses. By the same mechanism, the probability of recalling a List-2 image decreases relative to a control condition (proactive interference). Thus, the model predicts an increase in proactive interference as a function of the retention interval.

A second phenomenon that is due to the contextual fluctuation assumption is "normal" forgetting, that is forgetting in single-list paradigms. As the retention interval increases, the expected overlap between the storage and test contexts, and hence the probability of recall, decreases. Mensink and Raaijmakers (1988) showed that the model predicts that forgetting curves for lists differing in initial associative strength (due to e.g., differing numbers of study trials) fall off more or less in parallel, a somewhat controversial phenomenon observed by Slamecka and McElree (1983).

Recently, this contextual fluctuation model has been used to explain results concerning the spacing of repetitions. Suppose an item is presented twice for study (P1 and P2) and tested at a later time T. If the retention interval (i.e., the interval P2-T) is relatively long, the probability of recall increases as a function of the spacing between the two presentations (the interval P1-P2). With short retention intervals, however, the probability of recall decreases as a function of the spacing between the presentations. With intermediate retention intervals, the results are more complicated, often showing a nonmonotonic effect of spacing.

Unpublished work by Raaijmakers and van Winsum-Westra shows that this complicated state of affairs can be predicted by the present version of the SAM model (supplemented by a few assumptions appropriate for the paradigm). This is in large part due to contextual fluctuation. The reasons for this are basically similar to those described by Estes (1955b). As the interpresentation interval increases, the context at P2 will include more new, not yet encoded, elements that may be added to the memory image. Encoding more elements in the image increases the expected overlap between the test context and the context elements on the image.

Although this sounds very simple, the actual model requires supplementary assumptions that complicate matters. Crucial in this version of SAM is what happens on the second presentation, P2. It is assumed that on P2 an implicit retrieval attempt is made for the image stored on P1 (a study-phase retrieval assumption). New context elements that are present on P2 are only added to the image formed on P1 if that image is successfully retrieved on the second presentation. If it is not retrieved, a new storage attempt is made, based only on the information present on P2; if the attempt succeeds, a new image is stored. In addition, in order to accommodate dependencies due to differential storage strengths, it is assumed that each storage attempt is either successful or not. If it is not successful, the probability of sampling that image on a future retrieval attempt is zero. It is also assumed that no new storage takes place for any item that is still in STS on P2.

In this model, spacing of repetitions has a number of effects. As mentioned, due to context fluctuation more new context elements are stored, provided the item is "recognized" on P2. Second, as the spacing interval increases, there is a corresponding decrease in the probability that the item is still in STS on P2. Both of these effects lead to an increase in the probability of recall at test. However, spacing also has an opposite effect. That is, the longer the spacing interval, the lower the probability that the image is successfully retrieved on P2. This is a simple forgetting effect: As the interval increases, the expected overlap between the context at P1 and that at P2 decreases and this implies a decrease in the strength of the context cue at P2. Together, these factors produce a nonmonotonic effect of spacing. The spacing function shows an initial increase followed by a decrease, the maximum point depending on the length of the retention interval (P2 to T).

This version of the model has been used to fit the results of a number of well-known experiments (e.g., Glenberg, 1976; Rumelhart, 1967; Young, 1971). Although the success of this enterprise is perhaps not surprising (as most of these data have already been fitted by other models), these analyses again show the value of incorporating hypotheses about contextual fluctuation in SAM. In addition, the fact that it can handle data from experiments with many study trials (e.g., Rumelhart, 1967), demonstrates that SAM can handle the basic learning data that were the main focus of the Markov models of the 1960s.

The present model can also explain the intriguing results of Ross and Landauer (1978). According to their analysis, most theories that explain the effects of spacing by some sort of encoding or contextual variability assumption predict that there should not only be a beneficial effect of spacing for two presentations of the same item but also for the two presentations of two different items. That is, there should be an effect on the probability of recalling either of the two items. They showed that such a result is not obtained: A typical spacing effect is only obtained for one item presented twice, not for two items each presented once. The model handles this result because the second presentation of a single item is often stored within the trace formed for the first presentation, but two different items are never stored in the same trace. Because the probabilities of sampling and recovery depend on the overlap in elements with each image separately, the spacing of the presentations by and large only matters for the single item case (the model predicts only a very minor deviation from independence for the two item case).

Taken together, these studies show that contextual fluctuation hypotheses greatly extend the range of phenomena that can be handled by the SAM theory. Of course, this important step is only a start. Issues such as contextual fluctuations within list, and the ability of subjects to select probe context appropriate for the test situation (in autobiographical memory tests, to take one obvious example), are yet to be examined theoretically within the SAM framework.

Composition, Differentiation, and the List-Strength Effect

The previous section discusses interference in the traditional sense, between lists; this type of forgetting is based in part on context shifts and context fluctuations. Interference also occurs within lists, as demonstrated by the list length effect:

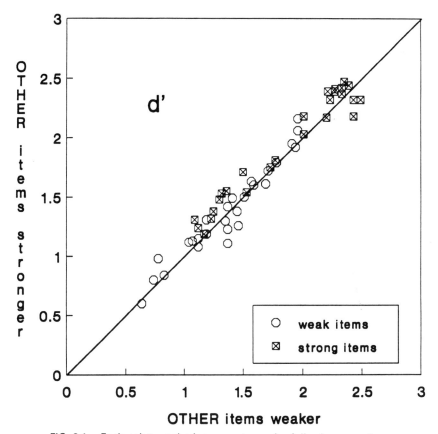

FIG. 3.1.   Each point graphed represents a pair of d' values, one from
each of two conditions that are matched for presentation time and
number of presentations, total number of different items on the list,
serial presentation position, test position, and lag from study to test,
but differ in the strength of *other* items on the list. Data from many
conditions in several studies is accumulated in this figure, and strong
and weak test items are indicated separately. A positive list-strength
effect is represented by points below the diagonal.

Longer lists produce poorer memory in recognition, free recall, and cued recall.
Ratcliff, Clark, and Shiffrin (1990) studied a related effect. The strengths of
some items on a list are varied: If the unchanged list items are harmed by strength
increases for other items (or helped by strength decreases), then a (positive) list-
strength effect is said to have occurred. A list-strength effect occurs for free recall
(e.g., Tulving & Hastie, 1972; Ratcliff et al., 1990). However it is weak at best
for cued recall, and missing or negative for recognition (Ratcliff et al., 1990). In
seven studies, strength was varied either by the number of spaced repetitions or
by the amount of study time. The results are summarized in Fig. 3.1. Points
below the diagonal represent positive list-strength findings. None were signifi-

cantly below, but several were significantly above (although of small magnitude).

Before drawing conclusions it is necessary to establish that the results are not due to some artifact of experimental design or between-list strategy differences. In the course of the first seven studies, and subsequent experiments by Murnane and Shiffrin (in press-a, in press-b), we ruled out contamination by serial position effects at study or test, delay between study and test, within-list context shift effects, and redistribution of rehearsal or coding effort from strong to weak items in mixed lists.

We take the list-strength findings to provide strong prima facie evidence against the hypothesis that structural interference occurs in the process of storing multiple inputs in memory. Most composite storage models store items in such a way that the successive inputs interact and produce mutual degradation. According to these models it is assumed that many items are stored (in part) in the same units of memory, in such a way that increases in the number of items stored reduces the quality of representation of the individual items. One simple example comes from Anderson (1973); he represented an item by a vector of feature values; multiple items are stored by adding the vectors together to form a single vector. The resultant vector is correlated with the individual item vectors, but the correlations keep dropping as new items are added. Almost all current composite models have this character (e.g., Ackley, Hinton, & Sejnowski, 1985; Anderson, 1973; Metcalfe Eich, 1982; Murdock, 1982; Pike, 1984). Shiffrin, Ratcliff, and Clark (1990) showed that these models could not handle the list-strength findings; in addition, they could not find variants retaining structural interference that could be made to fit the results. Although Shiffrin et al. (1990) argued for separate rather than composite storage, this phrasing might be slightly misleading. The results really argue for models in which events are stored in noninterfering fashion. However, even models with this characteristic, like SAM, may not be able to predict the findings. For example, the traditional version of SAM could not do so. This led us to the following revision.

To simplify the exposition, suppose we are interested in recognition of a target item, A, or a distractor item, X, when an item B not rehearsed with A is varied in strength (B+ and B- will be used to refer to strong and weak items, respectively). The effect of B is produced by the activation of the image of B when A or X is tested. Suppose X is tested; then the cues used to probe memory are X and C (where C is the context cue). In the old version of SAM, the mean and variance of activation of B+ by C is greater than the activation of B-, but the activation of B+ by X is same as the activation of B-. As the net activation is produced by the product of these, the mean and variance of activation of B+ is more than of B-. The variance increase produces the predicted recognition deficit produced by stronger items.

To revise SAM, we settled upon a *differentiation* hypothesis: The activation (e.g., of B) produced by an unrelated item cue (e.g., A or X) is posited to be less when the image being activated is stronger (e.g., X activates B+ less than B-). This assumption has precedent in the literature and is also fairly plausible: As the cue and the image are in fact quite different, one can argue that the stronger is the stored image, the more salient will be the differences between it and the cue, and hence the less will be the activation. If so, the item cue and context cues will roughly counteract each other, strong and weak B's will be activated about equally, and list-strength effects near zero can be predicted.

It should be noted that the explanation of the list-strength effect within SAM requires a composite-like assumption, that repetitions of a given item are accumulated into a single, stronger image; otherwise, separate images would each be activated to a "standard" level, and their sum would reflect the number of repetitions. Murnane and Shiffrin (in press-a) induced separate storage of repeated words by placing them in the context of different sentences; as predicted, this manipulation produced a positive list-strength effect.

The differentiation assumption itself is a fairly modest modification of SAM (the residual strength parameter, d, is allowed to depend on the strength of the image), altering previously derived predictions only in small ways. The main result of the change is a magnification of the predicted effect of increasing list study time, so that we would need to assume that the increase in stored strength as study time increases would have to be highly damped.

In sum, we take the list-strength findings as evidence in favor of noninterfering rather than structurally interfering storage of events, and as evidence that interference in memory arises during retrieval rather than during storage. (Perhaps this is the answer to the question posed by Estes to the first author over 20 years ago.)

The differing results for free recall and recognition are accounted for by the model because free recall is assumed to involve some search cycles with only the context cue in the probe set. Similarly, the small effects in cued recall are predicted because both context and item cues are used in this paradigm. Thus both the findings and our theoretical account support different retrieval mechanisms for (free) recall and recognition.

The Units of Storage and Retrieval

The list strength results provide evidence for separate storage of events; what then are the units of event storage? We have been exploring this issue for several years. The difficulty lies in distinguishing a single higher order unit like a sentence from an interassociated collection of lower order units like the words making up a sentence. A related issue is the nature of unit used as the probe of memory. For example, when a sentence is presented for test, context will presumably be one of the cues used to probe memory, but what will be the other cues in the probe? All the words may be used jointly and separately in the probe, or the words may join into a single unit that is then used in the probe, or there may be successive probes each using one word at a time. Shiffrin et al. (1989) examined these model variants and tested them empirically. They presented five word sentences and examined cued recall for a word in a designated sentence position. The number of cues varied from one to four, and accuracy and response time were measured.

The results provided strong evidence for sentence units in both storage and test. As number of test cues increased, accuracy of response increased but latency of response decreased. The better match of the sentence unit cue to the stored sentence unit would cause such a result. However, separate storage of words would lead to slower latencies as the cues themselves would tend to be sampled during retrieval. In a subsequent study, the cue words were presented in scrambled positions. In this case accuracy increased with number of cues, but latency was flat. It was assumed that the scrambling of word order at test reduced the cue to image match, offsetting the advantage of extra cues, and thereby producing a flat latency function. However, once the relevant sentence image had been sampled, recovery from it depends on the number of sentence words in the cue much more than the order of those words, leading to the accuracy increase. This argument represents another extension of SAM in which sampling and recovery processes are at least somewhat disassociated.

Several other studies provided supporting evidence. In one, sentences, scrambled sentences, or nonsense sentences were studied. In response to the cue(s), the subject responded with as many of the remaining words as possible. Of the many salient results, we mention only one: When all the remaining words in a sentence were recalled correctly, the latencies for successive recalls were constant. We took this for evidence of a serial read out process from a sentence image, when the sentence image was well stored. If the sentence were stored as separate words, it should have taken increasing times to locate the remaining words as recall proceeded. These findings by no means exhaust the evidence in Shiffrin et al. (1989) for sentence level units. It would be pointed out, however, that their results also included evidence for word level storage in certain conditions when sentence encoding was difficult.

The sentence studies provide evidence for higher order sentence units, but the results may be generalized much further. That is, SAM must be construed as a flexible model in which the level of unit at storage and retrieval is determined by coding operations at these times. Shiffrin et al. (1989) outlined such an extension of SAM for recall tasks:

1. Grouping and coding operations in short-term store determine the units of storage. Often higher order units require longer and deeper encoding operations; if these do not succeed, lower order units may be stored, quite possibly with interassociations.

2. A variety of retrieval strategies may be used by subjects in different

situations. When the test items are easy to combine into a higher order unit, the probe set will tend to consist of context plus this unit. When the test items are hard to combine (as when sentence words are presented for test in scrambled order), the items may be used separately and jointly at first (along with context), but may be combined into a higher order unit later in the memory search. When higher order units are even more difficult to form (as when nonsense sentences are tested) only lower order units may be used in the probe sets.

3. Once a higher order image is sampled, recovery is not generally based on the same strength that governs sampling (previous versions of SAM used the same strength for both, but did not consider the possibility of units at several levels). Overall match of cue set to image may determine sampling strength, but component strengths may determine recovery (if, e.g., the test sentence consists of words in scrambled order, sampling strength may be weak, but recovery strength may be quite high).

4. It seems likely that information is stored at several different levels simultaneously.

Evidence for higher order units may also be found in recognition tasks. Humphreys, Pike, Bain, and Tehan (1989) have argued for such units on the basis of tasks in which doubles and triples of items are studied and tested. Suppose the subject studies AB, AC, BC, and DEF. Suppose the task requires an "old" response when each of the test items is old. Recognition of DEF can be superior to ABC even when recognition of AB, AC, BC is superior to DE, DF, and EF. This suggests that recognition of DEF is not based on pairwise associations, and that DEF may be a unit (the argument is not airtight because the subject might have inverted the normal decision rule, but Gronlund, 1986, reported in Shiffrin et al., 1989, added some additional conditions and obtained quite strong evidence for higher order units).

Clark and Shiffrin (1987) studied many types of recognition tasks after study of word triples. They examined an alternative to higher order images as a basis of explaining findings not fitting the standard SAM model: *context sensitive encoding*. Suppose an item's encoding at study is different depending upon the other items with which it is studied. Suppose that the encoding of that item at test also depends upon the other test items. Then when test groups match study groups, the encodings will match better than otherwise, producing effects similar to those that would have occurred had the group of items been stored as a higher order unit. The context sensitive encoding model did fit the data well, but no attempt was made to fit the higher level unit model, and it is likely that this model would have done well also. We think both hypotheses are probably correct; certainly the weight of evidence from all the studies argues for multiple levels of units.

FUTURE DIRECTIONS

Despite the notable successes of the SAM theory to date, there are many opportunities for future developments, and large sets of findings that must be handled before the theory can be fairly assessed. These findings and issues include: (a) reaction times in all the basic paradigms (free and cued recall and recognition), including times for all the types of responses observed, correct and incorrect; (b) probabilities of responses in signal-to-respond paradigms (e.g., Dosher, 1984); (c) the way in which the subject or the memory system choose recognition criteria (including the "mirror" effect; see Glanzer & Adams, 1990); (d) the way in which memory is accessed for the purposes of categorization; (e) how information should be represented, and similarity among items taken into account; (f) how information is stored in and retrieved from semantic memory (can an accumulation of episodic images appear to act as a semantic image?); (g) how SAM may be best applied to the data concerning implicit and explicit memory tasks.

At the present stage of development of the field, the SAM theory is certainly one of the best worked out and most self-consistent approaches to the basic phenomena of memory. However, there are numerous strong theoretical competitors, including those couched in distributed, composite form. The field continues to evolve rapidly, and exciting prospects lie on the near horizon.

ACKNOWLEDGMENTS

This research was supported by NIMH Grant 12717 and AFOSR grant 870089 to the first author.

REFERENCES

Ackley, D. H., Hinton, G. E., & Sejnowski, J. J. (1985). A learning algorithm for Boltzmann machines. *Cognitive Science, 9,* 147–169.

Anderson, J. A. (1973). A theory for the recognition of items from short memorized lists. *Psychological Review, 80,* 417–438.

Atkinson, R. C., & Shiffrin, R. M. (1968). Human memory: A proposed system and its control processes. In K. W. Spence & J. T. Spence (Eds.), *The psychology of learning and motivation: Advances in research and theory, Vol. 2* (pp. 89–195). New York: Academic Press.

Bjork, R. A. (1988). Retrieval inhibition as an adaptive mechanism in human memory. In H. L. Roediger & F. I. M. Craik (Eds.), *Varieties of memory and consciousness: Essays in honour of Endel Tulving.* Hillsdale, NJ: Lawrence Erlbaum Associates.

Bjork, R. A., & Richardson-Klavehn, A. (1989). On the puzzling relationship between environmental context and human memory. In C. Izawa (Ed.), *Current issues in cognitive processes: The Tulane Flowerree symposium on cognition,* (pp. 313–344). Hillsdale, NJ: Lawrence Erlbaum Associates.

Clark, S. E., & Shiffrin, R. M. (1987). Recognition of multiple-item probes. *Memory and Cognition, 15,* 367–378.

Dosher, B. A. (1984). Degree of learning and retrieval speed: Study time and multiple exposures. *Journal of Experimental Psychology: Learning, Memory, and Cognition, 10,* 541–574.

Eich, J. Metcalfe. (1982). A composite holographic associative recall model. *Psychological Review, 89,* 627–661.

Estes, W. K. (1955a). Statistical theory of spontaneous recovery and regression. *Psychological Review, 62,* 145–154.

Estes, W. K. (1955b). Statistical theory of distributional phenomena in learning. *Psychological Review, 62,* 369–377.

Gillund, G., & Shiffrin, R. M. (1984). A retrieval model for both recognition and recall. *Psychological Review, 91,* 1–67.

Glanzer, M., & Adams, J. K. (1990). The mirror effect in recognition memory: Data and theory. *Journal of Experimental Psychology: Learning, Memory, and Cognition, 16,* 5–16.

Glenberg, A. M. (1976). Monotonic and nonmonotonic lag effects in paired-associate and recognition memory paradigms. *Journal of Verbal Learning and Verbal Behavior, 15,* 1–16.

Godden, D. R., & Baddeley, A. D. (1975). Context-dependent memory in two natural environments: On land and underwater. *British Journal of Psychology, 66,* 325–331.

Gronlund, S. D. (1986). *Multi-level storage and retrieval: An empirical investigation and theoretical analysis.* Unpublished doctoral dissertation. Indiana University.

Gronlund, S. D., & Shiffrin, R. M. (1986). Retrieval strategies in recall of natural categories and categorized lists. *Journal of Experimental Psychology: Learning, Memory, and Cognition, 12,* 550–561.

Humphreys, M. S., Pike, R., Bain, J. D., & Tehan, G. (1989). Global matching: A comparison of the SAM, MINERVA II, Matrix, and TODAM models. *Journal of Mathematical Psychology, 33,* 36–67.

Mensink, G. J. M., & Raaijmakers, J. G. W. (1988). A model for interference and forgetting. *Psychological Review, 95,* 434–455.

Mensink, G. J. M., & Raaijmakers, J. G. W. (1989). A model of contextual fluctuation. *Journal of Mathematical Psychology, 33,* 172–186.

Murdock, B. B., Jr. (1982). A theory for the storage and retrieval of item and associative information. *Psychological Review, 89,* 609–626.

Murnane, K., & Shiffrin, R. M. (in press-a). Interference and the representation of events in memory. *Journal of Experimental Psychology: Learning, Memory and Cognition.*

Murnane, K., & Shiffrin, R. M. (in press-b). Word repetitions in sentence recognition. *Memory & Cognition.*

Pike, R. (1984). Comparison of convolution and matrix distributed memory systems for associative recall and recognition. *Psychological Review, 91,* 281–294.

Postman, L., & Underwood, B. J. (1973). Critical issues in interference theory. *Memory & Cognition, 1,* 19–40.

Raaijmakers, J. G. W., & Shiffrin, R. M. (1980). SAM: A theory of probabilistic search of associative memory. In G. H. Bower (Ed.), *The psychology of learning and motivation: Advances in research and theory* (Vol. 14, 207–262). New York: Academic Press.

Raaijmakers, J. G. W., & Shiffrin, R. M. (1981). Search of associative memory. *Psychological Review, 88,* 93–134.

Ratcliff, R., Clark, S., & Shiffrin, R. M. (1990). The list-strength effect. I. Data and discussion. *Journal of Experimental Psychology: Learning, Memory, and Cognition, 16,* 163–178.

Ross, B. H., & Landauer, T. K. (1978). Memory for at least one of two items: Test and failure of several theories of spacing effects. *Journal of Verbal Learning and Verbal Behavior, 17,* 669–680.

Rumelhart, D. E. (1967). *The effects of interpresentation intervals on performance in a continuous paired-associate task.* (Tech. Rep. No. 16). Stanford, CA: Stanford University, *Institute for Mathematical Studies in Social Sciences.*

Shiffrin, R. M. (1970). Memory search. In D. A. Norman (Ed.), *Models of memory* (pp. 375–447). New York, Academic Press.

Shiffrin, R. M., & Atkinson, R. C. (1969). Storage and retrieval processes in long-term memory. *Psychological Review, 79,* 179–193.

Shiffrin, R. M., Murnane, K., Gronlund, S., & Roth, M. (1989). On units of storage and retrieval. In C. Izawa (Ed.), *Current issues in cognitive processes: The Tulane Floweree symposium on cognition* (pp. 25–68). Hillsdale, NJ: Lawrence Erlbaum Associates.

Shiffrin, R. M., Ratcliff, R., & Clark, S. (1990). The list-strength effect: II. Theoretical mechanisms. *Journal of Experimental Psychology: Learning, Memory, and Cognition, 16,* 179–195.

Slamecka, N. J., & McElree, B. (1983). Normal forgetting of verbal lists as a function of their degree of learning. *Journal of Experimental Psychology: Learning, Memory, and Cognition, 9,* 384–397.

Smith, S. M. (1979). Remembering in and out of context. *Journal of Experimental Psychology: Human Learning and Memory, 5,* 460–471.

Tulving, E., & Hastie, R. (1972). Inhibition effects of intralist repetition in free recall. *Journal of Experimental Psychology, 92,* 297–304.

Young, J. L. (1971). Reinforcement-test intervals in paired-associate learning. *Journal of Mathematical Psychology, 8,* 58–81.

4 The Long-Term Retention of Skills

Alice F. Healy
David W. Fendrich
Robert J. Crutcher
William T. Wittman
Antoinette T. Gesi
K. Anders Ericsson
Lyle E. Bourne, Jr.
University of Colorado, Boulder

For the last 4 years we have been engaged in a study of the long-term retention of skills. Our research project has had as its overarching goal finding ways to optimize long-term retention, particularly the long-term retention of skilled performance. We started with the assumption that some part of acquired knowledge or skill is, for reasons that remain to be identified, permanent. Bahrick (1984), among others, demonstrated that whereas a large part of acquired knowledge is lost rapidly, a significant portion can last a lifetime, even if that knowledge is not intentionally rehearsed or accessed in the meantime. In a theoretically noncommittal way, we adopted Bahrick's concept of a permastore as a fundamental fact of memory and we looked for conditions of training or attributes of learned material that lead to permastore. Indeed, in a number of our lines of investigation, we have found evidence for a surprising degree of retention of acquired performance. We first provide an overview of three of these investigations, and then we discuss a general theoretical framework that helps us understand this impressive memory performance. In contrast, in other studies we have conducted, we found considerable forgetting over even relatively short retention intervals. We next review three of these studies, with an attempt to place them in the same general theoretical framework developed to account for the earlier studies. The aim of this review is to derive indications of the specific factors that facilitate retention. Thus, we try in this chapter to provide an integrated theoretical account of the many different facets of our research program.

As indicated in Table 4.1, we have divided our investigations into two broad

TABLE 4.1
Studies Demonstrating Remarkable Memory (on Left) and Considerable Forgetting (on Right)

High Retention	Low Retention
target detection	memory for numerical calculations
mental multiplication	vocabulary learning
data entry	components of memory for course schedules

categories: those showing some evidence for permanent retention of acquired performance and those showing evidence instead for substantial forgetting. Although Table 4.1 suggests a sharp boundary separating these two categories, we do not imply that there is a clear separation, or that long-term retention is all or none. But this categorization should highlight the factors most crucial in facilitating memory over a long interval. Our studies demonstrating remarkable memory used target detection, mental multiplication, and data entry tasks. Our studies demonstrating considerable forgetting assessed memory for numerical calculations, for vocabulary, and for components of course schedules.

STUDIES DEMONSTRATING REMARKABLE MEMORY

Target Detection

In our studies of target detection (Healy, Fendrich, & Proctor, 1990), subjects sat at a computer terminal where they saw displays containing 16 random characters grouped to resemble three words. Half of the displays contained the letter H, which was the target, and half did not. The subjects' task was to press a response button every time they saw a target, and both response accuracy and latency were used as dependent variables. A major independent variable was frame size. There were either 2, 4, or 16 letters in the display with the other characters replaced by number signs. A sample display of each frame size is shown in Fig. 4.1. Previous studies have shown that subjects generally respond less accurately and more slowly as frame size increases (see, e.g., Schneider & Shiffrin, 1977), and we took the loss of this frame size effect with practice as our index of automaticity. We wondered whether retention of target detection skill would be related to the degree of skill automaticity achieved during training.

In our first experiment examining the retention of the detection skill, we employed three groups of subjects. Subjects in the control group received no detection training, those in the limited training group performed 10 blocks of training over two sessions, and those in the extensive training group received 24 blocks of training over four sessions. A retention interval of 3 to 5 weeks then elapsed before subjects returned for the final (retention) session. At that time subjects in all three groups performed five blocks of the detection task to evaluate retention of the letter detection skill.

FRAME SIZE

2   ## ###### #####HI#

4   ##O ## H###I##M###

16   WYSEYIG PEO PCNUHE

FIG. 4.1. Sample displays of each frame size in the target detection study by Healy, Fendrich & Proctor (1990). Reprinted by permission of the American Psychological Association.

The results of detection training for the limited and extensive training groups are shown as a function of day of training and frame size in Fig. 4.2 for hit proportions. For both groups hit rates increased during acquisition. A substantial frame size effect was evident even at the end of training, but the effect was significantly reduced with practice, even in the limited training group. In contrast, although response latencies (shown in Fig. 4.3) decreased during acquisition, they showed no reduction in the frame size effect. Hence, by this measure, there was no evidence that automatic processing had been achieved. Comparisons of performance on the last day of training versus the retention test showed no decrease in accuracy or speed for either group, suggesting essentially perfect retention of the detection skill over the delay interval.

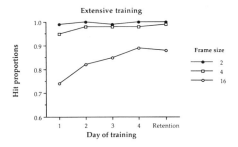

FIG. 4.2. Hit proportions as a function of day of training and frame size in Experiment 1 of the target detection study by Healy, Fendrich, & Proctor (1990), with data from the limited training group in the top panel and data from the extensive training group in the bottom panel. Adapted by permission of the American Psychological Association.

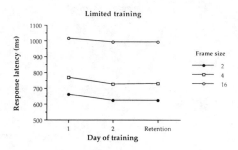

FIG. 4.3. Average response latency as a function of day of training and frame size in Experiment 1 of the target detection study by Healy, Fendrich, & Proctor (1990), with data from the limited training group in the top panel and data from the extensive training group in the bottom panel. Adapted by permission of the American Psychological Association.

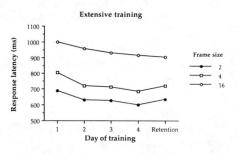

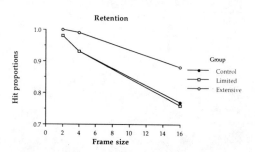

FIG. 4.4. Retention data from the limited and extensive training groups in Experiment 1 of the target detection study by Healy, Fendrich, & Proctor (1990) compared to data from the control group, with hit proportions in the top panel and average response latency in the bottom panel. Adapted by permission of the American Psychological Association.

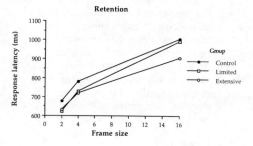

The retention-test data are replotted in Fig. 4.4 where they are compared to the analogous data from the control group, in terms of both hit proportions and response latencies as a function of frame size. Hit rate was significantly better overall for the extensive training group than for either of the other groups. Also, for response latencies as well as hit rate, the frame size effect was significantly smaller for the extensive training group than for the other two, suggesting that indeed responding did become more automatic after extensive training.

One purpose of our next experiment was to determine whether more intensive practice would lead to more dramatic changes in the frame size effects and, therefore, a greater degree of automaticity. A second purpose was to assess retention of the detection skill over delays considerably longer than the one-month interval used in our first study.

This study employed only two subjects, so we must be cautious in making generalizations based on our findings. Both of the subjects were given 12 days of practice on the detection task. The two subjects were recalled 6 months later for a retention test, and one of the subjects (A. G.) was also recalled 9 months after that (i.e., 15 months after the initial training) for a subsequent retention test. The results in terms of accuracy are shown in Fig. 4.5. Large improvements in performance are evident during training, so that before the end of training both subjects have attained essentially perfect accuracy, even with the largest frame size. Most interesting is the observation that this maximal level of performance is maintained across the long retention intervals. Although no forgetting was evident, some forgetting could have been masked by a ceiling effect because ac-

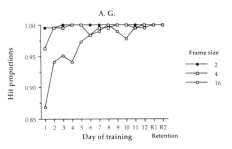

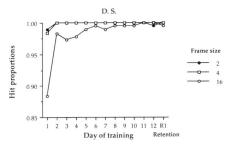

FIG. 4.5. Hit proportions as a function of day of training and frame size in Experiment 2 of the target detection study by Healy, Fendrich, & Proctor (1990), with data from subject A. G. in the top panel and data from subject D. S. in the bottom panel. (R1 stands for the first retention test, and R2 for the second retention test.) Adapted by permission of the American Psychological Association.

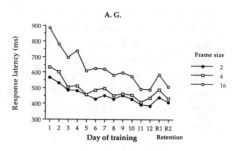

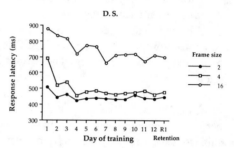

FIG. 4.6. Average response latency as a function of day of training and frame size in Experiment 2 of the target detection study by Healy, Fendrich, & Proctor (1990), with data from subject A. G. in the top panel and data from subject D. S. in the bottom panel. (R1 stands for the first retention test, and R2 for the second retention test.) Adapted by permission of the American Psychological Association.

curacy was so high. This problem does not exist, however, when we examine response latencies, which are shown in Fig. 4.6. Again there are large improvements in performance with practice, but the functions for the three frame sizes do not completely converge, especially for D. S. Thus, the subjects became more automatic with practice but did not achieve full automaticity. Nonetheless, performance on the retention tests showed a remarkable degree of memory. Specifically, after 6 months D. S. showed absolutely no forgetting, and although A. G. did show some loss at that point, the initial retention test may have served as a reminder, because her response latencies after the 15-month retention interval were no different than at the end of training.

Mental Multiplication

We have also found remarkable retention in a paradigm involving mental multiplication (Fendrich, Healy, & Bourne, in press). In this task as well, we were examining whether retention is related to automaticity. Subjects were shown single-digit multiplication problems, like 3 × 5, and they responded with the answers, either by typing them into the computer or saying them aloud into a microphone. This is a natural task that subjects learned initially outside of the laboratory, but with training subjects showed considerable improvement, at least in terms of speed of responding (accuracy was in some cases on the ceiling). We first report the data from two subjects given extensive training and tested after substantial retention intervals. Both of these subjects were given 11 training sessions with the typing response and a final training session with the oral response. The subjects were then retested at retention intervals up to 14 months, and each retention test involved the oral response. On each training and testing session the subjects were shown all 81 problems with single-digit operands. Individuals typically respond more slowly as the size of the operands increases. For example, responses are typically slower to 8×9 than to 2×3. Hence, we used as our index of automaticity the function relating the speed of responding to the size of the operands. We reasoned that as subjects' performance became automatic, this function would flatten, so that there would be little effect of problem difficulty on response time.

Figure 4.7 presents the acquisition functions for the two subjects with the typing response method. Response times are shown as a function of multiplication column and session. Both subjects showed large effects of multiplication column, large decreases in response time as sessions increased, but essentially no change in the effect of multiplication column with practice. Hence, the subjects improved at this skill, but their performance did not become more automatic by the previously stated criterion. Figure 4.8 shows the retention data. Specifically, Fig. 4.8 includes functions for the last day of training and each of the retention tests with the oral method of responding. Note that as with the target detection

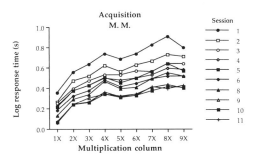

FIG. 4.7. Average log response time as a function of multiplication column and training session number for the acquisition trials in Experiment 1 of the mental multiplication study by Fendrich, Healy, & Bourne (in press), with data from subject M. M. in the top panel and data from subject S. M. in the bottom panel. Adapted by permission of Lawrence Erlbaum Associates.

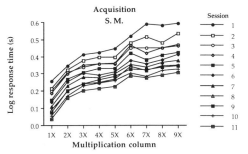

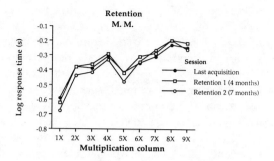

FIG. 4.8. Average log response time as a function of multiplication column and session number for the last acquisition and retention trials in Experiment 1 of the mental multiplication study by Fendrich, Healy, & Bourne (in press), with data from subject M. M. in the top panel and data from subject S. M. in the bottom panel. Adapted by permission of Lawrence Erlbaum Associates.

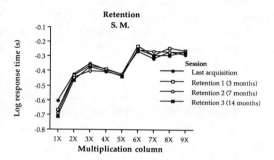

task, subjects showed essentially no forgetting, despite the fact that their performance had not become automatic by our criterion.

In two follow-up experiments, our goal was to gain a better understanding of what subjects learn when they are given training in the mental multiplication task. In the first of these experiments, we tried to determine how specific was the information learned by the subjects. In particular, we wondered whether subjects simply strengthened the correct answers and the associations between each answer and the two operands that produce it, or whether, instead, the multiplication operations themselves were strengthened. In order to explore this issue, subjects in this experiment were given training on only half of the multiplication problems. Specifically, during training subjects were shown multiplication problems with single-digit operands. Square problems, such as 2 × 2, were excluded. The remaining 72 problems were divided into pairs, with the two problems in a pair differing only in operand order (for example, 6 × 5 and 5 × 6). Two subsets of problems were constructed with one problem from each pair in each subset. In each of three acquisition sessions, subjects were shown problems from one of the two subsets depending on their counterbalancing group. A retention test occurred 1 month later during which all subjects were shown the complete set of 72 problems. During all four sessions, subjects responded by typing their answers

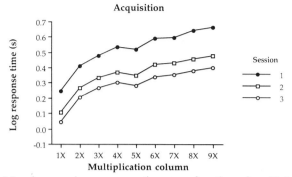

FIG. 4.9. Average log response time as a function of multiplication column and training session number for the acquisition trials in Experiment 2 of the mental multiplication study by Fendrich, Healy, & Bourne (in press). Adapted by permission of Lawrence Erlbaum Associates.

using the numeric keypad on the terminal. Figure 4.9 summarizes the acquisition response times as a function of multiplication column and session. This figure reveals the typical problem-size effect found in earlier studies, including our first experiment. Also, as in that previous experiment, response times declined as training progressed. Thus, subjects' performance improved but did not become more automatic with training.

Figure 4.10 summarizes the retention response times as a function of multiplication column and whether the problem was old (shown during the training phase) or new (not shown earlier). The figure reveals a consistent advantage for the old relative to the new problems across problem size with the single exception

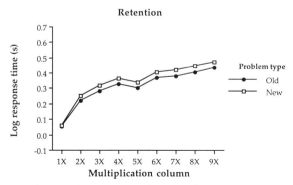

FIG. 4.10. Average log response time as a function of multiplication column and problem type for the retention trials in Experiment 2 of the mental multiplication study by Fendrich, Healy, & Bourne (in press). Adapted by permission of Lawrence Erlbaum Associates.

of problems in the 1× multiplication column. Presumably the lack of an old/new difference for the 1× problems is due to the fact that subjects do not truly compute the answer to these problems but rather use a simple rule—namely, if one of the operands is 1, the answer is the other operand. Because the new problems differed from the old ones only in operand order, the old/new difference found for all but the 1× problems suggests that the information learned by the subjects during training was very specific and concerned the multiplication operations themselves, not just the correct answers or the associations between each answer and the two operands that produce it. Alternatively, a very specific association may be learned by the subjects; the answer may be learned in response to a specific order of the operands.

Although this experiment revealed that the new problems with operands in the reverse order were responded to less quickly than the old problems, it is not clear from this study whether there was any facilitation for these new problems due to the practice with the matching problems that had similar multiplication operations. In our second follow-up study, we addressed that question. The design was similar to that used in the last experiment except that during acquisition subjects were shown a smaller subset of problems. Instead of pairs, the problems were divided into quadruples, with the four problems in each quadruple including two pairs with problems differing only in operand order. For some of the quadruples, the two pairs had the same answer (for example, 2 × 6, 6 × 2, 3 × 4, 4 × 3). For the remaining quadruples, the two pairs were matched for difficulty as closely as possible. Four subsets of problems were constructed with one problem from each quadruple in each subset. During each of three acquisition sessions, subjects were shown problems from one of the four subsets. During the retention session 1 month later, all subjects were shown the complete set of problems.

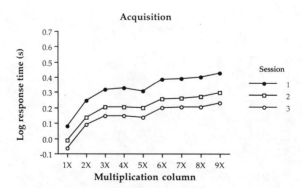

FIG. 4.11. Average log response time as a function of multiplication column and training session number for the acquisition trials in Experiment 3 of the mental multiplication study by Fendrich, Healy, & Bourne (in press). Adapted by permission of Lawrence Erlbaum Associates.

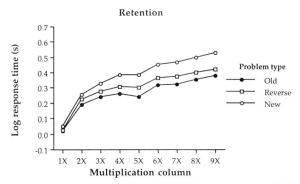

FIG. 4.12. Average log response time as a function of multiplication column and problem type for the retention trials in Experiment 3 of the mental multiplication study by Fendrich, Healy, & Bourne (in press). Adapted by permission of Lawrence Erlbaum Associates.

Figure 4.11 summarizes the acquisition response times. As in the last experiment, the typical problem-size effect is maintained, although response times decline across the three sessions. Figure 4.12 summarizes the 1-month retention response times as a function of multiplication column and problem type. There are three types of problems in this experiment: old, reverse, and new. The reverse problems were identical to the old ones except that the order of the operands was reversed; these problems had been classified as "new" in the previous experiment. New problems in the present experiment were ones that contained a new combination of operands. All three types of problems showed the expected effect of problem size. There was also a consistent advantage for the old relative to the other two types of problems and for the reverse relative to the new problems for all problem sizes except those in the $1 \times$ multiplication column, as in the previous experiment. The difference between the reverse and new problems in the present experiment was significant even when considering only those quadruples in which the new problems had the same answers as the old and reverse problems. This finding indicates that subjects learned more than an association between the answer and the specific order of the operands. This result also suggests that practice on problems transfers to those with similar multiplication operations, thereby lending further support to the hypothesis that the information learned and retained by the subjects concerned the multiplication operations themselves.

Data Entry

The third task we studied in which subjects showed remarkable retention was a motor task involving data entry (Fendrich, Healy, & Bourne, 1991). Subjects were shown lists of digits and typed them with the keypad of a computer termi-

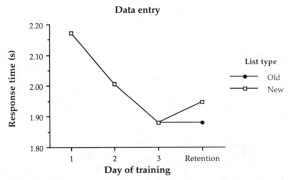

FIG. 4.13.   Average response time as a function of day of training and test list type in Experiment 1 of the data entry study by Fendrich, Healy, & Bourne (1991). Adapted by permission of the American Psychological Association.

nal. In our first experiment, subjects were given 3 days of training at entering lists of 10 three-digit numbers. A given list was repeated either once or five times during training, with the repetitions either spaced or massed. One month later they were given a retention test in which they entered some of the old lists of numbers along with some new lists. Unexpectedly, we found in this experiment no reliable effects of either the amount or spacing of repetitions, but we did find a significant advantage for the old lists relative to the new ones at the retention test. Response times as a function of day of training and test list type are summarized in Fig. 4.13. Subjects improved at the data entry task, and their performance on the old lists was maintained across the month-long retention interval. Although performance at test was worse on the new lists than on the old lists, even with new lists performance was better than at the start of training.

It was most surprising to us that after a one-month interval there was a difference between the old and new lists of digits, despite the fact that subjects were given no instructions to memorize the lists. However, we noted that our index of memory—namely, changes in response time—was an indirect or "implicit" measure, to use the term first proposed by Graf and Schacter (1985). In a follow-up experiment, we addressed the question whether subjects under the same circumstances could also exhibit reliable memory for the lists using a direct or "explicit" measure. If not, we would demonstrate a clear independence or dissociation between the two types of memory measures. Alternatively, perhaps subjects would demonstrate significant memory by the explicit as well as the implicit measure of memory, in which case the question would arise whether the memory processes underlying these two types of measures interact in any way.

In order to investigate these issues in our second experiment, we modified the procedures of the first study to include a recognition test as an explicit measure of memory. Specifically, subjects were asked to give a recognition rating on a six-

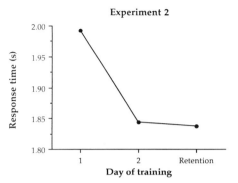

FIG. 4.14. Average response time as a function of day of training in Experiment 2 of the data entry study by Fendrich, Healy, & Bourne (1991). Adapted by permission of the American Psychological Association.

point scale for each digit list shown at the retention test. Subjects were not told about the recognition rating until the beginning of the retention test, so that acquisition still involved incidental learning. For half of the subjects, the rating for each list was given immediately after the list was entered on the keypad, and for the other subjects the rating was made before the list was typed.

As in the first study, we found that subjects' typing times significantly decreased as training progressed and changed very little over the one-month delay interval, as shown in Fig. 4.14. Also, we found that the response times on the retention test were significantly faster for the old lists than for the new lists, as shown in Fig. 4.15. Unlike our first experiment, we found a significant difference between the old and new items only for old items that were repeated five times (old5 lists), not for those that were shown only once (old1 lists).

Most crucial is the signal detection analysis of data from the recognition test. The sensitivity statistic we used was d_a. As shown in Fig. 4.16, subjects' accuracy was significantly greater than chance for the items shown five times, but not for those shown only once. This result indicates that subjects did have

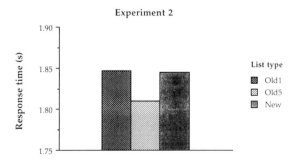

FIG. 4.15.   Average response time as a function of test list type for the retention test in Experiment 2 of the data entry study of Fendrich, Healy, & Bourne (1991). Adapted by permission of the American Psychological Association.

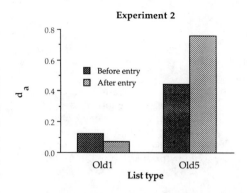

FIG. 4.16. Recognition accuracy (d_a) as a function of number of repetitions and order of the recognition and entry tasks in Experiment 2 of the data entry study by Fendrich, Healy, & Bourne (1991). Adapted by permission of the American Psychological Association.

significant memory for the digit lists presented 1 month earlier by our explicit as well as our implicit measure. Hence, it is interesting to determine whether there is any interaction between the memory processes underlying these two different measures. In fact, there was a significant interaction of repetitions by the order of the recognition and entry tasks. Recognition for the repeated items was better when the recognition test came after, rather than before, the subjects entered the numbers. Hence, typing the digit lists aided the subjects in making their recognition decisions. This finding is consistent with the hypothesis that relative motoric fluency can support recognition judgments. More generally, these results suggest that the memory processes reflected by the explicit and implicit measures are not independent but instead mutually support each other.

To explore further the relation between the two measures of memory, we examined the entry times for subjects in both task orders contingent on whether or not the subjects correctly classified the digit lists on the recognition test, collapsing the rating scale into a binary "old/new" response. As shown in Fig.

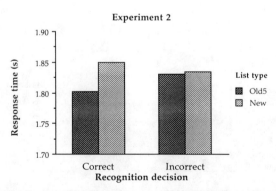

FIG. 4.17. Average response time as a function of recognition decision accuracy and test list type for the retention test in Experiment 2 of the data entry study by Fendrich, Healy, & Bourne (1991). Adapted by permission of the American Psychological Association.

CALCULATOR   TELEPHONE

7 8 9   1 2 3

4 5 6   4 5 6

1 2 3   7 8 9

FIG. 4.18.   Two different keypad orientations used in Experiment 3 of the data entry study by Fendrich, Healy, & Bourne (1991). Reprinted by permission of the American Psychological Association.

4.17, which presents the mean response times for the new lists and the old lists repeated five times, the difference in typing times between old and new digit lists was significant only when those lists were correctly classified, not when subjects made incorrect recognition judgments. This pattern of results further indicates that memory processes underlying the explicit and implicit measures go hand in hand. Evidence for reliable memory by the implicit measure is only available when there is also evidence of reliable memory by the explicit measure.

In a subsequent experiment, we sought to determine the locus of our long-term priming effect. In particular, we wondered whether the remarkable retention we found was reflecting only a motor component of the data entry task or whether a perceptual component was involved as well. In order to separate the motor and perceptual components, we made use of the fact that there are two different conventional orientations of the keypad. As shown in Fig. 4.18, one keypad orientation is used on most computer and calculator keyboards, and the other orientation is used on the standard touch tone telephone. Subjects were trained on one of these keypads and then switched to the other at the retention test 1 week later. We included new lists of digits as well as two different types of old lists on the final test. The "old digit" lists included the same sequences of digits as shown during training but required new motor responses. In contrast, the "old motor" lists included new sequences of digits but ones that required the same sequence of motor responses. For example, for the sequence 7539 shown during training, the old digit list would also be 7539, but the old motor list would be 1593, which requires the same sequence of finger movements on the alternate keypad. The times to initiate the first digit of each sequence are shown in Fig. 4.19 for the new, old digit, and old motor lists on the retention test. Subjects showed a significant advantage relative to the new lists for both types of old lists, thereby locating the long-term priming effect at both the motoric and perceptual stages of processing.

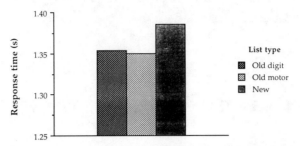

FIG. 4.19.   Average time to initiate the first digit of each sequence as a function of test list type for the retention test in Experiment 3 of the data entry study by Fendrich, Healy, & Bourne (1991). Adapted by permission of the American Psychological Association.

Possible Bases of Permastore.   We have now discussed three different tasks, all of which show evidence for strong long-term skill retention implicating Bahrick's (1984) notion of permastore. At this point we can ask what these three tasks have in common, so that we can generate an hypothesis concerning the factors responsible for entry into permastore. We start by ruling out several hypotheses that are inconsistent with our findings.

First, the results from the target detection and mental multiplication studies are clearly inconsistent with our original idea that entry into permastore is necessarily associated with automaticity. In those two tasks we found essentially perfect retention with little or no indication that subjects' performance had achieved automaticity.

Second, we can rule out the hypothesis that only implicit memory measures can reveal evidence for permastore. Although changes in response times were our primary indices of learning and retention in our three tasks and such changes are implicit or indirect measures of memory, our study of data entry clearly demonstrated long-term retention using an explicit memory measure as well. In fact, the processes underlying the implicit and explicit memory measures were shown to be interdependent in that task.

Third, we can rule out the hypothesis that only motor learning yields superior long-term retention. This hypothesis has some support in the early literature comparing verbal and motor learning (see, e.g., Naylor & Briggs, 1961). Indeed, motor learning was implicated to some degree in the data entry experiments, but perceptual information was also shown to be well retained in those studies. Further, motor learning presumably played only a minor role in the largely perceptual target detection task. Most crucial in this regard are the results of the mental multiplication study. Motor learning was eliminated as a contributing factor in that case, because the subjects given extensive training in the first experiment were tested using an oral response, although they were trained with a typing response. Also, the typing response was used in the retention session as well as the training sessions for the follow-up multiplication experiments, but in those cases the subjects answered the old problems more rapidly than the corresponding reverse problems even though the answers, and hence the motor responses, were the same. The mental multiplication task is probably best described as a cognitive skill rather than a perceptual or motor skill, so perceptual, motor, and cognitive skills can all gain entrance into permastore.

What do the three tasks we studied have in common? It seems to us that the most important common feature shared by these tasks is a major or overriding procedural—as opposed to declarative—component, to use the distinction made by Anderson (1983), among others. In agreement with the theoretical position and arguments put forth by Kolers and Roediger (1984), we propose that memory representations cannot be divorced from the procedures that were used to acquire them, and that the durability of memory depends critically on the extent to which the learning procedures are reinstated at test. Tasks like target detection, mental multiplication, and data entry, all of which require the direct storage, retrieval, and use of specific procedures, should, according to this argument, be acquired and maintained with much greater facility than tasks that involve procedural memory more indirectly and that place a greater emphasis on events, facts, or declarative components, such as the standard list learning experiments. In the traditional studies involving list learning, even those tapping short-term memory (see, e.g., Estes, 1972), the memory coding procedures used by subjects to store the list are not easily retrieved or reinstated at the time of test, unless the subjects employ specific mnemonic procedures, such as the method of loci or the chunking method used by Ericsson and Chase's (1982) expert S. F. In contrast, the procedures used by subjects in our three tasks during acquisition are easily reinstated during the retention test because the subjects are performing the same task (e.g., letter detection) in both cases.

This characterization of memory is consistent with Morris, Bransford, and Franks' (1977) theory of transfer appropriate processing and Tulving and Thomson's (1973) encoding specificity principle, both of which postulate that memory performance will be best when the retrieval operations required at the retention test match or overlap the encoding operations employed during learning. One of our experiments on data entry provides direct support in this domain for the importance of transfer appropriate processing or test appropriateness (Gesi, Fendrich, Healy, & Bourne, 1989). In this study subjects were presented with four-digit sequences on a computer screen. Half the sequences were shown only once, and the other half were shown three separate times in the study session. In one condition the subjects simply read each sequence and pressed the space bar once for each digit in the sequence. In the second condition they entered the sequence using the numeric keypad of the terminal, and in the third condition they entered the sequence using the horizontal number row on the console key-

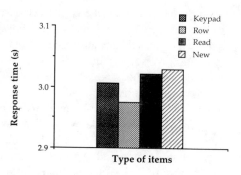

FIG. 4.20. Average response time as a function of study task in the retention test phase of the data entry experiment by Gesi, Fendrich, Healy, & Bourne (1989).

board. One week after the training session, subjects were given a retention test. This test required them to enter old and new sequences using, in some cases, the number row and, in other cases, the keypad configuration. After entering each sequence, the subjects also made an old/new recognition decision. The theory of transfer appropriate processing would predict that subjects' recognition would be most accurate for the sequences entered in the same way at acquisition and at test. In other words, using the row at study and at test or using the keypad at study and at test should be better than either reading at study or using a different key configuration at study and at test.

Our initial analyses examined the typing times during the study phase. Most interesting in these analyses is the effect of repetitions on response times. Subjects were faster at entering digit sequences that were repeated ($M=2.333$ s) than those that were only presented once ($M=2.365$ s), showing that subjects had implicit memory for the digit sequences, even though they were only four digits long and, hence, considerably less complex than the lists of 10 three-digit numbers used in our earlier studies of data entry.

The second set of analyses examined typing times during the retention test phase of the experiment. Of primary concern is whether subjects exhibited memory for the digit sequences after the one-week retention interval. Indeed, response times were significantly shorter for the old sequences shown previously during the study phase ($M=3.002$ s) than for the new sequences ($M=3.029$ s). This advantage for the old items occurred for the sequences entered at study with either the keypad or the row, but not for those only read at study, as shown in Fig. 4.20. This production effect is similar to the generation effect found for episodic memory (see, e.g., Slamecka & Graf, 1978) but points to the crucial role of procedural memory. Although there was a strong production effect on response times, the effect of test appropriateness was only marginally reliable for this implicit measure of memory. Figure 4.21 compares response times for sequences entered the same way at study and test, a different way at study and test, or simply read at study. The response times for these three conditions were statis-

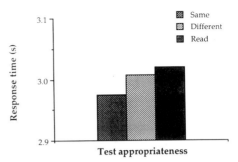

FIG. 4.21. Average response time as a function of test appropriateness in the retention test phase of the data entry experiment by Gesi, Fendrich, Healy, & Bourne (1989).

tically different, but when the read condition was excluded, the difference was only marginally significant.

The third set of analyses was concerned with the explicit recognition data. The d' scores were computed for each subject in each condition. Overall recognition was reliably greater than chance, indicating that subjects did have explicit, as well as implicit, memory for the digit sequences. Of most interest in these analyses is the effect of test appropriateness. Although there was only a marginal effect of this factor on typing times, it did have the expected strong effect on recognition responses. As revealed in Fig. 4.22, subjects showed highest d' scores for the sequences entered with the same key configuration at test as used at study, in accordance with the principle of transfer appropriate processing. Interestingly, when sequences were entered with a different response at study and at test, subjects' recognition memory was no better than when they simply read the sequences at study. Entering the sequence at study only aided explicit recognition if the sequence was entered in the same way on the retention test. Therefore, this production effect can be seen as limited to the situation when the items were produced in the same way at study and at test.

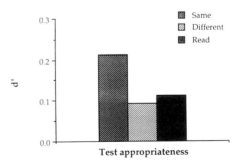

FIG. 4.22. Recognition accuracy (d') as a function of test appropriateness in the retention test phase of the data entry experiment by Gesi, Fendrich, Healy, & Bourne (1989).

STUDIES DEMONSTRATING CONSIDERABLE FORGETTING

Memory for Numerical Calculations

We now turn to our studies showing considerable forgetting over even relatively short retention intervals. In our work on memory for numerical calculations (Crutcher & Healy, 1989), we provided a more general test of the importance to memory of procedures or mental operations. This work followed from the phenomenon known as the *generation effect*. A growing number of experiments since the initial study by Slamecka and Graf (1978) have demonstrated a distinct retention advantage for material that is generated by an individual rather than simply read. If it is assumed that the generation effect is due to the activation in the subjects of auxiliary cognitive operations or mental procedures, then a task leading the subjects to perform such cognitive operations but not necessarily overt generation of an item may show equivalent retention to a generate task. Likewise, a task involving overt generation by the subjects but no auxiliary cognitive operations may not result in any better retention than a read task. In other words, according to this formulation, it is not essential that the subjects generate or produce the stimulus; rather, it is essential that the subjects engage in the auxiliary cognitive operations or mental procedures linking the stimulus to other information stored in memory.

To test this cognitive operations hypothesis, we devised an experimental paradigm that allowed for the orthogonal variation of stimulus presence (absent or present) and auxiliary cognitive operations (self or other). Four tasks were included, which we called the "read," "generate," "verify," and "calculate" tasks. Subjects in all four tasks were given single-digit multiplication problems. A sample problem for each task is shown in Table 4.2. In the read task, the answers were present in the problems and the multiplication operations were performed by another agent (the experimenter), whereas in the generate task the answers were absent and the multiplication operations were performed by the

TABLE 4.2
Illustration of Sample Problems for the Four Tasks in the Study of Memory for Numerical
Calculations by Crutcher and Healy (1989)

Task	Subject Sees	Calculator Available	Subject Responds
Read	6 x 8 = 48	no	"6 x 8 = 48"
Generate	6 x 8 = ?	no	"6 x 8 = 48"
Calculate	6 x 8 = ?	yes	"6 x 8 = 48"
Verify	6 x 8 = 48	no	"6 x 8 = 48, correct"

Note. Reprinted by permission of the American Psychological Association.

TABLE 4.3
Correct Response Proportions on the Free Recall Test as a Function of Cognitive Operations and
Stimulus Presence in Experiment 1 of the Study of Memory for Numerical Calculations
by Crutcher and Healy (1989)

	Cognitive Operations	
Stimulus Presence	Self	Other
Present	Verify .68	Read .38
Absent	Generate .68	Calculate .42

Note. Reprinted by permission of the American Psychological Association.

subjects themselves. The verify and calculate tasks were the ones crucial for testing the cognitive operations hypothesis. In the verify task, the subjects were given a problem with its answer but were required to verify that the answer was correct. Contrastingly, in the calculate task, the subjects had to provide the answers to the problems but they were told to use a calculator rather than perform the arithmetic themselves. After completing all the problems, subjects were asked to recall the answers to all the problems they had been shown. The cognitive operations hypothesis yields the prediction that retention on the verify and generate tasks would be superior to that on the read and calculate tasks, because in the former two tasks the multiplication operations are performed by the subjects themselves whereas in the latter two tasks the multiplication operations are performed by another agent (either the experimenter or a calculator). In contrast, no difference is expected between the generate and verify tasks or between the calculate and read tasks because whether the answers are absent or present in the problems is not thought to be of much consequence. The results of primary interest are summarized in Table 4.3 in terms of correct response proportions on the free recall test. In accordance with our hypothesis, recall was greatly affected by whether or not the subjects performed the mental operations themselves but not by whether they were shown the answers with the problems.

In a follow-up experiment, we aimed to assess the generalizability of these results. Our goal was to replicate and extend the findings from our first experiment along two dimensions. First, we sought to determine whether the same pattern of results would obtain for retention over considerably longer delays than were involved in the immediate testing situation of the first experiment. Second, we aimed to assess whether a recognition test procedure would lead to the same findings as the recall procedure used in the first experiment.

The method was similar to that in the first experiment except that subjects were tested either immediately, after a two-day delay or after a seven-day delay. Right after the recall task subjects were given the recognition test. Subjects were

TABLE 4.4
Correct Response Proportions on the Recognition Test as a Function of Cognitive Operations,
Stimulus Presence, and Retention Interval in Experiment 2 of the Study of
Memory for Numerical Calculations by Crutcher and Healy (1989)

Stimulus Presence and Retention Interval	Cognitive Operations	
	Self	Other
Present	Verify	Read
Immediate	.59	.42
Two-day	.40	.24
Seven-day	.24	.10
Mean	.41	.25
Absent	Generate	Calculate
Immediate	.55	.34
Two-day	.49	.16
Seven-day	.40	.14
Mean	.48	.21

Note. Reprinted by permission of the American Psychological Association.

shown pairs of multiplication products and for each pair they were to circle the one number in the pair that was an answer to one of the multiplication problems they were given during the study phase.

The results of the recall task are summarized in Table 4.4 in terms of correct recall proportions for the four tasks in each of the three retention interval conditions. As in Experiment 1, recall levels for the generate and verify conditions were higher than those for the read and calculate conditions, and the same pattern of results was found for each of the three retention interval conditions, although increased delay between study and test did depress performance levels considerably.

The results of the forced-choice recognition task are summarized in Table 4.5 in terms of correct recognition proportions. Although performance levels for the recognition task were higher than for the recall task, the same pattern of results was found for recognition as for recall. Specifically, recognition levels were higher for shorter delays between study and test and, most crucially, mean recognition rates were higher for the generate and verify conditions than for the read and calculate conditions, with essentially no differences between the generate and verify or between the read and calculate conditions.

It is important to note that although performance was influenced by the use of cognitive operations in this task, in no case was performance at the ceiling, and we did find substantial decreases in performance over retention intervals up to a week, so that permastore contributes little to these results.

TABLE 4.5
Correct Response Proportions on the Recognition Test as a Function of Cognitive Operations,
Stimulus Presence, and Retention Interval in Experiment 2 of the Study of
Memory for Numerical Calculations by Crutcher and Healy (1989)

Stimulus Presence and Retention Interval	Cognitive Operations	
	Self	Other
Present	Verify	Read
Immediate	.82	.81
Two-day	.76	.61
Seven-day	.72	.52
Mean	.77	.65
Absent	Generate	Calculate
Immediate	.81	.65
Two-day	.75	.66
Seven-day	.69	.64
Mean	.75	.65

Note. Reprinted by permission of the American Psychological Association.

Vocabulary Learning

Although we did not provide a direct test of our hypotheses in our studies of other task domains, the results in these other domains are also consistent with our theoretical framework. For example, our work with vocabulary retention (Crutcher, 1989; Crutcher & Ericsson, 1988) provides important support for the hypothesis that the durability of memory depends critically on the extent to which the encoding generated during learning can be reinstated at test. This work is also of particular relevance to the conception of permastore, because it involves the same domain studied by Bahrick (1984). In these studies subjects were given the task of learning Spanish-English vocabulary items using the keyword method, which is a two-part mnemonic procedure that has been shown in the past to be effective in the teaching of foreign vocabulary. This method is illustrated in Fig. 4.23. In this example, subjects are given the Spanish word (doronico), a mediating keyword (door), and the English translation (leopard). The subject's task is first to form a phonological (or orthographic) link between the Spanish word and keyword and then to form an interactive image linking the keyword and the English word.

In our initial experiments with this method, we tested the subjects on each of the two subtasks as well as the complete task. Specifically, in the phonological test we provided the Spanish word as a cue and required subjects to produce the keyword as a response; in the image test we provided the keyword as a cue and

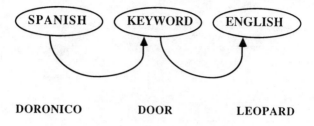

FIG. 4.23.   Illustration of the keyword method used in the vocabulary learning study by Crutcher and Ericsson (1988).

required subjects to produce the English word as a response; and in the full task the Spanish word was provided as a cue and subjects were required to produce the English word as a response. In our first experiment we tested two groups of subjects, both of whom acquired the vocabulary items followed by an immediate test. One group of subjects was then retested after a one-week retention interval, whereas the other group was retested after a one-month delay. The results for the two groups of subjects on the immediate and delayed tests are summarized in Fig. 4.24 in terms of correct response proportions. Although there was little difference among the three tasks on the immediate test, the phonological task (in which subjects are given the Spanish word and respond with the keyword) was best retained after the delay, especially for the one-month delay interval. This result suggests that it is the image component of the full task that is largely responsible for the forgetting observed when the keyword method is employed. We propose as an explanation for the difference between the phonological and image components that the procedures used in the phonological task to generate the keyword from the Spanish word are easily reinstated at the time of the test, whereas the procedures used in the image task to generate the English word from

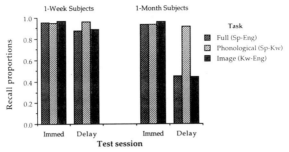

FIG. 4.24.   Correct recall response proportions for the two groups of subjects as a function of test session and task in the vocabulary learning study by Crutcher and Ericsson (1988).

the keyword are not easily reinstated. In other words, subjects given the Spanish word can easily use inferencing to generate the keyword by thinking of words that sound like the Spanish word, because there are only a limited number of words that meet this relatively strict phonological constraint. On the other hand, subjects given the keyword cannot easily derive the English word by thinking of words that can be imaged together with the keyword, because there are a very large if not infinite number of different words that meet this much looser image constraint.

Two new experiments by Crutcher and Ericsson provide support for this explanation. In the first experiment we recalled 4 of the original 24 subjects from our earlier study, two initially tested after 1 week and two after 1 month. In the present experiment these subjects were tested after a retention interval of approximately 1 year. In this case, forgetting would be expected to be considerable, so that subjects would have to rely more on the inference or generating procedures than they would at the earlier tests. Indeed it was found, as shown in Fig. 4.25, that the performance of these subjects on the image and full tasks was very depressed, whereas their performance on the phonological task, though clearly lower than that after the initial delayed tests, was still extremely high. Note, however, that even for the image and full tasks, there was some retention after a year. This observation is consistent with Bahrick's (1984) findings concerning permastore, especially given the relatively limited amount of practice by our subjects.

In the second experiment, a new group of subjects was asked to generate keywords given the same Spanish words as used previously. The subjects were given 40 seconds for each item to produce as many keywords as possible. The subjects were told to generate words that were phonologically or orthographically similar to the Spanish words. Both the proportion of trials on which the original keywords were produced by the subjects as their first response and the proportion of trials on which the original keywords were produced as any re-

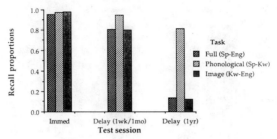

FIG. 4.25. Correct recall response proportions as a function of test session and task in the vocabulary learning study by Crutcher and Ericsson.

sponse within the 40 seconds were computed and are shown in Fig. 4.26. Fig. 4.26 includes a conservative estimate of subjects' retention of the keywords after one year. This estimate is based on recall accuracy for the first trials of the retention test before the subjects from the first new experiment were exposed to the keywords as part of any other test stimuli. On only 15% of the trials did subjects produce an incorrect response, which implies substantial memory of the keywords even after corrections for guessing. These results suggest that the subjects primarily relied on a generate-and-test method to retrieve the presented keywords.

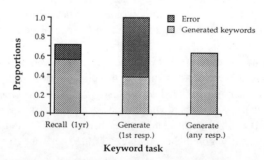

FIG. 4.26. Proportions of trials on which subjects recalled the presented keywords correctly (light bar) or recalled an incorrect word (dark bar) in response to the Spanish word after a one-year delay in the first new vocabulary learning study by Crutcher and Ericsson. In addition, proportions of trials in which a different group of subjects cued by the Spanish word correctly generated English words matching the original keywords (light bar) and other nonmatching words (dark bar) as their first response or as any matching response within 40 seconds in the second new study by Crutcher and Ericsson.

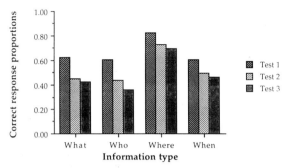

FIG. 4.27.   Correct response proportions as a function of test number and information type in Experiment 1 of the study of components of memory for course schedules by Wittman (1989).

Components of Memory for Course Schedules

Our last task domain involves the recall by undergraduate students of information about their course schedules. In this study (Wittman, 1989), we examined the retention of four different types of course schedule information: the actual title of the course ("what"), the instructor's name ("who"), the location of the class building on a campus map ("where"), and the class start time ("when"). In our first experiment we used both a cross-sectional and longitudinal design to assess the relative forgetting rates of these four different types of information. We tested three groups of subjects on each of three different occasions, with the three tests for each group occurring on consecutive semesters. Subjects were initially tested after completing at least 2 years of course work at the University of Colorado. During each of the three tests they were questioned about their course schedule from a previous semester, with a different semester tested on the three occasions, so that on average there was a six-month retention interval separating the three tests. The testing made use of a cued recall procedure. Subjects were probed about three courses taken during the test semester. Across subjects each type of information was used equally often as a cue to recall the other three types of information. Partial credit was allowed for an incomplete answer, such as providing only the course number when the course title was requested. The results are summarized in Fig. 4.27 in terms of mean correct response proportions for the four different types of information at the three testings. There was considerable forgetting of this course schedule information. This finding is evident in two different ways. First, the overall levels of performance are quite low. For example, at the second and third testings, subjects recall less than half of the time the course title, the instructor's name, and the class time. Second, there is a significant overall decrease in performance on the second and third tests relative to the first test. Hence, it is clear that the course schedule information, although learned naturally and with considerable reexposure during the semester in question, is not well retained, and certainly does not rely on permastore to any great extent. The most interesting observation concerns the differences among the four types of information. On all three tests, subjects' performance was much better on the spatial, or where, information than on the other three types (which is consistent with the finding that spatial information is retained better than temporal information in studies of short-term memory; see, e.g., Healy, 1975).

In accordance with the theoretical framework outlined earlier, we propose as an explanation for the superiority of spatial location recall in this case that subjects learned this information by using procedures that were repeated throughout the semester. Specifically, subjects walked through the campus to the classroom each time the class was held. A similar type of procedural learning was not as readily available for the course title, instructor's name, or class start time.

In order to provide an initial test of this hypothesis, we conducted a follow-up experiment in which subjects had to learn course schedules in the laboratory. We compared two test conditions, the map test and the class-listing test, which differed in the amount of procedural memory required. During the study phase of the experiment, subjects were provided with both a map of the campus and a course schedule in a format similar to that naturally provided to students at the university. This schedule included the four types of information studied in the first experiment along with some ancillary information such as the classroom number. Subjects were given nine training trials followed by a pair of retention tests 1 week later and then another pair of tests after approximately 5 more weeks. In both tests subjects were required to provide from memory the course title and the instructor's name. The tests differed in the type of temporal and spatial information required. In the map test the subjects provided the order of their classes during the school week and the location of each class on the campus map. In contrast, in the class-listing test, subjects provided the start time of each course and the building name where the class was held. Although it is difficult to specify precisely the kinds of learning that involve procedural information, the map test was meant to mimic as closely as we could with paper and pencil the procedures naturally used to retrieve course locations, whereas the class-listing test was meant to remove any procedural component from the recall of course locations.

The results are summarized in Fig. 4.28 in terms of correct response proportions on our two tests as a function of retention interval (1 week for the first test and 6 weeks for the retest) and information type. The comparison of the two retention intervals makes it clear that, as in the natural situation, subjects showed forgetting of the course schedule information overall. Of most interest is the observation that the superiority of spatial information occurred only in the map test, which involved procedural memory. In fact, there was almost no sign of forgetting the spatial information on the map test over the six-week retention interval. In the class-listing test, spatial information showed no superiority in

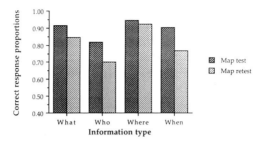

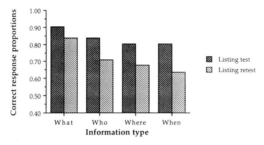

FIG. 4.28.   Correct response proportions as a function of test time and information type in Experiment 2 of the study of components of memory for course schedules by Wittman (1989), with results of the map test in the top panel and results of the class-listing test in the bottom panel.

retention at test and showed significant loss at retest. Thus, we have initial support for our hypothesis that the superiority of spatial memory is due to the fact that procedures are used to learn that information and these procedures can be readily reinstated at test.

FINAL COMMENTS

Conclusions

Although the theoretical framework we have proposed, which is centered around the notion of procedural reinstatement, is able to throw considerable light on the long-term maintenance of knowledge and skills, it can by no means account for all important retention phenomena. Other theoretical constructs are needed to provide a more complete account of long-term retention, and the constructs we have outlined need to be fleshed out in greater detail and require more rigorous experimental tests that also determine their generalizability to other tasks and situations. Nevertheless, we have been impressed with the wide variety of memory studies that already fit into this framework and the remarkably large range of forgetting rates found in these studies. Recall that information about course schedules was quickly forgotten, so that many of our subjects could not report, even in approximate form, the name of the instructor, the course title, or the class meeting time for a course they had taken previously, even though that information was learned in a natural setting, had importance to the individuals, and was presumably given considerable rehearsal during a semester-long interval. In contrast, for example, our two subjects who were given extensive training in the laboratory on a target-detection skill were able to maintain their performance level without any noticeable decrease at all over a period as long as 15 months. If procedural reinstatement can indeed help to explain these large differences in forgetting rates, the practical significance of this finding is substantial. The implication is clear that if we wish to retain knowledge or skills over a long delay interval, it is crucial that we make sure that the procedures we use when learning the information are reinstated at the time we need to recall the information.

A Personal Note from the First Author

I want to end this chapter by discussing the relation between this work and my earlier work with Bill Estes. The research I did with Bill was very different in several ways; nevertheless, it served as an important inspiration for the present study. My dissertation research under Bill's supervision concerned short-term recall for temporal and spatial information (see, e.g., Healy, 1975). Probably the most intriguing aspects of that research involved two related observations. First, as had been demonstrated initially by Peterson and Peterson (1959), there was a steep retention function for temporal order recall. After a delay of approximately 7 seconds, I found that subjects could remember only about two of four letters they had been shown. It was this rapid forgetting coupled with a symmetrical bow-shaped serial position function that led Bill to his highly insightful and influential perturbation model of short-term memory (see, e.g., Estes, 1972). The second, related observation I made in my dissertation was that this dramatic forgetting was evident for temporal but not for spatial order recall, which showed instead a retention function that was much flatter. I used this observation as the basis for my own Markov model of spatial order retention (see, e.g., Healy, 1978).

It was the first of these two observations, the rapid forgetting of temporal order information, that led to my initial interest in Bahrick's (1984) notion of permastore and my subsequent amazement at our own findings of remarkable memory over very long retention intervals of the target detection, mental multiplication, and data entry skills. Although subjects cannot remember four letters shown to them after a delay of 7 seconds, they can easily retain over a delay as long as 15 months their acquired ability to perform a skill such as letter detection. The second observation, that spatial order information is lost from memory more slowly than temporal order information, motivated our study comparing the retention of temporal and spatial information about course schedules (Wittman, 1989). The naturalistic course schedule task was very different from the controlled short-term memory task I conducted in the laboratory. Nevertheless, the pattern of results are in agreement; in both cases spatial information is retained better than temporal information.

These, however, are only superficial ways in which Bill has influenced my research. He has had a much more profound and pervasive influence as well. Throughout the years I have kept in close contact with him, and when making decisions about my research, I always try to think of what he would do in the same situation.

A number of years ago I had a discussion with a group of scientists about the relationship we had with our dissertation advisors. The general consensus seemed to be that as students the others were initially awed by their advisors but, as time progressed, the gap between their advisor's knowledge and their own markedly decreased. I explained that my experience was quite different: Although I perceived the same initial gap, for me that gap seemed to grow with time as my appreciation for my advisor's wisdom steadily increased. Another psychologist in the group responded, "That's no surprise, Alice; your advisor was Bill Estes."

ACKNOWLEDGMENTS

This research was supported in part by United States Air Force Human Resources Laboratory Contract VE5744–022–001 and United States Army Research Institute Contracts MDA903–86–K–0155 and MDA903–90–K–0066 to the Institute of Cognitive Science at the University of Colorado and by National Institute of Mental Health Training Grant MH14617–08 to the University of Colorado. We are grateful to Bill Marmie for help with the preparation of the figures and to Elizabeth Bjork and Stephen Kosslyn for helpful comments on an earlier version of this chapter.

REFERENCES

Anderson, J. R. (1983). *The architecture of cognition.* Cambridge, MA: Harvard University Press.

Bahrick, H. P. (1984). Semantic memory content in permastore: Fifty years of memory for Spanish learned in school. *Journal of Experimental Psychology: General, 113,* 1–29.

Crutcher, R. J. (1989). *The role of mediation in knowledge acquisition and retention: Learning foreign vocabulary using the keyword method.* Unpublished master's thesis, University of Colorado, Boulder, CO.

Crutcher, R. J., & Ericsson, K. A. (1988, April). *A componential analysis of the keyword method.* Paper presented at the American Educational Research Association Convention, New Orleans, LA.

Crutcher, R. J., & Healy, A. F. (1989). Cognitive operations and the generation effect. *Journal of Experimental Psychology: Learning, Memory, and Cognition, 15,* 669–675.

Ericsson, K. A., & Chase, W. G. (1982). Exceptional memory. *American Scientist, 70,* 607–615.

Estes, W. K. (1972). An associative basis for coding and organization in memory. In A. W. Melton & E. Martin (Eds.), *Coding processes in human memory* (pp. 161–190). Washington, DC: Winston.

Fendrich, D. W., Healy, A. F., & Bourne, L. E. (1991). Long-term repetition effects for motoric and perceptual procedures. *Journal of Experimental Psychology: Learning, Memory, and Cognition, 17,* 137–151.

Fendrich, D. W., Healy, A. F., & Bourne, L. E. (in press). Mental arithmetic: Training and retention of multiplication skill. In C. Izawa (Ed.), *Cognitive psychology applied.* Hillsdale, NJ: Erlbaum.

Gesi, A. T., Fendrich, D. W., Healy, A. F., & Bourne, L. E. (1989, April). *Episodic and procedural memory for digit sequences.* Paper presented at the Joint Annual Convention of the Western Psychological Association and the Rocky Mountain Psychological Association, Reno, NV.

Graf, P., & Schacter, D. L. (1985). Implicit and explicit memory for new associations in normal and amnesic subjects. *Journal of Experimental Psychology: Learning, Memory, and Cognition, 11,* 501–518.

Healy, A. F. (1975). Coding of temporal-spatial patterns in short-term memory. *Journal of Verbal Learning and Verbal Behavior, 14,* 481–495.

Healy, A. F. (1978). A Markov model for the short-term retention of spatial location information. *Journal of Verbal Learning and Verbal Behavior, 17,* 295–308.

Healy, A. F., Fendrich, D. W., & Proctor, J. D. (1990). Acquisition and retention of a letter-detection skill. *Journal of Experimental Psychology: Learning, Memory, and Cognition, 16,* 270–281.

Kolers, P. A., & Roediger, H. L. (1984). Procedures of mind. *Journal of Verbal Learning and Verbal Behavior, 23,* 425–449.

Morris, C. D., Bransford, J. D., & Franks, J. J. (1977). Levels of processing versus transfer appropriate processing. *Journal of Verbal Learning and Verbal Behavior, 16,* 519–533.

Naylor, J. C., & Briggs, G. E. (1961). *Long-term retention of learned skill: A review of the literature* (ASD–TR–61–390). Wright-Patterson AFB, OH: Advanced Systems Division.

Peterson, L. R., & Peterson, M. J. (1959). Short-term retention of individual verbal items. *Journal of Experimental Psychology, 58,* 193–198.

Schneider, W., & Shiffrin, R. M. (1977). Controlled and automatic human information processing: I. Detection, search, and attention. *Psychological Review, 84,* 127–190.

Slamecka, N. J., & Graf, P. (1978). The generation effect: Delineation of a phenomenon. *Journal of Experimental Psychology: Human Learning and Memory, 4,* 592–604.

Tulving, E., & Thomson, D. M. (1973). Encoding specificity and retrieval processes in episodic memory. *Psychological Review, 80,* 352–373.

Wittman, W. T. (1989). *A long-term retention advantage for spatial information learned naturally and in the laboratory.* Unpublished doctoral dissertation, University of Colorado, Boulder, CO.

5 The Perturbation Model of Short-Term Memory: A Review and Some Further Developments

Catherine L. Lee
Harvard Medical School

It was my good fortune to meet Bill Estes in 1972, the same year in which his description of an associative coding model of forgetting in short-term memory was published (Estes, 1972). With Bill's encouragement and guidance, I soon found myself absorbed in attempts to understand and expand upon this model, which came to be known as the *Perturbation Model*. Most of my efforts in this regard over subsequent years were an attempt to understand the relationship between primary and secondary memory processes as they influenced short-term memory forgetting. Much of this work was done in collaboration with Bill Estes. In the following chapter I review the basic model and trace its development in the work of Estes, Healy, and Lee and Estes. I also present two previously unpublished experimental studies that expand the application of the Perturbation Model to describe short-term memory rehearsal processes and memory for sentences.

THE PERTURBATION MODEL

An impetus for the development of the Perturbation Model was Estes' dissatisfaction with the existing models of memory based on association theory or coding conceptions alone. He noted that whereas basic association theory was able to describe a broad variety of memory phenomena, it was not well adapted to deal with the phenomena of organization. For instance, in analyzing confusion errors in memory for strings of letters, the pattern of errors appeared to be best predictable on the basis of critical features (i.e., phonemes) that are shared by pairs of letters, that is, a coded representation of the stimuli. Coding also is useful in understanding how "memory span" can be extended by presenting or rehearsing items of a sequence in groups or "chunks" (Miller, 1956). The idea is that chunking of items simplifies the learner's task by permitting assignment of codes to the subgroups of a sequence, thus reducing the number of items to be remembered; the codes can be decoded later to reproduce the original sequence (Johnson, 1970). Estes was not impressed with the suggestion that association theory be cast aside and that theories of memory be based on concepts of coding and information processing alone. He felt that coding was useful for dealing with what is remembered, but was less useful with regard to the dynamics of forgetting. What he proposed was a model that drew on both association theory and coding models. The aim was a model with a conceptual structure rich enough to handle in detail the processes responsible for retention loss with regard to identity and order of letters, syllables, and words—and one that would be pertinent to a broader range of memory events in complex cognitive activities.

As a starting point for his model, Estes chose to focus on describing the processes underlying memory for strings of random letters or digits. In particular, he was interested in the fact that in situations in which short-term recall of items and their order could be measured separately, in certain cases item and order information display different relationships with different experimental operations. He reported the results of an experiment using a modified Brown–Peterson paradigm in which order errors were in predominance at short retention intervals, but noted that this gradually shifted to a slight predominance of other error types (confusion, nontransposition) at long retention intervals. Similarly, Healy (1974) has shown that the relation between order errors and serial position was different from the relation of item errors and serial position. In her findings, order errors showed symmetrical bow-shaped serial position curves, whereas item errors showed serial position curves that were relatively flat.

The basic paradigm used in investigations of the Perturbation Model was one in which a short sequence of letters was presented rapidly (at approximately a .5 sec rate) followed by a retention interval filled with varying numbers of digits. Typically the items were presented on a screen one at a time and, to prevent rehearsal, the subject shadowed them as they appeared. At a recall signal, the subject wrote his or her recall (beginning with the first item of the sequence and continuing in order) on an answer sheet with spaces for each of the presented items. If an item was forgotten, its space was left blank or the subject guessed.

For the case of four-item letter strings, some typical findings for order and item recall are shown in Fig. 5.1. Serial position curves for recall of items correct in position are typically bowed and symmetrical (Fig. 5.1A). Curves for recall of items (regardless of position) have the same shape but tend to be much flatter (Fig. 5.1B).[1] The overall levels of recall for both position and item information will vary with the length of the retention interval, but the basic shape of the serial position curves will be constant. Position gradients (Fig. 5.1C) show that the

---

[1]The hypothetical curves for item recall shown here are typical of the findings for the studies in this series. However, other studies (e.g., Bjork & Healy, 1974), have obtained item curves that are less symmetrical and show an advantage for primacy but not recency items. Minor adjustments in the model's assumptions can accommodate the latter finding.

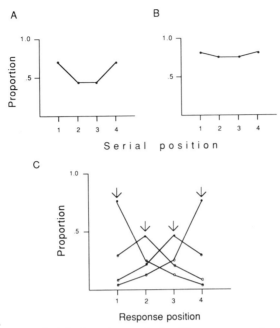

FIG. 5.1. Typical findings for recall of a 4-item sequence for a) recall correct in position, b) item recall (regardless of position), and c) position gradients.

probability of reporting items in their presentation position is high (points with arrows) and that the probability of reporting these items in other positions is a decreasing function of the distance between presentation and recall positions.

In order to account for these findings, Estes developed an associative coding model that is hierarchical and in which the elements of an ordered chain are not associated with each other. Instead, they are connected to higher order nodes called *control elements*. This principle is applied simultaneously at several levels. For instance, each letter may be thought of as composed of a number of features (e.g., phonemes) and the letter name could be the control element for the phonemic elements. The letter name in turn is associated to a control element for a letter group (i.e., syllable or word). This, in turn, is connected to a control element specifying the context in which the memory event was presented. This structure may be presented as follows:

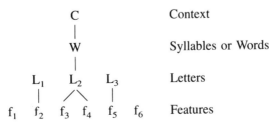

Memory for order is described in terms of a repetitive recycling process. Memory elements and their control elements are connected in a reverberatory loop and this produces a recurrent reactivation of the representation of the memory event at a rate determined by the refractory phase of the system, represented thus:

$$
\begin{array}{c}
C \\
| \\
f_1
\end{array}
$$

If the sequence of memory elements (or items) has become associated with a single control element as a result of the input of a single experimental trial, a similar reverberatory loop is established for each item, with the consequence that the items will be reactivated in sequence thus providing for the representation of order information in short-term memory.

If this process were deterministic, memory would be permanent. To account for forgetting, it is assumed that there is a certain amount of random error in the recurrence times owing to differences in the refractory times of different items and to perturbations arising from other concurrent activity in the nervous system. The result of these random variations is that over time, the timing of recurrent activations of the individual elements of a sequence will come to deviate sufficiently from the original relationship so that eventually interchanges in order will begin to appear between adjacent items.

In the model, item errors can be accounted for in at least two ways. First, they can occur by perturbation at the level of features and here, order errors will most likely produce impossible combinations (Estes, 1972); second, item errors can result from perturbations of the to-be–remembered items with some other events in the experimental situation (e.g., distractor digits, items from previous trials), resulting in unavailability at the time of recall (Lee & Estes, 1981).

From this description it is relatively easy to see how the model predicts bow-shaped symmetrical serial position curves for recall of order information based on the relative opportunities for transpositions of order at each serial position. For instance, in the sequence ABCD, A is most likely to transpose with the letter in the just adjacent position, B, and less likely to transpose with items C and D, which are farther away. Item B is likely to transpose with letters in the two just adjacent positions, A and C, and less likely to transpose with item D. Item A has only one neighbor with which it is likely to transpose, whereas B has two immediate neighbors and thus has a higher probability of being reported out of order at the time of recall. Overall, an item in an interior serial position has more chances to transpose with an adjacent item than an item at an end position does. Thus, we would expect bow-shaped serial position curves for recall of order information entirely on the basis of perturbation (and transpositon) probabilities. The form of position gradients also follows nicely from this conception.

In the simplest case, item errors were assumed to be the result of perturbations acting at the level of features of items and the probability of these perturbations was assumed to be constant over serial positions. Thus, the curves for item recall would be expected to be flat. Later conceptions of the model allowed for more complexity and alternative means by which items might be lost from recall; these are discussed in a later section.

Extension of the Model

In 1977, Lee and Estes expanded the model to take into account the experimental situation in which order and position information are distinguishable. According to the Perturbation Model, order information should be derivative of position information (that is, if only primary memory processes are assumed to be operating). Also of interest was the interaction of primary and secondary memory processes. Therefore, a situation was created in which primary memory processes were assumed to be predominant, that is, sequences with letters spaced out among distractors. For example:

$$4 \; \underline{B} \; 8 \; 1 \; \underline{X} \; 2 \; 4 \; \underline{G} \; 3 \; 9 \; \underline{K} \; 6$$

Then variations on this situation, with letters clustered to varying degrees within the distractor strings, were produced. For example:

$$2 \; 3 \; \underline{B} \; 9 \; 4 \; \underline{X \; G} \; 6 \; 1 \; \underline{K} \; 5 \; 8$$

$$3 \; 9 \; 2 \; 1 \; \underline{B \; X \; G \; K} \; 8 \; 4 \; 5 \; 7$$

These variations on the basic situation were to allow for the possibility of secondary memory processes (such as the recognition of familiar letter sequences or spelling groups) interacting with the underlying primary memory processes. In this conception, secondary memory was thought of as a network of associations among nodes or control elements corresponding to attributes of previously experienced events or situations (e.g., letter names, syllables). Primary memory was limited to information that such previously established events were activated in a particular context.

The results showed that under conditions contrived to maximize the contribution of primary memory processes (i.e., the spaced condition), memory for order appeared to be entirely derivative to memory for temporal position. All principle trends in the data were predicted from the model. However, under conditions in which secondary memory was expected to play some role (i.e., clustered conditions), memory for order turned out to be better than predicted on the basis of memory for position. Similar trends were seen for item information although the results were not as unambiguous.

In a later version (Lee & Estes, 1981), the model was revised and expanded to provide a comprehensive treatment of the interrelations of item, order, and position information. It provided for multiple levels of encoding and perturbation of memory information in primary memory and it gave a major role to schemata based on information in secondary memory that actively enters into the performance of a short-term memory task. All of this was spelled out mathematically to provide for vigorous testing of the model.

In this experimental series, the format was an extended trial made up of minitrials (i.e., a 12-item string with 3 groups of four items, each set off by distinct markers). For example:

$$! F J B H ! 4 6 9 3 ! Z R M S ?$$

Recall was cued for one or all of the groups. Also the extent to which the subject was provided with a priori information about the structure of the sequence was varied across experiments. In the most highly constrained situation, a particular set of letters was assigned to each segment and the subject was informed of this. In the least constrained situation, stimulus items from the set of stimuli could occur in any one of the 12 string positions. Other conditions with intermediate levels of constraint were included in the design.

The model assumed encoding with control elements at the level of items, segments, and trials. The memory representation of an item was conceived as a vector of attribute information including the current remembered position of the item within a sequence of trials, its segment within a trial, and its position within a segment. The control elements at each level were thought to be subject to perturbations that lead at recall to transposition errors, that is, incorrect reports of the trial, segment or position within a segment in which the item occurred. The experimental design thus described allowed the perturbation process at various levels to be observed independently or in combination by varying the information available in secondary memory about the structure of the trials.

This version of the model specified in greater detail the manner in which loss of item information can occur. One way is by errors of recoding at the trial level. That is, when the encoded relation between an item and the control element for the trial on which it occurred is perturbed, it may be remembered to have occurred earlier or later. Similarly, loss of item information may occur if the relation between the item and the control element for the segment in which it occurred is perturbed. That is, the item will be remembered in some other segment and will be "lost" when partial report for the original segment is given. (Of course, under full report conditions, the "lost" item may be located again.) The other mechanism for item loss is operative if during reactivations of the items of the trial, the position code of a given item is perturbed but in a way that does not result in a recognizable code for any position.

The basic results of this study were as expected from the model. Bow-shaped symmetrical position curves were found for each individual segment, with the overall level of recall increasing across the three segments. Item recall showed essentially flat serial position curves within each chunk with the overall level of item recall increasing across segments from first to last. These results were obtained regardless of the level of constraint imposed upon stimulus items' assignment to segment. The findings suggest that each segment is remembered as a unit and that the most elementary perturbation processes described in earlier studies are operative for items within a segment or "chunk." At this basic level, items do not perturb across chunks (e.g., the final item of one segment does not tend to transpose with the first item of the next) because the basic structure of the trial (segments divided by markers) provides a schemata that limits the process. However, that is not to say that perturbations across chunks do not occur. The observed position gradients (for conditions in which items were not constrained to occur only in particular segments) show that transposition errors can occur across chunks. This is the case in which the subject was cued to report items from a particular chunk but remembered incorrectly items from another chunk. The results suggest that when items perturb across chunks, they do so into their correct relative positions with the greatest likelihood (e.g., the first item of one segment transposes with the first item of the next one) and into other positions as a decreasing function of distance from the correct relative position. What is more, these transpositions of items from chunk to chunk appear to occur independently (i.e., it is just as likely that one item of a chunk will transpose as it is that more than one will). This later finding reinforces the model's basic assumption that the representations of items are associated with higher order nodes rather than with each other.

TWO EXPERIMENTAL STUDIES
OF THE PERTURBATION MODEL

Overall, the Perturbation Model has proved useful in generating predictions about major trends and patterns in the data from a variety of experimental situations involving short-term recall of sequences of letters and digits. The two experimental studies to be reported in detail in the next sections were intended in part as attempts to expand the scope of the model even further. The first of these examines rehearsal processes in short-term memory by instructing the subject to rehearse aloud and by recording these overt rehearsals for later analysis. A comparison of the ultimate products of overt rehearsal could then be compared to those of covert rehearsal to begin to get a closer look at the perturbation process in operation. In the second study, the application of the model was expanded to include short-term recall of words and sentences.

Rehearsal Processes in Primary Memory

Models of short-term memory tend to give rehearsal processes a primary role. They are the activities that maintain representations of stimulus events in memory over time. In the Perturbation Model, the reverberatory reactivation process is essentially an automatic, covert rehearsal process that produces a reactivation of the representation of an item and thus maintains the item in short-term memory. However, because it is subject to perturbation arising as the result of noise in the system, it is not expected that memory will be perfect (unless the subject is able to bring his or her conscious attention to the rehearsal, unhindered by distraction). Techniques like the Brown–Peterson Task aim to prevent rehearsal by introducing distractor activity between presentation and test, thus providing a means for studying forgetting. Without distraction we would expect rehearsal to be an accurate replica of the stimulus. However, if rehearsal is prevented following presentation and only permitted after a delay, we would expect it to be a very imperfect copy of the original stimulus (because there would have been an opportunity for perturbation). In the study that follows, our purpose was to obtain a description of rehearsal based on memory that is not perfect.

In a modification of the Conrad (1967) procedure, we presented sequences of letters followed by three successive delays filled with distractor digits. Immediately after each delay, there was an interval of overt rehearsal. For instance, a sequence might be as follows:

HBTQ659352? - - - - 437563? - - - - 851934? - - - -
      (Rehearse)   (Rehearse)   (Rehearse)

In this example, there are four letters in the stimulus and 6 distractor digits in each delay. Items for a trial were chosen without replacement from a set of 12 consonants. In the experiment, stimulus lists of five and six letters and a delay interval of 18 digits were also used. The stimulus strings were presented in blocks of a single list length. Stimulus items and distractors were presented one at a time at a .5 sec rate, and subjects were instructed to read each character aloud as it was presented. The rehearsals were paced by a series of markers, one for each item of the stimulus sequence and these also appeared at .5 sec rate. Subjects were instructed to rehearse the stimulus items out loud in the correct sequence and to guess if necessary. If they were unable to report an item, they said the word "blank" to mark an empty position. These rehearsals were monitored by the experimenter and recorded on tape.

The data analysis focused on the extent to which the content of each successive rehearsal reflected memory for the stimulus sequence. Also of interest was the extent to which each rehearsal was like the previous rehearsals. To make these comparisons, each rehearsal protocol was scored in two ways; first, according to the total number of items that were reported correctly, and second, according to the number of these items that were recalled correct in position. These comparisons were made with the original stimulus and with previous rehearsals (e.g., Rehearsal 2 with Rehearsal 1).

Table 5.1 shows examples of a stimulus sequence and three rehearsals along

TABLE 5.1
Stimulus Sequence and Three Rehearsals from a Trial of the Rehearsal Experiment

Stimulus	Rehearsal 1	Rehearsal 2	Rehearsal 3
HBTQ	HTBQ	HBQK	HRQK
Compared to stimulus			
ITEM			
C in P	100	75	50
	50	50	25
Compared to			
Rehearsal 1			
ITEM		75	50
C in P		25	25

Shown are scores for percent recall of stimulus items and of items reported in rehearsal 1, and for percent recall of each of these correct in position (C in P).

with the recall scores they would receive according to our scoring method. In this example, on Rehearsal 1, all stimulus items are reported and the item score is 100%. But two of the items (B and T) are out of position so that the position score is only 50%. In the second rehearsal, only three stimulus items (H, B, and Q) are reported, so the item score is down to 75%. Of these, two (H and B) are in the same positions in which they were in the stimulus sequence, so the correct position score is 50%. Moving along to a comparison of the second rehearsal with the first one, here three items (H, B, and Q) are reported from Rehearsal 1 but only one of these (H) is reported in the same position. Therefore, the item score for Rehearsal 2 compared to Rehearsal 1 is 75% and the position score is 25%.

Serial position curves for item recall for sequences of four, five, and six items are shown in Fig. 5.2. (Depicted are scores for the long delay only: scores for the short delay are essentially similar except that all scores are higher.) On the left side of the figure are curves for recall of the stimulus in Rehearsals 1, 2, and 3. It can be seen that the pattern of recall is similar across the three rehearsals and

FIG. 5.2. Serial position curves for item recall for sequences of 4, 5, and 6 items for the long-delay condition of the rehearsal experiment. On the left are results for recall of the stimulus at Rehearsals 1, 2 and 3; on the right are results for recall of Rehearsal 1 items at Rehearsals 2 and 3.

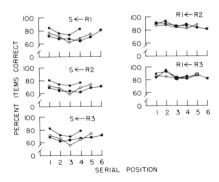

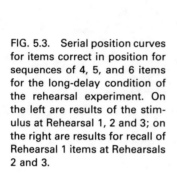
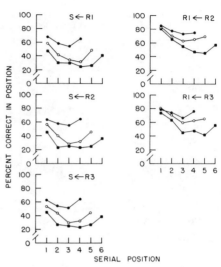

FIG. 5.3. Serial position curves for items correct in position for sequences of 4, 5, and 6 items for the long-delay condition of the rehearsal experiment. On the left are results of the stimulus at Rehearsal 1, 2 and 3; on the right are results for recall of Rehearsal 1 items at Rehearsals 2 and 3.

there is a small but significant decrease in the level of recall with each successive rehearsal. On the right side of the figure are curves for recall of the items of a previous rehearsal (Rehearsal 1) in the current one. A comparison of the curves in the two panels across the top of the figure is appropriate as equivalent delay intervals have occurred between the rehearsal and the items being reported (i.e., the delay between the stimulus and Rehearsal 1 is 18 digits and likewise the delay between Rehearsal 1 and Rehearsal 2 is 18 digits). The most obvious difference between recall of the stimulus and recall of Rehearsal 1 is in the absolute level of recall; that is, scores for recall of Rehearsal 1 are higher than for recall of the stimulus. The same comparison can also be made for the curves in the middle two panels. Here the interval between the rehearsal and the sequence it is being compared to is even longer and the differences are more accentuated. Another important difference between recall of the stimulus and recall of Rehearsal 1 is in the shape of the serial position curves. They are symmetrical and bowed for recall of the stimulus with roughly equivalent levels of recall for primacy and recency items. For the recall of Rehearsal 1 the curves are flat and decline with serial position.

The next figure (Fig. 5.3) shows the serial position curves for recall of items correct in position. (Again, these are the results of the long delay condition and they differ from the short delay only in the absolute level of recall.) On the left are curves for recall of the stimulus sequence and on the right are curves for recall of the first rehearsal. A comparison of the curves on the top left and right panels shows considerably higher recall of Rehearsal 1 items than of stimulus items. This comparison can also be made for the two middle panels, and here the difference between the level of recall of the stimulus and of Rehearsal 1 is even

TABLE 5.2
Examples of Pairs of Stimulus Sequences and the Rehearsals Produced by a Subject in the
Rehearsal Experiment

Stimulus	Rehearsal 1	Rehearsal 2	Rehearsal 3
CFLR	CFLR	CLFR	CLFR
KJSQ	CSJR	CSJR	CSJR
KQNF	KNQL	KNQL	KNQL
BTSH	KTCL	KTCL	KTCL
NKBJ	SQBJ	SQBJ	SQBJ
FHJR	FQJR	SQJR	SQJR

greater. The pattern for all of these position curves is similar. They are bowed and skewed, with the advantage for primacy items. However, the curves for Rehearsal 1 tend to be less bowed and more skewed than those for recall of the stimulus.

Taken together, the results from Fig. 5.2 and 5.3 indicate that Rehearsal 2 and Rehearsal 3 are more like the first rehearsal than they are like the stimulus. Although the second rehearsal contains about 70% of the items that were presented in the stimulus string, it contains 90% to 95% of the items reported in Rehearsal 1. Clearly the items that are intrusions in Rehearsal 1 are well retained on subsequent rehearsals. The next question that arises concerns the nature of these intrusions. An examination of the subject protocols will indicate that the great majority of intrusions are from rehearsals on the previous trial.

In order to illustrate this finding, some examples of actual stimulus sequences and the rehearsals that followed them are shown in Table 5.2. These trials are typical of the overall pattern of responding and have been selected because they illustrate some key points about recall in this experimental situation. Examination of the rehearsals of the second trial of each pair will show that recall is a mixture of items from the stimulus on that trial and items from the rehearsals of the previous trial. For example, on the trial with stimulus KJSQ (second row of the table) on the first rehearsal, only two items from the stimulus (S and J) were reported and their order is inverted. The other reported items (C and R) appear to be intrusions from the previous trial. Of special significance is the fact that these items intrude into the positions in which they were previously rehearsed. But as the next two examples in the table illustrate, intruded items almost never come from the previous trial's stimulus if they are also not present in its rehearsals. Furthermore, intrusions on the previous trial's rehearsals are often intrusions on the current trial as well. Examination of the third row shows that items K, Q, and N of the stimulus KQNF are reported in the first rehearsal. The F is lost and is replaced by L, which persists in subsequent rehearsals. It is the case that stimulus

TABLE 5.3
Error Percentages on the Three Rehearsals (R1, R2, and R3) of a Trial for Intrusions from the Final
Rehearsal of the Previous Trial for the Rehearsal Experiment

| | | | | Short Delay | | | Long Delay | |
		chance	R1	R2	R3	R1	R2	R3
List Length 4								
	Item	33	77	75	75	72	74	75
	C in P	25	68	62	65	62	55	48
List Length 5								
	Item	42	77	81	84	79	77	79
	C in P	20	62	63	66	64	53	56
List Length 6								
	Item 50	50	71	70	75	65	64	70
	C in P	17	46	46	44	52	51	49

letters that are not reported on the first rehearsal are almost never recovered on subsequent rehearsals. On the next trial (fourth row) only one letter of the stimulus BTSH, namely T, is reported. The other items are intrusions, two of which (K and L) can be traced back to the previous trial. K was also in the stimulus on that trial, but L was always an intrusion. The last pair of trials provides another example in which intrusions on the current trial are also intrusions on the previous trial. Here the items S and Q are intrusions on both trials.

In brief, it is the case that intrusion errors can often be traced to the previous trial, specifically to rehearsals on that trial. Intruded items may also be members of the stimulus on the previous trial but not unless they were also in its rehearsals. Overall, approximately 25% of the responses in rehearsal are errors. The next table (Table 5.3) shows the percentage of these errors that can be accounted for by intrusions from rehearsals on the previous trial. This count was based on the total opportunities for errors, that is, all those cases in which a stimulus item was not reported, suggesting that there is an empty slot in memory. These percentages indicate that items from Rehearsal 3 of the previous trial were reported in the rehearsals of the current trial with much greater than chance likelihood.[2] In addition they were more likely than chance to be reported in the same position as on the previous trial's rehearsal. These values change little across the three rehearsals of the current trial, suggesting that most intrusions occur on the very first rehearsal of the trial and simply persist in the later ones.

At this point it is possible to account for the great majority of responses in this experiment. Approximately 75% of reported items are from the stimulus on the

---

[2]Chance for item recall is the probability of choosing any four letters out of the total stimulus set of 12 for list length 4, and likewise for lists of 5 and 6 items. For position (C in P), chance was the likelihood of placing the item in the correct one out of 4 (5 or 6) positions.

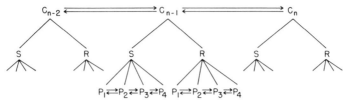

FIG. 5.4.   A conceptual framework based on the Perturbation Model for describing the findings of the rehearsal experiments.

current trial. Of the 25% that are errors, about three fourths of them are intrusions from rehearsals of the previous trial. The remaining 5% or so errors can be accounted for as the result of acoustic confusion and omissions. Clearly, very few errors can be considered simple guesses.

In Fig. 5.4 a conceptual framework is presented, from which the results can be understood. It is a modification of the Perturbation Model using the hierarchical structure and multilevel encoding and perturbation processes introduced by Lee and Estes (1981). In the current version, memory control elements representing the positions of items in the sequence are at the bottom of the network. The arrows between them in the figure represent the potential for perturbations in order and the related loss of items. At the next higher level are separate control elements for the stimulus and rehearsal sequences. These have been represented separately as the results indicate that the memory representation of rehearsal is qualitatively different from the memory representation of the stimulus. Moreover, the rehearsals of a trial tend to be more like each other than they are like the stimulus; that is, items reported in the first rehearsal rarely drop out in subsequent rehearsals, and stimulus items not reported in the first rehearsal are seldom recovered in later ones. However, whether the stimulus representation continues to exist in parallel with the rehearsal representation is open to question. It does appear that a new representation is generated at the first rehearsal and other sorts of measures would be required to discover whether the stimulus is still alive and is a distinct memory channel.

Finally, at the top of the network are the control elements for the trial context. These nodes are connected by arrows indicating that their order is subject to perturbation. When perturbations happen at the level of trial representations, they lead to intrusion errors. Because rehearsals tend to share context with other rehearsals, it is expected that intrusions will come from rehearsals of previous trials rather than from the stimuli of those trials. In short, we have a model that predicts that rehearsals will not be simple replicas of the stimulus but rather that they will be a synthesis of memory traces from several different sources. The use of overt rehearsals has allowed us to examine processes that are usually covert and probably automatic and, so it appears, ones that are well described by the Perturbation Model.

The model as described here favors a multiple channel interpretation of primary rehearsal. Another version of the Perturbation Model proposed by Cunningham, Healy, and Williams (1984) provides an interesting alternative. They utilized the Lee and Estes (1981) description of the model and added to it the explicit distinction between two kinds of rehearsal processes—a passive, automatic reactivation process (as described in the original model) and an active, conscious rehearsal process that acts to crystallize memory and reduce perturbations. As applied to the rehearsal study, it could be assumed that stimulus items are encoded passively at presentation, and when they are reported during the rehearsal interval, they receive the memory advantage provided by active rehearsal. Intrusions which make their way into the rehearsal have their representations elaborated and strengthened along with those of the remembered stimulus items. However, stimulus items that fail to be reported in the rehearsal have no special advantage and may be lost as they continue to suffer perturbations during the subsequent retention interval. This conception seems to do quite well in explaining many of the results reported here for overt rehearsals. A definitive choice between these versions of the model would require further quantitative elaboration and tests; however, the findings of the next experiments to be reported here may have some relevance to this choice.

The experimental situation created for this study of rehearsal is an unusual one for short-term recall experiments. Typically, rehearsal processes proceed covertly or overtly, without tampering by the experimenter, or they are actively discouraged by giving the subject a distractor task. A question arises as to the generalizability of the findings of this study in which subjects rehearsed aloud to other short-term recall situations. An attempt to provide some answers on this score was made in two follow-up experiments that are reported here briefly.

The design of these experiments was similar to that of the study just presented with the exception of instructions to the subjects regarding rehearsal. Subjects always rehearsed aloud at the third and final rehearsal interval but on Rehearsals 1 and 2, this was not always the case. In the "covert" rehearsal experiment, they might be cued to rehearse silently on Rehearsal 1, Rehearsal 2, or both. For instance:

> !BQJF546392 - - - -   216583 $ $ $ $ 392468 - - - -
>   (rehearse)   (silent)   (rehearse)
>
> !RXFJ259463 $ $ $ $ 934521 $ $ $ $ 243968 - - - -
>   (silent)   (silent)   (rehearse)

The first example is a trial in which the subject was cued to rehearse silently on the second rehearsal and to rehearse aloud on Rehearsals 1 and 3. The second example is a trial in which the subject would rehearse silently on both Rehearsals 1 and 2 but rehearse aloud on the final rehearsal interval. In the "suppressed" rehearsal experiment, subjects were cued to recite "La" repeatedly during the

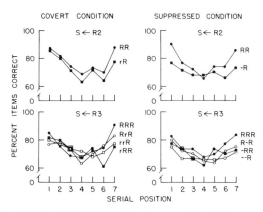

FIG. 5.5.   Serial position curves for item recall on Rehearsals 2 and 3 of the covert and suppressed rehearsal experiments ("R" = overt, "r" = silent, "-" = suppressed; referring to the instruction on each rehearsal of a trial.

rehearsal interval as a means of actively suppressing rehearsal on Rehearsal 1, Rehearsal 2, or both. In the sample trials shown, subjects would say "La" aloud when cued with "$." Otherwise, in both versions of the experiment, rehearsal was aloud as in the previous "overt" rehearsal study. We were fairly confident that subjects complied with instructions and made the effort to rehearse silently or to suppress rehearsal when so cued as they were highly practiced and well-motivated members of the research staff.

The results for covert and suppressed rehearsal experiments were essentially similar. Perhaps surprisingly, it made relatively little difference in the overall level of recall at the final (overt) rehearsal, whether the preceding intervals on a trial were composed of active but "silent" rehearsal or of passive, "suppressed" rehearsal. What is more, the results of these experiments were similar in all major trends to the results of the previous study in which subjects always rehearsed aloud. As expected, serial position curves for recall of the stimulus sequence were bowed and symmetrical for recall of items correct in position. Equivalent curves for item recall were flatter (see Figs. 5.5 and 5.6). Overall, recall on Rehearsal 3 tended to be slightly better if the previous two rehearsals had been overt than if they had been silent or suppressed.

Curves for recall of a prior rehearsal (1 or 2) on Rehearsal 3 were similar to those for recall of the stimulus but in all cases flatter. Figure 5.7 shows serial position curves for recall on Rehearsal 3 of items previously reported on Rehearsal 1. Similar functions were obtained for recall of items from Rehearsal 2 at the final overt rehearsal. As in the previous study, recall on Rehearsal 3 tended to be more like recall on an earlier rehearsal (2 or 1) than it was like the stimulus. When stimulus items were not recalled, their places tended to be occupied by items reported on the previous trial's rehearsals. And, as previously, the likelihood of recalling an

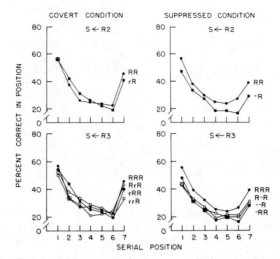

FIG. 5.6. Serial position curves for items recalled correct in position on Rehearsals 2 and 3 of the covert and suppressed rehearsal experiments. ("R" = overt, "r" = silent, "-" = suppressed; referring to the instruction on each rehearsal of a trial).

item in the same relative position as it had been reported on the previous trial was considerably above chance (for both silent and suppressed conditions).

From these results it appears that silent and even suppressed rehearsal have essentially the same effects on memory for sequences that overt rehearsal does.

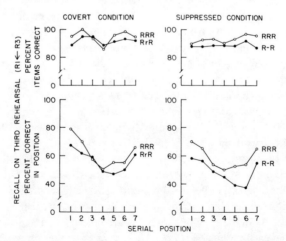

FIG. 5.7. Serial position curves for recall of Rehearsal 1 items on Rehearsal 3 for the covert and suppressed rehearsal experiments. ("R" = overt, "r" = silent, "-" = suppressed; referring to the instruction on each rehearsal of a trial).

Thus it does not appear to be inappropriate to conclude that the model presented here to describe the perturbation process for stimulus and rehearsal representations within and across trials of an experiment has general applicability to short-term recall situations. The alternative dual rehearsal model of Cunningham et al. (1984) receives equivocal support. As expected, recall on Rehearsal 3 is better if the previous two rehearsals were overt; however, there was no advantage for rehearsal that is active but silent over rehearsal that is passive and suppressed.

Short-term Memory for Sentences

In this section, the results of two experiments that examine short-term verbatim recall of words presented in sentences is examined. A motivation for the study was the question of how to account for memory for order of the words of a sentence. In some ways, the answer may seem obvious, as it is the meaning and syntax of the sentence that constrain the order of the words. Still, it is not supposed that these words are firmly welded together. So if memory for a sentence is fallible and words are lost or get out of order, some other mechanism is needed to account for this forgetting. One hypothesis is that processes that have been brought out in examination of short-term memory for simple letter sequences also may have application in the case of sentence memory. The experiments of Lee and Estes (1977, 1981) show that for sequences of letters, errors of order occur in a predictable manner when there are few constraints on the structure of the sequence. When the letters are grouped or "chunked," then recall of order tends to be better than expected on the basis of primary memory processes alone. In the latter case, we assumed that secondary memory processes or schemata are playing a role in recall. In recall of sentences, when constraints of order are not high, a similar pattern of order and item errors may be seen.

In two experiments, memory for sentences that were specially constructed to provide opportunities for order errors in the report of words, both within a sentence and between sets of sentences, was studied. Tables 5.4 and 5.5 show examples of stimulus sentences from the first experiment of this series. These sentences may seem a bit artificial but they are convenient for the purpose of our analysis. The sentences had multiple subject and object nouns and the order of the words within these clusters was not constrained by either meaning or syntax. Because memory load is high and constraints on order are relatively low, it was

TABLE 5.4
Examples of Stimulus Sentences for the Three Sentence Frame Conditions (4-1, 2-2, and 1-4)
from Sentence Experiment 1

4 – 1	The mother, the doctor, the child, and the therapist sat with the father.
2 – 2	The butler and the cook stole the jewelry and the furs.
1 – 4	The dictionary contains definitions, dates, places, and abbreviations.

TABLE 5.5
Examples of Stimulus Pairs for Between-Sentence Semantic Similarity Conditions of
Sentence Experiment 1

Similar

The banker and the actress walked by the store and the tavern.
The sailor and the nurse visited the museum and the restaurant.

Different

The plates and the bowls are stored with the napkins and the towels.
The dog and the raccoon ran through the river and the field.

expected that recall of these sentences would not be perfect. Presentation of the stimulus sentences was auditory: each sentence was spoken at a normal conversational pace and a pair of sentences was presented on a trial. Subjects recalled out loud, and guessed or said "blank," when they forgot a word.

An important variable here is the format or frame of the sentence. Examples of the three frame conditions are illustrated at the top of Table 5.4. The first example shows a sentence with a cluster of four subject nouns; the second shows one with two clusters, two subject nouns, and two object nouns; and the third shows one with one cluster of four object nouns. Also varied were the semantic similarity of the words in the subject or object of a sentence and the semantic similarity of words across sentences of a trial pair. The first sentence of the table shows an example of within-sentence semantic similarity. Here all nouns are from the same semantic category. The second sentence shows an example of the different condition and here subject and object nouns are from different semantic categories. Between-sentence semantic similarity variation is shown in the examples in Table 5.5.

Figure 5.8 shows serial position curves for the three sentence frame conditions (item recall and items correct in position, conditionalized on item recall). Each sentence type has a curve with the distinct shape reflecting the underlying structure. The sentences with four-item clusters of subject or object nouns show bowed serial position curves for the cluster, reminiscent of the curves for letter strings. The patterns suggest that words in these clusters are recalled as memory units. The curves for item recall are flatter but also reflect the unique structure of each sentence type.

Figure 5.9 shows position gradients for the frame condition with four subject nouns and one object. (Similar results were obtained for the other two conditions.) The curves show that words in the cluster of subject nouns follow a distance function similar to that seen for random letter sequences. Confusions of order are seen within the cluster, the probability of these declining with the

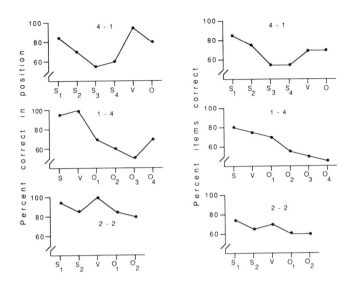

Position in sentence

FIG. 5.8. Serial position curves for items correct in position (conditionalized on item recall) and item recall for the three sentence frame conditions of Sentence Experiment 1.

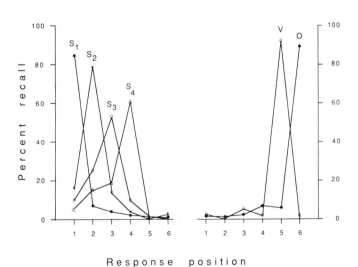

Response position

FIG. 5.9. Position gradients for the 4-1 condition of Sentence Experiment 1. (Subject noun positions are presented separately from verb and object noun positions for clarity.)

distance between presentation and report position. However, subject nouns are not recalled in the positions of verbs or object nouns or vice versa. This constraint on position of report can be attributed to the role of syntax.

From studies of memory for letter strings, a good deal is known about the effects of similarity, particularly acoustic similarity, on short-term recall. In general, similarity has been shown to have detrimental effects on memory for the order of items. In this experiment, within-sentence semantic similarity led to a slight but significant trend toward lower recall for the order of words, specifically for the order of subject or object nouns within a cluster of similar items. There were also detrimental effects of within-sentence similarity on item recall, but these were smaller and only marginally significant. Table 5.6 (left) shows the results for variations in within-sentence semantic similarity.

When the effect of similarity is considered in terms of between-sequence effects, the findings for recall of letter strings lead to the expectation of detrimental effects of similarity, this time for item recall but not order. In this experiment between-sentence similarity had no effect on memory for order, but large detrimental effects on memory for items. Table 5.6 (right) shows the findings for between-sentence similarity.

Further analyses revealed that at least a portion of this decline in recall due to sentence similarity is due not to item loss per se, but rather to transpositions of words from one sentence of a pair to the other. The next experiment was carried out to get a clearer picture of intersentence transposition errors. Examples of stimulus sentences from the second experiment for the sentence memory series are shown in Table 5.7. On each trial, four sentences were presented, this time visually instead of auditorially. Otherwise the procedure was similar to that of the previous experiment. Sentence frame was kept constant here, but between sentence similarity was manipulated. In the blocked condition, the words in the corresponding serial positions of each sentence were semantically similar. In the mixed condition, sentences from two different semantic categories alternated. In the example, the first and third sentences are similar to each other and different from the second and fourth ones. The results of the experiment show again that

TABLE 5.6
Percent Item and Position (Conditionalized on Items) Recall of Words from Clusters of Four Subject or Object Nouns in the Within-Sentence and Between Sentence Semantic Similarity Conditions of Sentence Experiment 1

		Within-Sentence	Between-Sentence
Position			
	Similar	59	58
	Different	69	58
Item			
	Similar	55	50
	Different	62	68

TABLE 5.7
Examples of Stimulus Sentences for the Blocked and Mixed Semantic Similarity Conditions of Sentence Experiment 2

Blocked

An expensive ring was donated by the pretty actress.
An intricate tapestry was owned by the rich dancer.
A fabulous clock was sold by the successful writer.
An antique mirror was purchased by the brilliant student.

Mixed

A yellow jacket was laid on the kitchen chair.
The sleepy puppy chewed on the old string.
A blue sweater was thrown on the bedroom shelf.
The noisy hamster chased after the new ball.

---

semantic similarity is detrimental to recall. Sentences in the mixed condition are recalled better than those in the blocked condition (see Table 5.8).

Table 5.9 shows the results of the analysis of intrusion errors. These points describe position gradients but with a difference; these are for transposition errors between sentences rather than within. Each value represents an average across the items of a sentence. Looking across the rows for the blocked condition, it can be seen that for a given output sentence position, words from sentences in the corresponding presentation positions (e.g., second presented sentence recalled second) are most likely to be reported (note the underlined values). When the correct words are not reported, then words from other sentences tend to intrude into recall (off diagonal values). The probability that words from a given sentence will intrude is a function of how far they were at presentation from the sentence the subject is attempting to report.

However, when we look at the mixed condition, the orderly distant gradient is gone. This is as expected because the semantic categories of words in a sentence should constrain the quality of errors that can occur in recall. Here it appears that

TABLE 5.8
Percent Recall Correct in Position for the Blocked and Mixed Conditions of Sentence Experiment 2

	Serial Position in Sentence					
	1 A_1	2 S	3 V	4 A_2	5 O	Mean
Blocked Condition	64	62	49	57	65	59
Mixed Condition	66	69	61	67	73	67

Note. A_1 and A_2 are adjectives.

TABLE 5.9
Position Gradients for Recall of Sentences in Sentence Experiment 2

Output Sentense	Input Sentence				
	1	2	3	4	Extra-List
Blocked Condition					
1	.65	.13	.09*	.06	.07
2	.10	.50	.19	.14*	.07
3	.08*	.11	.60	.16	.05
4	.06	.07*	.12	.68	.07
Mixed Condition					
1	.73	.03	.10*	.02	.12
2	.03	.58	.09	.13*	.17
3	.14*	.03	.67	.06	.10
4	.01	.09*	.03	.77	.10

Underlined entries (diagonals) are proportions correct for words from a particular stimulus sentence output in the corresponding sentence at recall. Off diagonal values are transposition errors (i.e., recall of words from a particular stimulus sentence output in a different sentence). Starred entries are corresponding values from the blocked and mixed conditions showing transpositions between similar sentences.

transposition errors are most likely, not between adjacent sentences, but between those two positions away at input—those, in fact, that are semantically similar in this condition. A comparison of the values for the mixed condition with the corresponding cells for the blocked condition suggests that an underlying distance gradient is camoflaged by response editing for semantic appropriateness. The starred values are for transposition errors from semantically similar sentences occurring at the identical output positions of each condition.

In conclusion, the results of these two sentence experiments give strong support to the hypothesis that memory for order in sentences is influenced by the same set of factors that influence memory for simple sequences. When the constraints of structure are relaxed, order errors that follow predictable patterns are evidenced. Nevertheless, semantic and syntactic structure constrain memory in important ways—and ways that are again predictable from studies of the role of structure in short-term memory for letter sequences.

CONCLUSION

The Perturbation Model has proved to be useful in predicting findings from a number of different short-term recall situations. It has provided a basis for a quantitative model that has allowed for considerable precision in testing assumptions about primary memory processes in recall of item, order, and position information (Lee & Estes, 1977, 1981). It has been useful for distinguishing the contributions of primary and secondary memory to short-term recall. Moreover, the model can in many instances generate a priori predictions about major trends and patterns in the data (even without quantitative elaboration), as it has for the experiments reported here. The model has been used to describe memory for letters, letter groups, and words in sentences. It has described not only the short-term memory processes affecting recall of items (and their order) within a single trial context, but also the way in which these processes interact across different contexts to produce a unique reactivation of memory elements for recall. In his original conception of the model, Estes had intended that the Perturbation Model have a relatively broad application, including the role of short-term memory in complex cognitive activities such as reading or listening to discourse. It seems possible at this point to contemplate such further expansions; it is hoped that this review of the model will interest other students of memory in exploring this possibility.

ACKNOWLEDGMENTS

The research reported here was supported by Grant BNS 79–21028 from the National Science Foundation.

REFERENCES

Bjork, E. L., & Healy, A. F. (1974). Short-term order and item retention. *Journal of Verbal Learning and Verbal Behavior, 13,* 80–97.

Conrad, R. (1967). Interference or delay over short retention intervals? *Journal of Verbal Learning and Verbal Behavior, 6,* 49–54.

Cunningham, T. F., Healy, A. F., & Williams, D. M. (1984). Effects of repetition on short-term retention of order information. *Journal of Experimental Psychology: Learning, Memory and Cognition, 10,* 575–597.

Estes, W. K. (1972). An associative basis for coding and organization in memory. In A. W. Melton & E. Martin (Eds.), *Coding processes in human memory* (pp. 161–190). New York: Halstead Press.

Healy, A. F. (1974). Separating item from order information in short-term memory. *Journal of Verbal Learning and Verbal Behavior, 13,* 644–655.

Johnson, N. F. (1970). The role of chunking and organization in the process of recall. In G. H. Bower (Ed.), *The psychology of learning and motivation* (Vol. 4, pp. 171–247). New York: Academic Press.

Lee, C. L., & Estes, W. K. (1977). Order and position in primary memory for letter strings. *Journal of Verbal Learning and Verbal Behavior, 16,* 395–418.

Lee, C. L., & Estes, W. K. (1981). Item and order information in short-term memory: Evidence for multilevel perturbation processes. *Journal of Experimental Psychology: Human Learning and Memory, 7,* 149–169.

Miller, G. A. (1956). The magical number seven, plus or minus two: Some limits on our capacity for processing information. *Psychological Review, 63,* 81–97.

6 A Simultaneous Examination of Recency and Cuing Effects

Michael S. Humphreys
Gerald Tehan
University of Queensland

In the Brown–Peterson paradigm, short lists of items are briefly presented. Then the subject's attention is diverted for a few seconds before she or he is asked to recall the list. After one or more previous lists have been learned, there is a very rapid rate of forgetting (Keppel & Underwood, 1962). The traditional explanation for the very rapid forgetting in this paradigm is similar to the explanations for the disappearance of the recency effect after a filled delay in the free recall paradigm. That is, it is assumed that items are displaced from a short-term store by the activity that intervenes between the end of the study period and the start of the recall period. Such an explanation, however, can no longer be considered viable. In general there has been a gradual eroding of the evidence for a distinction between primary and secondary memory (Crowder, 1982; Brannelley, Tehan, & Humphreys, 1989; Humphreys, Lynch, Revelle, & Hall, 1983.) More particularly there have been clear demonstrations of recency and other time-dependent effects that cannot be attributable to displacement from a short-term store.

Thus Loess and Waugh (1967) showed that the recency of the interfering material in the Brown–Peterson paradigm affected recall. They used a 9-second retention interval and varied the intertrial interval over a wide range. As the intertrial interval increased, the amount of proactive interference (PI) decreased until it was negligible at a 90-second interval. Because the interfering material would not have been in a short-term store (the subjects had no reason to continue remembering an already recalled list), this decline in the amount of interference produced is a time-dependent effect, not due to a displacement from a short-term store.

Bjork and Whitten (1974) also found strong time-dependent effects when each item in a free recall list was separated from the other items by distractor activity. This recency effect persisted even when there was a period of distractor activity following the presentation of the last item, which should have displaced all to-be-remembered items from the short-term store. Further research with the continuous distractor paradigm tended to rule out such explanations as surreptitious rehearsal during the final filled interval and variations in output order (Glenberg, Bradley, Stevenson, Kraus, Tkachuh, Gretz, Fish, & Turpin, 1980; Greene, 1986; Whitten, 1978). Glenberg et al. (1980) also showed that the recency effect depended on the ratio of the length of the interpresentation interval to the length of the retention interval (the ratio rule).

Glenberg et al. (1980; see also Glenberg, Bradley, Kraus, & Renzaglia, 1983) have proposed a theory for this effect that has its origins in a theory proposed by Estes in 1955. In the Glenberg theory, rapidly changing contextual cues, instead of fluctuating stimulus elements, are responsible for the recency effects in the continuous distractor paradigm. Additionally, there are several contextual components that can become associated with a list item. Some of these components are assumed to remain unchanged during list learning (e.g., the study room); others change more or less rapidly (e.g., hypotheses about the purpose of the experiment). The contextual components present when an item is studied are encoded as part of the episodic representation of that item. Item retrieval then depends on two factors. One is the number of contextual components common to both the retrieval cue and the episodic representation of the item. The other factor is the number of list items associated with each component of the retrieval cue. The more items, the less effective is that component. The contextual cue, hypothesis, is certainly a parsimonious and internally consistent explanation for these effects. It explains the ratio rule and the superior recall of the last items in the list. However, the continuous distractor paradigm is not well suited for further explorations of the hypothesis that recency should be conceptualized as a cuing effect. The problem is that none of the cues that are presumably employed in the recall of these lists are observable or manipulable.

Cues can be manipulated in the Brown–Peterson paradigm and, in fact, this manipulation provides the strongest support for a cuing interpretation of the buildup and release from PI. Keppel and Underwood (1962) first showed that forgetting in this paradigm depended on the learning of previous lists. That is, there was essentially no forgetting over 18 seconds on the very first list. The rapid rate of forgetting that had seemed characteristic of this paradigm only occurred after two or three prior lists had been learned. This increase in forgetting over the first few lists is referred to as the *buildup of proactive interference*. Wickens, Born, and Allen (1963) then showed that this forgetting was specific to the class of material employed. That is, when the material used to construct the lists is changed (e.g., from animal names to vegetable names), recall improves. This improvement in performance with a change in material is referred to as *release from PI*.

To support a cuing interpretation of the buildup and release from PI, Gardiner, Craik, and Birtwistle (1972) shifted from indoor games to outdoor games or from wild flowers to garden flowers. For those subjects who were not informed of the shift, there was no release from PI. There was release, however, when subjects were informed, and it did not matter whether they were informed at the time of study or at the time of test. Dillon and Bitner (1975) extended these findings by providing a subset cue in the absence of a shift. That is, their subjects received four trials using the names of eastern Canadian cities, but were only informed that the cities were eastern Canadian cities on the fourth trial. The provision of a more specific cue than the one the subjects were presumably using (e.g., Canadian cities or cities) at either study or test improved performance[1].

The conclusions drawn from these studies are: (a) that category labels can be used as cues in the Brown–Peterson paradigm, and (b) that the use of category label as a cue increases the probability of retrieving/generating the correct targets because the provision of the category label could not have improved discrimination in Dillon and Bitner's (1975) study. Dillon and Bitner are correct, however, when they point out that showing that category labels can be used as cues is not the same as showing that they are normally used as cues to produce release from PI. Nevertheless, the demonstrations that category labels can be used as cues should be considered along with the success of cuing explanations in other paradigms (cf. M. J. Watkins, 1981) and the failures of alternative hypotheses such as differential storage (cf. Loftus & Peterson, 1975; Watkins & Watkins, 1975).

Whereas the Brown–Peterson paradigm is suited to demonstrating cuing effects, it is not well suited to demonstrate recency effects because the manipulation of the interlist interval is constrained by the time needed to recall. The subjects also have a substantial incentive to perform at less than their maximum capacity on the interfering task and to continue rehearsing the to-be-remembered material, making it impossible to get an accurate picture of the true forgetting rate.

The BPRMS Paradigm

The paradigm that we developed to study recency effects in conjunction with known cueing effects was designed to incorporate the complementary strengths

---

[1]It could be argued that the provision of a more specific cue should not have improved performance in Dillon and Bitner's (1975) experiment. That is, if the sole determiner of cue effectiveness was the number of study items subsumed under the cue the same number would be subsumed under the cue *cities* and the cue *eastern Canadian cities*. However, the number of preexperimental associates of a cue has also been shown to be inversely related to its effectiveness (Nelson & McEvoy, 1979). Thus the improvement in recall in the Dillon and Bitner experiment probably occurs because the preexperimental set size of the cue *eastern Canadian cities* is smaller than the cue the subjects had been using.

of the Brown–Peterson and continuous distractor paradigms. In addition, we believe that it achieves a greater degree of control over surreptitious rehearsals than has previously been possible. The paradigm is essentially a cross between a Brown–Peterson and a running-memory-span paradigm (Pollack, Johnson, and Knaff, 1959) and is abbreviated accordingly (BPRMS). It is also similar to a paradigm used by Cunningham, Healy, and Williams (1984), which in turn was based on a paradigm used by Lee and Estes (1981). Results using an early version of this paradigm were briefly reported in Humphreys and Revelle (1984). Our current version, however, incorporates many refinements over the early version.

The experiment is computer controlled with memory items and feedback displayed on a video terminal. The subject initiates the presentation of each string of alpha numeric characters by pressing the return key. Letters (consonants only) and digits are presented sequentially in blocks of five letters or five digits. Each character within a block is presented for 600ms and there is an additional 50ms between characters and an extra 200ms between blocks. Perceptibly there is a slight pause at the end of each block. When the sequence terminates, subjects are cued to recall the last block of digits or the last block of letters. The last block of a particular kind (e.g., digits) may have occurred just prior to the cue. We refer to this situation as an *immediate test*. Alternatively, the last block of digits might have been followed by one or more blocks of letters or vice versa. In this case a cue to recall the earlier block (digits followed by letters or letters followed by digits) is referred to as a *delayed test*.

In devising this paradigm, we tried to insure that subjects only paid attention or rehearsed the items in the block that was currently being presented. They were instructed to do this and these instructions were reinforced by training and feedback. We told subjects that they must achieve an average of 80% correct (to be scored as correct, an item had to be recalled in position) on the immediate tests. Throughout the experiment they were given immediate feedback on these tests. If they recalled four out of five they were told their performance was acceptable but they were urged to do better. If they recalled three or fewer they were admonished to be better. In most experiments, a few subjects were discontinued after the first session for not meeting the 80% criterion. The Session 1 results for the remaining subjects were treated as practice and never included in the analysis. The block size and presentation rate had also been selected so that an immediate test on digits was just barely on ceiling for our subjects (the probability of ordered recall was in the mid-nineties). Letters were somewhat harder to recall than digits and an immediate test on letters was generally just below ceiling (the probability of ordered recall was in the high eighties to mid nineties).

In the BPRMS paradigm, PI is manipulated by the presence or absence of a prior block of the same kind of item. The spacing between the interfering block and the to-be-remembered block can also be manipulated. For example, a no-interference condition might consist of three blocks of letters and a block of digits (*LLLD*). The comparable adjacent interference condition would consist of two block of letters followed by two blocks of digits (*LLDD*), and the separation interference condition would consist of blocks of digits separated by two blocks of letters (*DLLD*). In all of these sequences the fourth block is critical. It is tested (subjects are cued to recall the most recent block of digits) after some number of letters intervening between the end of the digit block and the recall cue. The number of intervening letters (the retention interval) can also be manipulated. As the number of prior blocks is the same in the interference and no-interference conditions, with only the category membership of the items in the prior blocks differing, we refer to lower performance in the interference conditions as *category specific interference*.

If it is assumed that rehearsal is a control process (Atkinson & Shiffrin, 1968) that is affected by payoffs and instructions, it is extremely unlikely under the conditions obtaining in the BPRMS paradigm that subjects would continue to rehearse a block of digits that was followed by a block of digits or a block of letters that was followed by a block of letters. The subjects knew that they would never be tested on the earlier block as soon as the first item from the next block of the same kind was presented. When a block of digits was followed by a block of letters or vice versa there may, however, have been a tendency to continue rehearsing the earlier block because the subjects knew they would sometimes be tested on these blocks. Subject reports (including our own subjective reactions to being subjects) suggest, however, that such rehearsal were only possible during the first one or two presentations in the succeeding block. Furthermore, immediate recall is so demanding that any significant attempt to continue rehearsing items from an earlier block should be detectable. In addition, a comparison between recalling the critical block in a separated and an adjacent interference condition (e.g., the recall of block four in sequences *DLLDL* and *LLDDL*) is only attenuated by a tendency to continue rehearsing the earlier block, because such a rehearsal strategy will reduce the amount of time spent rehearsing the critical block in the separated interference condition.

Experimental Plan

There were three purposes to the present series of experiments. The first was simply to calibrate the BPRMS paradigm. That is, we needed to determine the retention intervals where performance would not be affected by floor and ceiling effects. The second purpose was to demonstrate a continuity in performance between the immediate serial recall and the Brown–Peterson paradigm. We felt that such a demonstration would help to support a role for cues in immediate serial recall. The final purpose was to demonstrate that kind of recency effects that Glenberg et al. (1980) summarize under the term "ratio rule" could occur in conjunction with cuing effects (category specific interference). To do this, we simultaneously manipulate the intervals between the interfering material and the to-be-remembered material and between the study and the test on the to-be-remembered material. The analogue to the ratio rule in an interference paradigm should consist of the following three results: (a) at short retention intervals interference should be observable when there is little separation between the interfering block and the to-be-remembered (TBR) block, but not when there is a longer separation; (b) at longer retention intervals, PI should be observable with longer separations; and (c) with a sufficiently long retention interval, the amount of PI should be the same for short and long separations.

EXPERIMENTS 1A AND 1B

In Experiment 1A an adjacent interference condition was compared to a separated interference condition (two blocks intervening between the TBR and the interfering block) at three retention intervals (0, 1, and 2 intervening blocks). In Experiment 1B an adjacent interference condition was compared to a no interference condition at the same three retention intervals. This design potentially provides complete information about the ratio rule and the between experiment separation of the two comparisons (separation vs. adjacent and adjacent vs. no interference) reduced the time required from each subject.

METHOD

Subjects

There were 10 subjects in Experiment 1A and 12 subjects in Experiment 1B. They all were students in an introductory psychology course at the University of Queensland and they served in the experiment as part of a course requirement.

Design and Procedure

Both experiments used completely within-subject designs. In Experiment 1A, adjacent interference sequences (LLDD, LLDDL, and LLDDLL) were compared with separated interference sequences (DLLD, DLLDL, and DLLDLL). These six sequences are referred to as the *critical sequences*. The retention interval was manipulated by either testing the fourth block immediately (LLDD cue for digits or DLLD cue for digits), after one block of letters (LLDDL cue for digits or DLLDL cue for digits), or after two blocks of letters (LLDDLL cue for digits or DLLDLL cue for digits). The blocks of letters that followed the fourth block were also tested (immediate tests). Filler sequences were also used to ensure that subjects paid attention to the blocks that preceded the critical fourth

TABLE 6.1
Sequences, Cues, and Probability Correct for all Sequences Used in Experiment 1a

Separated Interference and Control Sequences			Adjacent Interference and Control Dequence		
Sequence	Cue	Probability Correct	Sequence	Cue	Probability Correct
D	d	.97	L	l	.88
DL	l	.86	LL	l	.77
DLL	l	.83	LLD	d	.96
DLLD	d	.93	LLDD	d	.94
DLLDL	d	.59	LLDDL	d	.49
DLLDL	l	.85	LLDDL	l	.86
DLLDLL	d	.30	LLDDLL	d	.27
DLLDLL	l	.81	LLDDLL	l	.84

Sequences, cues, and probability correct for all sequences used in Experiment Ib.

No Interference and Control Sequences			Adjacent Interference and Control Sequences		
L	l	.89			
LL	l	.84	LD	d	.98
LLD	d	.98	LDD	d	.96
LLDL	d	.61	LDDL	d	.48
LLDL	l	.87	LDDL	l	.86
LLDLL	d	.29	LDDLL	d	.31
LLDLL	l	.83	LDDLL	l	.84
LLL	l	.86			
LLLL	l	.88			

Note. D = block of five digits, L = block of five letters, d = digits.

block. There were a total of 16 sequence-cue combinations. A complete list is provided in Table 6.1.

Each subject served in four one-hour sessions on separate but not necessarily consecutive days. Each session consisted of 4 practice trials and 128 experimental trials. During the 128 experimental trials, each of the 16 sequence-cue combinations was presented 8 times. The order of presentation was randomly determined for each subject and each session. Subjects recorded their answers by typing the sequences on the keyboard. They were required to depress five keys before their answer was recorded.

In Experiment 1B, adjacent interference sequences (LDD, LDDL, and LD-DLL) were compared with no interference sequence (LLD, LLDL, and LLDLL). Again the retention interval was manipulated by either testing the third block immediately (LDD cue for digits or LLD cue for digits), after one block of letters (LDDL cue for digits or LLDL cue for digits), or after two blocks of letters (LDDLL cue for digits or LLDLL cue for digits). In this experiment there were a total of 15 sequence-cue combinations, which are also given in Table 6.1. Each session consisted of 4 practice trials and 120 experimental trials. During the 120 experimental trials, each of the 15 sequence-cue combinations was presented 8 times. All of the other details were the same as in Experiment 1A.

RESULTS

The probability correct for each of the 16 sequence-cue combinations in Experiment 1A is presented in Table 6.1. To be scored as correct an item had to be recalled in its correct position.

There were six critical sequences involving digit recall among the 16 sequence-cue combinations in Experiment 1A (see Fig. 6.1). A 2 × 3 ANOVA involving conditions (adjacent vs. separated) and retention interval (0, 1, or 2 blocks of letters) was conducted on the critical sequences. The effect of retention interval was significant, $F(2,18) = 148.53$, $MSe = .01$. In this and all subsequent analyses, the significance level was p< .05. There was also a significant effect of conditions, $F(1,9) = 12.54$, $MSe = .002$ and a significant interaction between conditions and retention interval, $F(2,18) = 11.35$, $MSe = .001$. An analysis of the simple effects showed that the adjacent and separation conditions only differed after one intervening block of letters, $F(1,9) = 37.53$.

The probability correct for each of the 15 sequence-cue combinations in Experiment 1B is presented in the bottom panel of Table 6.1. Again the six critical conditions involving digit recall were analyzed as a 2 × 3 ANOVA involving conditions (adjacent vs. no interference) and retention interval (0, 1, or 2 blocks of letters). There was a significant effect of retention interval $F(2,22) = 232.15$, $MSe = .01$, a significant effect of conditions $F(1,11) = 10.23$, $MSe = .004$, and a significant retention interval by conditions interaction, $F(2,22) = 14.00$, $MSe = .003$. An analysis of simple effects showed that the adjacent and no interference conditions only differed after one block of intervening letters, $F(1,11) = 31.24$.

These results did not appear to be due to a trade off between trying to remember the previous blocks of digits and trying to learn the following block of letters. A 2 × 2 ANOVA (in Experiment 1A the sequences were LLDDL cue for letters, LLDDLL cue for letters, DLLDL cue for letters, and DLLDLL cue for letters, and in Experiment 1B they were LDDL cue for letters, LDDLL cue for letters, LLDL cue for letters, and LLDLL cue for letters) was conducted on the recall data for the blocks of letters following the critical block of digits. The variables were conditions (adjacent vs. separated in Experiment 1A and adjacent vs. no interference in Experiment 1B) and block position (the first vs. the second block following the critical block of digits). There were no significant differences between conditions $F(1,9) = .19$; $MSe = .001$ and $F(1,11) = .92$; $MSe = .002$ for Experiments 1A

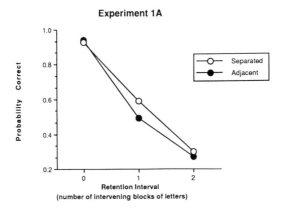

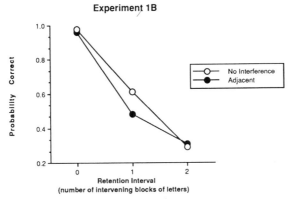

FIG. 6.1.   Digit recall as a function of the interfering condition and retention interval.

and 1B, respectively. There was, however, a marginally significant effect of block position in Experiment 1A, $F(1,9) = 4.19; MSe = .003, p < .07$, and a significant effect in Experiment 1B, $F(1,11) = 7.78; MSe = .001$. Performance was better on the first block than on the second block.

The superior performance in the separation condition as opposed to the adjacent condition (Experiment 1A) was also not due to a failure to learn the interfering digits. When a digit recall cue was given after the first block of digits, the probabilities of recall were .97 and .96 in the separation (sequence D) and adjacent (Sequence LLD) conditions, respectively. In Experiment 1B, the probability of recall on an immediate test for the first block of digits in the adjacent condition (sequence LD) was .98.

DISCUSSION

The BPRMS paradigm seemed to work in controlling rehearsals, as performance declined very rapidly as a function of the number of intervening blocks. In addition, there was clear evidence for PI, at least when the retention interval was one intervening block. There was, however, only limited support for the ratio rule. The strongest support comes from the finding that with a retention interval of one block there was more interference in the adjacent than in the separation interference condition (Experiment 1A). The failure to find a difference between the adjacent and no interference condition on an immediate test (Experiment 1B) is also consistent with the ratio rule. However, an effect could have been obscured by the very high level of recall. The failure to find any difference between the adjacent and no separation condition after two intervening blocks (Experiment 1A) is also consistent with the ratio rule, although this finding is marred by the failure to find a difference between the adjacent and no interference conditions at this interval. That is, with a long enough retention interval, the separation interval should not matter but there should still be some interference.

After two intervening blocks performance was, however, relatively poor, and this may have prevented us from finding interference at this retention interval. The disadvantage of the between experiment design we used is that we cannot be certain that the adjacent conditions in the two experiments were comparable. Thus, we cannot tell whether this result is due to an unusual level of recall in the adjacent condition in one of the two experiments. Consequently a complete within subject design was used in Experiments 2A and 2B. In these experiments we also decided to look for evidence for the ratio rule at shorter retention intervals. The retention intervals chosen ranged from zero (an immediate test) to five (one intervening block), in steps of one. With this range of retention intervals we could also look for a continuity in performance between an immediate test, where no interference had been observed, and a delayed test, where interference was observed. We felt that this continuity in performance would support a continuity in process across these retention intervals. We also shortened the separation interval in the separation interference condition from two blocks to one. This allowed us to bracket the ratio of retention interval to separation interval at which we had observed differential interference in Experiment 1A.

EXPERIMENTS 2A AND 2B

METHOD

Subjects

There were 10 subjects in Experiment 2A and 11 subjects in Experiment 2B. They were students in an introductory psychology class at the University of

Queensland. They served in the experiment as part of a course requirement and they were paid for any hours that were additional to the course requirement.

Design and Procedure

Experiments 2A and 2B were basically the same. In both experiments all subjects received a no interference condition (*LLD*), a separation interference condition (*DLD*), and an adjacent interference condition (*LDD*). The third block was followed by zero, one, two, three, four, or five letters. If fewer than five letters followed the third block, the subject was cued to recall digits (the third block should be recalled). If five letters followed the third block there were five cues to recall letters (the fourth and final block should be recalled) for each cue to recall digits (the third block should be recalled). The extra letter cues were provided to determine whether the subjects were paying attention to the final block of letters. A complete list of the sequence-cue combinations is provided in Table 6.2. Each of the 10 subjects in Experiment 2A and the 11 subjects in Experiment 2B served in eight one-hour sessions. No subject was used in both experiments. In Session 1 of both experiments, each subject received 117 practice trials. In the remaining sessions of Experiment 2A it was planned that each subject should have received 5 practice trials and 156 experimental trials. However, all 20 trials of sequence LDDL cue for letters were omitted. This was corrected in Experiment 2B where the number of experimental trials was also reduced from a planned 156 in Experiment 2A to 117 in Experiment 2B.

RESULTS AND DISCUSSION

For both experiments the probability of recalling the digits in the third block (in position) as a function of the retention interval (0–5 intervening letters) is presented in Figure 6.2. In both experiments there is no evidence for PI on the immediate test (zero intervening letters) and there is substantial PI in both conditions after five intervening letters. Furthermore, PI may develop earlier in the adjacent than in the separation condition. (Experiment 2A only.)

  To assess the reliability of these trends, we compared the average of the two interference conditions to the no interference condition at each retention interval. Then we compared the separation and adjacent conditions at each interval. In Experiment 2A the average of the two interference conditions differed significantly from the no interference condition after three ($F(1,18) = 10.63$, $MSe = .004$) and after five ($F(1,18) = 44.47$, $MSe = .003$) intervening letters. The adjacent condition differed from the separation condition after two ($F(1,18) = 6.43$, $MSe = .004$) and after four ($F(1,18) = 8.20$, $MSe = .008$) intervening letters. In Experiment 2B the average of the interference conditions differed from the no interference condition after two ($F(1,20) = 7.58$, $MSe = .001$), three

TABLE 6.2
Sequences, cues, and Probability Correct for All Sequences Used in Experiments 2A and 2B

	No Interference			Separation Interference			Adjacent Interference	
Sequence and Cue	Experiment 2A	2B	Sequence and Cue	Experiment 2A	2B	Sequence and Cue	Experiment 2A	2B
L 1a	.93	.97	D d	.97	.99	L 1a	.93	.97
LL 1	.85	.96	DL 1	.92	.95	LD d	.98	.99
LLD d	.97	.99	DLD d	.96	.99	LDD d	.96	.99
LLD1 d	.95	.98	DLD1 d	.94	.98	LDD1 d	.92	.98
LLD2 d	.93	.98	DLD2 d	.93	.95	LDD2 d	.86	.96
LLD3 d	.85	.94	DLD3 d	.79	.91	LDD3 d	.74	.89
LLD4 d	.74	.87	DLD4 d	.75	.82	LDD4 d	.66	.81
LLDL d	.65	.74	DLDL d	.52	.69	LDDL d	.50	.65
LLDL 1	.91	.96	DLDL 1	.92	.96	LDDL 1	-	.96

Note D = block of five digits, L = block of five letters, 1-4 = the number of letters following the last block of digits, d = digit cue, l = letter cue.
aThe results from the two sequences of this type have been combined.

Experiment 2A

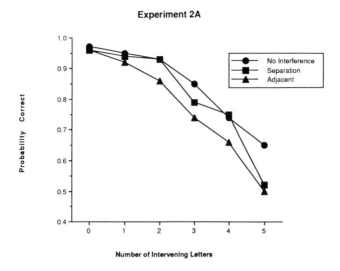

Experiment 2B

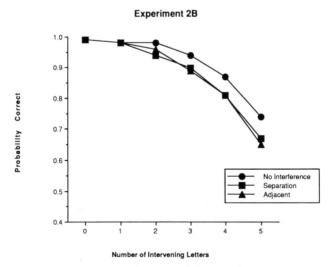

FIG. 6.2.   Digit recall as a function of the interfering condition and retention interval.

$(F(1,20) = 6,77, MSe = .002)$, four $(F(1,20) = 5.62, MSe = .004)$, and five $(F(1 ,20) = 8.49 MSe = .005)$ intervening letters. Unlike Experiment 2A, the adjacent condition did not differ from the separation condition at any of the retention intervals. In both experiments signs of interference were detected after two intervening letters, and in Experiment 2A interference developed more rapidly in the adjacent condition than in the separation condition.

These results do not appear to be due to trade offs between remembering the digits in the third block and learning the final block of letters, nor to failures to learn the interfering blocks of digits. In Experiment 2A, the probability of recalling the final block of letters was .91 and .92 in the no interference and separation conditions, respectively (this test was omitted in the adjacent condition). In Experiment 2B the probability of recalling the final block of letters was .96, .96, and .96 in the no interference, separation, and adjacent conditions, respectively. Digit recall was also cued after a single block of digits (D) and after an LD sequence. These blocks of digits constitute the interference in the separation and adjacent conditions, respectively. In Experiment 2A the recall probabilities were .97(D) and .98(LD), and in Experiment 2B they were .99(D) and .99(LD). Thus, subjects were clearly attending to the digit blocks that would become the interfering blocks. On an immediate test for letters there was evidence for interference. In Experiment 2A an immediate test on the second block in a DL sequence (.92) was better than an immediate test on the second block in an LL sequence (.85). This difference was reliable, $(F(1,9) = 22.27, MSe = .001$. There was no difference in Experiment 2B (sequence DL = .95 and sequence LL = .96).

Furthermore, the omission of a sequence in Experiment 2A does not seriously affect the interpretation of the results. The omitted sequence (LDDL cue for letters) was the control sequence for the adjacent interference condition. It was designed to detect subjects who were not paying attention to the final block of letters because they were continuing to rehearse or pay attention to the critical third block. If any subject was doing this, it means that we have underestimated the amount of interference in the adjacent interference condition in this experiment, and this condition already produces the largest amount of interference. Note that there is no reason to believe that differential rehearsal is occurring in the separated and no interference conditions. Performance on the control sequences in these conditions (LLDL cue for letters and DLDL cue for letters) does not differ from performance on sequence DL cue for letters.

GENERAL DISCUSSION

In these experiments recall performance declined by almost 50% over one intervening block. This very rapid decline indicates that there is a very substantial control over displaced rehearsals. Furthermore, PI effects were clearly observable in Experiments 2A and 2B after two intervening letters. This corresponds to a retention interval of 1550ms (the time between the onset of the recall cue and the offset of the last digit in the third block). We also have evidence that the separation interval (the interval between the TBR block and the interfering block) has an effect. That is, with a retention interval of one block we found a significant difference between no separation and a separation of two blocks in Experiment 1A. In addition, with a retention interval of between two and four items we found a significant difference between no separation and a separation of one block in Experiment 2A. Furthermore, in Experiment 2A there was no effect of separation with a retention interval of five items (one block). These results are consistent with the ratio rule.

Unfortunately, in Experiment 2B we could not replicate the separation effect that we found in Experiment 2A. Given these results we cannot claim support for the ratio rule in the BPRMS paradigm. Nevertheless, we now have a good idea as to where to look. The most promising prospect would involve a separation interval of two blocks with retention intervals between two and five items. Performance in Experiment 2B was also a little bit too good. This makes it difficult to detect displaced rehearsals. It may also have tempted a few subjects to continue rehearsing the second block in sequence DLD when they should have been paying attention to the third block. Further attempts to find evidence for the ratio rule should increase the difficulty of the task by increasing the block size or the rate of presentation.

Although we have not been able to find consistent evidence for an effect of the separation interval on PI we think that these results still contribute to a changing perspective of the relationship between long-term and short-term memory. Long-term memory has generally been seen as being cue dependent (e.g., Tulving, 1983), whereas short-term memory has not (Wickens, Moody, & Dow, 1981). The proposal that recency is a cuing effect (Glenberg, et al., 1980) and the proposal that in probe recognition memory access starts with the probe, not a search of the memory set (Brannelley et al., 1989) are direct challenges to this distinction. The eroding distinction between short-term and long-term memory that has been documented by Crowder (1982) also challenges it. In our experiments we could find no sharp distinction between a retention interval at which PI effects were not observed and one at which they were observed. Instead it looked like PI effects started to emerge whenever performance was off the ceiling. Thus there was PI on an immediate test for letters in Experiment 2A where the probability of recall for sequence DL was .92, but no interference in Experiment 2B where the probability of recall was .95. Similarly, when immediate recall for the first block of letters following the TBR block of digits was relatively poor (.85 in Experiment 1A and .87 in Experiment 1B), there was evidence for interference, as an immediate test on the second block was worse (.81 in Experiment 1A and .83 in Experiment 1B). Although it was not significant, PI looks like it starts to emerge after one intervening letter in Experiment 1A where the probability of recall in the no interference condition is .95. There is no sign of PI after one intervening letter in Experiment 2B, but the probability of recall in the no interference condition is .98.

Given the almost continuous changes that are observed in this experiment, we find it difficult to believe that a cue dependent memory access process is responsible for PI and that some process (e.g., search) is responsible for immediate serial recall. Instead it appears that we need models in which multiple cues work together to provide access to memory. That is, we need models in which the concepts such as control elements that are used to explain item and order information in short-term memory (Lee & Estes, 1981) can be seen to work together with cues such as category labels and fixed and/or changing contextual cues.

At this point the senior author admits to being biased in favor of multiple cues and cue dependent processes, especially when they are incorporated into a distributed storage or connectionist model. The kind of thinking involved in this enterprise seems to have evolved very naturally from the work on stimulus sampling theory to which he was exposed when he was a graduate student of Bill Estes in the mid1960s.

ACKNOWLEDGEMENTS

This research was supported by a grant from the Australian Research Grants Scheme to the first author. We would like to thank John Bain for his comments on earlier drafts.

REFERENCES

Atkinson, R. C., & Shiffrin, R. M. (1968). Human memory: A proposed system and its control processes. In K. W. Spence and V. T. Spence (Eds.), *The psychology of learning and motivation: Advances in research and theory, Vol. 2* (pp. 89–195). New York: Academic Press.

Bjork, R. A., & Whitten, W. B. (1974). Recency-sensitive retrieval processes in long-term free recall. *Cognitive Psychology, 6,* 173–189.

Brannelley, S., Tehan, G., & Humphreys, M. S. (1989). Retrieval plus scanning: Does it occur? *Memory & Cognition, 17,* 712–722.

Crowder, R. G. (1982). The demise of short-term memory. *Acta Psychologica, 50,* 291–323.

Cunningham, T. F., Healy, A. F., & Williams, D. M. (1984). Effects of repetition on the short-term retention of order information. *Journal of Experimental Psychology: Learning, Memory and Cognition, 10,* 575–597.

Dillon, R. F., & Bitner, L. (1975). Analysis of retrieval cues and release from proactive inhibition. *Journal of Verbal Learning and Verbal Behavior, 14,* 616–622.

Estes, W. K. (1955). Statistical theory of spontaneous recovery and regression. *Psychological Review, 57,* 99–107.

Gardiner, J. M., Craik, F. I. M., & Birtwistle, J. (1972). Retrieval cues and release from proactive inhibition. *Journal of Verbal Learning and Verbal Behavior, 11,* 773–778.

Glenberg, A. M., Bradley, M. M., Stevenson, J. A., Kraus, T. A., Tkachuh, M. J., Gretz, A. L., Fish, J. H., & Turpin, B. M. (1980). A two-process account of long-term position effects. *Journal of Experimental Psychology: Human Learning and Memory, 6,* 355–369.

Glenberg, A. M., Bradley, M. M., Kraus, T. A., & Renzaglia, G. J. (1983). Studies of the long-term recency effect: Support for contextually guided retrieval hypothesis. *Journal of Experimental Psychology: Learning, Memory and Cognition, 9,* 231–255.

Greene, R. L. (1986). Sources of recency effects in free recall. *Psychological Bulletin, 99,* 221–228.

Humphreys, M. S., Lynch, M. J., Revelle, W., & Hall, J. W. (1983). Individual differences in short-term memory. In R. F. Dillon & R. R. Schmeck (Eds.), *Individual differences in cognition, Vol. I* (pp. 45–64). New York: Academic Press.

Humphreys, M. S., & Revelle, W. (1984). Personality, motivation, and performance: A theory of the relationship between individual differences and information processing. *Psychological Review, 91,* 153–184.

Keppel, G., & Underwood, B. J. (1962). Proactive inhibition in short-term retention of single items. *Journal of Verbal Learning and Verbal Behavior, 1,* 153–161.

Lee, C. L., & Estes, W. K. (1981). Item and order information in short-term memory: Evidence for multiple perturbation processes. *Journal of Experimental Psychology: Human Learning and Memory, 7,* 149–169.

Loess, H. & Waugh, N. (1967). Short-term memory and intertrial interval. *Journal of Verbal Learning and Verbal Behavior, 6,* 455–460.

Loftus, G. R., & Patterson, K. K. (1975). Components of short-term proactive interference. *Journal of Verbal Learning and Verbal Behavior, 14,* 105–121.

Nelson, D. L., & McEvoy, C. L. (1979). Encoding context and set size. *Journal of Experimental Psychology: Human Learning and Memory, 5,* 292–314.

Pollack, I., Johnson, L. B., & Knaff, P. R. (1959). Running memory span. *Journal of Experimental Psychology, 57,* 137–146.

Tulving, E. (1983). *Elements of episodic memory.* New York: Oxford University Press.

Watkins, M. J. (1981). Human memory and the information-processing metaphor. *Cognition, 10,* 331–336.

Watkins, O. C., & Watkins, M. J. (1975). Build-up of proactive inhibition as a cue overload effect. *Journal of Experimental Psychology: Human Memory and Learning, 104,* 442–452.

Whitten, W. B. (1978). Output interference and long-term serial position effects. *Journal of Experimental Psychology: Human Learning and Memory, 4,* 685–692.

Wickens, D. D., Born, D. G., & Allen, C. K. (1963). Proactive inhibition and item similarity in short-term memory. *Journal of Verbal Learning and Verbal Behavior, 2,* 440–445.

Wickens, D. D., Moody, M. V., & Dow, R. (1981). The nature of timing of the retrieval process and of interference effects. *Journal of Experimental Psychology: General, 110,* 1–20.

7 The Role of Visible Persistence in Backward Masking

George Wolford
Hwa-Young Kim
Dartmouth College

We have been exploring practice effects in various visual information processing paradigms. Some visual processing paradigms show little improvement with practice; other paradigms, such as backward pattern masking, yield striking improvement with practice. We would like to understand the source(s) of such improvement. We have considered a variety of possible explanations, from fairly cognitive mechanisms (e.g., stimulus learning and attention) to more sensory mechanisms. One promising candidate that we entertained from the latter category was that visible persistence changed with practice. We explore that hypothesis in this chapter after describing early visual information processing research in Estes' lab, and our previous work on practice effects.

The work that we describe is somewhat tangential to most of the work that Estes is associated with. Nevertheless, it has its roots in Estes' laboratory. In the mid1960s, Estes and various of his students developed and explored a new paradigm (Estes, 1965; Estes & Taylor, 1964, 1966; Estes & Wessel, 1966; Wolford, Wessel, & Estes, 1968). That paradigm, labeled the *detection method,* was used to measure the amount of information extracted in a single fixation. Following Sperling (1960), it was assumed that subjects could see more than was revealed by their reports in span of apprehension experiments. The detection paradigm consisted of a tachistoscopic flash of several letters. A pair of letters (such as B and F) were designated as targets and one or more instances of one of the pair members would be present in each display. The subject's task was to identify the presented target on each trial.

The detection paradigm was developed, in part, to test certain aspects of Estes' stimulus sampling theory. Individual letters were thought of as the elements. The detection paradigm yielded estimates of the number of elements sampled without the contamination of memory limitations. These estimates were relevant to the application of stimulus sampling theory in other domains. In addition to obtaining estimates of sample size, tests were carried out to determine if sample size was 'fixed' or 'variable' across trials. This also was an important issue in various learning models based on stimulus sampling theory.

Unfortunately, the estimates of sample size, the questions about fixed versus variable sample size, and all of the models tested rested on assumptions that are no longer tenable. Perhaps the most crucial of these assumptions was that each letter constituted a single element and that each of those elements was sampled on an all-or-none basis. Evidence rapidly accumulated that whole letters weren't 'elements' or the primitives of visual information processing. For instance, a robust finding in such experiments is that subjects often confuse similar letters and that their errors often resemble the correct letter visually (Rumelhart, 1970; Wolford & Hollingsworth, 1974). If letters were sampled on an all-or-none basis, it would be difficult to explain why a given letter would yield errors similar to itself. Several models soon appeared based on the assumption that letters were composed of features and that it was possible to sample a subset of the features of a given letter (Estes, 1972; Gardner, 1973; Rumelhart, 1970; Shiffrin & Geisler, 1973; Wolford, 1975). The response that a subject might give to a subset of a letter's features depended on the set of letters in the experiment, the task, and the decision rule used, but confusions would often result.

A corollary to the finding that letters are composed of lower level primitives was that different tasks might require different amounts and/or types of information to produce a correct response. In the span of apprehension paradigm, subjects must extract enough information per letter to identify that letter uniquely. In the detection paradigm, subjects only need to extract enough information to discriminate the target letter from noise letters and to identify which target letter was present; a single feature might allow accurate performance on some trials.

Because letters are not necessarily extracted as wholes and because the tasks have different information requirements, it is extremely difficult to compare performance on detection versus span of apprehension. Certainly the estimates provided in the early papers of the number of letters actually 'seen' in a tachistoscopic exposure were unrealistic. Related arguments apply to estimates of the number of letters actually seen from the partial report procedure developed by Sperling (1960; see Wolford, 1975). In fact, we believe that it is possible that the classic span of apprehension provides accurate estimates of the number of letters 'seen' in a single glance.

Another shortcoming of the early work on the detection paradigm is that we failed to appreciate sufficiently the importance of the *visual system* in these visual information processing tasks. In particular, little attention was paid to the role of retinal locus and contour interaction in that early work. It became apparent that both were powerful variables and some effects that had been ascribed to cognitive processes (such as attention, inference, and scanning) were better understood in terms of visual processes (see Wolford, 1975). Much of our subsequent work has been to understand those visual effects especially in the spatial domain. More recently, we have been exploring various visual processes in the temporal domain and their impact on visual information processing. We have made heavy use of the presence or absence of practice effects and the relationship among paradigms to aid our exploration.

PRACTICE EFFECTS IN VISUAL TASKS

We are interested in the kinds of practice effects that can be observed in various visual information-processing paradigms. Although these practice effects are receiving increased attention in the literature (Salthouse & Prill, 1983; Salthouse & Somberg, 1982), most investigators pay little attention to them, often considering such effects an annoyance. However, not all visual information-processing tasks yield practice effects and we believe that a careful consideration of which tasks do and which do not will address important questions about the nature of visual information processing: How is information integrated across displays? What causes backward masking? Can practice facilitate the early stages of visual processing or are practice effects confined to later stages of processing? What limits performance in different paradigms? Is attention necessary for improvement to occur? and so on.

Some tasks appear readily to afford practice effects. For instance, tasks involving complex skills or motor performance often lead to substantial improvement; paradigms using latency as the primary dependent measure show sustained and substantial improvement; tasks involving perceptual discrimination with novel or complex stimuli or novel mapping of stimuli onto responses also lead to substantial improvement (Gibson, 1953, 1969; LaBerge & Samuels, 1974; Salthouse & Somberg, 1982; Shiffrin & Schneider, 1977).

The effect of practice on simple perceptual tasks with accuracy as the dependent measure and well-learned stimuli, mapped in familiar and consistent ways onto responses, is less clear. Some investigators have reported practice effects in these paradigms. For instance, Johnson and Leibowitz (1979) and McKee and Westheimer (1978) report strong practice effects on hyperacuity. Others, however, have claimed that practice effects are minimal in simple visual tasks (Green & Swets, 1964). Our experience with various visual information processing paradigms had been consistent with the latter. We found little or no improvement in accuracy in a tachistoscopic letter detection task across 15 days; in lateral masking experiments across 8 and 10 days respectively; and in a whole report paradigm after 8 days (Wolford & Chambers, 1983, 1984; Wolford & Porter, 1976; Wolford, Wessel, & Estes, 1968).

We do find robust practice effects in paradigms that use a backward pattern mask. Except for the presence of the mask, these paradigms are similar to those in which we failed to observe practice effects (i.e., the tasks were simple, the exposures were brief, the stimuli were highly familiar, and accuracy was the dependent measure). Other investigators have observed practice effects in backward masking (Hertzog, Williams, & Walsh, 1976; Ward & Ross, 1977). Schiller and his colleagues noted differential practice effects for different kinds of masking. In particular, they found that there were substantial practice effects with pattern masks but no practice effects with brightness masks (Schiller, 1965; Schiller & Wiener, 1963).

PRACTICE EFFECTS IN BACKWARD MASKING

One question, then, is why we and others see robust practice effects in some visual information processing paradigms (such as backward pattern masking) and not in other seemingly similar paradigms (whole report, lateral masking, and backward masking with a brightness mask). We carried out a series of experiments to examine the practice effect in backward pattern masking (Wolford, Marchak, & Hughes, 1988). The experiments shared several methodological details. Subjects received 7 to 45 days of practice at varying SOAs, with the number of training days varying across experiments. Each trial began with a fixation point. The subject's keypress led to a target consisting of three letters or digits presented on the computer screen. In most of the experiments, the targets were centered on the fixation point. Following the designated SOA, a mask, consisting of three noise characters, was presented. Subjects responded with as many of the target characters as possible.

In those experiments we demonstrated a variety of phenomena and eliminated some possible explanations of the practice effects. Practice effects of considerable magnitude are possible. For example, one subject was able to identify only 17% of the target characters on the first day, but after 45 days of practice could identify over 90% of the characters. Improvement occurs gradually over days and is not confined to a particular SOA but is evident at a range of SOAs including ones not used during training. Target learning and task familiarity are not sources of the improvement effect in backward masking. Learning about the mask appears to be responsible for some of the improvement as switching masks at the end of training reduces the improvement. It only appears to account for a fraction of the improvement, however.

What, then, is responsible for the improvement? There were some indications that subjects had learned to process the target more rapidly, so that more of the information was extracted prior to the onset of the mask. For instance, a simple model based on that assumption adequately predicted performance at different SOAs before and after training. In addition, the improvement transfers to a new task in which speed is critical (i.e., threshold performance for two-flash judgments). In this paradigm, an LED was flashed for two 10 ms pulses with some interflash interval (IFI). At short IFIs, subjects always report seeing a single flash; at long IFIs, they always report two flashes. The threshold is generally in the neighborhood of 50–70 ms. On the first day of the experiment, we determined the two-flash threshold for each subject (i.e., the IFI at which the subject reported seeing two flashes on one half of the trials). On the second day, we measured the performance of the subjects on a whole-report task. The subjects, then, were trained for 20 days on backward masking and, finally, we measured their two-flash thresholds and whole-report performance again. We found that the training on backward masking led to a significant reduction of the two-flash threshold but had no effect on whole-report performance.

THE ROLE OF ATTENTION

There are indications that the practice effects that we and others observe are related to attention. Lindsley and Griffiths (cited in Lindsley, 1958) examined the two-flash threshold in humans and monkeys. In humans, they observed two-flash thresholds that averaged approximately 73 ms. Similarly, Lindsley and Griffiths found that monkeys exhibited two distinct evoked potentials to two flashes separated by over 100 ms and only one evoked potential to two flashes separated by 50 ms. The evoked potentials were recorded from the visual cortex. When the reticular system of the monkeys was stimulated, however, two distinct evoked potentials were recorded with a 50 ms interstimulus interval. Presumably, the stimulation of the reticular system led to improved temporal resolution. Hoyman and Kelsey (1977) replicated these findings using additional controls and using rats as subjects. Most investigators believe that the reticular formation is critically involved in alertness and arousal (Moruzzi & Magoun, 1949; Vierck, 1965).

These studies are important in two respects: They show that it might be possible to enhance visual processing, and they implicate attention (arousal, alertness) as a potential mediator of the enhancement. The important role of attention in these early studies is consistent with the reports of subjects in our laboratory and other laboratories. Many of our subjects reported that they felt their improvement in backward masking resulted from learning how to concentrate more effectively. McKee and Westheimer (1978) made a similar observation in their report of large practice effects in vernier acuity. We have recently completed a series of studies in our laboratory to explore the possible role of attention in the practice effect (Wolford, Schwartz, & Kim, 1991).

The experiments were based on the cuing paradigm developed by Posner (1978). Using that paradigm, we had subjects participate for several days in a backward masking study in which the three-letter target and mask were presented, at random, 2° into the left or right visual field and the likely location of the target and mask was indicated with a precue (a left or right arrow). Trials on

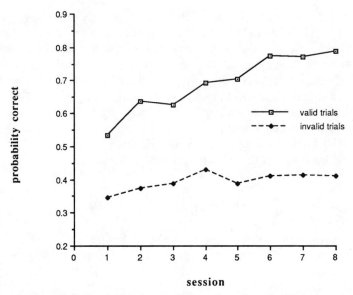

FIG. 7.1. The role of attention in the practice effect. Performance on valid versus invalid trials.

which the target appeared in the predicted visual field were referred to as *valid trials* and trials on which the target appeared in the unpredicted visual field were referred to as *invalid trials*. Eye movements were monitored, and trials on which eye movements occurred were discarded. Based on the work of Posner, we assumed that subjects would attend to the predicted location. If attention is a necessary or important ingredient in the improvement effect, then we would expect to see more learning on the valid than on the invalid trials. In a series of four experiments, we found that improvement only occurred on the valid trials. Performance remained constant on the invalid trials. In other words, subjects only improved at the location where they were attending. The respective learning curves are shown in Fig. 7.1. We believe that these findings strongly implicate attention in the practice effect.

THE ROLE OF VISIBLE PERSISTENCE

Although we have identified attention as an important ingredient in the practice effect, it isn't obvious what mechanisms or processes are affected by attention. We were interested in the possibility that practice, with attention, might lead to a decrease in visible persistence. Visible persistence is one of several forms of persistence identified by Coltheart (1980). Visible persistence refers to the fact that a stimulus remains visible after its offset. According to Coltheart, the two defining features of visible persistence are the inverse duration effect and the inverse intensity effect (i.e., judged persistence decreases as a stimulus is made longer or brighter).

Two lines of evidence led us to consider visible persistence as a possible mechanism. One was our finding of a significant reduction in the two-flash threshold with practice on backward masking and the other was the demonstration by Hoyman and Kelsey (1977) of a reduction in two-flash threshold through stimulation of the reticular system. What role would visible persistence play in backward masking? We reasoned that if the visible persistence of the target overlapped the onset of the mask, the subject might have trouble separating the two. If the visible persistence of the target could be reduced, separation would be enhanced and performance improved. This view would be consistent with the views of Eriksen and Schultz (1978) on the roles of integration in backward pattern masking.

Although this hypothesis has some plausibility, there are reasons for being skeptical. Visible persistence is probably a fairly low level sensory process and it's a bit hard to imagine affecting it with a few days of practice. In addition, according to Turvey's (1973) classification, we are employing backward pattern masking and this type of masking is only marginally affected by the physical variables, such as intensity, that affect visible persistence (see also Michaels & Turvey, 1979).

The temporal characteristics of the visual system are placed in interesting relief by comparison with the auditory system. Looking at the work on two-flash threshold, flicker-fusion thresholds, temporal order judgments, and so on, it is evident that even under optimal conditions the temporal resolution of the visual system is in the neighborhood of 50 ms (see Kelly, 1971). In contrast, several investigators have shown that the gap detection threshold in audition is an order of magnitude shorter (2 to 5 ms) (e.g., Moore, Glasberg, Donaldson, McPherson, & Plack, 1989). The superior temporal resolution of the auditory system is due in part to the use of mechanical receptors in audition and photochemical processes in vision. The photochemical process is relatively slow and it leaves traces long after the signal is terminated (Baylor, 1987). The difference between the two systems makes evolutionary sense. The information in audition is specified in the temporal domain so the neural substrata are optimized to extract that information. Although some of the information in vision is temporal, the bulk of the information is carried in the spatial domain. The neural structures in vision then are optimized to extract spatial information, and further to extract information in low levels of illumination. It remains to be seen if the temporal properties of vision are malleable.

SYNCHRONY PARADIGM

We had shown previously that training on backward masking lowered the two-flash threshold. Based on that finding we wanted to see whether training would affect other measures of persistence. We began with a paradigm developed by Sperling (1967) and examined in detail by Efron (1970). In this paradigm, a subject synchronizes the offset of a visual target stimulus with the onset of a second stimulus, either another visual stimulus or an auditory click. Investigators found that subjects set the click at a substantial distance after the offset of the target. This offset-to-click distance is used as a measure of visible persistence.

Estimates of visible persistence are influenced by dark adaptation, target intensity, and target duration. Somewhat surprisingly, Efron found that visible persistence is an inverse function of both target intensity and target duration. As target duration increased from 10 to 150 ms, estimates of persistence decreased from 120 to 0 ms. (Using a visual second stimulus rather than a click, persistence decreases from 230 to 100 ms.) Similar inverse functions have been recorded from single cells in cat visual cortex (Duysens, Orban, Cremieux, & Maes, 1981).

We used a procedure similar to Efron's in two experiments. The first was a control experiment to confirm that we could replicate Efron's inverse relationships. Six subjects participated in the experiment. We used two intensities of an LED (0.41 cd/m^2 and 8.71 cd/m^2) and two exposure durations (60 and 120 ms). Subjects were seated in a darkened room and allowed 5 minutes for dark adaptation. They were asked to adjust a chin rest to a comfortable height for viewing a panel containing nine LEDs. The center LED was kept on at a low level of luminance ($.051$ cd/m^2) to serve as a fixation point. A panel, tilted at a $45°$ angle and containing three microswitches, was placed in front of the subjects. Each trial began with a 1000 cycle tone. One second after the tone, the LED $10°$ into the right or left visual field flashed for the designated duration. At some random interval after the offset of the flash, a 5 ms click sounded. The subject responded with the righthand switch (of the two middle switches) to move the click farther from the offset of the flash and the lefthand switch to move it closer. The subject was instructed to go back and forth past the point of apparent synchrony. At the beginning, the click moved 10 ms with each button press; following the fourth reversal of direction, the click moved in 1 ms steps; following the seventh reversal, the trial was terminated and the estimate of persistence recorded. Subjects provided 12 estimates of persistence in each of the four conditions.

The results of the first synchrony experiment are presented in Fig. 7.2. We replicated the inverse relationships of Efron, although the luminance effect did not reach significance. The effect of duration was consistent across subjects and highly significant ($F[1,5] = 32.67$, $p < .01$); the effect of luminance was not significant ($F[1,5] = 2.33$, $p > .05$); there was no interaction.

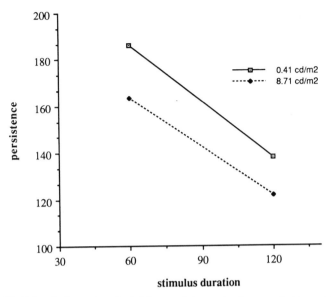

FIG. 7.2. Judgments of visible persistence in the synchrony paradigm as a function of duration and luminance.

In the main synchrony experiment, we obtained persistence estimates from
four subjects on the first day, trained the subjects for 8 days on backward pattern
masking (using the same procedure as Wolford, Marchak, & Hughes, 1988) and,
finally, collected new persistence estimates. Based on the previous experiment,
we used two durations for the synchrony judgments, but held the luminance
constant at 3.79 cd/m².

The subjects improved on the backward masking paradigm from an average of
36% correct on the first day of training to an average of 71% correct on the eighth
day. This is the range of improvement that we have observed in similar experiments. The results of the synchrony judgments are presented in Fig. 7.3. We
replicated the duration effect from the control experiment and Efron ($F[1,3] =
12.63$, $p < .05$). Importantly, there was a significant transfer effect from the
training on backward masking ($F[1,3] = 12.75$, $p < .05$). Persistence estimates
averaged 150 ms before training and dropped to 139 ms after training.

The results of the synchrony experiments were consistent with our speculation
that the improvement that occurs with training on backward masking might result
from a decrease in visual persistence. We had some reservations about the paradigm, though. Subjects found the task extremely difficult and had little or no
confidence in their synchrony judgments. Although the averages of the subjects'
12 judgments in each condition were consistent and sensible, the variation within
the 12 judgments was quite large. In addition, the synchrony paradigm is vul-

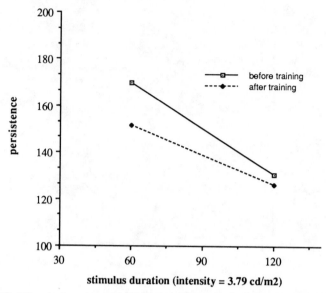

FIG. 7.3. Judgments of visible persistence in the synchrony paradigm as a function of duration and practice.

nerable to explanations in terms of criterion shifts. There is no correct answer,
making it difficult to employ catch trials or a signal detection analysis. It is
possible, therefore, that subjects' criteria change with practice rather than their
persistence. We, therefore, pursued our exploration of visible persistence using
an integration paradigm developed by DiLollo and his colleagues (DiLollo,
1980).

DiLollo's Integration Paradigm

In DiLollo's integration paradigm, subjects are presented with a matrix of small
squares in two successive displays, half of the squares per display. For example,
12 cells from a 5 × 5 matrix of squares are presented for a specified duration,
followed by a blank interval, followed by a different set of 12 squares from the
matrix. The subjects' task is to identify the one square that was not presented in
either the leading or trailing display. If the blank interval is sufficiently short, it
appears as if 24 of the squares are present simultaneously and the decision is
easy. As the delay increases, it begins to appear as if many squares are missing
and performance drops.

All of the standard features of visible persistence are evident in the DiLollo
paradigm. Performance decreases as the duration of the leading flash increases,
performance decreases as the intensity of the leading flash is increased, and

performance decreases as the delay between the leading and trailing display is increased. Dixon and DiLollo (1989) also showed that performance decreases as the duration of the trailing display is increased. (In a similar fashion, Kelly [1971] showed that the two-flash threshold decreased as the duration of the second flash was increased.) The integration paradigm minimizes the problems with the synchrony paradigm already mentioned. There is a correct answer on each trial, performance is stable, subjects understand the paradigm, and the influence of criterion shifts is minimized.

On the surface, backward pattern masking is the opposite of the integration paradigm: performance increases as target duration increases and performance increases as the delay between the target and mask increases. Our goal over the remaining experiments was to compare performance with the same subjects on the backward masking and integration paradigms and to examine the effect of variables on backward masking that are known to influence the integration paradigm. We predicted that if visible persistence plays a role in backward pattern masking and the practice effect, then transfer between the two paradigms should be negative and variables should affect performance on the two paradigms in opposite ways.

Transfer Between Masking and Integration.   We began by looking for negative transfer between the two paradigms. If practice on backward masking leads to finer temporal resolution, then practice on backward masking should hurt performance on any task requiring integration. There were two groups: One group was tested on the first day on the integration paradigm, then trained for 6 days on backward masking, and finally tested again on the integration paradigm. The second group had the reverse order. Both paradigms were implemented on a Mac II; all displays were black on white.

The procedure for the backward masking sessions was similar to those of the earlier experiments. Each session consisted of 160 trials. The SOA was randomly varied among 30, 45, and 60 ms[1]. Each trial began with a fixation point; subjects initiated each trial with a keypress. The keypress was followed by a target consisting of three consonants (each .32° by .40°), centered on the fixation point. Thirty, 45, or 60 ms after the onset of the target, a mask consisting of three noise characters was presented. Subjects then typed in the three target letters, guessing when necessary. Feedback on accuracy was provided after each block of 32 trials.

The display for the integration paradigm consisted of a 4 by 4 matrix of small squares. The individual squares were .45° by .34° and the entire matrix was 4.35° by 3.20°. Each of the 160 trials per session began with a fixation point, and subjects initiated the trial with a keypress. Following the keypress, the subject

---

[1]The Mac II uses a refresh rate of 68 hz or approximately 15 msec per refresh.

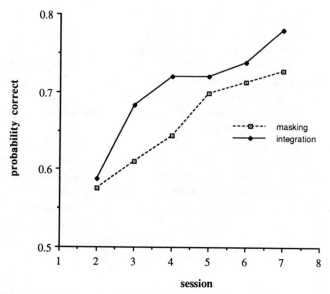

FIG. 7.4. A comparison of improvement in the masking and integration paradigms over days.

was shown eight of the small squares for 30 ms followed by a blank interval randomly chosen from 15, 30, or 45 ms. After the blank interval, the subject was shown seven of the remaining small squares for 30 ms. After a delay of 1000 ms the entire 4 by 4 matrix was presented and subjects were instructed to indicate the missing square with the mouse.

Our first question was whether practice effects would be obtained in the integration paradigm. Figure 7.4 shows the learning curves for the masking and integration paradigms obtained during the middle 6 days. Performance improved approximately the same amount in each paradigm. The best fit log regression line was fitted to each subject's performance over the middle 6 days. The slopes of those regression lines were significantly greater than zero for both paradigms (t[5] = 3.54, p < .05, for masking and t[5] = 6.07, p < .05, for integration). The slopes for the two paradigms did not differ from one another (t[10] = .22, p > .10).

Figure 7.5 shows the transfer between the two paradigms. There was no evidence for negative (or positive) transfer. Performance increased from the first day to the transfer day in both paradigms between 3% and 4%, but the increases were not significant (t[5] = 1.16, p > .10, for masking and t[5] = .39, p > .10, for integration).

Intermixed Paradigms. Although this experiment provided no evidence of negative transfer between paradigms, we pursued the question with a second

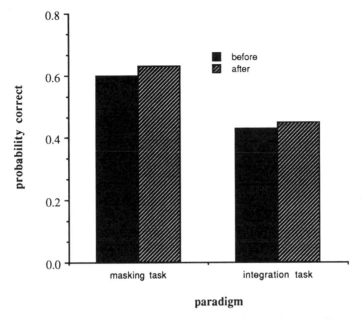

FIG. 7.5.   Transfer between the masking and integration paradigms.

experiment. We had subjects participate in a task in which backward masking and integration were randomly intermixed on a trial-by-trial basis. The question was whether subjects would improve at both paradigms over days. If improvement on backward masking was due, in part, to a decrease in visible persistence, and if improvement in integration was due, in part, from an increase in visible persistence, then it should be difficult to improve at both tasks when they are intermixed.

There were 240 trials on each day for a period of 4 days. Each trial began with a fixation cross centered on the screen. The four subjects initiated each trail with a keypress. Following the keypress, the fixation cross was replaced with equal probability with a backward masking trial or an integration trial. No cues were available to the subject as to the trial type until the target or leading display of squares appeared. The displays and procedures for the two tasks were identical to those used in the preceding experiment.

The results of the experiment were quite clear. There was significant improvement across days ($F[3,9] = 8.21$, $p < .01$) and no interaction between days and tasks ($F < 1$). There was a highly significant difference between the two tasks, but that probably had to do with the choice of various parameters ($F[1,3] = 31.95$, $p < .01$). The learning curves from the two tasks are presented in Fig. 7.6. Clearly, the intermixing of the two tasks did not prevent normal improvement in either task.

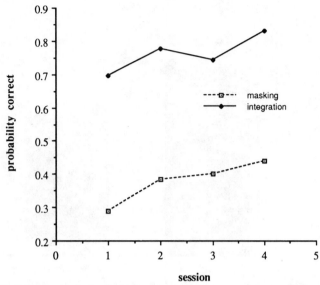

FIG. 7.6. A comparison of improvement in the masking and integration paradigms over days when the two are randomly intermixed.

Mask and Target Intensity.   At this point it seemed a little bit like beating a dead horse, but we wanted to best backward masking for the two defining characteristics of visible persistence. In this experiment, we varied the intensity of the target and mask. Again, if visible persistence limits performance in backward masking then we would predict that increased target intensity would lead to better performance, as increased intensity leads to shorter persistence. To parallel the integration paradigm, we set the target and mask at equal intensities. Ignoring persistence, we would predict that increased target intensity would improve performance, but we would also predict that increased mask intensity would lead to a decrease in performance. With the two varied together, it is difficult to know what to predict if we don't consider persistence.

Target intensity varied randomly among three levels: 11.18cd/m2, 41.1 6cd/m2, and 79.92 cd/m2; the background was set at 0.3cd/m2. SOA was chosen randomly from either 30 or 60 ms on each trial. Ten subjects were run for a single session of 192 trials. The remaining details were as in the previous masking experiments.

The results are presented in Fig. 7.7. SOA had its usual big effect ($F[1,9] = 235.06$, $p < .01$). The effect of luminance was also significant but in the opposite direction from the visible persistence prediction (multivariate $F[2,8] = 10.49$, $p < .01$). There was no interaction, $F < 1$. There was only a small effect of mask luminance and it was opposite to the predicted direction. The significant dif-

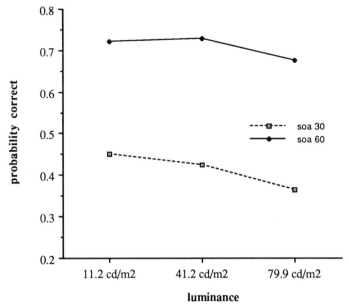

FIG. 7.7.   Performance on backward masking as a function of luminance and SOA.

ference was attributable to the drop in performance at the highest luminance. We believe that there was some modest blur at the highest luminance that eliminated some of the high spatial frequencies.

Mask Duration.   As mentioned, both two-flash thresholds and performance on the integration paradigm decrease as the duration of the second flash increases. Although data on the effect of mask duration in backward pattern masking may exist, we are not aware of it. If visible persistence is one of the causes of backward pattern masking, then increasing the duration of the mask might lead to increased performance. Our intuitions suggested that this hypothesis was implausible, and that increased duration of the mask should increase the effectiveness of the mask and reduce performance.

The experiment was similar to the preceding masking experiments. Subjects participated in one session of 160 trials. The SOA was set at 45 ms. Mask duration varied among 15, 30, 120, and 450 ms. Mask durations were randomly intermixed. Each trial began with a fixation point; subjects initiated each trial with a keypress. The keypress was followed by a target consisting of three consonants, centered on the fixation point. Forty-five ms after the onset of the target, a mask consisting of three noise characters appeared for the specified duration. Subjects, then, typed in the three target letters.

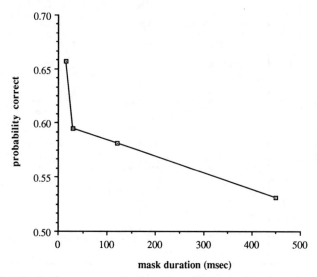

FIG. 7.8. Performance on backward masking as a function of mask duration.

The results of this experiment appear in Fig. 7.8. As is apparent, our intuitions were much saner than our hypothesis. Performance decreased significantly as mask duration increased (multivariate $F[3,9] = 23.98$, $p < .01$). The effect was consistent across subjects and was in the opposite direction of the prediction based on visible persistence.

CONCLUSIONS

We began with some suggestive evidence that practice effects in backward masking might result from a change in visible persistence with practice. That evidence consisted primarily of a significant drop in two-flash thresholds and a reduction in persistence judgments using the synchrony paradigm after training on backward masking. The evidence from both of those paradigms is somewhat indirect and possibly subject to criterion changes. We had also shown that focal attention plays an important role in the practice effect.

In the remaining research presented here we attempted to test the role of visible persistence more directly. We predicted that persistence might play a negative role in backward masking such that longer persistence led to worse performance. We predicted that if visible persistence were involved in backward masking, then practice on backward masking should interact negatively with the integration paradigm as DiLollo has shown that visible persistence plays a major role in that paradigm. We failed to find any relationship or transfer between the two paradigms. We also tested backward masking for the defining characteristics of visible persistence: inverse relationships between persistence and the variables of duration and intensity. We found significant effects in the opposite direction. Based on these direct tests, we conclude that visible persistence plays little role in backward masking or in the practice effects that we observe.

While preparing this chapter we came across some references that helped put our practice effects into perspective. Boring (1942) discusses a number of German scientists from the 19th century who showed that the two-point limen in touch decreased with practice (Camerer, 1881; Tawney, 1897; Volkmann, 1858; all cited in Boring, 1942, p. 480). The scientists at that time following Weber were interested in measuring two-point limens at different points on the body. They showed that there were huge differences in the two-point threshold at different locations ranging from a few millimeters at the fingertips to 100 millimeters at the shoulder. They assumed that their measurements reflected the underlying density of pressure-sensitive nerve endings. These investigators found the robust practice effects quite disturbing. Tawney (1897), for instance, measured two-point limens over 20 successive days and observed gradual decreases over days as large as from 50 mm to .5 mm (two orders of magnitude). It's difficult to imagine that the density of nerve endings changes with practice! It's also difficult to call a threshold that changes so dramatically with practice a threshold.

If visible persistence and the density of nerve endings don't change, what does lead to these robust effects in such paradigms as backward masking in vision and two-point thresholds in touch? Coincidentally given the nature of this volume, we are beginning to develop a model that could be viewed as a variant of a stimulus sampling model to describe our data and related data. The basic premise of the model is that the stimulus consists of a number of elements; the elements certainly being smaller than individual letters. Further, the elements are not equally easy to sample. Imagine a can filled with mixed nuts. In such a can, the larger nuts have a tendency to be on top and the smaller nuts sink to the bottom. In order to get some of the smaller nuts you have to exert some effort and dig fairly deep.

In a task like the two-point threshold for touch, we assume that there are a variety of cues that signal the presence of two versus one stimulus, but some of the cues are more obvious than others. The role of attention (or concentration) is to yield a deeper sampling of the cues so that some of the subtler (smaller, fainter, less valid, etc.) cues are included in the sample. The link between the subtler cues and the correct answer might be less obvious and, therefore, requires learning or practice. Practice effects would result from learning to associate less obvious cues with the correct response and attention would be required to include the less obvious cues in the sample.

Two questions, at least, come to mind about the developing model. One is: What type of feedback is required to allow the association between the less obvious cues and the correct answer? The second is: Why do some tasks *not* yield practice effects? Most of the tasks that we are interested in do not provide trial-by-trial feedback on the correct answer. Those same tasks, however, include trials that vary in difficulty. On some two-point trials the stimuli are far apart and the judgment is easy. If the subject is paying attention and including less obvious cues on the sample set on those easier trials, then there are opportunities to form the necessary associations. We are less certain about the tasks that do not yield robust practice effects. Possibly the tasks either do not provide a range of possible cues or sufficient opportunities to associate the cues with the correct answer. If the former were true, we would predict that attention would not play an important role in tasks that did not yield practice effects. We are currently testing those ideas.

ACKNOWLEDGMENT

This material is based on work supported by the National Science Foundation under Grant No. BNS-8820653. We would like to thank William Cohen for carrying out the first experiment, Carol Fowler for her helpful comments on the manuscript, and Bennett Schwartz for his assistance with the final experiment.

REFERENCES

Baylor, D. A. (1987). Photoreceptor signals and vision: Proctor lecture. *Investigative Opthamology & Visual Science, 28,* 30–49.

Boring, E. G. (1942). *Sensation and perception in the history of experimental psychology.* New York: D. Appleton-Century.

Coltheart, M. (1980). Iconic memory and visible persistence. *Perception & Psychophysics, 27,* 1, 83–228.

DiLollo, V. (1980).Temporal integration in visual memory. *Journal of Experimental Psychology: General, 109,* 75–97.

Dixon, P., & DiLollo, V. (1989). Visual integration and stimulus duration. Paper presented at the annual meeting of the Psychonomic Society, Atlanta, GA.

Duysens, J., Orban, G. A. Cremieux, J., & Maes, M. (1985). Visual cortical correlates of visible persistence. *Vision Research, 25,* 171–178.

Efron, R. (1970). The relationship between the duration of a stimulus and the duration of a perception. *Neuropsychologica, 8,* 37–55.

Eriksen, C. W., & Schultz, D. W. (1978). Temporal factors in visual information processing. In J. Requin (Ed.), *Attention and performance, VII* (pp. 3–23). Hillsdale, NJ: Lawrence Erlbaum Associates.

Estes, W. K. (1965). A technique for assessing variability of perceptual span. *Proceedings of the National Academy of Sciences, 54,* 403–407.

Estes, W. K. (1972). Interactions of signal and background variables in visual processing. *Perception and Psychophysics, 12,* 278–286.

Estes, W. K., & Taylor, H. A. (1964). A detection method and probabilistic models for assessing information processing from brief visual displays. *Proceedings of the National Academy of Sciences, 52,* 446–454.

Estes, W. K., & Taylor, H. A. (1966). Visual detection in relation to display size and redundancy of critical elements. *Perception and Psychophysics, 1*, 9–16.

Estes, W. K., & Wessel, D. L. (1966). Reaction time in relation to display size and correctness of response in forced-choice visual signal detection. *Perception and Psychophysics, 1*, 369–373.

Gardner, G. T. (1973). Evidence for independent parallel channels in tachistoscopic perception. *Cognitive Psychology, 4*, 130–155.

Gibson, E. J. (1953). Improvement in perceptual judgments as a function of controlled practice or training. *Psychological Bulletin, 50*, 401–431.

Gibson, E. J. (1969). *Principles of perceptual learning and development*. New York: Appleton-Century-Crofts.

Green, D. M., & Swets, J. A. (1964). *Signal detection theory and psychophysics*. New York: Wiley.

Hertzog, C. K., Williams, M. V., & Walsh, D. A. (1976). The effects of practice on age differences in central perceptual processing. *Journal of Gerontology, 31*, 428–433.

Hoyman, L., & Kelsey, J. E. (1977). Facilitation of flicker discriminability by electrical simulation of mesencephalic reticular formation of the rat. *Journal of Comparative and Physiological Psychology, 91*, 951–961.

Johnson, C. A., & Leibowitz, H. W. (1979). Practice effects for visual resolution in the periphery. *Perception and Psychophysics, 25*, 439–442.

Kelly, D. H. (1971). Theory of flicker and transient responses. 1. Uniform fields. *Journal of the Optical Society of America, 61*, 537–546.

LaBerge, D., & Samuels, S. J. (1974). Toward a theory of automatic information processing in reading. *Cognitive Psychology, 6*, 293–323.

Lindsley, D. B. (1958). The reticular system and perceptual discrimination. In H. H. Jasper (Ed.), *Reticular formation of the brain* (pp. 513–534). Boston: Little, Brown.

McKee, S. P., & Westheimer, G. (1978). Improvement in vernier acuity with practice. *Perception and Psychophysics, 24*, 258–262.

Michaels, C. F., & Turvey, M. T. (1979). Central sources of visual masking: Indexing structures supporting seeing at a single, brief glance. *Psychological Research, 41*, 1–61.

Moore, B. C. J., Glasberg, B. R., Donaldson, E., McPherson, T., & Plack, C. J. (1989). Detection of temporal gaps in sinusoids by normally hearing and hearing-impaired subjects. *The Journal of the Acoustical Society of America, 85*, 266–275.

Moruzzi, G., & Magoun, H. W. (1949). Brain stem reticular formation and activation of the EEG. *Electroencephalography and Clinical Neurophysiology, 1*, 455–473.

Posner, M. L. (1978). *Chronometric explorations of mind*. Hillsdale, NJ: Lawrence Erlbaum Associates.

Rumelhart, D. E. (1970). A multicomponent theory of the perception of briefly exposed visual displays. *Journal of Mathematical Psychology, 7*, 191–218.

Salthouse, T. A., & Prill, K. (1983). Analysis of a perceptual skill. *Journal of Experimental Psychology: Human Perception and Performance, 9*, 607–621.

Salthouse, T. A., & Somberg, B. L. (1982). Skilled performance: Effects of adult age and experience on elementary processing. *Journal of Experimental Psychology: General, 111*, 1, 76–207.

Schiller, P. H. (1965). Monoptic and dichoptic visual masking by patterns and flashes. *Journal of Experimental Psychology, 69*, 193–199.

Schiller, P. H., & Wiener, M. (1963). Monoptic and dichoptic visual masking. *Journal of Experimental Psychology, 66*, 386–393.

Shiffrin, R. M., & Geisler, W. S. (1973). Visual recognition in a theory of information processing. In R. L. Solso (Ed.), *Contemporary issues in cognitive psychology: The Loyola symposium* (53–101). Washington, D. C.: V. H. Winston & Sons.

Shiffrin, R. M., & Schneider, W. (1977). Controlled and automatic human information processing: 11. Perceptual learning, automatic attending, and a general theory. *Psychological Review, 84*, 127–190.

Sperling, G. (1960). The information available in brief visual presentations. *Psychological Monographs, 74*, no. 11.

Sperling, G. (1967). Successive approximations to a model for short-term memory. *Acta Psychologica, 27*, 285–292.

Turvey, M. T. (1973). On peripheral and central processes in vision: Inferences from an information-processing analysis of masking with patterned stimuli. *Psychological Review, 80*, 1–52.

Vierck, C. J. (1965). Reticular stimulation and generalized drive. *Experimental Neurology, 12*, 463–467.

Ward, T. B., & Ross, L. E. (1977). Laterality differences and practice effects under central backward masking conditions. *Memory and Cognition, 5*, 221–226.

Wolford, G. (1975). Perturbation model for letter identification. *Psychological Review, 82*, 184–199.

Wolford, G., & Chambers, L. (1983). Lateral masking as a function of spacing. *Perception and Psychophysics, 33*, 129–138.

Wolford, G., & Chambers, L. (1984). Contour interaction as a function of retinal eccentricity. *Perception and Psychophysics, 36*, 457–460.

Wolford, G., & Hollingsworth, S. (1974). Evidence that short-term memory is not the limiting factor in tachistoscopic full report procedure. *Memory & Cognition, 2*, 796–800.

Wolford, G., Marchak, F., & Hughes, H. C. (1988). Practice effects in backward masking. *Journal of Experimental Psychology: Human Perception and Performance, 4*, 101–112.

Wolford, G., & Porter, G. (1976). Simultaneous and sequential presentation of visual arrays. Paper presented at the annual meeting of the Psychonomic Society, St. Louis, MO.

Wolford G., Schwartz, B., & Kim, H-Y. (1991). The role of attention in the practice effect with visual backward masking. Manuscript submitted for publication.

Wolford, G., Wessel, D., & Estes, W. (1968). Further evidence concerning scanning and sampling assumptions of visual detection models. *Perception and Psychophysics, 3*, 439–444.

8 Category Membership, Similarity, and Naive Induction

Edward E. Smith
Alejandro Lopez
University of Michigan

Daniel Osherson
I.D.I.A.P.

A question of continuing concern to psychology is how people make predictions about uncertain events. One line of research on this question has its origins in studies of learning and memory, and focuses on cases in which people have had ample opportunity to observe the relative frequencies of the uncertain events. This tradition is exemplified by Estes' (1976) cognitive analysis of probability learning, which holds that judgments of probability are based on judgments of frequency. Another line of research has its roots in decision theory and classical studies of induction, and focuses on cases in which people base their probability judgments more on the contents of the events than on their relative frequencies. Within psychology this tradition is illustrated by the work of Kahneman and Tversky (e.g., 1973). The work that we present here is more closely aligned with the decision-induction tradition, though it is informed by the learning-memory tradition as well.

Our starting point is that many probabilistic predictions—or "inductive inferences" as we refer to them—are based on categories. An obvious way in which categories support inductive inferences is that if we know that an object belongs to a category we can infer that the object has the properties that characterize the category. For example, if we know that a particular creature is a bird, we may infer that it flies and nests in trees. A second way in which categories figure in inductive reasoning is that if we know that some members of a category have a particular property, we can infer that other members of the category also have the property. For example, if we know that robins and bluejays have sesamoid bones, we may infer that sparrows do too (or with less certainty, that all birds have sesamoid bones). It is this second kind of category-based induction that is of concern in the present chapter.

Category-based induction develops early. This fact was established by an experiment of Gelman and Markman's (1986), which is illustrated as follows. Four-year-old children were told that a pictured flamingo feeds its young mashed food, whereas a pictured bat feeds its young milk. They were then shown a pictured blackbird, whose appearance resembled the bat more than the flamingo. When asked what the blackbird fed its young, the children favored the flamingo-like mashed food rather than the bat-like milk. Very early in development, then, we know that members of the same category are likely to share many invisible properties even when the members do not physically resemble one another.

Gelman and Markman concluded that category membership rather than perceptual similarity governed the inferences they observed. This cannot be the whole story, though. In an earlier study, Rips (1975) had demonstrated that when adults draw an inference from one category member to another, the judged strength of their inference increases with the overall similarity of the members involved; for example, subjects are more willing to conclude that sparrows have some particular property when told that robins have it than when told that geese do. And Gelman and Markman (1987), in a follow-up to the study mentioned earlier, found results like those of Rips with four-year-olds.

Our goal is to provide a detailed account of category-based induction, one that will reconcile the contributions of similarity and category membership. Such an account should include on the empirical side a determination of the factors that affect category-based induction, and on the theoretical side a specification of the mental computations that underlie the inductions. In what follows, we report some progress that we have made on this goal. (A good deal of what we report is based on the work presented in Osherson, Smith, Wilkie, Lopez, & Shafir, 1990; the interested reader should consult that work for details.)

To structure our report, we must introduce some terminology and distinctions. Note first that any inductive inference can be characterized as an argument, where the known beliefs used to derive the inference are the *premises* of the argument and the inference itself is the *conclusion* of the argument. To illustrate, two of the inferences about birds mentioned earlier amount to the following arguments (where statements above the line are premises, and the one below the line is the conclusion):

1. Robins have sesamoid bones
   Bluejays have sesamoid bones
   Sparrows have sesamoid bones
2. Robins have sesamoid bones
   Bluejays have sesamoid bones
   All birds have sesamoid bones

Arguments like Argument 1 are distinguished by the fact that the category in their conclusion, SPARROW, is at the same hierarchical level as the categories in their premises, ROBIN and BLUEJAY (we use capitals to indicate categories).

Such arguments are said to be "specific." In contrast, in Argument 2 the conclusion category, BIRD, is at a more abstract level than the premise categories, and in fact includes the premise categories as proper subsets. Such an argument is said to be "general." Intuitively, it seems that specific and general arguments may be evaluated by somewhat different psychological processes, and for this reason we keep them distinct.[1,2]

A second distinction concerns the property in Arguments 1 and 2. *Having sesamoid bones* is a plausible (though not necessarily true) biological property of animals. It is not a property that most people know much about. Such plausible but unfamiliar properties are referred to as "blank properties"; they are to be distinguished from nonblank properties like *eats insects,* about which we have many prior beliefs. Because our goal in the research we report here is to focus on the role of categories in induction, we are concerned only with blank properties.

With this as background we can state our agenda. In the next section we focus on general arguments. We first demonstrate some factors that influence how people evaluate general arguments, then present a model of the evaluation of general arguments, and lastly provide an experimental test of the model. In the third section we turn our attention to specific arguments. First we extend the model for general arguments to specific ones. Next we show how the extended model can handle factors that affect how people evaluate specific arguments, and then we provide an experimental test of the extended model. In the fourth and final section, we consider some alternative explanations of our results.

EVALUATION OF GENERAL ARGUMENTS

Factors that Affect Evaluation

Of interest here are four phenomena, where each one demonstrates a particular factor that affects the evaluation—that is, the judged strength—of a general argument. Each phenomenon (factor) is described and illustrated by a contrasting pair of arguments. All these pairs were presented to 80 University of Michigan undergraduates who were asked to choose from each pair the argument whose premises "provide a better reason to believe its conclusion." To illustrate, one pair in the study consisted of:

3a. [73] Robins have a higher potassium concentration in
          their blood than humans
          All birds have a higher potassium concentration in
          their blood than humans

---

[1]A more stringent definition of a specific argument is: An argument is specific if any category that properly includes either one of the premise categories or the conclusion category properly includes all the others as well.

[2]Arguments that are neither general nor specific are referred to as "mixed." For a discussion of mixed arguments, see Osherson, Smith, Wilkie, Lopez, & Shafir (1990).

TABLE 8.1
Four Phenomena Involving General Arguments

Phenomenon	Stronger Argument	Weaker Argument
1. Premise typicality	ROBIN/BIRD [73]	PENGUIN/BIRD [7]
2. Conclusion homogeneity	BLUEJAY, FALCON/BIRD [75]	BLUEJAY, FALCON/ ANIMAL [5]
3. Premise diversity	HIPPO, HAMSTER/MAMMAL [59]	HIPPO, RHINO/ MAMMAL [21]
4. Premise monotonicity	HAWK, SPARROW, EAGLE/BIRD [75]	SPARROW, EAGLE/ BIRD [5]

Number of subjects preferring each argument is given in brackets.

3b. [7] Penguins have a higher potassium concentration in
their blood than humans
All birds have a higher potassium concentration in
their blood than humans

The numbers in brackets indicate the number of subjects that chose each argument. The two arguments differ only with respect to the typicality of their premise category, robins being more typical than penguins, and clearly the more typical the premise category, the stronger the argument; that is, the stronger the inductive inference, or generalization, that all birds have the property in question. This phenomenon indicates that Premise Typicality is one factor that affects category-based induction.

Table 8.1 lists four of the phenomena that emerged from the study. The first column of the table names the phenomenon, the second column gives the premise and conclusion categories used in the stronger of the two arguments, and the third column gives the premise and conclusion categories used in the weaker of the arguments. The arguments are presented in the format "Premise Category . . . / Conclusion Category," with the blank property being suppressed. The number of subjects choosing each argument is again in brackets. In all four cases, the difference between the stronger and weaker argument is significant at the .05 level by a two-tailed sign test.

After Premise Typicality the next factor listed in Table 8.1 is Conclusion Homogeneity; that is, for fixed premises, the more homogeneous the conclusion category, the stronger the argument. For example, the fact that both bluejays and falcons require vitamin K provides more inductive support for all birds requiring vitamin K than for all animals requiring it, where BIRD is a more homogeneous category than ANIMAL. Conclusion Homogeneity may reduce to Premise Typicality in that a given premise category is usually more typical of a homogenous category than of a variable one. The third phenomenon in Table 8.1, however, makes it clear that more than typicality is involved in category-based induction. This phenomenon shows that the more diverse, or dissimilar, the premise categories, the stronger the inductive inference. Hippos and hamsters having some property provides more inductive support for all mammals having it than does hippos and rhinos having the property. This is true even though hamsters are less typical of MAMMAL than are rhinos. In this case, the factor of Premise Diversity has overwhelmed that of Premise Typicality.[3] The final phenomenon in Table 8.1 is Premise Monotonicity. It says: the more premise categories that have a particular property, the stronger the inductive inference to the conclusion category.

The Coverage Model

The Notion of Coverage.   The model that we have developed to account for these phenomena centers on the notion of *coverage*. To gain an intuitive grasp of this notion, a spatial metaphor may be helpful. Figure 8.1 contains a two-dimensional representation of the similarities between various instances of the concept FRUIT, and between the instances and the concept itself. (The representation was obtained by Tversky and Hutchinson, 1986, by applying standard multidimensional scaling techniques to pairwise similarity ratings.) Suppose you were interested in whether all fruits had a particular property but could examine only a limited number of instances. If you could examine just one instance, it is likely that you would choose a typical instance like APPLE or PLUM. This is because typical instances are close to the category itself, and, on average, are relatively close to all other instances. So you would be more confident that all FRUIT have a particular property if you know that APPLE has it than if you know that OLIVE has it. Now suppose you could examine another instance. Should it also be typical? Intuition suggests not, that, instead, you would choose an instance in a different region of the space, such as GRAPEFRUIT or BLUEBERRY (see Fig. 8.1). The first instance you selected already covers the center of the space, and now you want *coverage* elsewhere. The idea of coverage, then, is that you will be more confident about an inference to a general category to the extent that any member of that category is covered by at least one known case.

The last statement may be rephrased as follows: You will be more confident about an inference to a conclusion category to the extent that any member of that category is *similar* to at least one premise category. This phrasing allows us to define the notion of coverage algebraically. Let $CAT(P_1) \ldots CAT(P_m)/CAT(C)$ be an argument with premise categories $CAT(P_1) \ldots CAT(P_m)$ and general conclusion category $CAT(C)$. Furthermore, let $c_1 \ldots c_n$ be instances of $Cat(C)$

---

[3]The factor of premise diversity is closely related to the notion of diversity of evidence, which figures in philosophy of science treatments of normative inference procedures like Bayes Theorem. For a discussion of this point, see Lopez (1989).

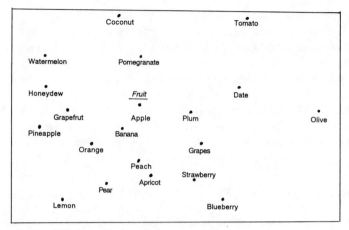

FIG. 8.1.   A two-dimensional space for representing the similarity relations among 20 instances of fruit and FRUIT itself. From Tversky and
Hutchinson (1986).

that a person evaluating the argument tends to think of. And let $SIM(CAT(P_i), c_j)$
be the similarity between premise-category P_i and conclusion-category-instance
c_j. Then the coverage of an argument, which we denote by
$COV(CAT(P_1) \ldots CAT(P_m); CAT(C))$, is defined as the average of:

$$MAX(SIM(CAT(P_1), c_1),\ldots,SIM(CAT(P_m), c_1))$$
$$MAX(SIM(CAT(P_1), c_2),\ldots,SIM(CAT(P_m), c_2))$$
$$\bullet$$
$$\bullet$$
$$\bullet$$
$$MAX(SIM(CAT(P_1), c_n),\ldots,SIM(CAT(P_m), c_n)).$$

In words: (a) sample some instance of the conclusion category; (b) determine its
similarity to each of the premise categories, and take the maximum similarity; (c)
repeat these two steps for other instances of the conclusion category that you
happen to think of; and (d) when you are done sampling, take an average of the
maximum similarities that you have calculated. Note that (b) determines the
extent to which an instance of the conclusion category is similar to at least one
premise category; so the use of a MAX similarity function is at the heart of the
coverage notion. Coverage, then, is the average maximum similarity between
(sampled) conclusion-category instances and premise categories.

An example may be helpful. Suppose you are evaluating an argument of the
form, SPARROW, CARDINAL/SONGBIRD, and that the songbirds you happen
to think of include: ROBIN, BLUEJAY, SPARROW, and ORIOLE. Then
COV(SPARROW, CARDINAL; SONGBIRD) equals the average of:

MAX(SIM(SPARROW, ROBIN), SIM(CARDINAL, ROBIN))
MAX(SIM(SPARROW, BLUEJAY), SIM(CARDINAL, BLUEJAY))
MAX(SIM(SPARROW, SPARROW), SIM(CARDINAL, SPARROW))
MAX(SIM(SPARROW, ORIOLE), SIM(CARDINAL, ORIOLE)).

Our intuitions are that the preceding reduces to the average of:

SIM(SPARROW, ROBIN)
SIM(CARDINAL, BLUEJAY)
SIM(SPARROW, SPARROW)
SIM(CARDINAL, ORIOLE).

Note that coverage may be interpreted as the similarity of categories at one hierarchical level to a category at a higher level. Thus COV(SPARROW, CARDINAL; SONGBIRD) gives the similarity of SPARROW and CARDINAL on the one hand, to SONGBIRD on the other, where similarity is computed by a Maximum rule. Indeed, what we term $COV(CAT(P_1),...,CAT(P_m)$; $CAT(C))$, Osherson, Smith, Wilkie, Lopez, & Sharif (1990) term $SIM(CAT(P_1),...,CAT(Pm)$; $CAT(C))$. We later exploit this equivalence between coverage and similarity when we explain certain phenomena.[4]

One more point about coverage. In the special case of single-premise arguments, P/C, there is no maximum to consider, and COV(CAT(P); CAT(C)) is simply the average of:

$$SIM(CAT(P), c_1)$$
$$SIM(CAT(P), c_2)$$
$$\bullet$$
$$\bullet$$
$$\bullet$$
$$SIM(CAT(P), c_n).$$

In words, coverage is simply the average similarity of the premise category to conclusion-category instances. Returning to the preceding example, if ROBIN were the only premise category, the coverage of ROBIN in SONGBIRD would simply be ROBIN's average similarity to SONGBIRD instances. This, however, is how some researchers interpret the *typicality* of ROBIN in SONGBIRD (e.g., Smith & Medin, 1981; Tversky, 1977). Hence, for single-premise arguments, coverage reduces to typicality.

---

[4]In the Osherson, Smith, Wilkie, Lopez, & Shafir analysis, coverage is defined for a particular individual whereas in our treatment coverage is assumed to be the same for all individuals under consideration so as to facilitate exposition.

Application of the Coverage Model.   We now show that the coverage model predicts the four phenomena we described earlier. The first phenomenon was Premise Typicality. We demonstrated it by showing that an argument with premise category ROBIN and conclusion category BIRD is judged stronger than an argument with premise category PENGUIN and conclusion category BIRD; that is, ROBIN/BIRD > PENGUIN/BIRD. For the model to predict this result, the coverage of (ROBIN; BIRD) must exceed that of (PENGUIN; BIRD). As noted earlier, coverage for single-premise arguments reduces to typicality. For the model to predict the result of interest, then, the typicality of ROBIN in BIRD must exceed that of PENGUIN in BIRD. This, of course, is the case.

The second phenomena was Conclusion Homogeneity, and we demonstrated it by showing that the argument BLUEJAY, FALCON/BIRD is judged stronger than the argument BLUEJAY, FALCON/ANIMAL. Computation of coverage for the stronger argument would include terms such as,

MAX(SIM(BLUEJAY, ROBIN), SIM(FALCON, ROBIN)),

assuming that ROBIN is an available BIRD instance. In contrast, coverage for the weaker argument would include terms such as,

MAX(SIM(BLUEJAY, HORSE), SIM(FALCON, HORSE)),

assuming that HORSE is an available ANIMAL instance (ROBIN may not even be sampled in this case). Obviously the similarities will be higher in the former case than in the latter one, which predicts the phenomenon.

The third phenomenon was Premise Diversity, and we illustrated it by showing that HIPPO, HAMSTER/MAMMAL is stronger than HIPPO, RHINO/MAMMAL. Coverage for the stronger argument might include terms such as,

MAX(SIM(HIPPO, HORSE), SIM(HAMSTER, HORSE)), and
MAX(SIM(HIPPO, MOUSE), SIM(HAMSTER, MOUSE)).

Coverage for the weaker argument might include terms such as,

MAX(SIM(HIPPO, HORSE), SIM(RHINO, HORSE)), and
MAX(SIM(HIPPO, MOUSE), SIM(RHINO, MOUSE)).

When the sampled conclusion instance is HORSE, there should be little difference between the two arguments; that is, it is doubtful that RHINO is appreciably more similar to HORSE than HIPPO is. However, when the sampled instance is MOUSE, the maximum similarity will be greater in the more diverse argument because HAMSTER is more similar to MOUSE than RHINO is. To put it another way, because the two premises of the HIPPO, RHINO argument are very similar, the second premise does not really cover anything that is not already covered by the first premise. In contrast, because the premises of the HIPPO, HAMSTER argument are dissimilar, there will be some conclusion instances that are covered by the second premise but not by the first one. Considerations like these account for the Premise Diversity phenomenon.

The final phenomenon was Premise Monotonicity, which we illustrated by showing that HAWK, SPARROW, EAGLE/BIRD > SPARROW, EAGLE/ BIRD. Coverage for the stronger argument includes terms such as,

MAX(SIM(HAWK, ROBIN), SIM(SPARROW, ROBIN), SIM(EAGLE, ROBIN)),

whereas coverage for the weaker argument includes terms such as,

MAX(SIM(SPARROW, ROBIN), SIM(EAGLE, ROBIN)).

Because the former term properly includes the latter one, the value of the former term must always be at least as great as that of the latter one. That is, the addition of another premise to a general argument can never decrease its coverage. This consideration suffices to predict the phenomenon of interest.

An Experimental Test of the Model

Rationale.   The preceding derivations constitute prima facie support for the coverage model. However, the four phenomena involved are demonstrational in character and thus have certain limitations. For one thing, the two arguments in each pair were selected to show the phenomenon; that is, our sampling was biased. Another matter is that our derivation of strength differences between arguments relies on our own intuitions of similarity rather than on those of unbiased subjects. Finally, our derivations provide no indication of the *degree* of strength predicted by the model for various arguments; that is, the evidence from our four phenomena is qualitative rather than quantitative. To remedy these problems and provide a more rigorous test of the model, we performed an experiment that involved the evaluation of 15 different arguments, in which all of the arguments had MAMMAL as the conclusion category and an arbitrarily selected pair of mammals as the premise categories.

In the first part of the experiment, one group of subjects rated the similarity of pairs of mammals; these ratings were later used to estimate coverage of the relevant arguments. In the second part of the experiment, another group of subjects judged the strengths of 15 arguments. An argument's judged strength was correlated with its estimated coverage to determine how well the coverage model quantitatively describes the inductive judgments.

TABLE 8.2
Similarity Scores for Pairs of Mammals, along with Judged Strength and Estimated Coverage for the Corresponding General Arguments

Pair	Similarity	Strength	Coverage
DOG WOLF	.94	.41	.51
DOG MOUSE	.23	.64	.72
DOG HAMSTER	.35	.64	.72
DOG RHINO	.22	.67	.72
DOG HIPPO	.23	.67	.72
WOLF MOUSE	.25	.68	.72
WOLF HAMSTER	.24	.61	.72
WOLF RHINO	.25	.67	.71
WOLF HIPPO	.20	.68	.71
MOUSE HAMSTER	.91	.29	.46
MOUSE RHINO	.07	.72	.70
MOUSE HIPPO	.09	.80	.70
HAMSTER RHINO	.06	.75	.72
HAMSTER HIPPO	.08	.83	.72
RHINO HIPPO	.81	.28	.44

Procedure. The arguments were based on the category MAMMAL and a "base set" of six instances that were selected to vary in typicality. The set included DOG, WOLF, MOUSE, HAMSTER, RHINO, and HIPPO. In Part 1 of the experiment, the following rating procedure was employed. All 15 pairs of mammals drawn from the base set were typed on a single page in the following manner:

mice, dogs   Dissimilarity:_____

The subjects, 60 University of Michigan undergraduates, were asked to rate the dissimilarity of the mammals on a scale of 0 to 10 (0 for similar, 10 for dissimilar). In order that the ratings of different subjects weigh equally in the group average, a linear transformation was applied to the data of each subject so that the highest number assigned by that subject was 10 and the lowest was 0. Subsequent to this transformation, for each pair of mammals, the average dissimilarity rating was calculated and divided by 10. This number was then subtracted from 1 to yield similarity scores that run from 0 to 1. These similarity scores are presented in the second column of Table 8.2.

In Part 2 of the experiment, the procedure used was designed to obtain judgments of strength for arguments falling under the following schema,

X BLANK PRED.
Y BLANK PRED.
All mammals BLANK PRED,

where BLANK PRED is a dummy variable filled by a particular blank predicate. To create an argument that falls under this schema, X and Y are replaced by two distinct mammals from the base set and BLANK PRED is replaced by one of the following 15 blank predicates,

    have an ulnar artery

    need carbon for producing blood cells

    have three middle-ear ossicles

    need insulin to move glucose into their muscle cells

    produce THS by their pituitary

    regulate their coordination by their cerebellar system

    produce hydrochloric acid in their stomachs

    secrete antibodies in their mucus

    have 12 cranial nerves coming out of their brain stems

    have higher body temperature as newborns than as adults

    have enamel in their teeth

    have choroid membranes in their eyes

    have a left aortic arch

    have sesamoid bones

    have seven cervical vertebrae

Each subject evaluated 15 arguments falling under the stated schema, corresponding to the 15 possible pairs of distinct instances from the base set. Each argument involved a different blank predicate from the foregoing list. Across all subjects, the 15 blank predicates were counterbalanced so that each pair of premises occurred an equal number of times with each blank predicate.

The 15 arguments assigned to a subject were bound into a typewritten booklet. For each argument, subjects were asked to estimate the probability of the conclusion on the assumption that the premises were true. The arguments were to be evaluated independently of one another, and there was no time limit. The subjects were 30 University of Michigan undergraduates, none of whom had participated in Part 1 of the experiment.

The probability, or strength, ratings assigned to arguments that involved the same pair of mammals in their premises were averaged. The average strength ratings are presented in the third column of Table 8.2.

Results.   All arguments are of the form X,Y/MAMMAL. We determined the coverage of each argument by making the simplifying assumption that subjects sampled only the base set of mammals. The coverage of X,Y/MAMMAL is therefore given by the average of:

MAX(SIM(X, DOG), SIM(Y, DOG))
MAX(SIM(X, WOLF), SIM(Y, WOLF))
MAX(SIM(X, MOUSE), SIM(Y, MOUSE))
MAX(SIM(X, HAMSTER), SIM(Y, HAMSTER))
MAX(SIM(X, RHINO), SIM(Y, RHINO))
MAX(SIM(X, HIPPO), SIM(Y, HIPPO)),

where, for example, SIM (X, DOG) is the similarity score for the pair (X, DOG) obtained in Part 1. These estimated coverage scores are presented in the fourth column of Table 8.2. The correlation between coverage and the strength ratings of Part 2 is .92 ($N = 15$, $p < .01$). Clearly the model provides a satisfactory quantitative account of the data.

Replication. In an effort to increase the generality of our results, the preceding experiment was replicated in Spain, using University of Sevilla students as subjects. All the materials were translated into Spanish, and 30 subjects provided similarity ratings in Part 1 of the study, and 60 different subjects gave strength ratings in Part 2. The correlation between estimated coverage and judged strength of an argument was .76 ($N = 15$, $p < .01$).

EVALUATION OF SPECIFIC ARGUMENTS

Extension of the Model

Our concern now is with specific arguments, such as

4. Beavers require oxydilic acid for digestion
   Raccoons require oxydilic acid for digestion
   Bears require oxydilic acid for digestion

It seems likely that the judged strength of such an argument increases with the similarity of the premise categories to the conclusion category, and Rips (1975) has provided empirical evidence for this relation. We suspect, however, that people also consider in their reasoning the lowest-level general category that includes the premise and conclusion categories (MAMMAL in the case of Argument 4). That is, we suspect that people reason that bears have the property in question if beavers and raccoons do both because: (a) bears are similar to beavers or raccoons, and (b) bears, like beavers and raccoons, are mammals, and all mammals may have the property in question given that beavers and raccoons do. This dual-process view leads to the following claim. The judged strength of a specific argument increases with (a) the maximum similarity of the premise categories to the conclusion category, and (b) the coverage of the premise categories in the lowest-level category that includes the premise and conclusion categories. For example, the strength of Argument 4 is determined by: (a) the maximum similarity of BEAVER and RACCOON to BEAR, and (b) the coverage of BEAVER and RACCOON in the category MAMMAL.

This dual-process view extends the coverage idea to specific arguments. Because we have two distinct processes or terms—hereafter referred to as the "similarity" and "coverage" terms—we need to allow for the possibility that they are differentially weighted in determining the strength of a specific argument. Accordingly, we introduce a positive constant α ($0 \leq \alpha \leq 1$) that indicates the weight given to the similarity process: the weight given to the coverage process will simply be $1 - \alpha$. Our final model for the strength of specific arguments is given by:

$$(\alpha)MAX(SIM(CAT(P_1),CAT(C)),\dots,SIM(CAT(P_m),CAT(C)))+$$
$$(1 - \alpha)\ COV(CAT(P_1),\dots,CAT(P_m); \text{ Lowest Level Category That Includes}$$
$$CAT(P_1),\dots,CAT(P_m) \text{ and } CAT(C)).$$

The coverage term reduces to $(1 - \alpha)$ times the average maximum similarity between, on the one hand, premise categories and, on the other hand, sampled instances from the lowest-level category that includes the premise and conclusion categories. For example, the coverage term for Argument 4 reduces to $(1 - \alpha)$ times the average of terms like,

MAX(SIM(BEAVER, DOG), SIM(RACCOON, DOG))
MAX(SIM(BEAVER, HORSE), SIM(RACCOON, HORSE))
MAX(SIM(BEAVER, MOUSE), SIM(RACCOON, MOUSE))
and so on.

We refer to this final model as the "similarity-coverage" model of argument strength.[5]

The similarity-coverage model includes the coverage model for general arguments as a special case. For example, the argument BEAVER, RACCOON/MAMMAL, yields the similarity term,

(α) MAX(SIM(BEAVER, MAMMAL), SIM(RACCOON, MAMMAL)).

As noted earlier, coverage may be interpreted as specifying the similarity of lower-level categories on the one hand, to a higher level category on the other. So

---

[5]In Osherson, Smith, Wilkie, Lopez, & Shafir's (1990) analysis, α is defined for each individual. As before, we assume the same term for all individuals under consideration so as to facilitate exposition.

the preceding term can be shown to be equivalent to the coverage of BEAVER and RACCOON in MAMMAL. For this argument, then, we end up with,

$$(\alpha) \text{ COV(BEAVER, RACCOON; MAMMAL)} +$$
$$(1 - \alpha) \text{ COV(BEAVER, RACCOON; MAMMAL)},$$

which is just,

$$\text{COV(BEAVER, RACCOON; MAMMAL)}.$$

Applications of the Similarity-Coverage Model

Our first tests of the similarity-coverage model involve a number of phenomena like those discussed earlier, only this time they deal with specific arguments rather than general ones. Again each phenomenon will be illustrated by a contrasting pair of arguments, where each pair was presented to 80 University of Michigan undergraduates who were asked to choose the argument whose premises "provide a better reason to believe its conclusion." The five phenomena of interest are listed in Table 8.3. For each phenomenon, the number of subjects who chose each argument is given in brackets, and the difference between the stronger and weaker argument in a pair is significant at the .05 level by a two-tailed sign test.

The first phenomenon in Table 8.3 is different in kind from those we considered earlier. It is Premise-Conclusion Similarity; that is, the more similar the premise categories to the conclusion category, the stronger the argument. Thus, if we know that robins and bluejays use serotonin as a neurotransmitter, this provides more inductive support for a conclusion about sparrows using serotonin than for one about geese using serotonin. The question of interest is how this phenomenon fits with the similarity-coverage model. According to the model, the strengths of the two arguments are given by:

1. (α) MAX(SIM(ROBIN, SPARROW), SIM(BLUEJAY, SPARROW)) +
   $(1 - \alpha)$ COV(ROBIN, BLUEJAY; BIRD), and
2. (α) MAX(SIM(ROBIN, GOOSE), SIM(BLUEJAY, GOOSE)) +
   $(1 - \alpha)$ COV(ROBIN, BLUEJAY; BIRD).

Although the coverage terms for the two arguments are identical, the similarity term is clearly greater for (1.) than (2.). This explains why the argument that has SPARROW as its conclusion is stronger than the one that has GOOSE as its conclusion.

The preceding derivation shows that the model predicts the phenomenon of interest, but it does not show the need to consider general categories in the evaluation of specific arguments. The next few phenomena will attest to this need. The second phenomenon in Table 8.3 is a Premise-Diversity one (compara-

TABLE 8.3
Five Phenomena Involving Specific Arguments

Phenomenon	Stronger Argument	Weaker Argument
1. Premise-conclusion similarity	ROBIN, BLUEJAY/ SPARROW [76]	ROBIN, BLUEJAY/ GOOSE [4]
2. Premise diversity	LION, GIRAFFE/ RABBIT [52]	LION, TIGER/ RABBIT [28]
3. Premise monotonicity	FOX, PIG, WOLF/ GORILLA [66]	PIG, WOLF/ GORILLA [14]
4. Premise-conclusion asymmetry	MICE/BAT [40][a]	BAT/MICE [20]
5. Inclusion fallacy	ROBIN/BIRD [52]	ROBIN/OSTRICH [28]

Number of subjects preferring each argument is given in brackets.
[a]Only 60 subjects were tested on this phenomenon.

ble to the Premise-Diversity phenomenon considered with general arguments). The more diverse the premise categories, the stronger the specific argument. For example, LION and GIRAFFE provide more support for a conclusion about RABBIT than do LION and TIGER. According to the similarity-coverage model, the strengths of the two arguments are given by:

1. (α) MAX(SIM(LION, RABBIT), SIM (GIRAFFE, RABBIT)) + $(1 - \alpha)$ COV(LION, GIRAFFE; MAMMAL), and
2. (α) MAX(SIM(LION, RABBIT), SIM(TIGER, RABBIT)) + $(1 - \alpha)$ COV(LION, TIGER; MAMMAL).

The similarity terms of the two arguments are likely to be roughly equal. But the coverage term should be greater for (1.) than (2.) inasmuch as (LION, GIRAFFE) covers MAMMAL better than (LION, TIGER) does. These facts predict the phenomenon.

The next phenomenon in Table 8.3 is the specific analogue of the Premise-Monotonocity phenomenon considered earlier. In this case, the more premises, the stronger the specific argument. For example, FOX, PIG, and WOLF support a conclusion about GORILLA more than do just PIG and WOLF. According to the model the strengths of the two arguments are as follows:

1. (α) MAX(SIM(FOX, GORILLA), SIM(PIG, GORILLA), SIM(WOLF, GORILLA)) +
   $(1 - \alpha)$ COV(FOX, PIG, WOLF; MAMMAL), and
2. (α) MAX(SIM(PIG, GORILLA), SIM(WOLF, GORILLA)) +
   $(1 - \alpha)$ COV(PIG, WOLF; MAMMAL).

Because the similarity and coverage terms of the longer argument include those of the shorter argument, the longer argument must be at least as strong as the shorter one. This fact suffices to explain the phenomenon at issue.

The next-to-last phenomenon in Table 8.3, Premise-Conclusion Asymmetry, has no exact analogue among those considered with general arguments, though it is related to the Typicality phenomenon. The Asymmetry phenomenon is defined only for single-premise arguments, and reveals that such arguments need not be symmetric. In particular, a single-premise argument will be stronger when the more typical category is in the premise than the conclusion. For example, mice having the property of a low body temperature provides more support for bats having a low body temperature, than vice versa. According to the model the strengths of the two arguments are given by:

1. (α) SIM(MOUSE, BAT)+
   (1 − α) COV(MOUSE; MAMMAL)
2. (α) SIM(BAT, MOUSE)+
   (1 − α) COV(BAT; MAMMAL).

Presumably the two similarity terms are equal. But the coverage term should be greater in (1.) than (2.) because MOUSE is more typical than BAT of MAMMALS, and hence covers MAMMAL better. This consideration accounts for the phenomenon.

The final phenomenon in Table 8.3 involves a comparison of specific and general arguments. It consists of some counternormative reasoning known as the *Inclusion Fallacy* (see Shafir, Smith, & Osherson, 1990). A specific argument can sometimes be made to appear stronger by increasing the generality of its conclusion, even though the objective probability of a conclusion must decrease as its generality increases. For example, if we know that robins have an ulnar artery, we may erroneously think that this provides more support for *all* birds having an ulnar artery than for just ostriches having an ulnar artery. The fallacy is derivable from the similarity-coverage model. According to the model, the strengths of the two arguments are given by:

1. (α) SIM(ROBIN, BIRD)+
   (1 − α) COV(ROBIN; BIRD), and
2. (α) SIM(ROBIN, OSTRICH)+
   (1 − α) COV(ROBIN; BIRD).

With regard to the general argument, even though SIM(ROBIN, BIRD) and COV(ROBIN; BIRD) are equal, we have chosen to display the strength of this argument in separate similarity and coverage terms so as to facilitate comparison to the specific argument. This comparison shows that the coverage terms for the two arguments are identical. However, the similarity term for the general argument should exceed that for the specific argument. This is because SIM(ROBIN, BIRD) is the average similarity of robins to other birds, including other songbirds like sparrows, cardinals, and orioles. These similar songbirds should boost the average, which should exceed SIM(ROBIN, OSTRICH), as ostriches are highly dissimilar to robins.

In addition to the preceding, there is one other phenomenon involving specific arguments that deserves mention. This is the development finding that we mentioned at the outset of the chapter. Recall that Gelman and Markman (1986) presented young children with, for example, a pictured flamingo that fed its young mashed food, a pictured bat that fed its young milk, and asked the children which kind of food a blackbird fed its young. Though the blackbird resembled the bat more than the flamingo, inductions about the blackbird generally were based on the flamingo. Comparable results were obtained with adult subjects.

To see how our model would handle the Gelman–Markman finding, note that their task amounts to having a subject choose between the following arguments:

5a. <u>Flamingos feed their young mashed food</u>
     Blackbirds feed their young mashed food
5b. <u>Bats feed their young milk</u>
     Blackbirds feed their young milk[6]

According to the similarity-coverage model, the strengths of the two arguments are given by:

1. (α) SIM(FLAMINGO, BLACKBIRD)+
   (1 − α) COV(FLAMINGO; BIRD)
2. (α) SIM(BAT, BLACKBIRD)+
   (1 − α) COV(BAT; ANIMAL)

A comparison of the similarity terms favors the BAT argument. Regarding the coverage terms, however, note first that whereas the lowest level category that includes FLAMINGO and BLACKBIRD is BIRD, the lowest level category that includes BAT and BLACKBIRD is ANIMAL. This fact leads to a coverage advantage for the FLAMINGO argument, because FLAMINGO covers BIRD better than BAT covers the varied category ANIMAL. As a consequence of these considerations, the FLAMINGO argument will be judged stronger than the BAT argument as long as: (a) not too much weight is given to the similarity term (i.e., α is not too large), and (b) FLAMINGO's coverage advantage is not greatly outweighed by BAT's similarity advantage. These latter two assumptions seem

---

[6]Pretesting established that the children had no prior knowledge about which property applied to which animal, so the properties were essentially blank ones.

plausible, which suggests that the Gelman–Markman results are compatible with a model that considers both similarity and category membership in evaluating inductive inferences.

An Experimental Test of the Extended Model

Rationale.   Again we want to go beyond our demonstration of qualitative phenomena and show that our model provides a quantitative account of inductive judgments. The structure of the present experiment is very similar to that of the study presented earlier. Again there are two parts, with Part 1 being devoted to similarity ratings and Part 2 to inductive judgments.

Procedure.   The arguments were based on the category MAMMAL and a base set of eight instances, including: DOG, WOLF, MOUSE, HAMSTER, RHINO, HIPPO, FOX, ELEPHANT. In Part 1, all 28 pairs of mammals drawn from the base set were rated for similarity by a group of 30 undergraduates from the University of Michigan. The rating procedure and derivation of similarity scores was the same as in the earlier experiment with general arguments. The similarity scores for the present study are given in the second column of Table 8.4.

In Part 2 of the experiment, another group of 30 University of Michigan undergraduates gave probability judgments (used as a measure of strength) for arguments falling under the following schema:

X BLANK PRED.
Y BLANK PRED.
Elephants BLANK PRED.

To create an argument that falls under this schema, X and Y are replaced by two distinct mammals from the base set excluding FOX and ELEPHANT (this gives 15 premise pairs), and the variable BLANK PRED is replaced by one of 15 particular blank predicates (the same 15 used in the earlier experiment). All other procedural details were the same as in the earlier experiment. The obtained strength judgments are given in the third column of Table 8.4.

Results.   All arguments are of the form X,Y/ELEPHANT. We determined the similarity term for each argument directly from the similarity ratings obtained in part 1; for example, the similarity term for DOG, RHINO/ELEPHANT is the maximum of SIM(DOG, ELEPHANT) and SIM(RHINO, ELEPHANT). These maximum similarity scores are presented in the fourth column of Table 8.4. We determined the coverage term for each argument by the same procedure used in the earlier experiment except that the sampled conclusion instances were assumed to consist of the current base set (which includes eight rather than six

TABLE 8.4

Similarity Scores for Pairs of Mammals (Sim), Judged Strength of the Corresponding ELEPHANT Argument (Strength/ELE), Maximum Similarity of Pair to ELEPHANT (Sim/ELE), Estimated Coverage of Argument (Cov), Maximum Similarity of Mammal Pair to FOX (Sim/FOX), and Judged Strength of the Corresponding Fox Argument (Strength/FOX)

Pair	Sim	Strength/ ELE	Sim/ ELE	Cov	Sim/ FOX	Strength/ FOX
DOG HAMSTER	.26	.33	.17	.63	.78	.63
DOG HIPPO	.16	.67	.72	.71	.78	.68
DOG MOUSE	.24	.35	.17	.63	.78	.71
DOG RHINO	.18	.66	.66	.70	.78	.64
DOG WOLF	.92	.40	.19	.50	.91	.92
WOLF HAMSTER	.23	.35	.19	.65	.91	.81
WOLF HIPPO	.16	.71	.72	.72	.91	.77
WOLF MOUSE	.20	.36	.19	.65	.91	.80
WOLF RHINO	.20	.71	.66	.71	.91	.76
RHINO HAMSTER	.08	.67	.66	.63	.25	.45
RHINO HIPPO	.77	.82	.72	.44	.20	.24
RHINO MOUSE	.07	.64	.66	.62	.27	.46
HIPPO HAMSTER	.11	.59	.72	.64	.25	.51
HIPPO MOUSE	.08	.62	.72	.63	.27	.46
HAMSTER MOUSE	.85	.27	.11	.38	.27	.38
ELEPHANT DOG	.17					
ELEPHANT FOX	.18					
ELEPHANT HAMSTER	.11					
ELEPHANT HIPPO	.72					
ELEPHANT MOUSE	.08					
ELEPHANT RHINO	.66					
ELEPHANT WOLF	.19					
FOX DOG	.78					
FOX HAMSTER	.25					
FOX HIPPO	.13					
FOX MOUSE	.27					
FOX RHINO	.20					
FOX WOLF	.91					

mammals). These estimates of coverage are in the fifth column of Table 8.4. We then tested the similarity-coverage model by determining the multiple correlation between the estimated similarity and coverage terms on the one hand, and the obtained strength judgments on the other. The multiple correlation was .96 ($N = 15$, $p < .01$). The model obviously provides a satisfactory quantitative account of the judgments.

Replications.   We replicated the preceding study, but using FOX rather than ELEPHANT as the specific conclusion. All procedural details were the same as in the preceding study (15 arguments involving 15 distinct premise pairs combined with 15 distinct blank predicates, etc.). The coverage term for each argument was the same as in the preceding study. Also, the same set of similarity ratings was used to estimate the similarity terms for each argument; the maximum similarity scores to FOX are in the sixth column of Table 8.4. The same group of subjects used in the previous study gave the probability judgments.

These judgments are presented in the last column of Table 8.4. The multiple correlation between the estimated similarity and coverage terms on the one hand, and the obtained strength judgments on the other, was .93 ($N = 15, p < .01$).

We have also replicated both the ELEPHANT and FOX versions of this study in Spain. The same 30 University of Sevilla students provided strength judgments for both the ELEPHANT and FOX arguments (the relevant similarity ratings had been obtained in a previous study). The multiple correlation between the estimated similarity and coverage terms on the one hand, and the obtained strength judgments on the other, was .88 for the ELEPHANT arguments and .95 for the FOX arguments ($N = 15, p < .01$ in both cases).

Other Evidence for the Model. We note that there is even more empirical support for the similarity-coverage model than that just summarized. Osherson, Smith, Wilkie, Lopez, & Shafir (1990) present an additional four qualitative phenomena involving general, specific, and mixed arguments (see Footnote 2) that are predicted by the model. This same paper also mentions the results of several additional experiments that show that the similarity-coverage model provides a good quantitative account of strength judgments to general and specific arguments. In subsequent work (Osherson, Stern, Wilkie, Stob, & Smith, 1991), we have shown that a variant of the similarity-coverage model does a good job of quantitatively predicting inductive judgments on an individual subject basis. This same work also shows that the model can be readily extended to handle arguments that contain: (a) negative premises (e.g., Robins have sesamoid bones, Bluejays *don't* have sesamoid bones/Eagles have sesamoid bones), and (b) intermediate level premises (e.g., Hawks have sesamoid bones, Songbirds have sesamoid bones/Eagles have sesamoid bones). There is, then, an appreciable body of data that supports the model.

ALTERNATIVE MODELS

It is of interest to consider two alternative accounts of category-based induction. One alternative views induction as rule-based, the other views induction as explanation-based.

A Rule Model

A number of theorists have proposed that drawing an inductive inference is largely a matter of applying certain rules, often rather abstract ones (e.g., Collins & Michalski, 1989; Holland, Holyoak, Nisbett, & Thagard, 1986). Of particular interest is the Collins and Michalski report, because it deals with cases of category-based induction. The Collins and Michalski approach to the phenomena that we have reported would be to assume that they directly reflect the application of rules. Thus the Premise-Conclusion Similarity phenomenon suggests a Similarity rule that might look like this:

If CAT_1 and CAT_2 are both members of the same category,
    and CAT_1 has property P,
    and CAT_1 is similar to CAT_2 to degree s,
Then CAT_2 has P to a degree that is proportional to s.

Likewise, the Premise Diversity phenomenon with general arguments suggests a Diversity rule that looks like:

If CAT_1 and CAT_2 are members of CAT_3,
    and CAT_1 and CAT_2 both have property P,
    and CAT_1 and CAT_2 are similar to degree s,
Then all members of CAT_3 have P to a degree that is inversely proportional to s.

Similarly, the Premise Typicality phenomenon suggests a Typicality rule that goes roughly as follows:

If CAT_1 is a member of CAT_2,
    and CAT_1 has property P,
    and CAT_1 is typical of CAT_2 to degree t,
Then all members of CAT_2 have P to a degree that is proportional to t.[7]

Although the preceding might suggest that any particular argument is handled by a single rule, in fact any particular argument will satisfy the conditions of multiple rules. Thus, often a reasoner will have to amalgamate the results from various rules. Because, according to Collins and Michalski, the outcome of a rule being applied to an argument is a numerical indication of the strength of that argument, the reasoner can amalgamate the results from various rules by combining their strengths. To appreciate the subtleties of amalgamation, consider the following two argument pairs (both of which were studied by Osherson, Smith, Wilkie, Lopez, & Shafir, 1990):

6a. Robins secrete uric acid crystals
     <u>Ostriches secrete uric acid crystals</u>
     All birds secrete uric acid crystals

---

[7]In addition to s and t, Collins and Michalski's (1989) rules include other parameters. Thus, there is a parameter that reflects the extent to which a person believes a premise (or conclusion) is true, another parameter that reflects the frequency of the predicate, and still another parameter that reflects the extent to which the features used to calculate similarity between categories are related to the predicate. We have ignored these parameters because the factors they reflect tend to be constant in our experiments.

6b. Robins secrete uric acid crystals
     <u>Sparrows secrete uric acid crystals</u>
     All birds secrete uric acid crystals

7a. Robins secrete uric acid crystals
     <u>Sparrows secrete uric acid crystals</u> [Same as 6b]
     All birds secrete uric acid crystals

7b. Pelicans secrete uric acid crystals
     <u>Albatrosses secrete uric acid crystals</u>
     All birds secrete uric acid crystals

All of these arguments satisfy the conditions of both the Diversity and Typicality rules. In the first pair, the ROBIN, OSTRICH argument is judged stronger than the ROBIN, SPARROW one; because ROBIN and OSTRICH are more diverse but less typical than ROBIN and SPARROW, the outcome of the Diversity rule must dominate the outcome of the Typicality rule. In the second pair, the ROBIN, SPARROW argument is judged stronger than the PELICAN, AL-BATROSS argument; because ROBIN and SPARROW are less diverse but more typical than PELICAN and ALBATROSS, now the outcome of the Typicality rule must dominate that of the Diversity rule. This pattern of results obviously depends on the specific parameters involved in the Diversity and Typicality rules.

This, then, is a rough sketch of a rule model of category-based induction. Compared to the similarity-coverage model, the rule model has a major disadvantage: it is unparsimonious. For one thing, the rule model seems to require numerous rules. We have seen a glimmer of why we need Similarity, Diversity, and Typicality rules to account for the corresponding phenomena, and we may well need Conclusion-Homogeneity and Monotonicity rules to account for other phenomena. We could even end up positing a separate rule for each phenomenon we considered. And there are phenomena that we have not discussed here (see Osherson, Smith, Wilkie, Lopez, & Shafir, 1990), and they may require additional rules.

Moreover, the rule model needs more than just rules. It requires parameters, such as that for the degree of similarity in the Similarity and Diversity rules, or that for typicality in the Typicality rule. These parameters are needed to explain why, for example, there is a relatively continuous relation between the degree of similarity between two categories and the extent to which a property known to be true of one of the categories will be judged true of the other (see Table 8.4 for evidence of this). The parameters in question are also needed to account for the details of the process that amalgamates the outcomes of the various rules (see Arguments 6a–7b). Because these parameters do much of the work in explaining inductive judgments (see Rips, 1990), and because these parameters resemble the critical entities in the similarity-coverage model (namely, pairwise-similarity estimates), one wonders about the need to postulate the rules themselves.[8]

However, we do not claim that rules of some sort *never* play a role in category-based induction. Perhaps simple versions of the rules sketched earlier— that is, rules without parameters—might be used as heuristics for judging the strength of arguments, as long as the outcomes of the relevant rules do not conflict. Consider the contrasting pair of arguments we used to demonstrate a monotonicity effect, HAWK, SPARROW, EAGLE/BIRD versus SPARROW, EAGLE/BIRD. The longer argument is likely to be favored by any rule we apply (including simplified versions of the Diversity rule, the Typicality rule, or a Monotonicity rule that says that belief in a conclusion should increase with the number of premises). This might explain why the just-mentioned contrast yielded such a substantial effect (75 of 80 subjects chose the longer argument), even though it does not manifest a substantial difference in coverage.

An Explanation Model

The basic idea behind an explanation model of category-based induction is as follows. Evaluation of an inductive argument consists of trying to determine the best explanation of why the premise categories have the property that they do, where an explanation amounts to membership in some relatively simple category. To illustrate, consider the general argument:

8a. Bluejays have sesamoid bones
     Falcons have sesamoid bones
     All animals have sesamoid bones

The reasoner is trying to determine the best or strongest explanation of why bluejays and falcons have sesamoid bones. One possible explanation is given by the conclusion itself, namely, that all animals have sesamoid bones. An alternative explanation is available, however, namely, that all birds have sesamoid bones. Because the BIRD explanation is more specific than the ANIMAL one, and because the strength of a simple explanation may increase with its specificity, the BIRD explanation discounts the ANIMAL explanation. Consequently Argument 8a is considered less strong than Argument 8b, where no simple alternative explanation discounts the one given in the conclusion:

---

[8]We note that a detailed rule model (one with specific values for the parameters) has yet to be applied to inductive judgments. Consequently it is still an open question whether such a model would yield as good an account of the data presented in this chapter as does the similarity-coverage model.

8b. Bluejays have sesamoid bones
     <u>Falcons have sesamoid bones</u>
     All birds have sesamoid bones

An explanation model therefore naturally predicts the Conclusion Homogeneity phenomenon.

Thus in the context of category-based induction, an explanation is strong if the category it consists of: (a) is available; (b) is relatively simple (e.g., natural categories such as BIRD and ANIMAL); (c) includes all the premise categories; and (d) is not discounted by more specific categories that meet criteria a, b, and c. Criteria a, b, and c capture part of a mode of induction (called "Reverse Deduction") that has been suggested as an alternative to similarity-based induction (Osherson, Smith, & Shafir, 1986), and criterion d figures centrally in discussion of causal induction (e.g., Holland, Holyoak, Nisbett, & Thagard, 1986).

In addition to accounting for the Conclusion Homogeneity phenomenon, an explanation model can also account for our demonstration of the Premise Diversity phenomenon with general arguments. Recall that we showed that an argument of the form HIPPO, HAMSTER/MAMMAL is stronger than one of the form HIPPO, RHINO/MAMMAL. Whereas MAMMAL may be the best explanation for HIPPO and HAMSTER, an alternative explanation for HIPPO and RHINO comes to mind, something like LARGE JUNGLE MAMMAL. This alternative will discount MAMMAL, and hence weaken the HIPPO, RHINO argument.

The preceding analysis, however, considers only one instance of the Premise Diversity phenomenon, and an extreme one at that. With more subtle variations in premise diversity, the explanation model runs into trouble. For example, in an experiment presented earlier, we found that an argument of the form RHINO, HAMSTER/MAMMAL was judged stronger than one of the form RHINO, DOG/MAMMAL; this is an instance of the Premise Diversity phenomenon because RHINO and HAMSTER are less similar than RHINO and DOG (see Table 8.2). But there do not seem to be more alternative explanations of the RHINO, DOG argument than of the RHINO, HAMSTER one (no alternatives come readily to mind for either argument). More generally, the problem is that inductive judgments are sensitive to variations in similarity that are too fine-grained to be captured by the notion of an explanation.

An explanation model also has trouble with the other phenomena associated with general arguments. We demonstrated the Premise Typicality phenomena by showing that an argument of the form ROBIN/BIRD is stronger than one of the form PENGUIN/BIRD. There is no reason to believe that there are more available, alternative explanations for the PENGUIN argument than for the ROBIN argument (e.g., WATERBIRD and LARGE BIRD are two available alternatives for the PENGUIN argument, whereas SONGBIRD and SMALL BIRD are two available alternatives for the ROBIN argument). Likewise, we demonstrated the Premise Monotocity phenomenon by showing that HAWK, SPARROW, EAGLE/BIRD is stronger than SPARROW, EAGLE/BIRD. Again there do not seem to be more alternative explanations for the weaker argument.

A similar story holds when we apply an explanation model to specific arguments (except that now the explanation must account for why both the premises and conclusion have the property that they do). To deal with such arguments, an explanation model must first posit that people generate general categories that include the premise and conclusion categories (as no general category is given). This much is uncontroversial, as the similarity-coverage model had to make the same assumption to account for the same phenomena. Problems arise, however, when we focus on a particular phenomenon. Consider Premise-Conclusion Similarity, which we demonstrated by showing that ROBIN, BLUEJAY/SPARROW is stronger than ROBIN, BLUEJAY/GOOSE. An explanation model can be made consistent with this result by adding to the model the assumption that, other things being equal, more specific explanations are favored over less specific ones. A category likely to be generated for the SPARROW argument, namely SONG-BIRD, is a more specific explanation than the category likely to be generated for the GOOSE argument, namely BIRD. However, the model runs into trouble with more subtle instances of the Similarity phenomenon. For example, in an experiment presented earlier, we found that the argument DOG, HAMSTER/ELEPHANT was judged stronger than the argument MOUSE, HAMSTER/ELEPHANT; this is an instance of Premise-Conclusion Similarity inasmuch as DOG is more similar to ELEPHANT than MOUSE is (see Table 8.4). But there does not seem to be any difference between the two arguments with respect to available explanations; MAMMAL is the only available explanation in both cases.

The situation is even bleaker when we consider the other phenomena involving specific arguments. The explanation model fails to handle even our demonstrations of Premise Diversity and Premise Monotonicity. With regard to the latter, FOX, PIG, WOLF/GORILLA is stronger than PIG, WOLF/GORILLA, even though there is no apparent difference between the two arguments with respect to available explanations; MAMMAL seems to be the most available alternative in both cases. Lastly, an explanation model has nothing to say about the Asymmetry and Inclusion Fallacy phenomena.

In summary, an explanation model fails to account for much of the data that the similarity-coverage model handles readily. And the explanation model fails because its fundamental unit—that of an explanatory category—is not fine-grained enough to capture subtle variations in inductive strength. Explanations, however, may play more of a role in category-based induction when the properties involved are nonblank ones. Propositions involving nonblank properties (e.g., Sharks have sharp teeth) often are causally connected to other beliefs (e.g., Sharks eat meat), and such connections provide a means by which explanations can enter the induction process.

SUMMARY

The similarity-coverage model provides a more parsimonious and accurate account of the relevant data than other plausible models of category-based induction. Moreover, the constructs invoked by the similarity-coverage model—similarity and category membership—are ones that have always figured centrally in previous analyses of induction. Indeed, these constructs have played a major role in Estes' theorizing about various aspects of cognition (e.g., Estes, 1976, 1986), and this, too, suggests we may be on the right track.

ACKNOWLEDGMENTS

The research reported in this chapter was supported by NSF grants Nos. 8609201 and 870544 to Osherson and Smith, respectively, and by Air Force Contract No. AFOSR-91-0265 to Smith. We thank Alice Healy and Jay Rueckle for helpful comments on the manuscript.

REFERENCES

Collins, A. M., & Michalski, R. (1989). The logic of plausible reasoning: A core theory. *Cognitive Science, 13*, 1–50.

Estes, W. K. (1976). The cognitive side of probability learning. *Psychological Review, 83*, 37–64.

Estes, W. K. (1986). Array models for category learning. *Cognitive Psychology, 18*, 500–549.

Gelman, S. A., & Markman, E. (1986). Categories and induction in young children. *Cognition, 23*, 183–209.

Gelman, S. A., & Markman, E. (1987). Young children's inductions from natural kinds: The role of categories and appearances. *Child Development, 58*, 1532–1541.

Holland, J., Holyoak, K., Nisbett, R. E., & Thagard, P. (1986). *Induction: Processes of inference, learning, and discovery*. Cambridge, MA: MIT Press.

Kahneman, D., & Tversky, A. (1973). On the psychology of prediction. *Psychological Review, 80*, 237–251.

Lopez, A. (1989). (Di)Similitud e inducción. *Revista í Chilena de Psicología, 10*, 5–13.

Osherson, D. N., Smith, E. E., & Shafir, E. (1986). Some origins of belief. *Cognition, 24*, 197–224.

Osherson, D. N., Smith, E. E., Wilkie, O., Lopez, A., & Shafir, E. (1990). Category based induction. *Psychological Review, 97*, 185–200.

Osherson, D. N., Stern, J., Wilkie, O., Stob, M., & Smith, E. E. (1991). Default probability. *Cognitive Science, 15*, 251–269.

Rips, L. J. (1975). Inductive judgments about natural categories. *Journal of Verbal Learning and Verbal Behavior, 14*, 665–681.

Rips, L. J. (1990). Reasoning. *Annual Review of Psychology, 41*, 321–353.

Shafir, E., Smith, E. E., & Osherson, D. N. (1990). Typicality and reasoning fallacies. *Memory and Cognition, 18*, 229–239.

Smith, E. E., & Medin, D. L. (1981). *Categories and concepts*. Cambridge, MA: Harvard University Press.

Tversky, A. (1977). Features of similarity. *Psychological Review, 84*, 327–352.

Tversky, A., & Hutchinson, W. (1986). Nearest neighbor analysis of psychological spaces. *Psychological Review, 93*, 3–22.

9 Abstraction and Selective Coding in Exemplar-Based Models of Categorization

Douglas L. Medin
Judy E. Florian
University of Michigan

Something surprising has been going on in the area of categorization, and going on for some time. It centers around the fundamental question of how abstract representations of concepts are derived from experience with examples of a category. One of the most prominent ideas has it that people learn from examples by abstracting out the central tendency for a category. The central tendency or prototype reflects what is typical, or on the average true, for category members. A robin is a typical bird because it sings, flies, builds nests, lays eggs, has wings, hollow bones, and a number of other characteristic features of birds. Prototype models appear to provide a natural way to handle fuzzy categories that do not have defining features—in fact, Medin and Smith (1984) go so far as to refer to such categories as "prototype concepts."

So what's so surprising? Well, there is an alternative model that ought to serve as a good foil for prototype models. One could assume that no abstraction takes place during category learning and that people simply store examples. New examples would be classified on the basis of similarity to stored examples, not in terms of how closely they match the prototype. What is surprising is that prototype and exemplar models have been repeatedly compared (e.g., Medin & Schaffer, 1978; Medin & Smith, 1981; Nosofsky, 1987, 1988a,b) and exemplar models consistently fare better! This differential success has been quite marked and one might be tempted to answer the question of how abstraction takes place by saying "It doesn't." Incidentally, there are formal proofs that classifying on the basis of the most similar stored example (so-called "Nearest Neighbor" classification), yields accuracies that are close to optimal performance (Cover & Hart, 1967).

This sort of sweeping conclusion, that abstraction does not occur, will not, however, hold up under closer scrutiny. First of all, there is a serious sense in which exemplar models *are* models of abstraction. Different variations of exemplar models make alternative claims about just what kinds of information determine classification. For instance, average distance exemplar models assume that a new example is classified by determining its average distance from stored examples of alternative categories and assigning the example to the category with smallest average distance (e.g., Reed, 1972). In effect, such a model would be constructing prototypes at the time of test, and under many conditions its predictions about categorization would be indistinguishable from those of prototype models (see also Estes, 1986a).

More generally, exemplar models do not assume that an example has unique access to its own representation. A stored exemplar representation may be activated by a similar, new example, and even an old example may access more than its own representation. Indeed, some of the strongest support for exemplar models comes from classification experiments where new-old recognition is barely above chance (e.g., Medin & Smith, 1981).

Finally, exemplar models provide for abstraction to the extent that they allow the notion of similarity to be flexible. Selective attention and associated learning strategies may lead some examples to be more similar than would be true in the absence of selective attention. If similarity is flexible and dynamic, then distinct examples may have nondistinct representations. We later provide an illustration of an exemplar model that embodies abstraction in all the senses mentioned here.

We suggest that the contrast between prototype models and the exemplar model that has received the greatest attention is about what is abstracted and how it is abstracted and not whether abstraction takes place. One must evaluate models in terms of how they actually work; no conclusions are licensed by how they are labeled.[1]

The organization of this chapter is as follows. We begin by briefly describing an exemplar model of categorization, referred to as the *context model,* noting the ways in which this model involves abstraction. Elaborations and modifications of this model are then described from this same perspective. Next we turn to a number of recent observations that suggest some new avenues for exploring abstraction within an exemplar-based framework. Finally, we summarize, offer some speculations, and attempt to draw some morals from our analysis.

---

[1]It is traditional to define abstraction by reference to representations alone. That is, typical models of abstraction (e.g., prototype models) posit the development of abstract *representations.* In contrast, we suggest that abstraction can be usefully defined at the level of representation-process pairs. Therefore, even when the representation is in terms of individual examples, the processes that operate on examples necessarily involve loss of individuating information, then we would claim that abstraction has taken place. By our definition abstraction may be a by-product of either storage or retrieval processes.

THE CONTEXT MODEL

Background: Components, Compounds, and Context

A long standing problem in the psychology of learning has been identifying and coordinating appropriate units of analysis. To account for the effects of similarity on learning and transfer or generalization, it is natural to take stimulus components or features as fundamental units. Thus, in Spence's (1936) theory of discrimination learning, when the choice of a large, red triangle on the left led to a reward, it was assumed that the components *large, red, triangle,* and *left* each accrued some habit strength. If the triangle were then shifted to a position on the right, the components of large, red, and triangle would be competing against the habit strengths for choosing left. Total habit strength was simply the sum of the habit strength of the components.

Although theories like Spence's provided straightforward stimulus generalization in terms of shared components, they failed to correctly describe certain results concerning learning. For example, Spence's theory could not account for the fact that what are referred to as "successive discrimination learning" problems could be mastered. Suppose we have a learning task where either two black circles are presented and the correct response is to go to the left or two white squares appear and the correct response is to go to the right. Over a series of trials each of the components left, right, black, white, circle, and square is rewarded equally often so that all of the composite stimuli should have roughly equal habit strength. For example, suppose that an organism is correct and rewarded on each of the two possible types of trials. The trial with the black circles will boost the strength of black, circle, and left, and the trial with the white squares will boost the strength of white, square, and right. On the next trial with the black circles, there will be no basis for preferring the black circle on the left because black, circle, left, and right will each have been rewarded once. Similarly, there should be no basis for preferring one choice to the other when the white squares appear because Spence's theory assumes that each component is independent of all the other components. Thus the problem should be impossible to solve (but it is not).

There is an obvious way to account for the observation that successive discrimination problems are learnable—pick different units of analysis. That is, one could assume that compounds (e.g., the composite of black, circle, and left) are the functional units for learning, and that habit strengths or associations are to compounds rather than to constituent components. Under this analysis the compounds, white-circle-on-the-left and black-square-on-the-right, would gain associative strength, but the compounds of white-circle-on-the-right and black-square-on-the-left would not. The problem with this solution is that if each compound is unique, one can no longer account for generalization and transfer. What is needed is some way to coordinate the use of components (to allow for generalization) with the use of compounds (to allow for discrimination).

A closely related issue concerns the effects of context on learning and transfer. Behaviors learned in a particular context often fail to transfer when the context is changed. Although the effects of context were widely acknowledged in the 1940s and 1950s, there were relatively few efforts to incorporate context effects into learning models. An exception was provided by Estes, Hopkins, and Crothers (1960) who proposed that ". . . probability of a response reinforced on a training trial is reduced on subsequent test trials if components of the training stimulus pattern, including contextual, or background, cues have been replaced by novel ones in the test pattern" (p. 338). Estes and his associates also developed and tested models aimed at integrating responding to components with responding to compounds (e.g., Atkinson & Estes, 1963; Estes & Hopkins, 1961).

Many of the difficulties with treatments of components, compounds, and context stem from the idea that there are direct associations between stimulus components and outcomes. The hierarchical association model of Estes (1972, 1973, 1976) represents a major innovation that abandons the notion of direct associations. Estes proposed that stimuli were *indirectly* linked by what he referred to as a *control element*. According to Estes, "The learning which results from the contiguous occurrence of two stimuli is conceived in the new theory to be, not the establishment of association between them, but rather the association of each with a control element" (1972, p. 175).

The context model has its intellectual origins in the hierarchical association model. Consider again the situation where some stimulus (e.g., large red triangle) is presented and some event (e.g., reward) occurs. In the context model (e.g., Medin, 1975) individual stimulus components, such as large or red or triangle, are not assumed to be directly and independently associated with the event. Instead, information concerning the cue, the context, and the event are assumed to be stored together in memory. Furthermore, for the representation of the event to be retrieved, both cue and context must be simultaneously activated. A change in either cue or context can reduce the accessibility of information associated with both. In addition, both serve as a basis for discrimination and generalization (see Medin, 1975 for further details).

This idea is depicted in Fig. 9.1 where R (cue), R (context), and R (event) refer to the representation of cue, context, and event, respectively. The cue-context node corresponds directly to a control element in the Estes' hierarchical associative model and illustrates the assumption that cue and context interact. The context model makes the further assumption that each stimulus component serves two roles: It represents a cue with which outcomes may be (indirectly) associated and it simultaneously provides or is part of the context for other cues. In our simple example, red is part of the context in which the triangle appears and vice versa. In short, the context model aims to account for the role of components, compounds, and context within the framework of the hierarchical association model. The context model was originally developed to apply to discrimination learning but the idea of cue and context interaction has direct implications for categorization.

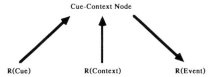

FIG. 9.1. Illustration of factors proposed to determine the accessibility of information associated with a cue presented in a particular context (R refers to the memory representation of the cue, context, or event; Medin, 1975).

Context Theory of Categorization

Basic Model. As applied to classification, the context model proposes that when an item is presented to be classified, that item acts as a retrieval cue to access information associated with similar stored exemplars. The various cue dimensions comprising stimuli in some context are assumed to be combined in an interactive, specifically multiplicative manner to determine the similarity of two stimuli. The theory states that the probability of classifying a test stimulus t as a member of Category A is given by the sum of the similarities of t to Category A members relative to the sum of the similarities of t to all stored examples:

$$P(A/t) = \frac{\sum_{a=A} S(t, a)}{\sum_{a=A} S(t, a) + \sum_{a \neq A} S(t, a)}$$

The individual similarities are computed by a multiplicative rule:

$$S(t, a) = \overset{n}{\underset{i}{\pi}} S_i,$$

where n is the number of dimensions and where $S_i = 1$ if $t_i = a_i$ and $S_i = p_i$, if $t_i \neq a_i$. The p_i parameters associated with mismatching values along dimensions are constrained to be between 0 and 1. Small values of p_i imply that differences along dimension i have a large influence on performance. In the limiting case of $p_i = 0$, the overall similarity will be zero, regardless of how many matching values there may be on other constituent dimensions.

The context model has ready application for binary-valued dimensions where components either match or mismatch. For multi-valued dimensions one could have a separate parameter for each possible difference, but this would have the undesirable consequence of a proliferation of parameters. For example, for six possible values on a dimension, potentially one could need up to 15 distinct values of p_i corresponding to each combination of value differences.

Nosofsky (1984) generalized the context model to continuous dimensions by bringing the multiplicative similarity rule into the framework of multidimensional scaling. Specifically, he showed that the multiplicative rule arises as a special case of psychological distance between stimuli conforming to the city block metric, and of stimulus similarity being an exponential function of psychological distance. An exponential function relating similarity to distance has received wide support; in fact, Shepard (1987) has proposed that the exponential function represents a universal law of generalization.

The multiplicative rule has the implication that an exemplar may be classified more efficiently if it is highly similar to one instance and dissimilar to a second than if it has medium similarity to two instances of a category. In addition, the context model reflects sensitivity to correlated attributes within a category (e.g., for the category birds there is a negative correlation between size and the probability that a bird can sing). Prototype models are insensitive to such density and correlation effects. Experiments with artificial and natural categories reveal that both density and correlated values affect people's categorization (Estes, 1986b; Malt & Smith, 1984; Medin, Altom, Edelson, & Freko, 1982; Medin & Schaffer, 1978; see also Nosofsky's chapter in this volume for further review). One should note that these problems for prototype models may be addressed by other theories of abstraction and that prototype and exemplar models do not exhaust the set of possible categorization models (e.g., Medin & Schaffer, 1978).

Although the basic context model certainly qualifies as an exemplar model, it always involves abstraction, except for the case where all similarity parameters (p_i) for nonmatching attributes have the value zero. In this special case, a stored example will only be retrieved when the stimulus corresponding to it appears as a probe and any new probe will fail to retrieve anything. As we noted earlier, generally a probe will access more than one example and exemplars do not have unique access to their associated representations. The contribution of stored examples to classification depends on their similarity to the probe. Where differences are salient (p_i values are small), performance will largely be determined by the most similar examples. Optimal values of p_i for classification will depend on factors such as category structure and exemplar frequency. Estes (1986a) points out that, even for the special case where all the p_i are equal, the absolute value of p_i observed may reflect not simply perceptual similarity but rather strategic adjustments in the importance attached to mismatching values in the service of improving categorization performance. Therefore, even the restricted form of the context model involves abstraction and adjustments in similarity values in response to category structures.

Selective Attention.   Both the original context model and the generalization of it due to Nosofsky make provision for differential weighting or selective attention to dimensions. The parameter reflecting the similarity of the two values on a dimension is assumed to be less when that dimension is attended to, or forms part of a hypothesis, than when it is not attended to or part of a hypothesis.

In general, one might expect that the weights on dimensions will vary as a function of their diagnostic value, that is, dimensions useful in distinguishing categories will receive greater attention than dimensions that are irrelevant to correct classification (Nosofsky, 1984, 1986).

Note that the assumption of selective attention carries with it the following implication: It is not necessarily the case that a distinct representation is set up for each individual exemplar. Consider a highly simplified classification task involving binary-valued dimensions where there are two Category A patterns ($a_1 = 1110$, $a_2 = 1010$) and two Category B patterns ($b = 0001$, $b_2 = 0010$). Suppose that a learner has selectively attended to the second and third dimensions, so that less information has been stored about the first and fourth dimensions. The learner's representation of exemplar information might be something like this:

$$?11?\text{-}A(a_1)\ 000?\text{-}B(b_1)$$
$$?010\text{-}A(a_2)\ ?010\text{-}B(b_2),$$

where the question marks indicate that information that would differentiate value 1 and value 0 on that dimension has not been successfully stored. Note that this representation is not sufficient to produce perfect performance because the representations associated with a_2 and b_2 cannot be distinguished. In this particular example, we have tied selective attention to partial learning, but the general point is, that however selective attention is implemented, it increases the similarity of some examples (to the point that different examples may not have distinctive representations) and decreases the similarity of others. In short, selective attention involves the "shrinking and stretching" of similarity space in the service of more effective classification. Medin and Smith (1981) showed that the very considerable performance differences associated with the use of different strategies could be qualitatively and quantitatively described by the context model where similarity parameters were allowed to vary across strategy conditions.

Presumably the context model qualifies as an exemplar model; thus we can state with confidence that exemplar models require neither unique access nor distinct storage for each example. The context model appears to be fully qualified as a model of abstraction and the main question is whether it contains abstraction mechanisms that correspond with observations from human category learning.[2] Although the context model has fared very well when contrasted with prototype and even rule-based models (e.g., Medin & Ross, 1989; Nosofsky, 1987; Nosofsky, Clark, & Shin, 1989), we think that several recent observations moti-

---

[2]Our illustration only informally corresponds to the version of the context model presented by Medin and Schaffer (1978). In the context model, the inability to distinguish values would correspond to higher similarity parameters. In the Medin and Schaffer model, however, similarity parameters are associated with dimensions, not examples. Therefore, the model would not correctly represent the cited situation because, in our example, question marks are associated with individual exemplars, not dimensions. Later on, we explore the idea of selective attention at the level of individual instances.

vate exploring further approaches to selective coding and abstraction within an exemplar framework. We now turn to them.

NEW AVENUES FOR EXEMPLAR-BASED ABSTRACTION MODELS

In this section, three sets of findings that pose problems for the context model are described. As shall be seen, these observations reinforce each other and together they suggest a new avenue for exploring exemplar-based abstraction. We first describe these findings and then draw out their implications.

Exemplar-Guided Encoding

Exemplar models allowing for selective attention to dimensions may not successfully capture certain generalizations that are formed during learning. For example, Elio and Anderson (1981, Experiment 2) varied the order in which the study items were presented. Items were either blocked, so that examples that would contribute to a category-level generalization occurred close together in the study sequence, or the items were randomly ordered. Study items were learned faster and transfer performance was better with blocked presentation than with random presentation. Because the category-level generalizations involved specific values on several dimensions, the notion of differential weighting at the level of dimensions cannot account for the advantage of blocked presentation over random presentation.

More recently, Ross, Perkins, and Tenpenny (1990) have demonstrated effects of both examples and generalizations on classification performance. In their studies, participants were taught about the category membership of several examples and then a test probe designed to elicit the retrieval of a specific example was given. For example, a participant may have learned that both an example with features a_1 and a_2 and another example with features b_1 and b_2 belong to the same category. Then a probe consisting either of a_1, a_2, and b_2 or one consisting of b_1, a_2, and b_2 was given. Note that a_2 and b_2 appear equally often. Nonetheless, participants ranked the feature a_2 as more typical of the category than b_2 when the probe consisted of a_1, a_2, and b_2 and yet ranked b_2 as more typical when the probe had been b_1, a_2, and b_2. Ross et al. suggested that the probes led to specific remindings of earlier examples and that features that were shared between the probe and the earlier example were strengthened. This specific result is also consistent with the idea that a reminding simply strengthened the entire earlier example. In further experiments, however, Ross et al. undermined this exemplar-strengthening explanation.

In some recent studies, Jeffrey Bettger, Dedre Genter, and the first author of this chapter have followed up the Elio and Anderson (1981) and Ross et al.

TABLE 9.1
Two Orders of Examples Used in the First Experiment Presented in Abstract Notation

Example	Small Change				Large Change			
	Dimension				Dimension			
Order	D1	D2	D3	D4	D1	D2	D3	D4
1	1	1	1	0	1	1	1	0
2	0	1	1	0	1	0	0	1
3	0	1	1	1	0	1	1	1
4	1	0	1	1	1	0	1	0
5	1	0	1	0	1	1	0	1
6	1	0	0	1	1	0	1	1
7	1	1	0	1	0	1	1	0
8	1	1	1	1	1	1	1	1

The binary values refer to alternative values on the dimensions.

(1990) research. Our general idea was that exemplar-guided encoding (e.g., Brooks, 1987; Jacoby, Baker, & Brooks, 1989; Jacoby & Brooks, 1984) may be an important source of selective encoding and abstraction (see also Watkins & Kerkar, 1985). Specifically, the order in which examples were presented was varied. The Anderson, Kline, and Beasley (1979) ACT model assumes that generalization occurs over items that are simultaneously present in working memory. In the basic procedure two groups see exactly the same set of examples but in two different orders. One order is set up to maximize the similarity of successive examples. The other order minimizes the similarity of successive examples. The instructions to the participants were to study the examples for a later memory test. (In other studies we have told people that the examples all belong to the same category and that their task is to learn about the category. Comparable results are observed for either type of instruction.) After the sequence of examples has been presented, participants are given a new–old recognition test.

Table 9.1 shows the two sequences of examples used in the one experiment, represented in abstract notation. Individual examples were distinguishable from each other only with respect to the combinations of properties they manifested. For each of the constituent dimensions one value (1) was more typical or frequent than the other (0). For the first and third dimensions the relative frequency was 6 to 2 and on the second and fourth dimensions it was 5 to 3. After participants saw the eight examples, they were given a new–old recognition test involving eight old stimuli and eight new stimuli. The new examples consisted of the remaining possible unique combinations of binary values on the four dimensions.

The Small Change sequence minimized differences across successive examples. Specifically, Example 2 differed from Example 1 only along the first dimension, Example 3 differed from Example 2 only along the fourth dimension, and so on. For the Large Change sequence, Example 2 differed from Example 1 along three dimensions and Example 3 differed from Example 2 along three dimensions, and so on. On the average, successive examples differed on 1.3 dimensions in the Small Change condition and differed on 2.7 dimensions in the Large Change condition. This design necessarily involves a confounding of particular examples with serial position in the list. To minimize the influences of primacy and recency effects, the first and last examples were the same for each list.

According to the idea of exemplar-guided encoding, participants ought to be able to use the previous example to guide the encoding of the current example more effectively in the Small Change condition than in the Large Change condition. Values shared by successive examples should be better encoded than values that differ across successive examples. (A variety of processing mechanisms might produce such a result but we confine our description of exemplar guided encoding to this general, somewhat vague level.) In our experiment the combinations of values shared by successive (old) exemplars tend not to be shared by new examples. This should facilitate new–old recognition. As shall be seen, a couple of new examples do have combinations of values shared by successive examples and we might expect participants in the small change condition to false alarm to these particular examples.

At least in a general way the ACT model is also able to predict interactions of order of presentation with the likelihood of false alarming to particular new examples (see also Forbus & Gentner, 1986; Hayes-Roth & McDermott, 1978; Skorstad, Gentner, & Medin, 1988 for other models that postulate on-line processes of pair-wise abstraction). Again the idea is that any of the values that two successive examples share get strengthened (i.e., a generalization is formed). Therefore, participants ought to be more likely to false alarm to the new examples 1000 and 0011 because 1000 is consistent with the generalization 10 ** (where * refers to any value) across the fourth, fifth, and sixth examples (see Table 9.1), and 0011 is consistent with a generalization ** 11 across the third and fourth examples. Note that we are assuming that all values in common across successive pairs are strengthened. The second and third examples fit the generalizations, 01**,*11*, and 0*1*, but our suggestion is that only the generalization 011* would be strengthened.

The stimuli were cartoon-like drawings of animals that differed in head shape (angular or round), body marking (spots or stripes), number of legs (four or eight) and tail length (long or short). As indicated in Table 9.1, participants saw the eight learning examples in one of the two orders and then were given the new–old recognition test. The distractor items were the remaining eight possible combinations of values (see Table 9.2).

The new-old recognition task revealed both a main effect of sequence and an interaction of sequence with particular examples. The Small Change group gave old patterns an average rating of 6.11 and new examples an average rating of 3.90, producing a difference of 2.21. The Large Change group gave old patterns

TABLE 9.2
Mean Recognition Rating for Each of the 16 Possible Examples for the Small Change and the
Large Change Conditions in the Experiment by Medin, Bettger, and Gentner.

Example				Condition	
Dimension					
D1	D2	D3	D4	Small Change	Large Change
Old					
1	1	1	0	6.50	5.31
0	1	1	0	6.00	4.12
0	1	1	1	5.94	5.12
1	0	1	1	5.94	5.94
1	0	1	0	6.18	5.00
1	0	0	1	5.75	5.88
1	1	0	1	6.00	6.06
1	1	1	1	6.62	6.12
New					
0	0	0	0	3.25	4.25
1	0	0	0	5.50	4.25
0	1	0	0	2.50	3.81
0	0	1	0	3.81	4.88
0	0	0	1	2.88	4.81
0	0	1	1	4.81	5.19
0	1	0	1	4.00	5.38
1	1	0	0	4.44	4.81

an average rating of 5.45 and new examples a rating of 4.68, yielding a substantially smaller difference of 0.77. In brief, new–old recognition was better for the Small Change group than for the Large Change group (the differences in new–old recognition were highly reliable).

The mean ratings for the two groups are given in Table 9.2. First of all, one may note that the more typical values an example possessed (the more 1's it had), the higher was its ratings. The overall mean ratings for 0, 1, 2, 3, and 4 typical values were 3.75, 4.08, 5.14, 5.85, and 6.37, respectively. More importantly, information order interacted with particular stimuli. Note especially that the new stimulus 1000, which was consistent with the 10** generalization but otherwise contained only one typical value, received a higher rating from the Small Change group (5.50) than from the Large Change group (4.25). In fact it was the highest rated new stimulus for the Small Change group despite the fact that it had only one typical value. For the Large Change group 1000 was among the lowest rated of the new stimuli. The tendency of the Small Change group to false alarm to this stimulus is consistent with the idea that values shared by successive example get strengthened. The other new stimulus that tests this idea was the example 0011, where the last two values are shared for the third and fourth examples, and it received the second highest rating (4.81) for the Small Change group for new stimuli.

Perhaps the most surprising finding was the main effect of order. The Small

Change group showed reliably better new-old recognition than the Large Change group. We say surprising because both groups saw the same examples over the same short time period (less than one minute) with the first and last examples being in the same order (see Ratcliff, 1978 for evidence that serial position per se showed has little effect on recognition). Yet there were large differences on the new–old recognition test given only a minute later. This general pattern of results held across each of three experiments.

In their most straightforward form, exemplar models of categorization cannot account for the effect of information order. If each example is encoded and stored separately, then memory should only be a function of the set of examples seen and the retention conditions. For both the Small Change and Large Change orders, however, the same set of examples was presented and the retention interval was the same for the two groups.

The only obvious way to account for order effects with independent coding and storage would be to argue that the effects of order arise at the time of retrieval. In illustration, Hintzman's (1986) MINERVA model is an exemplar model that allows memory traces to interact via an echo process whereby the initial output is fed back into memory as a new retrieval cue. This new retrieval cue produces a new output, which in turn may be fed back as a probe. Eventually the echo process settles down such that input and output agree. For this account to be viable, one would need to assume that one dimension of similarity is the set of temporal and contextual cues and that the similarity of these cues is very high for successive examples and much lower for nonsuccessive examples. Temporal features would be changing at the same rate for both the Small Change and Large Change condition, but temporal-contextual cues will make the most similar pairs of traces more similar in the Small Change condition than in the Large Change condition. These differences would need to persist for at least the duration of the study to test interval. These appear to be quite stringent requirements, especially given that people do not appear to have very good memory for item position or relative recency (e.g., Crowder, 1976).

Nonetheless, with the foregoing assumptions, the MINERVA model provides at least a qualitative account of our main findings. Using the echo process in simulating our first experiment, one obtains a greater difference in activation for old versus new examples in the Small Change condition than in the Large Change condition. At the same time, the activation for the new pattern 1000 is greater in the Small Change condition than in the Large Change condition, again in accord with our data. In our simulation these differences were quite small, but we have not systematically attempted to maximize them. The main difference between Hintzman's model and the exemplar-guided encoding account we are developing is not *whether* memory traces interact, but *when*. The exemplar-guided encoding position is that traces interact during encoding whereas MINERVA is based on trace interaction at the time of retrieval. (One could argue that MINERVA involves a storage-retrieval interaction by virtue of the assumptions made about contextual cues.) The data do not distinguish between these alternatives.

Although retrieval effects cannot be decisively ruled out, it seems to us more promising to argue that exemplar-guided encoding is responsible for nonindependent memory traces. Exemplar-guided encoding will favor properties that two successive examples share and thereby lead to selective coding of shared properties of the examples. It is also consistent with the finding that the Small Change group rated a new example (1000) that shared values on two dimensions that had appeared in three successive training examples much higher than the Large Change group, which did not see these examples in succession.

Both the original context model and its generalization by Nosofsky assume selective attention at the level of dimensions such that some dimensions may be weighted more than others. The present results suggest selectivity at the level of values of specific stimuli, namely those that are shared across successive examples. The same exemplar-specific attention would also account for the Ross et al. (1990) reminding results.

The ACT model is also generally consistent with the order by stimulus interaction observed in our studies. If one further assumes that memory can be based either on examples or generalizations, then the ACT model correctly predicts the better recognition by the Small Change group (see also Hayes-Roth & McDermott, 1978, and Skorstad, Gentner, & Medin, 1988). Better recognition follows from the claim by ACT that the Small Change group will have formed more generalizations than the Large Change group, generalizations that could be used to distinguish old from new examples. Such a mixed model would be difficult to distinguish from the exemplar models we have been discussing.

Base-Rate Effects and Competitive Learning

Experience and Base-Rates.   Imagine a physician who has noted a symptom that is only associated with two diseases, one of which appears a hundred times more frequently than the other. It would be quite surprising if the physician did not think that the disease with the larger base rate was much more likely to be present than the rare disease. Although there is evidence that base-rate information is not used properly when received in abstract form (e.g. Kahneman & Tversky, 1973), people appear to use base rate when it is conveyed through experience in classifying examples (e.g., Carroll & Siegler, 1977; Christensen-Szalanski & Beach, 1982; Christensen-Szalanski & Bushyhead, 1981; Manis, Dovilinia, Avis & Cardoze, 1980). One interpretation of these results on base-rate information and experience views them as by-products of learning processes that allow people to perform in a manner reflecting sensitivity to base rates without explicitly or directly using base-rate information. In the words of Christensen-Szalanski and Beach, "in some cases the use of perception and memory may be sufficient to behave in a 'Bayesian manner' (1982, p. 277).

Research on the use of base-rate information is relevant to categorization theories. For example, if categories are represented strictly in terms of prototypes, and classification decisions are based solely on distances from (similarity to) alternative prototypes, then one would not expect base-rate information (in the form of category size) to influence classification judgments. In contrast, many exemplar models that assume that an item is classified on the basis of its similarity to stored examples do predict category size effects. Furthermore, if multiple presentations of an example lead to multiple stored representations (e.g., Nosofsky, 1988b), then category probability effects will be predicted, even if the number of different examples does not vary across categories. Recently these predictions have been examined and they have led to some surprising and challenging results.

Base Rates and Competitive Learning.   Gluck and Bower (1988a,b) proposed and tested an adaptive network model that incorporates competitive learning. In their model, learning takes place only to the extent that outcomes (category assignment information) are not already anticipated by the information associated with features of an example. In essence, features compete to predict the appropriate categories (see also the chapters by Gluck and by Nosofsky).

Competitive learning can lead to base-rate neglect or underuse, and that is what Gluck and Bower observed, most clearly in a transfer task where participants were asked to estimate explicitly the probability of alternative diseases conditional upon the presence of different symptoms. Estes, Campbell, Hatsopoulos, and Hurwitz (1989) also found some evidence for base-rate neglect, and clear evidence favoring a network model employing competitive learning.

Medin and Edelson (1988) found that, depending on the structure of the learning task and the nature of the test, people were sensitive to, ignored, or even inappropriately used base-rate information. In their paradigm participants were presented with sets of symptoms (usually pairs) that were associated with alternative (disease) categories. The categories could differ in their relative frequencies (base rates) of occurrence. For example, Symptoms A and B might be associated with Disease 1, Symptoms A and C with Disease 2, and Disease 1 might appear three times as often as Disease 2. After participants learned to correctly classify examples from symptom information, they were given transfer tests designed to index their use of base-rate information. Three of the principle transfer tests were: Symptom A alone; Symptom B paired with Symptom C; and Symptoms A, B, and C together. Each of these tests is ambiguous in that each involves symptoms that had been associated with two different categories. The pattern of results depended on the particular transfer test. For Symptom A alone, participants tended to predict the more frequent category, showing sensitivity to experienced base rates. On the test with all three symptoms, people again used base-rate information appropriately. Surprisingly, however, on the B plus C test, an inverse base-rate effect was repeatedly observed as people tended to predict that the less frequent category was present, in this case Disease 2 (see also Binder & Estes, 1966). The context model predicts positive base-rate effects for all three tests, contrary to the data.

To account for this pattern of results, Medin and Edelson (1988) proposed that two processes were operating. The first is competition, although in a more indirect form than that proposed by Gluck and Bower (1988a,b) or Estes et al. (1989). The idea is that during learning, responses made on the basis of remindings of earlier trials, coupled with feedback about correctness or incorrectness, lead to selective attention favoring some symptoms over others. For example, when presented with Symptoms A and C during learning and asked to predict a disease, a participant may be reminded of AB and give the response associated with AB, which in the Medin and Edelson experiments would be incorrect. If feedback is given indicating that the response is incorrect, then participants may pay attention to what is different between the current and preceding situation— namely, Symptom C. When a reminding is successful, people may pay equal attention to both cues. The differential attention to Symptom C may create a situation where, in effect, participants have learned that AB predicts Disease 1 and that C predicts Disease 2 (this is an oversimplification in that the importance of A to Diseases 1 and 2 can be represented by a continuous function). The second process, context change, grows naturally from the first and comes into play on transfer tests. Because C has been studied apart from A more than B has, Symptom C will suffer less from the change in context associated with the BC test than will Symptom B. By the same token, Symptom B will benefit more than Symptom C from the presence of Symptom A on the ABC test.

Medin and Edelson showed that a modified form of the context model of classification embodying the competition and context change assumptions provided a good qualitative account of their results. For example, if the inverse base-rate effects are produced by remindings, then taking away the common symptom during training (e.g., AB defines a common disease and CD a rare one) should eliminate the inverse effect. This is what Medin and Edelson found (see their Experiment 2 and also Medin & Robbins, 1971). In addition, Joshua Rubinstein has successfully tested some implications of the idea that Symptom A is more closely tied to Symptom B than to Symptom C. First of all, when participants were given disease names at the end of learning and asked to recall the associated symptoms, they were more likely to recall Symptom C than Symptom B. Furthermore, when recall was perfect, they were more likely to recall C before A than they were to recall B before A. In a second study, Rubinstein recorded reaction times and found that an AB test led to quicker decisions than an AC test but that a test of B alone led to slower reaction times than a test of C alone. This support for competition and context change also supports the idea that exemplar models need more flexible encoding processes. We say more about this needed flexibility shortly.

Base-Rate Shifts.   The Gluck and Bower (1988b), Estes et al. (1989), and Medin and Edelson (1988) studies suggest that when base-rate information is conveyed through experience, processes come into play that indirectly influence its use. In particular, we have suggested that inverse base-rate effects are a by-

TABLE 9.3
Abstract Representation Base-Rate Shift Experiment

Learning Blocks: Relative Frequency	Symptoms	Disease
3, 3, 3, 3	a, b	1
1, 1, 1, 1	a, c	2
3, 3, 2, 2	d, e	3
1, 1, 2, 2	d, f	4
2, 2, 3, 3	g, h	5
2, 2, 1, 1	g, i	6
3, 3, 1, 1	j, k	7
1, 1, 3, 3	j, l	8

Transfer: Tests for base-rate information

1. Common cues: a, d, g, j
2. Conflicting tests: b, e, h, or k vs. c, f,i, or l (e.g., bc; ef; bf)
3. Combined tests: abc, def, ghi, jkl

product of learning processes. If this interpretation is correct, then the relative frequency patterns prevailing *during learning* should be critically important in determining transfer performance. In general, relative frequency early in training while learning is taking place should be more influential than the relative frequency later on. In some recent experiments (Medin and Bettger, in press), the training period was broken into quartiles and the relative frequency of a pair of diseases linked by a common symptom was held constant within a quartile but could vary between quartiles.

The design of one of our experiments is shown in Table 9.3. A pair of symptoms is associated with each disease category, where one of the symptoms is a perfect predictor (has a cue and category validity of 1) and the other is associated with exactly two diseases. The two diseases linked by a common symptom differ in their relative frequency by a 3 to 1 ratio or have equal frequency within any one learning block. For one pair of diseases the relative frequencies remain constant over blocks, whereas for the others the relative frequencies reversed after the second learning block. The former condition constitutes a replication of the Medin and Edelson experiments and provides a baseline for evaluating the effects of shifts in relative frequencies. The second condition starts with unequal frequency and shifts to equal frequency, whereas the third reverses this procedure. In the fourth condition, relative frequency reverses after the initial two blocks such that the overall relative frequency of the two diseases is equal. As Table 9.3 indicates, the transfer tests paralleled those used by Medin and Edelson.

Categorization models embodying competitive learning can predict effects of the distribution of relative frequencies. Specifically, relative frequencies during

TABLE 9.4
Transfer Results: Response Proportions from Base-Rate Shift Experiment

Shift Condition		Test Type		
	Disease	Common Cue	Within Conflicting Combined	
3, 3, 3, 3	1	.72	.42	.56
1, 1, 1, 1	2	.17	.47	.33
3, 3, 2, 2	3	.58	.31	.47
1, 1, 2, 2	4	.33	.56	.36
2, 2, 3, 3	5	.53	.58	.67
2, 2, 1, 1	6	.36	.36	.33
3, 3, 1, 1	7	.50	.44	.53
1, 1, 3, 3	8	.31	.56	.47

the early blocks should have a greater influence than relative frequencies in later blocks. Consider, for example, the j,k and j,l pairs that have equal overall frequency. By the interpretation suggested by Medin and Edelson, on a conflicting k,l test, people should predict Disease 8, because the key factor for the inverse base-rate effect should be relative frequencies while learning is taking place (the first half). On a test involving Symptom J alone, people should be more likely to predict Disease 7, which is more frequent than Disease 8 early on. Finally, on a combined j,k,l test, people should tend to predict Disease 7. Of course, these predictions hinge on the majority of learning taking place over the first two blocks.

The results indicated learning was largely complete by the end of the second training block. The overall average percentage correct was 53.5, 81.7, 92.8, and 95.1 for blocks one through four, respectively. The overall scores held for individual training pairs; there were no significant differences in the error rates for the various pairs on the final block of trials.

The main transfer results are shown in Table 9.4. Responses to the singly presented common cue conformed to overall relative frequency. For the pair with equal overall frequency, there was a trend for the disease category that had been frequent early in training to be selected. The within-conflicting trials reveal the separate contributions of early and late frequency. For the pair where frequencies did not shift there was a slight inverse base-rate effect.[3] This inverse effect was much stronger for the pair that had unequal frequency blocks followed by equal

---

[3]This slight inverse effect seems to only weakly replicate the robust inverse effects observed by Medin and Edelson. In the Medin and Edelson studies, however, training terminated when a learning criterion was met. Given that late frequency and early frequency effects appear to be opposite in character, the weaker inverse effects in the present study are not surprising.

frequency blocks. Just the opposite pattern appears for the pair that initially had equal frequency; here one observes a robust positive base-rate effect. The only observation that does not support the idea that early infrequency and late frequency contribute to a disease category's being selected is that the pair realizing both these conditions did not lead to the most extreme differences in responding. Overall, disease categories that were infrequent early in training were favored on transfer tests, whereas late frequency clearly helped for the pair that had appeared with equal frequency early in training. Finally, on the combined tests responses tended to mirror those shown on common cue tests, a pattern of performance in agreement with the Medin and Edelson (1988) results.

Obviously the emerging picture on the use of experience-derived base-rate information is quite challenging to theories. Most categorization models predict that base-rate information will be either uniformly used (e.g. Hintzman, 1986; Medin & Schaffer, 1978; Nosofsky, 1988a) or uniformly ignored (Rosch, Simpson, & Miller, 1976). The use of base-rate information depends not only on the type of test given but also on stage of training.

The Medin and Bettger results provide general support for theories that tie base-rate information to the details of learning. At a more specific level of detail, this support is not so strong. The Gluck and Bower (1988a,b) adaptation of the Rescorla–Wagner model includes competition among cues during learning but in its present form predicts no base-rate effects at the end of learning, and only positive base-rate effects preasymptotically (the suggestion to the contrary by Medin & Edelson, 1988, is simply wrong). Markman (1989) has shown, however, that a variation of a competitive learning model employing the explicit coding of missing symptoms (e.g., on an AB trial the absence of C is coded, and on an AC trial the absence of B is coded) can predict the A, BC, and ABC test results observed by Medin and Edelson (1988).[4] Markman's modifications, however, do not address the reversal of the effects of relative frequency as a function of training noted in the present studies.

Gluck (1989; this volume) has recently attempted to combine network models with earlier models associated with stimulus sampling theory (e.g., Estes, 1959). The main idea is that each symptom can be thought of as comprised of elements sampled with some probability. The principle of sampling variability implies that learning is never fully complete and the sampling-network model would allow for at least some contribution from late frequency (though it appears that the model will predict either no effect or an inverse

---

[4]Such mechanism could presumably operate only after expectations are built up from initial trials. Furthermore, these expectations would need to be tied to the common cues so that an AB trial is not also encoded involving the absence of D,E,F,G,H,I,J, and K. That is, the common cue C would retrieve the cues associated with it (B and C) and the absence of C (on an AB trial) would be noted. This assumption begins to sound very much like the reminding-based processing account we have been describing.

frequency effect on conflicting tests when frequencies are initially equal and unequal later on).

The Medin and Edelson (1988) competition and context change principles successfully predict that the inverse base-rate effects are linked to learning. Their formulation seems to be agnostic with respect to the effects of frequency late in training after learning is complete. It is not clear how reduced attention after learning is complete would trade off with forgetting and contextual changes to determine late frequency effects. What is clear is that the Medin and Edelson inverse base-rate effects depend on the base rate prevailing during learning and not only overall relative frequencies. Before attempting to draw out the implications of base-rate effects for selective attention and abstraction, we turn to some other recent results involving exemplar frequency.

Exemplar Frequency Effects

With respect to categorization performance, there is still some debate as to what role exemplar frequency plays. Rosch's family resemblance model predicts that the extent to which an exemplar's attributes are shared with other category members is a far better predictor of typicality than the frequency, or familiarity, of the category member (Rosch, Simpson, & Miller, 1976). In recent research, frequency of presentation of an exemplar has been found to increase typicality judgments for that exemplar and those similar to it (Nosofsky, 1986). Furthermore, Barsalou (1985) has found that people's judgment of frequency of instantiation of an example is highly correlated with typicality judgments.

Our own investigations of effects of exemplar frequency (Florian, 1989) reveal further complications. In one of our experiments investigating effects of exemplar frequency, subjects learned to distinguish two categories of items varying on four binary dimensions: pattern (striped or dotted), form (square or circle), size (small or large) and number (one or two forms). The design of this experiment is shown in Table 9.5. Category A consisted of exemplars of the abstract forms 1111, 0011, and 1100. Category B consisted of exemplars 0000, 0110, and 1001. The frequency of one exemplar (exemplar 0011 of Category A) varied among three conditions: In the first condition it was seen with the same frequency as every other exemplar. In Conditions two and three, the exemplar was presented twice and three times as often as all of the other exemplars learned respectively. We used three conditions so that nonmonotonic effects could potentially be observed.

On a categorization test administered after learning, new, similar items did not change in their likelihood of being categorized into the category with the frequent item as frequency increased. Figure 9.2 shows categorization performance on the most similar transfer items as a function of the frequency of the learned, similar exemplar. Frequency had no reliable overall effect on the classification of the similar transfer items. Furthermore, as shown in Figure 9.3, the probability of

TABLE 9.5
Design of Frequency Experiment

Item	PFS N	Frequency by Condition 123	Category A Categorization Probability 1	2	3	Probability (OLD) 1	2	3
Category A								
A1.	1111	333	1.00	1.00	.98	.97	1.00	1.00
A2	0011	369	.94	.94	.97	.97	1.00	.97
A3	1100	333	.95	.86	.89	1.00	1.00	1.00
Category B								
B1	0000	333	.05	.03	.03	.97	.97	.97
B2	0110	333	.05	.11	.06	.97	1.00	.88
B3	1001	333	.05	.01	.09	.97	1.00	1.00
Transfer Items								
1	1000		.39	.27	.19	.84	.78	.78
2	0100		.41	.34	.38	.56	.28	.34
3	0010		.25	.38	.38	.63	.47	.44
4	0001		.25	.25	.22	.63	.66	.53
5	0101		.31	.31	.48	.13	.22	.13
6	1010		.41	.44	.36	.13	.09	.13
7	1110		.53	.48	.55	.63	.59	.63
8	1101		.58	.48	.66	.69	.66	.59
9	1011		.77	.75	.64	.53	.25	.34
10	0111		.80	.78	.73	.78	.53	.66

Note. P, F, S, N refer to the dimensions of pattern, form, size, and number.

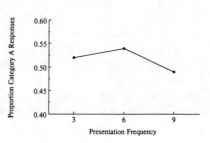

FIG. 9.2. Average probability of categorizing transfer items 1011, 0111, 0010, and 0001 into Category A, as a function of the presentation frequency of Category A item 0011.

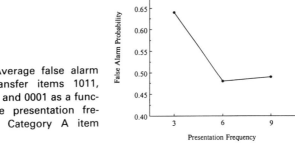

FIG. 9.3. Average false alarm rate to transfer items 1011, 0111, 0010, and 0001 as a function of the presentation frequency of Category A item 0011.

calling these new, similar items old *decreased* with an increase in presentation frequency, though this result was only marginally significant; ($p < .10$). (Table 9.5 shows the complete results on categorization and recognition tests.) This suggests that in learning to distinguish the two categories of this experiment, people are unaffected by seeing one exemplar an increased number of times, even though their encoding of that exemplar improves as reflected by fewer false alarms on a recognition test. An exemplar can be highly familiar and recognizable without making a large contribution to category structure. Likewise, Weber and Crocker (1983) have found that a person displaying behaviors that are inconsistent with members of a group will be highly remembered if the person is salient or frequently encountered, but this greater memorability will not affect the person's stereotypes of the category.

It appears the amount of influence an individual exemplar has in determining categorization depends on factors such as number of typical features. Other categorization experiments have found that attributes are more likely to be inferred from typical category members than from atypical category members, whether the attributes are category-consistent or category-inconsistent ones (Rips, 1975; Rothbart & Lewis, 1988). In an experiment by Rothbart and Lewis, the colors of more prototypical geometric figures were erroneously judged as more frequent of the category than the colors of less prototypical geometric forms. The more typical geometric figures received more weighting when determining color of category members than the atypical forms received (see also this volume's chapter by Smith on category-based induction).

The categorization results of our experiment can be predicted by the context model of categorization (Medin & Schaffer, 1978) when it is in the form of a type model; that is, when repetitions of an exemplar are not represented as additional traces. When the context model is fit to the results in the form of a token model (in which each presentation is represented by a new exemplar trace), the model does not adequately fit the data of Conditions 2 and 3. In contrast, studies presented by Nosofsky (1988b) have reported exemplar frequency effects on typicality using integral dimensions that would require a frequency-sensitive model to predict them. In other studies we have conducted we sometimes observe modest frequency effects that indicate that a pure type model is inadequate. We continue to be surprised with just how small these frequency effects are. Further research is needed to analyze the differences between our results and those by Nosofsky. What is clear is that simple frequency effects are not simple.

Investigators have suggested a straightforward way of linking exemplar recognition to categorization. The idea is that categorization depends on the comparison of summed similarity of an item to exemplars of one category versus other categories, but that recognition depends on the summed similarity of an item to all exemplars in memory (Estes, 1986b; Gillund & Shiffrin, 1984; Medin, 1986; Medin & Schaffer, 1978; Nosofsky, 1988a) or the summed activation of traces in memory (Gillund & Shiffrin, 1984; Hintzman, 1986). In the just-mentioned experiment, summed similarity of a test item to all old items was found to correlate with observed recognition data when a type model was used ($r^2 = 0.78$) better than when a token model was used ($r^2 = 0.44$). On the other hand, the type model could not account for the marginal *decrease* in false alarms to similar items as frequency increases.

Some experiments have reported frequency having an even more surprising effect on recognition performance. With increased frequency of an item's presentation, false alarms to new similar items increases. However, with continued frequency, false recognition to new distractor items decreases again (Hall & Kozloff, 1970). In the experiment discussed here, we obtained a decrease in false alarms to similar items with an increase in exemplar frequency. This effect could be well accounted for by selective attention to frequent exemplars. Similar new items would decrease in their similarity to the exemplar as it becomes more differentiated and as false recognition correspondingly diminishes.

Shiffrin, Ratcliff, and Clark (1990) have recently proposed a similar mechanism to produce differentiation within the framework of the SAM model (Gillund & Shiffrin, 1984). In several experiments they show the absence of the list-strength effect on recognition. A list-strength effect is manifest as lowered performance on once-presented (or weak) items when other items are presented more often. That is, strong items tend to inhibit memory for weak items. Although Shriffin et al. find no effect of list strength on recognition, they do find a reliable effect when free recall is tested. They are able to predict these results by incorporating differentiation into the SAM model by decreasing the parameter reflecting similarity between a distractor item and list items that change from moderate strength to high strength (i.e., those that appear frequently). This modification predicts the absence of the list-strength effect in tests of recognition. In addition, they increase the weighting of a context cue with increased trace strength. Because the context cue is used more in free recall according to this model, stronger traces are more likely to be activated and the predicted list-strength effect is observed. Their account of the phenomenon of differentiation, or little or negative effects of high strength of an exemplar on recognition, is identical to the frequency-sensitive context model previously presented. That is, by this account, the distinctiveness of exemplar encodings and, as a consequence, the similarity of new items to exemplars, is affected by frequency.

In summary, it appears that future exemplar models need some mechanism for providing increased weighting to particular exemplars over others, and this is affected by such factors as frequency, familiarity, and typicality. One possible way of achieving this is by varying the likelihood of an exemplar's being activated in response to a probe, or the similarity between a probe and an item in memory.

Implications for Exemplar-Based Abstraction

We believe that the observations on order effects, base-rate shifts, and frequency all point in the same direction. Specifically, they suggest that selective attention may operate not only at the level of dimensions (as in previous versions of the context model) but also at the level of individual examples or pairs of examples (see also Aha & Goldstone, 1990). The sequence effects are well described by the idea that when two items are together in working memory the properties they share are differentially strengthened. The various base rate effects we have been describing can also be described in terms of remindings and selective attention to properties of examples. We suggest that a successful reminding leads to differential attention to properties that a probe and the retrieved example share, and that a reminding that leads to an error is associated with attention to properties that are different between a probe and the retrieval example. Finally, our observations on exemplar frequency suggest that frequent examples may be better differentiated than infrequent examples. Again, selectivity is at the level of examples rather than dimensions overall.

It is not clear how to represent example-specific selective attention within a multidimensional scaling framework. Continuing the spatial analogy, one could posit highly local stretching and shrinking of the similarity space, but that still would not fully capture the idea of example-specific attention. The problem is that whether or not a difference makes a difference may depend on which stored example a probe is being compared with. For example, suppose one has stored examples 1100 and 1110 and that the probe is 1101. On logical grounds the probe is more similar to the first example than the second because it differs from the first example only along the fourth dimension, but it differs from the second example along the third and fourth dimensions. Suppose, however, that the first example was encoded precisely such that all four values were salient, but for the second example attention focused only on the first two dimensions. Effectively the second example could be encoded as 11**, where the asterisk means that the value differences do not diminish similarity. Then the probe would be more likely to access (or would access more strongly) the second example than the first. We see no straightforward way to represent example-specific similarity relationships with a multidimensional scaling framework (but see Nosofsky, 1988c for some initial speculations).

OVERVIEW

Abstraction and Learning

Coupling these new findings and interpretations with our initial observations, one can see that exemplar models may possess any or all of the three distinct mechanisms for abstraction: (a) integration during retrieval, (b) selective attention at the level of dimensions, and (c) selective attention at the level values associated with particular examples. We believe that these mechanisms are well-motivated by data, but that they make the task of distinguishing between exemplar models and alternative models of abstraction such as rule-based accounts even more difficult (see Medin, 1986, Nosofsky et al., 1989, for further discussion).

The results we have been discussing do not undermine an interest in distinguishing different models for category representation but they do place a renewed stress on learning process. A decade ago alternative classification models were contrasted almost exclusively in terms of their predictions concerning transfer performance *after* learning. Although transfer tests continue to have considerable diagnostic value, investigators are beginning to bring out the importance of learning data for theory development and testing (e.g., Estes, 1986b; Estes et al., 1989). The recent interest in adaptive network models of learning should only serve to further this trend.

Representation

The renewed focus on learning process should also have a salutary effect on our ideas about representation. Exemplar models have been shy on details concerning just how examples get encoded and one should at least consider the possibility that only fragments of a complex stimulus are successfully stored on a learning trial (for ideas along these lines, see Heit, 1990).

The next generation of exemplar models (and category learning models in general, for that matter) may also need to take further inspiration from Estes' hierarchical associative model of memory discussed earlier in this chapter. Current models assume only two levels of representation, dimension and value. Although researchers usually have restricted themselves to stimulus materials where this assumption seems viable, in the general case examples can be described at a number of hierarchical levels. Consider, for example, drawing of people as stimulus materials. One could attempt to force descriptions into a two-level framework (e.g., hair color, height), but such efforts might well not be successful. For example, if a hand were missing from one drawing and a foot from another, one would likely need to be able to indicate that "body part missing" was an important similarity between the two drawings. Furthermore, one would also need to be able to represent relations among properties such as "one arm longer than the other arm." Both multiple levels and relations point to the need for hierarchical, structured representations (Barsalou & Billman, 1989). In short, we need more powerful theories of similarity to extend our categorization theories to richer stimulus sets.

SUMMARY

We began our chapter with a puzzle about abstraction and category learning. Much of the theoretical debate in the categorization area has contrasted prototype models with exemplar models and some have taken this debate to be about whether or not abstraction takes place. We have argued that exemplar models *are* abstraction models and that they incorporate abstraction in at least three distinct ways. Recent research within the exemplar framework as well as other work contrasting exemplar models with alternative abstraction models has served to focus attention on the learning mechanisms and details of learning. In turn, this interest in learning is feeding back to suggest more realistic and powerful ideas concerning representation. Although the debate between exemplar-based abstraction models and alternative abstraction theories will likely not be resolved in the immediate future, we can anticipate that the background will be one of continued progress in understanding categorization and classification theories.

ACKNOWLEDGMENTS

The research reported in this chapter was supported by National Science Foundation Grants 88-12193 and 89-18701 to Douglas L. Medin. Larry Barsalou, Ed Smith, Rob Nosofsky, Tom Ward, Stephen Kosslyn, Gordon Bower, and Evan Heit provided helpful comments on earlier versions of this chapter. The first author also wishes to acknowledge several decades of excellent advice and support from William K. Estes.

REFERENCES

Aha, D. W., & Goldstone, R. L. (1990). Learning attribute relevance in context in instance-based learning algorithms. *Proceedings of the 12th Annual Conference of the Cognitive Science Society* (pp. 141–148). Hillsdale, NJ: Lawrence Erlbaum Associates.

Anderson, J. R., Kline, P. J., & Beasley C. M. (1979). A general learning theory and its application to schema abstraction. In G. H. Bower (Ed.), *The psychology of learning and motivation* (Vol. 13, pp. 227–319). New York: Academic Press.

Atkinson, R. C., & Estes, W. K. (1963). Stimulus sampling theory. In R. D. Luce, R. R. Bush, & E. Galanter (Eds.), *Handbook of mathematical psychology* (pp. 121–168). New York: Wiley.

Barsalou, L. W. (1985). Ideals, central tendency and frequency of instantiation as determinants of graded structure in categories. *Journal of Experimental Psychology: Learning, Memory, and Cognition, 11,* 629–654.

Barsalou, L. W., & Billman, D. (1989). Systematicity and semantic ambiguity. In D. Gorfein (Ed.), *Resolving semantic ambiguity* (pp. 146–203). New York: Springer-Verlag.

Binder, A., & Estes, W. K. (1966). Transfer of response in visual recognition situations as a function of frequency variables. *Psychological Monographs, 50,* (23, Whole no. 631).

Brooks, L. R. (1987). Decentralized control of categorization: The role of prior processing episodes. In U. Neisser (Ed.), *Concepts and conceptual development: The ecological and intellectual factors in categorization* (pp. 141–174). Cambridge: Cambridge University Press.

Carroll, J. S., & Siegler, R. S. (1977). Strategies for the use of base-rate information. *Organizational Behavior and Human Performance, 19,* 392–402.

Christensen-Szalanski, J. J. J., & Beach, L. R. (1982). Experience and the base-rate fallacy. *Organizational Behavior and Human Performance, 29,* 270–278.

Christensen-Szalanski, J. J. J., & Bushyhead, J. B. (1981). Physicians' use of probabilistic information in a real clinical setting. *Journal of Experimental Psychology: Human Perception and Learning, 7,* 928–935.

Cover, T. M., & Hart, P. E. (1967). Nearest neighbor pattern classification. *IEEE Transactions in Information Theory,* Vol. IT-13, pp. 21–27.

Crowder, R. G. (1976). *Principles of learning and memory.* New York: Wiley.

Elio, R., & Anderson, J. R. (1981). Effects of category generalizations and instance similarity on schema abstraction. *Journal of Experimental Psychology: Human Learning and Memory, 7,* 397–417.

Estes, W. K. (1959). Component and pattern models with Markovian interpretation. In R. R. Bush and W. K. Estes (Eds.), *Studies in mathematical learning theory* (pp. 9–52). Stanford, CA: Stanford University Press.

Estes, W. K. (1972). An associative basis for coding and organization in memory. In A. W. Melton and E. Martin (Eds.), *Coding processes in human memory* (pp. 161–190). Washington, DC: Winston.

Estes, W. K. (1973). Memory and conditioning. In F. J. McCuigan & D. B. Lumsden (Eds.), *Contemporary approaches to conditioning and learning* (pp. 265–286). Washington, D.C.: V. H. Winston.

Estes, W. K. (1976). Structural aspects of associative models for memory. In C. N. Cofer (Ed.), *The structure of human memory* (pp. 31–53). New York: W. H. Freeman.

Estes, W. K. (1986a). Array models for category learning. *Cognitive Psychology, 18,* 500–549.

Estes, W. K. (1986b). Memory storage and retrieval processes in category learning. *Journal of Experimental Psychology: General, 115,* 155–175.

Estes, W. K., Campbell, J. A., Hatsopoulos, N., & Hurwitz, J. (1989). Base-rate effects in category learning: A comparison of parallel network and memory storage-retrieval models. *Journal of Experimental Psychology: Learning, Memory, and Cognition, 15,* 556–571.

Estes, W. K., & Hopkins, B. L. (1961). Acquisition and transfer in pattern versus component discrimination learning. *Journal of Experimental Psychology, 61,* 322–328.

Estes, W. K., Hopkins, B. L., & Crothers, E. J. (1960). All-or-more and conservation effects in the learning and retention of paired associates. *Journal of Experimental Psychology, 60,* 329–339.

Florian, J. E. (1989). *Exemplar frequency effects on categorization and recognition.* Unpublished master's thesis, University of Illinois, Urbana, IL.

Forbus, K., & Gentner, D. (1986). Learning physical domains: Toward a theoretical framework. In R. M. Michalski, J. Carbonell, & T. Mitchell (Eds.) *Machine learning: An artificial intelligence approach* (Vol. 11, pp. 311–348). Los Altos, California: Morgan Kaufmann.

Gillund, G., & Shiffrin, R. M. (1984). A retrieval model for both recognition and recall. *Psychological Review, 91,* 1–67.

Gluck, M. A. (1989). Stimulus-sampling in a distributed network model: Effects of category frequency on generalizations. *Proceedings of the 11th Annual Conference of the Cognitive Science Society*. Hillsdale, NJ: Lawrence Erlbaum Associates.

Gluck, M. A., & Bower, G. H. (1988a). Evaluating an adaptive network model of human learning. *Journal of Memory and Language, 27*, 166–195.

Gluck, M. A., & Bower, G. H. (1988b). From conditioning to category learning: An adaptive network model. *Journal of Experimental Psychology: General, 117*, 227–247.

Hall, J. F., & Kozloff, E. E. (1970). False recognitions as a function of number of presentations. *American Journal of Psychology, 83*, 272–279.

Hayes-Roth, F., & McDermott, J. (1978). An interference matching technique for inducing abstractions. *Communications of the ACM, 21*, pp. 401–411.

Heit, E. (1990). The role of instance knowledge in memory for numerical distributions. Manuscript submitted for publication.

Hintzman, D. L. (1986). "Schema abstraction" in a multiple-trace memory model. *Psychological Review, 93*, 411–428.

Jacoby, L. L., Baker, J., & Brooks, L. (1989). Episodic effects on picture identification: Implications for theories of concept and learning theories of memory. *Journal of Experimental Psychology: Learning, Memory and Cognition, 15*, 275–281.

Jacoby, L. L., & Brooks, L. R. (1984). Non-analytic cognition: Memory, perception, and concept learning. In G. Bower (Ed.), *The psychology of learning and motivation* (Vol. 18, pp. 1–47). New York: Academic Press.

Kahneman, D., & Tversky, A. (1973). On the psychology of prediction. *Psychological Review, 80*, 237–251.

Malt, B., & Smith, E. E. (1984). Correlated properties in natural categories. *Journal of Verbal Learning and Verbal Behavior, 23*, 250–269.

Manis, M., Dovalina, I., Avis, N. E., & Cardoze, S. (1980). Base rates can affect individual predictions. *Journal of Personality and Social Psychology, 38*, 287–298.

Markman, A. (1989). LMS rules and the inverse base rate effect: Comments on Gluck and Bower. *Journal of Experimental Psychology: General, 118*, 417–421.

Medin, D. L. (1975). A theory of context in discrimination learning. In G. H. Bower (Ed.), *The psychology of learning and motivation* (Vol. 9, pp. 263–314). New York: Academic Press.

Medin, D. L. (1986). Commentary on "Memory storage and retrieval processes in category learning." *Journal of Experimental Psychology: General, 115*, 373–381.

Medin, D. L., Altom, M. W., Edelson, S. M., & Freko, D. (1982). Correlated symptoms and simulated medical classification. *Journal of Experimental Psychology: Learning, Memory, and Cognition, 8*, 37–50.

Medin, D. L., & Bettger, J. G. (1991). Sensitivity to changes in base-rate information. *American Journal of Psychology, 104*, 311–332.

Medin, D. L., & Edelson, S. M. (1988). Problem structure and the use of base-rate information from experience. *Journal of Experimental Psychology: General, 117*, 68–85.

Medin, D. L., & Robbins, D. (1971). Effect of frequency on transfer performance after successive discrimination training. *Journal of Experimental Psychology, 87*, 434–436.

Medin, D. L., & Ross, B. H. (1989). The specific character of abstract thought: Categorization, problem solving, and induction. In R. J. Sternberg (Ed.), *Advances in the psychology of human intelligence* (Vol. 5 pp. 189–223). Hillsdale, NJ: Lawrence Earlbaum Associates.

Medin, D. L., & Schaffer, M. M. (1978). A context theory of classification learning. *Psychological Review, 85*, 207–238.

Medin, D. L., & Smith, E. E. (1981). Strategies in classification learning. *Journal of Experimental Psychology: Human Learning and Memory, 7*, 241–253.

Medin, D. L., & Smith, E. E. (1984). Concepts and concept formation. *Annual Review of Psychology, 35*, 112–138.

Nosofsky, R. M. (1984). Choice, similarity, and the context theory classification. *Journal of Experimental Psychology: Learning, Memory, and Cognition, 10,* 104–114.

Nosofsky, R. M. (1986). Attention, similarity, and the identification categorization relationship. *Journal of Experimental Psychology: General, 115,* 39–57.

Nosofsky, R. M. (1987). Attention and learning processes in the identification and categorization of integral stimuli. *Journal of Experimental Psychology: Learning, Memory, and Cognition, 13,* 87–108.

Nosofsky, R. M. (1988a). Exemplar-based accounts of relations between classification, recognition, and typicality. *Journal of Experimental Psychology: Learning, Memory, and Cognition, 14,* 700–708.

Nosofsky, R. M. (1988b). Similarity, frequency, and category representations. *Journal of Experimental Psychology: Learning, Memory, and Cognition, 14,* 54–65.

Nosofsky, R. M. (1988c). On exemplar-based exemplar representations: Reply to Ennis (1988). *Journal of Experimental Psychology: General, 117,* 412–414.

Nosofsky, R. M., Clark, S. E., & Shinn, J. H. (1989). Rules and exemplars in categorization, identification, and recognition. *Journal of Experimental Psychology: Learning, Memory, and Cognition, 15,* 282–304.

Ratcliff, R. (1978). A theory of memory retrieval. *Psychological Review, 85,* 59–108.

Reed, S. K. (1972). Pattern recognition and categorization. *Cognitive Psychology, 3,* 382–407.

Rips, L. J. (1975). Inductive judgments about natural categories. *Journal of Verbal Learning and Verbal Behavior, 14,* 665–681.

Rosch, E., Simpson, C., & Miller, R. S. (1976). Structural bases of typicality effects. *Journal of Experimental Psychology: Human Perception and Performance, 2,* 491–502.

Ross, B. H., Perkins, S. J., & Tenpenny, P. L. (1990). Reminding-based category learning. *Cognitive Psychology, 22,* 460–492.

Rothbart, M., & Lewis, S. (1988). Inferring category attributes from exemplar attributes: Geometric shapes and social categories. *Journal of Personality and Social Psychology, 55,* 861–872.

Shepard, R. N. (1987). Towards a universal law of generalization for psychological science. *Science, 237,* 1317–1323.

Shiffrin, R. M., Ratcliff, E., & Clark, W. E. (1990). List-strength effect: II. Theoretical mechanisms. *Journal of Experimental Psychology: Learning, Memory and Cognition, 16,* 179–195.

Skorstad, J., Gentner, D., & Medin, D. L. (1988). Abstraction processes during concept learning: A structural view. In *Proceedings of the 10th Annual Conference of the Cognitive Science Society* (pp. 419–425). Hillsdale, NJ: Lawrence Erlbaum Associates.

Spence, K. W. (1936). The nature of discrimination learning in animals. *Psychological Review, 43,* 427–499.

Watkins, M. J., & Kerkar, S. P. (1985). Recall of a twice-presented item without recall of either presentation: Generic memory for events. *Journal of Memory and Language, 24,* 666–678.

Weber, R., & Crocker, J. (1983). Cognitive processes in the revision stereotypic beliefs. *Journal of Personality and Social Psychology, 45* 961–977.

10

A Fuzzy-Trace Theory of Reasoning and Remembering: Paradoxes, Patterns, and Parallelism

Valerie F. Reyna
Charles J. Brainerd
University of Arizona

In 1980, Estes published a paper that captured much of his "farewell" address at the Rockefeller University. The paper contrasted human and computer memory at a time when theoretical currents were flowing in the opposite direction. Departments of cognitive science were springing up, confederating those who studied humans and those who studied computers; after all, they both studied "memory" and "intelligence." The new cognitive scientists (of which the ever-ecumenical Estes was one) took the information-processing framework a step further. Not only was the computer a metaphor for human intelligence, but it increasingly became a proving ground for theories through simulations (Estes, 1982). Although one could debate the extent to which computational models and metaphors became reified in theories of human cognition, there is no doubt that similarities rather than differences were stressed.

In this chapter, we discuss Estes' (1980) views about human versus machine cognition. We outline a theory, *fuzzy-trace theory*, that takes seriously Estes' claim that human memory is "less than optimal for the special purposes of calculations and logical operations" (p. 68). Thus, our approach relies on Estes' characterization of memory, and its implications for reasoning. In contrast to thinking viewed as computation or as logical operations, then, fuzzy-trace theory takes intuition as its core metaphor (Brainerd & Reyna, 1990a; Reyna & Brainerd, 1990). As we discuss, this new perspective has led to the discovery of empirical phenomena that can only be described as paradoxical from conventional perspectives: that memory for problem information is often *independent* of problem-solving accuracy, that weakly remembered items *precede* stronger items in recall, that numerical problems are usually *not* solved numerically, that reasoners rely on *imprecision* to avoid errors, that development progresses from operating on details to an *increasing* use of gist, and so on.

Our discussion begins at encoding and continues through output, touching on issues of parallelism in processing and seriality at output (Estes, 1988). Although such information-processing stages provide an organizing framework for our presentation, as is often the case in contemporary theorizing, nothing serial is intended. Indeed, it is the interactions among these "stages," or better, aspects of thinking, that serve as the theory's focus. Central among these interactions is the relationship between reasoning and remembering. Preliminary to our input-to-output analysis, however, we present an overview of the fuzzy-trace theory approach.

METAPHORS OF THOUGHT

Paradoxes

For Piaget, information was construed as premises that were input to logico-mathematical rules, which, in turn, output conclusions. Although it is now well established that human logic has its limitations (e.g., Bell, Raiffa, & Tversky, 1988), reasoning of even minimal coherence is often assumed to conform to the Piagetian view—namely, that thought progresses from problem information, as premises, to conclusions. This implies linear thought in the sense that it is impossible to skip premises. In rule-based theories, Piagetian or otherwise, thinking must pass through premises in order to reach conclusions (Brainerd & Kingma, 1984, 1985; Reyna, in press-b; Reyna & Brainerd, 1990). Thus, the nature of thought from the rule-based or logicist perspective is a step-wise progression from premise-like inputs to conclusions.

The formalist approach characterizes thought as computation or abstract symbol manipulation (Brainerd & Reyna, 1990a). Much of cognitive science and information-processing psychology can be described as formalist in orientation because of the use of the computer as a predominant metaphor for human cognition (e.g., Shannon, 1988). Regarding computers, Estes (1980) noted that "the digital computer has characteristically been designed to preserve with a high degree of fidelity a very large number of discrete items of information, and to do so in a way that makes precise calculations possible" (p. 67). Thus, it is not coincidental that we see in formalist approaches to human cognition an emphasis on precision, richness of detail in representations, and complexity in processing (e.g., Kolodner & Riesbeck, 1986).

Neither the formalist view of thinking as computation nor the logicist rule-based approach, however, captures the impressionistic quality of thought, what Argyris (1988, p. 607) has called "rigorous sloppiness." In contrast to computers, the "memory system of the human being . . . has been designed, so to speak, to sacrifice high fidelity in favor of a capacity to maintain large amounts of approximate information" (Estes, 1980, p. 67). Such imprecision, as a father of the information-processing revolution, von Neumann (1958), pointed out, does have advantages, including decreased sensitivity to noise. Thus, the fuzziness of memory has inevitable consequences for processing, at least some of which are beneficial.

In the foundations of mathematics, there is a similar opposition between logicism, formalism, and a third approach, intuitionism (Brainerd & Reyna, 1990a). The intuitionist school argues that mathematical insights spring from manipulation of only the barest glimmers of ideas, and that such thinking does not progress in a linear, step-wise fashion. It is this sense of intuitionism that we intend (Reyna & Brainerd, 1991). An implication of intuitionism, then, is that reasoning, as Estes (1980) contended, is not intrinsically logical or computational. According to intuitionism, thinking acts on the global patterns in information. Precise inputs carry cues to these gist-like patterns, but simply presenting precise inputs does not imply that those facts in that form are used in reasoning (Reyna & Brainerd, 1990).

In transitive inference, for example, reasoners do not operate on verbatim premises of the form *The red stick is longer than the blue stick* and *The blue stick is longer than the yellow stick* (see Table 10.1 for descriptions of this and other tasks). Rather, they apprehend the gist of the incoming pattern of information. That is, as pairs of sticks are introduced, and their relationships described, they are laid down in order. Rather than remembering specific items or relationships, reasoners remember the overall flow that sticks were laid down so that "things get bigger to the right" (e.g., Brainerd & Kingma, 1984; Chapman & Lindenberger, 1988). Although reasoning must be based on memory for some information (because differences in length are imperceptible), the gist of the ordering is sufficient for accurate performance. Likewise in probability judgment, children are typically presented with two bins containing different numbers of a target object. Asked to select the bin from which the target is more likely to be drawn, subjects apparently do not process exact frequencies. Choices are based, instead, on the relational gist that one bin "has more" than the other (Brainerd, 1981; Brainerd & Kingma, 1985).

Evidence from these and other paradigms shows that the representations that subjects commonly use to solve problems fail to incorporate such details as counts of objects or information about individual items (e.g., specific relationships between sticks in transitive inference). Subjects do have representations of such verbatim details; they simply fail to use them in problem solving, leading to reasoning–remembering independence. Thus, according to fuzzy-trace theory, people prefer to extract the gist of the background facts in solving problems, rather than executing computations or logico-mathematical operations on precisely specified inputs.

The counterintuitiveness of such theoretical claims is related to the counterin-

TABLE 10.1
Verbatim Versus Gist Representations in Classic Problem-Solving Paradigms

Problem	Verbatim	Gist
Probability judgment	A = 7, and A' = 3.	A has more than A'.
Transitive inference	A = 18 cm, B = 17.5 cm, and C = 17 cm.	Things get longer to the left.
Class inclusion	A = 7, A' = 3, and B = 10	All As and all A's are Bs.
Conservation of number	A = 7, A' = 7, and B = 7.	A and A' are the same.
Framing of gains	Save 200 of 600 people or accept a one-third chance of saving 600, a two-thirds chance of saving none.	Save some people versus save some or save none.
Framing of losses	Let 400 of 600 people die or accept a one-third chance that none die, a two-thirds chance that 600 will die.	Some people die versus none die or some die.
Oddity discrimination	A = green triangle, A' = green square, and B = red circle.	A and A' are the same, and B is different.
Moral judgment	A has two cookies, and A' has one cookie.	A has more than A'.

Note. The verbatim level of representation also includes all encoded features, such as color, shape, and size, not specified here due to space limitations. Similarly, gist representations usually do not specify individual elements (designated here as A, A', B, and the like) if an external store is available.

In the standard version of the probability judgment task, A and A' are sets of familiar objects, and the indicated numbers of A and A' elements are displayed. Subjects are asked to predict the results of random draws from this sampling space.

In transitive inference, differing objects A, B, and C (e.g., colored sticks differing imperceptibly in length) are described pairwise, and placed down in order from left to right in front of the subject.

In class inclusion, A and A' are displayed sets of familiar objects (e.g., cows and horses), both of which are proper subsets of the superordinate set B (e.g., animals).

In conservation of number, two sets of objects are counted, A and B, and then A is transformed (spread out) to form A', and the experimenter asks the relationship between A' and B.

In framing problems of the lives saved/lost variety, subjects are told that 600 people are expected to die from an Asian disease, and are asked which of two programs to combat the disease is preferable; subjects choose between a sure thing and a gamble of equal expected value.

In oddity discrimination learning, subjects learn to pick the odd one (B) from a set based on dissimilarity along some dimension on which the remaining members (A and A') have identical values.

In moral judgment tasks, subjects are often asked to judge the rightness or wrongness of actions or states of affairs, in this case whether it is fair to distribute more cookies to one child, A, than to another, A'.

tuitiveness of the findings on which they are based. It is useful to note, then, that the standard threats to validity do not apply. The finding of reasoning–remembering independence, for example, is obtained when more, rather than less, sensitive techniques are used: Weaker techniques such as correlation and qualitative comparisons of the memory of accurate versus inaccurate reasoners suggest reasoning–remembering dependence, whereas more powerful tests such as conditional analysis of error data and response-time modeling indicate independence (e.g., Brainerd & Kingma, 1984, 1985; Callahan, 1989; Reyna & Brainerd, 1990). The fine-grain characteristics of the data across these tasks are also consistent with the fuzzy-trace theory account, but contradict traditional assumptions about memory dependencies.

Additionally, one might speculate that such paradoxical findings are confined to subjects who lack reasoning competence. That is, subjects might "downsize" problems, operate on gist, if they are incapable of more elaborate reasoning. It has been repeatedly demonstrated, however, that accurate reasoners prefer to operate on gist (e.g., Brainerd, 1981; Brainerd & Reyna, 1990b; Reyna & Brainerd, in press). Moreover, relying on gist, rather than operating on details or quantitative information, allows reasoners to avoid errors. In class-inclusion tasks, for example, children judge the relative numerosity of a superordinate set compared to its proper subset. Most children, until 9 or 10 years of age, judge the subset to be more numerous than the superordinate, a logical impossibility. Mature reasoners avoid this cognitive illusion by suppressing numerical information about sets given in the problem; by reasoning qualitatively from inclusional relationships to their implications for relative numerosity, they are able to avoid systematic processing errors (e.g., Reyna, in press-a).

Developmental trends also argue against the notion that gist processing is a default option for unsophisticated reasoners. On the contrary, reliance on gist increases with age, so that children are more likely to be verbatim processors (Reyna, in press-a; Reyna & Brainerd, 1990, 1991). For example, Perner and Mansbridge (1983) have shown that children better remember isolated sentences involving comparatives (e.g., *John is taller than Mary; Betty is taller than Fred*), but adults are superior at recalling the same types of sentences when they form a pattern, a transitive chain (e.g., *John is taller than Mary; Mary is taller than Fred*). Similarly, given verbatim memory tests, adults typically fall prey to the consistency between inferences and the overall gist of stories, and erroneously report having seen true inferences (Bransford & Franks, 1971). Children, however, are better able to reject inferences that were not directly presented (Liben & Posnansky, 1977).

This developmental pattern is not limited to verbal stimuli. The same trend has been reported, for example, with face recognition: Younger children tend to focus on piecemeal characteristics, but older children encode configurational patterns (e.g., Carey & Diamond, 1977). Gist-based processing appears to increase across diverse tasks during the early elementary years at about the same time that children's impressive verbatim memory has begun to decline. More children can be classified as gist processors as age increases (e.g., Marx, 1986; Schmidt & Welch, 1989), and there is a developmental shift from reliance on memory for details to gist. Simultaneously, reasoning errors decrease. In summary, increasing competence is associated with greater emphasis on gist in processing, rather than less.

Patterns and Parallelism

In this account of problem solving, both representation and processing are fuzzy. Like the description of thinking in the intuitionist school of mathematics, processing is not conceived as linear, but as parallel with local seriality, especially at input and output (see also Estes, 1988). People appear to begin extracting patterns from information before all of the information is actually presented (Brainerd & Reyna, 1990a; Townsend, 1990). For example, in transitive inference, they catch on to the pattern "things get bigger to the right" before all of the premises have been presented. This is, of course, a defining feature of a pattern, that information obeys certain regularities. Those regularities can then be exploited for the purposes of cognition, allowing processing to proceed, without the necessity of waiting for all details to be encoded. *Because* reasoning relies on vague pattern-like impressions, it can leap ahead in many directions at once, operating in parallel, to a degree. Thus, the assumption that people extract gist-like patterns coheres with observations of limited parallelism in their processing (e.g., McClelland, 1979).

The emphasis in fuzzy-trace theory, as in other recent models (McClelland & Rumelhart, 1986; Townsend, 1990), therefore, is on patterns and parallelism, rather than on discrete items processed sequentially. We claim that it is the gist-like patterns themselves, not the items that form the patterns, that are manipulated in reasoning. Such assumptions about vague patterns, together with parallelism, paint a portrait of thought as intuitive, a commitment contrasting with traditional computational approaches. (At present, the PDP approach appears to have elements of both computational formalism and intuitionism [Brainerd & Reyna, 1990a; Estes, 1988]). Advantages of fuzzy-processing, then, include parallelism, that processing proceeds unencumbered by incomplete information, in contrast to standard serial information-processing models or to the step-wise application of logical operations. Thus, thinking itself, not just representation, is fluid and ranging.

Patterns support parallelism because of their regularities, but problem information can contain many implicit regularities. Because reasoning involves manipulating these qualitative patterns, factors that affect which pattern is salient are crucial. The arrangement or presentation of information makes certain patterns conspicuous, while obscuring others (Reyna & Brainerd, in press). Consider a heterogeneous assortment of stuffed animals scattered on the floor versus a linear arrangement of those same animals according to size. A linear progression is salient in the latter arrangement, but it applies *equally,* in principle, to the prior one. Most observers would simply not notice the presence of a linear progression in the scattered arrangement, however.

Similarly, the "betweenness" relation (Bower, 1971) is salient in the following presentation from a children's book: "James was a new engine . . . [his wheels] weren't as big as Gordon's, and they weren't as small as Thomas's"

(Awdry, 1957 p. 4). Here, the betweenness relation can be seen immediately by children as young as 3. However, presenting children with a linear arrangement, and asking them about betweenness, creates difficulty. Rabinowitz and Howe (1990), for instance, presented children with three stimuli in a scrambled left-to-right sequence (e.g., squares of different sizes), and asked them to point to the "middle" one (e.g., the middle-sized square). In this sort of task, elementary schoolers do poorly, and results also fail to correspond to transitive inference tasks (that also involve linear orderings) in which pairwise asymmetries are presented (e.g., *The blue square is bigger than the red square*). Of course, any linear ordering implies all three relations: betweenness, progression, and pairwise asymmetry (Bower, 1971). Despite their logical equivalence, however, these patterns apparently differ psychologically, and a given presentation can highlight one pattern at the expense of others (Reyna, in press-a).

Framing (e.g., Reyna & Brainerd, in press; Tversky & Kahneman, 1986) and perceptual salience effects (e.g., Brainerd & Reyna, 1990b) are other examples of presentation or formatting effects on reasoning. Framing effects have typically been used to demonstrate cognitive shortcomings. In framing, two decision problems contain identical information, but one problem uses positive language (e.g., 200 people will be saved, of 600 potential fatalities), and the other uses negative language (e.g., 400 people will die, of 600 potential fatalities), and choices are shown to reverse (although changes are supposedly superficial). Perceptual salience manipulations, on the other hand, are often used to improve performance. In number conservation tasks, for example, in which children judge whether two rows have the same number of objects (e.g., beans), relative length tends to interfere with judgments. Reducing length differences among rows, or training children to selectively attend to numerical relationships, enhances performance (e.g., Brainerd & Reyna, 1990b). Thus, the manner in which information is presented can help or hinder performance, and such effects argue against machine-like cognition or abstract logical operations.

Such presentation effects are not confined to children. For example, some probability-judgment tasks involve two bins, each of which contains targets (e.g., black balls) and nontargets (e.g., white balls). A problem might consist of judging whether drawing a target is equally likely given three balls, of which one is black, versus six balls, of which two are black. When such a problem is graphically presented by stacking balls vertically, subjects who demonstrate an understanding of probability are not entirely indifferent between a black–white ratio of 1:2 versus 2:4 (Callahan, 1989). Despite *knowing* otherwise, there is a nagging sense that targets are more likely when there are more of them. This illusion seems less compelling when the same problem information is presented verbally as "half versus two fourths."

It is important to underline that formatting effects occur for competent reasoners, and reflect ordinary modes of thought (Reyna, in press-a). So, for example, in class-inclusion reasoning, children are typically presented with two subsets of objects belonging to a superordinate category, and are asked whether there are more members of the superordinate set or the larger subset. Perceptually tagging each member of the superordinate, for instance, by making them all the same color, dramatically improves performance" (Brainerd & Reyna, 1990b; Wilkinson, 1976). Whereas children in uncued conditions usually respond with the larger subset, in cued conditions, they correctly identify the superordinate as more numerous. Significantly, errors in uncued conditions are not due to failures to encode problem information, or to deficits in logic or memory (Reyna, in press-a). Instead, superordinate-set cuing makes the mechanics of processing easier; the vertical levels in inclusion hierarchies become distinctive, facilitating subset-superordinate comparisons. Once the inclusion hierarchy is represented this way, reasoners can apply the cardinality principle (that more inclusive sets must be more numerous), and solve the problem. In class-inclusion reasoning, superordinate-set cuing improves processing by configuring gist so that it can be operated on by an appropriate principle. Thus, presentation can affect the *configuration of gist,* and, consequently, the ability of reasoners to implement their competence (see Table 10.2).

By claiming that extracted gist depends on the format of information, we do not mean to imply that knowledge or prior learning play an unimportant role. Developmental data on the increasing use of gist with age certainly suggest that experience governs this kind of "pattern perception" (Liben & Posnansky, 1977; 1977; Perner & Mansbridge, 1983). Indeed, gist-like patterns seem to be acquired as the common denominator among related problems or situations, with learning sets a quintessential example (Brainerd & Reyna, 1990a). Learning sets are observed after many discrimination learning tasks, one after the other, are presented to subjects. Gradually, the number of trials required to learn each new task diminishes, until new problems are solved after one or two trials (e.g., Harlow, 1949). According to Harlow, prior experience, leading to formation of learning sets, accounts for apparently sudden insights in problem solving. The generalization involved in learning sets, moreover, occurs under conditions in which stimuli are dissimilar from task to task. In fact, specific transfer from one feature to another must be *minimized* in order to achieve a high level of performance. Thus, responses to verbatim details must be inhibited to form learning sets, a product of experience apparently based on gist.

Although variation across tasks may be present to a larger degree in the formation of learning sets, as Estes (1959) has taught us, all learning involves some variability in details across experiences. Gist is one way to bridge such superficially disparate experiences. As Estes (1980) points out, "approximate information . . . may be essential as a guide to actions when a situation previously experienced recurs with some variation" (p. 67). Thus, gist can be construed as the signal extracted across a range of specific exemplars of a pattern that differ in superficial details, the latter being the noise. The patterns perceived in information are, therefore, most likely a product of both experience (learning) and formatting (the way the problem is presented).

TABLE 10.2
Heuristics that are Typically Retrieved in Classic Problem-Solving Paradigms

Problem	Heuristic	Paraphrase
Probability judgment	Frequency	Greater frequency means more likely.
Transitive inference	Seriation	Anything to the left is more than anything to the right.
Class inclusion	Cardinality	Superordinate sets have more than (or the same as) subsets.
Conservation of number	Identity	Nothing added or taken away is the same.
Framing of gains	Values	Saving some lives is better than saving none.
Framing of losses	Values	Nobody dying is better than some dying.
Oddity discrimination	Similarity	Things are similar in the same way, except for one.
Moral judgment	Equality	Everyone should have the same.

Note. The term *heuristics* is used rather than *principles* because these are not true in the sense of being universally valid, and retrieval is probabilistic rather than deterministic, contrary to a rule-based or logicist approach.

PRINCIPLES OF FUZZY-TRACE THEORY

The major assumptions of fuzzy-trace theory include (a) gist extraction, (b) fuzzy-to-verbatim continua, (c) fuzzy-processing preference, (d) hierarchy of gist (task calibration), (e) simple readout versus reconstructive retrieval, (f) readout and reconstruction in both short- and long-term memory, (g) memory limitations as a function of the time courses of verbatim and gist representations, and (h) output interference. These assumptions track the flow of information processing from encoding of gist and verbatim representations at input, through processing and retrieval from memory, to output. We discuss these assumptions in turn, along with supportive data. Finally, we draw out some of their implications for accuracy in problem solving.

Gist Versus Verbatim Representations

Gist is often used to refer to the residue of information that remains after a delay (e.g., see Ellis & Hunt, 1989, chapter 8). As Estes (1980) put it, rather than an all-or-none loss, "forgetting takes the form of a progressive loss of precision or completeness of information about the original experience" (p. 67). In the psycholinguistics literature, gist is said to reflect the underlying structure or pattern of verbal information, for example a simpler, summary version of a story that selectively preserves ideas at higher nodes in a hierarchy (e.g., Kintsch, 1974). We have argued that quantitative, like verbal, representations can be ordered according to specificity: Some amount of money is more vague than $27.36 (Reyna & Brainerd, 1991).

Although memory dependence can occur in reasoning (e.g., Brainerd & Reyna, 1988; Reyna, 1991), independence is the more likely finding (Brainerd, 1985; Brainerd & Kingma, 1984, 1985). Reasoning–remembering independence presents a conundrum, namely that critical problem information does not appear to be used to solve problems: Empirically, reasoning performance and memory for verbatim background facts are stochastically independent, across different types of problems. The apparent conundrum is resolved by assuming that gist representations, independent from verbatim memory, are used in problem solving. It has been demonstrated that even when people remember the verbatim facts of a problem, they typically do not access those facts to solve it (e.g., Reyna & Brainerd, 1990).

Also illustrating reasoning–remembering independence, manipulations that affect memory often do not affect reasoning, nor vice versa. For transitive inference tasks, we can represent items with letters and relationships with symbols. So, for example, premises such as *John is taller than Mary* and *Mary is taller than Fred* can be represented as $A > B$ and $B > C$, respectively, and the inference question would take the form *is $A > C$?* We can lengthen the series $A > B > C$ by adding such premises as $C > D$ and $D > E$ to form $A > B > C > D > E$. According to the standard view, increasing the number of premises like this should affect both memory and reasoning. This is because subjects are assumed to answer transitivity questions by interrogating memory for the premises, each link being crucial to the logical inference. Thus, if $B > C$ is forgotten, then it is impossible to infer that $A > C$, $A > D$, or $A > E$. And, as memory load increases, that is, premises that must be remembered are added, memory errors are more likely, and, consequently, inferences should be compromised.

Increasing the number of premises increases memory load, but has no effect on problem solving (e.g., Chapman & Lindenberger, 1988; Reyna, in press-b; Reyna & Brainerd, 1990). Similarly, increasing the distance between items in a series (e.g., asking about $A > E$ as opposed to $A > C$), although there are more intervening links in the series, does not increase reasoning errors (Brainerd & Kingma, 1984). Distance between items should affect inferential accuracy because, as distance increases, there is more opportunity for memory loss to dissever the transitive chain, but, in fact, distance does not undermine accuracy. Neither does another memorial factor, the time interval between premise presentation and inference test. The memory dependency position would also predict that as delay increases, memory for premises should decline, and reasoning performance should suffer. However, the opposite trend has been observed (Brainerd & Kingma, 1985). More practice answering questions about premises and inferences increases accuracy, although the delay between premise presentation and test widens as questioning continues. In brief, although it can be demonstrated that verbatim memory reacts to such manipulations as delay and premise load, transitive reasoning does not.

The evidence supports the existence of *multiple* representations of the same problem information that vary along a fuzzy-to-verbatim continuum, allowing for cognitive options (e.g., Kintsch & van Dijk, 1978). Soon after problem presentation, both microscopic and macroscopic representations are available in memory, but the former become inaccessible. In line with this view, recent behavioral and physiological evidence from rats has demonstrated a shorter time course, and different neuromorphological substrata, for memory for details as opposed to gist in learning (e.g., Granger & McNulty, 1986; Staubli, Ivy, & Lynch, 1984).

The question of the degree of precision in reasoning can be broken down into three separate questions. First, when reasoners have options, do they rigidly respond to every problem with the same level of minute detail, or as fuzzy-trace theory would claim, do they take advantage of alternative gist-like representations? Evidence for fuzzy processing in certain tasks does not rule out the use of more precise representations in other contexts (nor vice versa). As we discuss, task demands, the form of response, and considerations of consequences bear on the level of precision at which the task is executed (Reyna & Brainerd, in press; Reyna & Brainerd, 1991).

Second, apparently precise responses should be distinguished from precise representation and processing. It is not necessary to posit precise representations and processes in order to achieve rigorous outputs. As Estes (1980) makes clear, people are better "general-purpose thinking machines" than computers because of, rather than in spite of, their representations being approximate. As noted earlier, empirically, accuracy has been associated with fuzzier processing. Last, levels of processing must be taken into account. Judgments at the periphery, for example perceptual judgments within short time frames, include degrees of detail that are not necessarily incorporated into higher levels of processing (see Estes, 1977).

Some assumption of global patterns operating in cognition is scarcely avoidable. Gist is the shared pattern when we can recall that letters rather than numbers occurred at approximate temporal positions, though we cannot recall which letters, or when we misremember "3, 4, 5" as "6, 7, 8," though they bear no literal similarity, or when we interpolate a memory item from the first position in one psychological chunk to the first position in another (see Estes, 1980, for a review of such findings). Even search and attention can be adjusted according to varying levels of gist. For example, people can respond to change in a global pattern, rather than to detection of specific signals.

Therefore, some phenomena are difficult to explain without assuming a level of global similarity that transcends superificial details. We have mentioned learning sets, but there are other well-documented examples, including transposition effects (intradimensional transfer), cross-model matching (cross-dimensional transfer; Bower, 1971; Marks, Hammeal, & Bornstein, 1987) and comprehension of metaphors (Reyna, 1985). In transposition studies, for example, the subject first learns to discriminate between two stimuli on some dimension such as size or intensity; for example, the larger or the darker stimulus may be correct. Then, two new stimuli varying along the same dimension are introduced. In this test, the subject often responds on a relational basis, for example, still picking the larger stimulus. The relationally correct choice is made, even when these particular stimuli have never been seen before, and when the nonselected stimulus (e.g., the smaller one) is closer in absolute terms to the original training stimuli. Indeed, subjects will avoid the formerly correct stimulus if it fails to bear the proper abstract relation in the new display. Thus, if subjects are trained to choose a 6″ circle over a 5″ one, and that 6″ circle is then tested against a 7″ circle, choices will shift to the 7″ circle. Consonant with our earlier discussion of developmental trends, young children behave like infrahumans in that transposition fails with increasing distance from the training stimuli, but in older children relational responding occurs even on far tests (e.g., Kuenne, 1946).

In cross-modal matching, abstract properties of experiences from different sensory modalities are compared. For example, resemblances can be mapped between loudness and brightness (soft equals dim; loud equals bright). Marks et al. (1987) showed that even very young children recognize similarities between hearing and vision, although the range of relations that could be mapped was broader in older children. Children made both perceptual and verbal cross-modal matches: "Just as young children match the higher pitched or the louder of two sounds to the brighter of two lights, so do they transfer meanings of words and phrases from either modality to the other, rating the adjective 'bright' . . . louder than the adjective 'dim' " (p. 70). As Marks et al. observed, cross-modal, and certain metaphorical, resemblances do not rest on any common properties of objects, "unlike calling a river a snake, where the perceptual similarity parallels a physical similarity in the objects themselves" (p. 84).

Bower (1971) found that transfer of stimulus-response assignments in paired-associate tasks was greatest for relationally similar assignments (which altered all specific S-R assignments), and was superior to assignments that had an absolute basis for transfer along a quantitative dimension. Reviewing results for intra-dimensional and cross-dimensional transfer, much like our arguments for gist, Bower (1971) concluded that such data require the assumption of abstract, "dimensionless" levels of representation (see pp. 199–200).

Processing

The availability of multiple representations that are versions of one another raises the question of which representation comes first, and whether some representations are derived from others (Brainerd & Reyna, 1990a). Comprehension and inference, for instance, would seem to depend on prior encoding of verbatim information. Linguistic results showing that loss of verbatim detail and conceptual integration both occur at clause boundaries in sentences appear to support such a verbatim-first account (e.g., Clark & Clark, 1977). However, it is important to stress that just because gist and verbatim representations can be related conceptually does not indicate that the gist is derived from encoded verbatim substrata. We have already discussed transitivity tasks, in which subjects catch on to the pattern before all of the premises have been presented, and therefore, before all of the verbatim information could *possibly* be encoded. In other tasks, prior practice with examples or familiarity with the task allow subjects to begin extracting relevant patterns immediately (Reyna & Brainerd, 1990). In text comprehension, global plausibility judgments can be made before verbatim verification (Reder, 1982). In pattern perception, global operators can extract patterns as local operators process features (e.g., Lamb & Robertson, 1989). Thus, a word can be named faster than one of its letters (Estes, 1977). Even numbers are apparently subject to a preliminary gist-like interpretation in terms of analog magnitudes (Restle, 1970). Thus, it cannot be assumed that global gist is derived from earlier verbatim input.

Despite having access to representations at different levels along a fuzzy-to-verbatim continuum, reasoners have a preference for fuzzy processing. Ostensibly numerical tasks, therefore, are frequently solved using *non*numerical gist (Brainerd, 1981; Reyna & Brainerd, in press). Reasoning does not depend on the exact *probabilities* in a probability judgment task, the *counts* for sets in class-inclusion problems (although subjects are asked about the numerosity of sets), and so on (Brainerd & Kingma, 1984, 1985). In probability judgment, for example, when problem-solving processes are diagnosed individually for each subject, or at the group level, there is no covariation between frequency sums, differences, or absolute magnitudes with either accuracy or response times (Callahan, 1989). In decision-making problems, qualitative comparisons among options guide choices, rather than the exact number of dollars won or lives saved. For example, in Allais-type problems, decreasing the dollars to be gained from millions to thousands does not change choices, as long as the qualitative relationships among quantities are preserved. Moreover, removing the numbers altogether, rather than merely decreasing amounts, does not eliminate standard effects. On the contrary, there are larger disparities across positive and negative frames, for example, when vague phrases are substituted for numbers (Reyna & Brainerd, in press).

In probability learning, Estes (1976) has shown that choices are not sensitive to absolute frequencies, but instead appear to be governed by relative frequencies. His probability learning task involved observation trials, in which a subject was presented with simulated results from a survey taken of different individuals' preferences between products, two at a time. A block of observation trials alternated with prediction trials, in which, for various pairs of products, subjects predicted the one that would be preferred by a sample of people from the same population that had been surveyed. By varying the absolute number of times a product is a winner, frequency of presentation as a winner could be unconfounded from probability of winning. In a critical experiment, the hypotheses that judgments are based on absolute versus relative frequencies were pitted against one another. Estes reasoned that predictions "should differ for the two models at the point of a shift in event frequencies" (p. 49). If absolute frequency information were being accumulated, a large number of preshift trials would require a correspondingly large number of postshift trials to yield a detectable change in performance. If frequency counts were small, however, only a few new trials would be needed to change the ratio of the counts, and, thus, to change performance. On the other hand, if relative rather than absolute frequencies governed performance, the rate of learning should be independent of the previous number of trials. Contrary to the idea that subjects use memory for "counts," performance for groups exposed to larger versus smaller preshift frequencies was strikingly similar (see Fig. 3, p. 50). Probability learning was related to relationships among frequencies, but exact information about absolute frequencies did not carry over into subsequent learning. Such indifference to absolute quantities cuts across problems that could be characterized as more and less quantitative (Brainerd & Reyna, 1990b; Reyna & Brainerd, in press).

One reason for a fuzzy-processing preference could be the memorial superiority of gist over detail. When detail is directly provided, the fuzzy-processing preference is not undone, however. When counts for items in each class are displayed in a class-inclusion task or when the exact lengths of sticks are shown in a transitive inference task, for example, subjects continue to rely on gist-based processing (e.g., Brainerd & Reyna, 1990b). Thus, as one might expect based on considerations of complexity, subjects apparently find it easier to manipulate gist, even when verbatim detail is accessible (see Table 10.3).

Although there is a preference for fuzzy processing, the task exerts some influence over the level of specificity used in reasoning. Such considerations as the form of response (e.g., point estimates versus forced choices), the amount of uncertainty surrounding quantities, and functional criteria concerning the consequences of assimilating nonidentical amounts apply in designating the lowest acceptable level in a hierarchy of gist (Reyna & Brainerd, in press). Consequently, judgment is not necessarily inaccurate or erratic, considered within the bounds of functional indifference. Thus, although distinctions without difference are typically ignored, as differences become larger, a threshold of sensitivity is reached. For example, as long as two alternatives in a preference task have nearly equivalent expected values (nontransparent dominance), choices may shift depending on wording (Tversky & Kahneman, 1986). As the difference between alternatives grows, however, there comes a point at which choices are no longer perturbed by wording (transparent dominance), and differences in expected value govern choices (Connolly & Northcraft, 1987; Reyna & Brainerd, in press). Inconsistency is not random, then, but appears to be confined to quantities seen as similar.

A sense of how gist varies across tasks can be gleaned from Table 10.1. This table reviews verbatim problem information and gist-level representations for

TABLE 10.3
The Advantages of Gist Versus Verbatim Detail in Reasoning

1. *Trace Availability/Accessibility.* Memory for gist is more persistent over time than memory for detail; therefore, the system is engineered around the kind of information that tends to be available.

2. *Generalizability.* The generality of gist-like representations makes them applicable to a wider variety of problem-solving contexts; particularized details are relevant to a narrower range of problems.

3. *Processing Simplicity.* All other factors being equal, elaborate detail usually makes processing more cumbersome and complicated. Therefore, gist processing tends to be less effortful, less error-prone, and more time-conserving (the latter because of the trade-off between precision and efficiency).

4. *No Necessary Loss in Accuracy.* The pervasive facts of random variation, measurement error, and uncertainty lead to an irreducible modicum of imprecision in everyday life; in such cases, increased precision merely reifies fluctuations rather than improving accuracy. Moreover, filtering of details usually occurs within the bounds of functional indifference for the individual. Finally, any increases in accuracy that precision might provide must be balanced against time and information costs, and increased errors associated with complication.

5. *Parallelism.* Because gist is based on patterns, or regularities in information, its construction does not depend on any one piece of information; therefore, gist can be constructed as information is being encoded.

some popular problem-solving paradigms. It is apparent in comparing tasks that certain kinds of gist tend to recur. For example, the relational gist that "one has more than the other" is implicated in probability judgment tasks, as well as in superficially dissimilar moral judgment tasks in which subjects judge the fairness of allocations. Although this relational gist differentiates, among some, between more and less, framing problems elicit an even cruder distinction, collapsing all amounts into some, in contrast to none (Reyna & Brainerd, in press). A critical consideration in understanding reasoning, then, whether moral or mathematical, according to fuzzy-trace theory, is not greater precision or increased quantitative subtlety, but the ability to reason using gist. Moreover, reasoners must select the appropriate gist from among many patterns present in problem information. In class inclusion, for example, the appropriate pattern is elusive. The subset relationships, say between seven horses and three cows, are readily apparent, but the superordinate relationships are implicit, creating an interference effect that depresses performance (Brainerd & Kaszor, 1974). Conservation tasks also typically involve competing patterns, for example in number, spreading out one set so that it appears to have more than the other (Brainerd, 1978). The presence of competing perceptual patterns is the feature that separates the two developmental paradigms in which children do well—transitivity and probability judgment—from the two in which they have more difficulty—conservation and class inclusion (Brainerd, 1973; Brainerd & Kaszor, 1974). And, an easier task can be converted to a harder one by presenting an interfering perceptual pattern; in transitive inference, for example, performance can be lowered by introducing competing visual illusions at test (Reyna & Brainerd, 1990). Thus, successful processing can turn on selecting appropriately configured gist from competing candidates.

Retrieval from Memory: Readout
Versus Reconstruction

Performance does not depend solely on the gist that is extracted, but also on retrieval of problem-solving principles from memory, such as cardinality for class inclusion or frequency for probability judgment (see Table 10.2; Brainerd, 1982; Brainerd & Reyna, 1990b). In framing problems, for instance, choices depend on retrieving principles (in both senses of the term) of the general form "saving some lives is better than saving none." In transitive inference, the principle of seriation is required to use the external array (plus memory for the gist that the array is ordered); subjects must be able to infer that any object to the right of another object, no matter the distance, is longer. In conservation, subjects retrieve the identity principle, that nothing added or taken away yields the same amount. In probability judgment, subjects invoke frequency or relative frequency principles (depending on age and task) to the effect that greater frequency implies greater probability. In class inclusion, the representation of the inclusion hierarchy is combined with the cardinality principle that a superordinate set always has more (or the same) as its subset. Knowledge of relevant principles consists not of computational algorithms, but of qualitative heuristics that are retrieved probabilistically.

In the literature on moral judgment, retrieval of moral principles has been discussed in similar terms, as an intuitive process based on imperfect retrieval of qualitative heuristics (e.g., Hare, 1981). This is contrasted with a more precise, elaborate process of critical thinking (but, unlike fuzzy-trace theory, the elaborate approach is seen as superior). The moral judgment and problem-solving literatures share a phenomenon to be explained—the failure to retrieve known principles (Brainerd, 1982). Children who fail problem-solving tasks, like those who succeed, often know the principle that should have been invoked, but do not retrieve it in the context of the task. Younger children who fail the class-inclusion task, for example, benefit from retrieval prompts for the cardinality principle (Reyna, in press-a).

Gist representations can act as retrieval cues for the principles in which they figure (Brainerd & Reyna, 1990a; Reyna & Brainerd, 1991). If the gist representation is felicitous, the probability of retrieving the correct principle appears to be enhanced. Under facilitating cuing conditions, these principles seem to be read directly out of long-term representations. The simplicity and straightforward application of these generic principles, especially among experienced reasoners, is a two-edged sword, however. Solutions may appear obvious that turn out to be wrong. On the other hand, the ready accessibility of principles has to do with their being gist-level representations, and this offers advantages in problem solving (see Reyna & Brainerd, in press). For instance, gist-level representations of problems are easily mapped onto similarly abstract gist-level representations of principles; thus, there is no need to assume elaborate combinatorial mechanics for mapping problem representations onto principles. Also, gist-level representations of principles are broadly relevant across specific problems that differ in superficial detail. Because these principles are so broadly applicable, it is advantageous to store them in a form that is resilient across time, and gist-level representations offer such resiliency. Last, gist-level representations provide a bridge between different problems that supports the induction of general principles. Although such problems differ at the verbatim level, they can be collapsed at the gist level, forming the basis for learning sets, and for overarching principles useful in problem solving. Thus, gist-level principles knit together representation and processing in that abstract problem representations can support the acquisition of principles, and they can also act as retrieval cues for general principles during problem solving.

The retrieval of these general principles from long-term memory, through direct readout, can be contrasted with reconstructive retrieval. Reconstruction involves the application of inference and other information-processing operations to restore or redintegrate the memory trace (e.g., Ellis & Hunt, 1989; Howe & Brainerd, 1989). As we have discussed, one way that the memory system compensates for its constraints is to rely on gist. Another way it compensates is through reconstruction, which can be applied to short-term, as well as long-term, memory. In a mental arithmetic task, for example, subjects can be questioned about their memory for the original problem information as they proceed to add and subtract additional quantities in series. If conditions are arranged so that it is easy to reconstruct the original information by reversing arithmetical operations, subjects will reconstruct rather than retrieve (Brainerd & Reyna, 1988). Probability judgment can be subject to the same kind of reconstruction effect: A prior judgment that A is more probable than B can serve as the basis for the answer to a memory question about the numerosity of A.

Short-and long-term memory are traditionally distinguished according to the permanence of storage (e.g., James, 1890). This distinction—between a blackboard that is constantly erased versus a permanent archive—has been a prime justification for positing two qualitatively different memory stores. For some time, however, there has been troublesome evidence that the temporary–permanent dichotomy was more like a continuum (Jones & Anderson, 1987). Fuzzy-trace theory captures this idea by describing forgetting as a gradual process of disintegration, a loss of coherence among bonds in a trace, so that it gradually fades out against the background of competing traces (Brainerd, Reyna, Howe, & Kingma, 1990c; Howe & Brainerd, 1989). The trace can be redintegrated, however, even when it has passed below the zero recall threshold by processes that reverse disintegration, a phenomenon that has important ramifications for a number of applied issues in memory development, such as children's eyewitness testimony (Brainerd & Ornstein, in press). Thus, storage failure can occur in the sense that the probability that the trace is stored can be (virtually) zero, yet the elements of the trace are *not lost* because the trace can be re-stored (Howe & Brainerd, 1989). Mathematical modeling techniques indicate that retrieval failure and storage failure are identifiable thresholds in an underlying continuous process of disintegration (Brainerd et al., 1990c).

The time course of disintegration for verbatim and gist representations is different, however. This appears to be the source of some of the variability in fixing exact time durations for short- versus long-term memory. We derive predictions about the fragility of a trace, not from any assumptions about the qualitative state of memory that it occupies, but from the nature of the representation itself. In general, verbatim information becomes quickly inaccessible, whereas memory for gist endures (Clark & Clark, 1977; Ellis & Hunt, 1989; Granger & McNulty, 1986). We take it as axiomatic that relational gist (e.g., associations among items) will be better remembered than verbatim elements (e.g., the items themselves), at least among adults (cf. Murdock, 1989).

Outputs: Speed, Scheduling, and Interference Effects

Another defining difference between short- and long-term memory is that the former is believed to have a limited capacity, whereas the latter is almost unlimited. The idea of working-memory capacity has increasingly been challenged (Brainerd & Reyna, 1989; Hulme & Tordoff, 1989; Reyna & Brainerd, 1989). We predict apparent "capacity effects" by reference to the *time courses* of different forms of representations, gist versus verbatim. Fading of verbatim information, for example in a digit span task, occurs rapidly, producing a limited subset of verbatim information in consciousness at any one time. Thus, the window of time will encompass only those verbatim representations presented recently enough that their contents are still accessible. (Input capacity also limits the system to some degree because we cannot, for example, simultaneously read an infinite amount of material.) The constant fading of information with time will produce a de facto limit on the ability to entertain numerous ideas simultaneously in working-memory tasks, but it is not necessarily the case that there is a qualitatively distinct state with a limited number of storage slots (Brainerd & Reyna, 1990a).

Critical evidence favoring this account comes from data on the effects of speech rate and item identification speed on short-term memory span (see Hulme & Tordoff, 1989, for a review). These results pose fundamental difficulties for the capacity construct, but fall naturally out of the assumption that representations have a time course of accessibility. When speech rate is included in a partial correlational analysis, for example, the paths from age and individual differences to span disappear; all of the variance is accounted for by speech rate (Hulme & Tordoff, 1989). There is no need to assume differences in short-term memory capacity across age or across individuals in order to explain such results, and it would be necessary to make ad hoc assumptions about effects of speech rate on capacity in order to retain the notion of capacity (see Reyna & Brainerd, in press-b).

Thus, in our view, speech rate (and correlated variables) covary with memory span because as rate increases, more items can beat the clock. The faster the output, the less time will have passed for each of the memory representations. Of course, the clock can be restarted if the item is recoded (e.g., is rehearsed), and recovery and redintegration effects can refresh the trace (Howe & Brainerd, 1989). But, these effects do not necessarily break down along a short- versus long-term memory axis. The idea of a continuous process of fading, that can be reenhanced, is broadly compatible with the workings of a biological system, as opposed to a mechanical or electronic system. Sensory memory, for example, is characterized in this way in terms of impressions on peripheral sense organs that wane with time, a process that is hastened when other inputs are overlapping.

Although output can be speeded up, there are physical limits on the number of outputs that can be made to fit in a given time period. We alluded earlier to the idea that all theories must contend with the fact that outputs are, by and large, constrained to be serial. Thus, emitting physically incompatible responses simultaneously produces output interference, a neglected concept in current theories. Obviously, output interference creates difficulties not only at the point of output, but further back in the system due to the necessity to schedule responses, and so on (Brainerd, Reyna, Howe, & Kevershan, 1990b). Dual-task interference effects, ordinarily used to support the concept of working-memory capacity, are straightforwardly handled by output interference (Brainerd & Reyna, 1989; Reyna & Brainerd, 1989). Using output interference to explain dual-task effects allows the assumption that processing is primarily parallel. Because the bottlenecks that occur in interference paradigms are localized near the response end of processing, significant parallelism can be permitted up to that point.

Output interference is implicated in other phenomena as well, for instance in the cognitive triage effect in which weakly remembered items are thrust to the front of a recall queue, ahead of more strongly remembered items (Brainerd, Reyna, & Howe, 1990a; Brainerd et al., 1990b). The cognitive triage effect would seem a natural candidate for strategic explanations, for example that subjects deliberately output weaker items first, before they become inaccessible. However, it appears that the effect is instead linked to such episodic factors as error-success histories in situ and output interference (Brainerd et al., 1990a). The triage effect is but one example of a growing number of cognitive phenomena for which strategic explanations are giving way to explanations stressing basic memorial and perceptual processes (Reyna & Brainerd, 1991).

Implications for Accuracy in Problem Solving

As Simon (1988) has argued, human reasoning should be evaluated in the context of its memorial and information-processing constraints. Because of such limitations, gist-based processing should have a favorable impact on the quality of reasoning. By relying on gist, an unreliable verbatim memory system can be bypassed (Table 10.3). Although fuzzy representations sacrifice details, such details are not necessarily significant. Precision may merely lead to the undue reification of uncertain estimates, random fluctuations, or measurement errors. In addition, gist is, relatively speaking, memorially stable, is broadly relevant across problems, requires uncomplicated processing (and is, therefore, unlikely to introduce errors arising from complication), is efficiently processed, and can be constructed in parallel as information is being encoded (Reyna & Brainerd, 1990; Reyna & Brainerd, in press). Although none of these properties is decisive in itself, it makes sense that cognition would be engineered around representations that are simple, flexible, efficiently processed, and that tend to be accessible in memory (Table 10.3; Brainerd & Reyna, 1990a; Simon, 1988). The fact that development progresses from verbatim representations to gist extraction in problem solving, rather than the other way around, similarly suggests a positive impact of gist on accuracy.

Resource-based theories of cognition stress that memorial constraints are sources of errors in thinking (Ellis & Hunt, 1989). In fuzzy-trace theory, memorial and processing limitations are thought to broadly influence the character of problem solving, but to produce little local variation across problems, due to compensation. In standard problem-solving tasks, such as conservation, class inclusion, transitive inference, and probability judgment, cognitive limitations are circumvented by, whenever possible, avoiding the need to remember details. In class inclusion, adults and older children will actively attempt to suppress numerical information, asking that the numbers for each set not be read to them, although the question being asked is ostensibly numerical (see Table 10.1). The numbers detract from the critical gist that an inclusion hierarchy is present (Brainerd & Reyna, 1990b).

As Estes (1980) pointed out, a capacity to tolerate variability across instances, and the flexibility with which representations can be made to fit diverse situations, allow human intelligence to address a broad range of functions. Thought is improved by sweeping away the clutter of irrelevancies (Vygotsky, 1962). And, as thinking encompasses an ever-greater number of considerations and contingencies, uncertainty increases (Russell, 1948). The organism who can winnow away details, for whom actions emerge from thought clearly and confidently, can act rapidly. The evolutionary benefits of rapid action, as opposed to muddled paralysis, are considerable (Brainerd & Reyna, 1990a). Evolutionary adaptability is also enhanced by introducing some tolerance to environmental variability (Estes, 1980).

Of course, accuracy is bounded in such a scheme. Some problems demand precision and elaboration, if solutions are to be accurate. Still, we claim that understanding a problem is governed by perception of the overall pattern of information, and even when artificial computation is elected, that perception influences the choice of specific computational procedures. The global perception of the problem, then, to some degree, stipulates its solution (Schon, 1979). From this perspective, presentation or formatting effects can be interpreted as biasing reasoners to perceive particular global patterns (Bell et al., 1988; Tversky & Kahneman, 1986). Thus, fuzzy-trace theory describes understanding a problem as pattern perception, though the pattern that is apprehended is vague, and expects attendant difficulties in reasoning such as mental set or the *Einstellung* effect, the tendency for perceived patterns to obscure the possibility of alternative patterns in the same information.

SUMMARY

Fuzzy-trace theory synthesizes recent empirical paradoxes in a revised framework. These findings include reasoning–remembering independence, the cognitive triage effect, nonnumerical solution of numerical problems, and increasing reliance on gist with age to reduce reasoning errors. The theory integrates these newer results with such well-established findings as learning sets, intradimensional and crossdimensional transfer (including transposition), *Einstellung* effects, framing and formatting biases, reconstructive and redintegrative memory, and dual-task interference effects. As an alternative to the logicist and computational approaches, fuzzy-trace theory implements intuitionism, emphasizing pattern perception and parallel processing in reasoning.

The theory's key explanatory concepts are gist extraction, fuzzy-to-verbatim continua, the fuzzy-processing preference, hierarchies of gist, readout versus reconstruction in retrieval, time courses of verbatim and gist representations, and output interference.

Gist extraction refers to the ubiquitous tendency, both in humans and infrahumans, to mine incoming information for its senses and patterns, a tendency that ultimately controls the nature of reasoning. *Fuzzy-to-verbatim continua* are families of memory representations that result from encoding information. The *fuzzy-processing preference* is the predisposition of reasoning to operate on traces that are as near as possible to the fuzzy extremes of fuzzy-to-verbatim continua. This predilection is constrained somewhat by task requirements, which means that processing is calibrated to the lowest level in a *hierarchy of gist* that will support accurate responding.

When traces are retrieved from storage, the retrieval process may vary in the extent to which the subject merely decodes the target traces (*simple readout*) or amplifies and enhances them in certain respects before decoding occurs (*recon-*

struction). The theory assumes that simple readout can occur for traces that have been in storage for protracted intervals and that reconstruction can occur for traces of recently encoded information, and vice versa. Further, empirical phenomena that have been used as bases for regarding short- and long-term memory as distinct stores are explained as by-products of the *time courses of verbatim and gist representations*. Finally, fuzzy-trace theory accounts for findings that have usually been interpreted as supporting the concept of a limited-capacity generic processing resource, such as dual-task deficits, as *output interference* effects.

ACKNOWLEDGMENTS

We would like to acknowledge the caring and support of Bill and Kay Estes. Their love, integrity, scientific ideals, and commitment to freedom and international understanding continue to inspire us. Preparation of this chapter and the conduct of some of the research reported herein were supported by a grant from the Spencer Foundation.

REFERENCES

Argyris, C. (1988). Problems in producing usable knowledge for implementing alternatives. In D. E. Bell, H. Faiffa, & A. Tversky (Eds.,), *Decision making: Descriptive, normative, and prescriptive interactions* (pp. 540–561). New York: Cambridge University Press.

Awdry, W. (1957). *James, the red engine*. London: Kay & Ward.

Bell, D. E., Raiffa, H., & Tversky, A. (Eds.). (1988). *Decision making: Descriptive, normative, and prescriptive interactions*. New York: Cambridge University Press.

Bower, G. H. (1971). Adaptation-level coding of stimuli and serial position effects. In M. H. Appley (Ed.), *Adaptation-level theory* (pp. 175–201). New York: Academic Press.

Brainerd, C. J. (1973). Order of acquisition of transitivity, conservation, and class inclusion of length and weight. *Developmental Psychology, 8,* 105–116.

Brainerd, C. J. (1978). *Piaget's theory of intelligence*. Englewood Cliffs, NJ: Prentice-Hall.

Brainerd, C. J. (1981). Working memory and the developmental analysis of probability judgment. *Psychological Review, 88,* 463–502.

Brainerd, C. J. (1982). Children's concept learning as rule-sampling systems with Markovian properties. In C. J. Brainerd (Ed.), *Children's logical and mathematical cognition* (pp. 177–212). New York: Springer-Verlag.

Brainerd, C. J. (1985). Do children have to remember to reason? In C. J. Brainerd & V. F. Reyna (Eds.), *Developmental psychology* (pp. 143–154). Amsterdam: North Holland.

Brainerd, C. J., & Kaszor, P. (1974). An analysis of two proposed sources of children's class inclusion errors. *Developmental Psychology, 10,* 633–643.

Brainerd, C. J., & Kingma, J. (1984). Do children have to remember to reason? A fuzzy-trace theory of transitivity development. *Developmental Review, 4,* 311–377.

Brainerd, C. J., & Kingma, J. (1985). On the independence of short-term memory and working memory in cognitive development. *Cognitive Psychology, 17,* 210–247.

Brainerd, C. J., & Ornstein, P. A. (in press). Children's memory for witnessed events: The developmental backdrop. In J. L. Doris (Ed.), *The suggestibility of children's memory*. Washington, DC: American Psychological Association.

Brainerd, C. J., & Reyna, V. F. (1988). Generic resources, reconstructive processing, and children's mental arithmetic. *Developmental Psychology, 24,* 324–334.

Brainerd, C. J., & Reyna, V. F. (1989). Output-interference theory of dual task deficits in memory development. *Journal of Experimental Child Psychology, 47,* 1–18.

Brainerd, C. J., & Reyna, V. F. (1990a). Gist is the grist: Fuzzy-trace theory and the new intuitionism. *Developmental Review, 10,* 3–47.

Brainerd, C. J., & Reyna, V. F. (1990b). Inclusion illusions: Fuzzy-trace theory and perceptual salience effects in cognitive development. *Developmental Review, 10,* 365–403.

Brainerd, C. J., Reyna, V. F., & Howe, M. L. (1990a). Children's cognitive triage: Optimal retrieval or effortful processing? *Journal of Experimental Child Psychology, 49,* 428–447.

Brainerd, C. J., Reyna, V. F., Howe, M. L., & Kevershan, J. (1991). Fuzzy-trace theory and cognitive triage in memory development. *Developmental Psychology, 27,* 351–369.

Brainerd, C. J., Reyna, V. F., Howe, M. L., & Kevershan, J. (1990b). The last shall be first: How memory strength affects children's retrieval. *Psychological Science, 1,* 247–252.

Brainerd, C. J., Reyna, V. F., Howe, M. L., & Kingma, J. (1990c). Development of forgetting and reminiscence. *Monographs of the Society for Research in Child Development, 53,* 2–3 (Whole No. 222).

Bransford, J. D., & Franks, J. J. (1971). The abstraction of linguistic ideas. *Cognitive Psychology, 2,* 331–350.

Callahan, P. (1989). *Learning and development of probability concepts: Effects of computer-assisted instruction and diagnosis.* Unpublished doctoral dissertation, University of Arizona, Tucson.

Carey, S., & Diamond, R. (1977). From piecemeal to configurational representation of faces. *Science, 195,* 312–314.

Chapman, M., & Lindenberger, U. (1988). Functions, operations, and decalage in the development of transitivity. *Developmental Psychology, 24,* 542–551.

Clark, H., & Clark, E. (1977). *Psychology and language.* New York: Harcourt Brace Jovanovich.

Connolly, T., & Northcraft, G. (1987). *The limits of decision framing.* Unpublished manuscript, University of Arizona, Department of Management and Policy, Tucson.

Ellis, H. C., & Hunt, R. R. (1989). *Fundamentals of human memory and cognition.* Dubuque: Brown.

Estes, W. K. (1959). The statistical approach to learning theory. In S. Koch (Ed.), *Psychology: a study of a science* (Vol. 2, pp. 380–491). New York: McGraw Hill.

Estes, W. K. (1976). The cognitive side of probability learning. *Psychological Review, 83,* 37–64.

Estes, W. K. (1977). On the interaction of perception and memory in reading. In D. LaBerge & S. J. Samuels (Eds.), *Basic processes in reading* (pp. 1–26). Hillsdale, NJ: Lawrence Erlbaum Associates.

Estes, W. K. (1980). Is human memory obsolete? *American Scientist, 68,* 62–69.

Estes, W. K. (1982). Issues in method and theory: Some afterthoughts. In W. K. Estes (Ed.), *Models of learning, memory, and choice* (pp. 313–336). New York: Praeger.

Estes, W. K. (1988). Toward a framework for combining connectionistic and symbol-processing models. *Journal of Memory and Language, 27,* 196–212.

Granger, R. H., & McNulty, D. M. (1986). Learning and memory in machines and animals: An AI model that accounts for some neurobiological data. In J. L. Kolodner & C. K. Riesbeck (Eds.), *Experience, memory, and reasoning.* Hillsdale, NJ: Lawrence Erlbaum Associates.

Hare, R. M. (1981). *Moral thinking: Its levels, method, and point.* Oxford: Oxford University Press (Clarendon Press).

Harlow, H. F. (1949). The formation of learning sets. *Psychological Review, 56,* 51–65.

Howe, M. L., & Brainerd, C. J. (1989). Development of children's long-term retention. *Developmental Review, 9,* 301–340.

Hulme, C., & Tordoff, V. (1989). Working memory development: The effects of speech rate, word length, and acoustic similarity on serial recall. *Journal of Experimental Child Psychology, 47,* 72–88.

James, W. (1890). *The principles of psychology.* Boston: Henry Holt.

Jones, W. P., & Anderson, J. R. (1987). Short- and long-term memory retrieval: A comparison of the effects of information load and relatedness. *Journal of Experimental Psychology: General, 116,* 137–153.

Kintsch, W. (1974). *The representation of meaning in memory.* Hillsdale, NJ: Lawrence Erlbaum Associates.

Kintsch, W., & van Dijk, T. A. (1978). Toward a model of text comprehension and production. *Psychological Review, 85,* 363–394.

Kolodner, J. L., & Riesbeck, C. K. (Eds.). (1986). *Experience, memory, and reasoning.* Hillsdale, NJ: Lawrence Erlbaum Associates.

Kuenne, M. R. (1946). Experimental investigation of the relation of language to transposition behavior in young children. *Journal of Experimental Psychology, 36,* 471–490.

Lamb, M. R., & Robertson, L. C. (1989, November). *An evaluation of the empirical bases underlying global precedence theory.* Paper presented at the Annual Meeting of the Psychonomic Society, Atlanta, GA.

Liben, L. S., & Posnansky, C. J. (1977). Inferences on inference: The effects of age, transitive ability, memory load, and lexical factors. *Child Development, 48,* 490–497.

Marks, L. E., Hammeal, R. J., & Bornstein, M. H. (1987). Perceiving similarity and comprehending metaphor. *Monographs of the Society for Research in Child Development, 52*(1, Serial No. 215).

Marx, M. H. (1986). More retrospective reports on event-frequency judgments: Shift from multiple traces to strength factor with age. *Bulletin of the Psychonomic Society, 24,* 183–185.

McClelland, J. L. (1979). On the time relations of mental processes: An examination of systems of processes in cascade. *Psychological Review, 86,* 287–330.

McClelland, J. L., & Rumelhart, D. E. (Eds.) (1986). *Parallel distributed processing* (Vols. 1 & 2). Cambridge, MA: MIT Press.

Murdock, B. B. (1989, November). *Item and associated information in a distributed memory model.* Paper presented at the Annual Meeting of the Psychonomic Society, Atlanta, GA.

Perner, J., & Mansbridge, D. G. (1983). Developmental differences in encoding length series. *Child Development, 54,* 710–719.

Rabinowitz, F. M., & Howe, M. L. (1990). *Betwixt and between: Neo-Piagetian theories and horizontal decalage in the development of the middle concept.* Manuscript submitted for publication.

Reder, L. M. (1982). Plausibility judgments versus fact retrieval: Alternative strategies for sentence verification. *Psychological Review, 89,* 250–280.

Restle, F. (1970). Speed of adding and comparing numbers. *Journal of Experimental Psychology, 83,* 274–278.

Reyna, V. F. (1985). Figure and fantasy in children's language. In M. Pressley & C. J. Brainerd (Eds.), *Cognitive learning and memory in children: Progress in cognitive development research* (pp. 143–179). New York: Springer-Verlag.

Reyna, V. F. (in press-a). Class inclusion, the conjunction fallacy, and other cognitive illusions. *Developmental Review.*

Reyna, V. F. (in press-b). Reasoning, remembering, and their relationship: Social, cognitive, and developmental issues. In M. L. Howe, C. J. Brainerd, & V. F. Reyna (Eds.), *Development of long-term retention.* New York: Springer-Verlag.

Reyna, V. F., & Brainerd, C. J. (1989). Output interference, generic resources, and cognitive development. *Journal of Experimental Child Psychology, 47,* 42–46.

Reyna, V. F., & Brainerd, C. J. (1990). Fuzzy processing in transitivity development. *Annals of Operations Research, 23,* 37–63.

Reyna, V. F., & Brainerd, C. J. (1991). Fuzzy-trace theory and children's acquisition of mathematical and scientific concepts. *Learning and Individual Differences, 3,* 27–60.

Reyna, V. F., & Brainerd, C. J. (in press). Fuzzy-trace theory and framing effects in choice: Gist extraction, truncation, and conversion. *Journal of Behavioral Decision Making.*

Russell, B. (1948). *Human knowledge: Its scope and limits.* New York: Simon & Schuster.

Schmidt, C. R., & Welch, M. (1989, April). *The development of rote and gist memory tendencies in young children.* Paper presented at the Biennial Meeting of the Society for Research in Child Development, Kansas City, MO.

Schon, D. A. (1979). Generative metaphor: A perspective on problem-setting in social policy. In A. Ortony (Ed.), *Metaphor and thought* (pp. 254–283). New York: Cambridge University Press.

Shannon, B. (1988). Semantic representation of meaning: A critique. *Psychological Bulletin, 104,* 70–83.

Simon, H. A. (1988). Rationality as process and product of thought. In D. E. Bell, H. Raiffa, & A. Tversky (Eds.), *Decision making: Descriptive, normative, and prescriptive interactions* (pp. 58–77). New York: Cambridge University Press.

Staubli, U., Ivy, G., & Lynch, G. (1984). Hippocampal denervation causes rapid forgetting of olfactory information in rats. *Proceedings of the National Academy of Sciences, 81,* 5885–5887.

Townsend, J. (1990). Serial versus parallel processing: Sometimes they look like Tweedledum and Tweedledee but they can (and should) be distinguished. *Psychological Science, 1,* 46–54.

Tversky, A., & Kahneman, D. (1986). Rational choice and the framing of decisions. *Journal of Business, 59,* 251–278.

Vygotsky, L. (1962). *Thought and language.* Cambridge: MIT Press.

von Neumann, J. (1958). *The computer and the brain.* New Haven: Yale University Press.

Wilkinson, A. C. (1976). Counting strategies and semantic analyses as applied to class inclusion. *Cognitive Psychology, 8,* 64–85.

11

How Readers Construct Situation Models for Stories: The Role of Syntactic Cues and Causal Inferences

Walter Kintsch
University of Colorado

It may appear unusual to write a Festschrift chapter in which the person honored is not cited, but discourse comprehension is not one of Bill's many research interests. Nevertheless, I hope that his influence on the work reported here is still discernible to the attentive reader. There are two rather direct lines that can be traced from Bill's work to this research. First, the theory described in the following is a computational model of a psychological process. Such models are (one of) the contemporary successors to the mathematical psychology that Bill helped to found when I was a graduate student. Secondly, the emphasis on associative processes and structures that characterizes my work as well as much of current connectionism, obviously owes something to older traditions. Bill's work has had an important bridging function in this respect: It demonstrated the strengths of associationistic theories, when precisely and explicitly formulated. Thus, I claim Bill as a model for both the computational approach and the associationist orientation.

The present chapter continues the development of a general theory of comprehension,[1] focusing on story understanding and the role that syntax plays therein. Partly as a reaction against the almost exclusive concern of some linguists and psycholinguists with syntax, syntactic questions play only a minor role in the current work on discourse processing, text comprehension, and conversation. Maybe this is too strong a statement as far as the field as a whole is concerned, but it certainly characterizes my own work in this area. Syntax plays a role in that it directs the reader how to parse a test into meaning units (proposi-

---

[1]From now on I speak about reading comprehension, because the experiments discussed in the following involve reading rather than listening.

tions), but all the most interesting processes psychologically seem to occur at the level of meaning and language use.

This imbalance needs to be redressed. Such an essential feature of language as grammar surely must be more important than we have given it credit for, and a recent paper by Givón (1989) in which he proposed that grammatical cues function as mental processing instructions, may give us some clues as to the manner in which syntactic cues are used in discourse processing. I show how Givón's ideas can be incorporated into a model of discourse comprehension, how such an extended model could account for some salient empirical results that have been reported previously by others as well as myself, and I argue that by paying attention to the role of syntactic cues in processing, we can greatly expand the power of our model and throw some light on currently controversial issues. Specifically, I show how only a single verbal signal may determine whether a text representation will be organized linearly or in terms of a topic–subtopic structure (in the second section), and how syntactic cues may indicate the presence of important causal relations in a text (in the third and fourth sections). Thus, it is possible to arrive at rather similar mental representations of a test either via weak but general syntactic strategies, or by by more powerful, knowledge-based, but domain-limited processing strategies.

A Theoretical Framework
for Discourse Comprehension

I first give some background concerning the view of text comprehension that underlies this discussion (Kintsch, 1988; Kintsch & van Dijk, 1978; van Dijk & Kintsch, 1983). At a very general level, the task of the comprehender can be considered as constructing a mental representation of the information provided by the text that is integrated with his or her knowledge, beliefs, and goals. We take this representation to consist of concepts and propositions (complex terms that establish some sort of relation between concepts and/or other propositions) forming an interrelated network. What is related to what in this network depends in part on properties of the to-be-comprehended text, and in part on the semantic and associative relations between concepts and propositions in the com-prehender's long-term memory (which includes general knowledge). In practice, we approximate these rich interrelationships by means of argument overlap: two propositions are related if they have a common argument (concept or proposi-tion). The rationale for this approximation is that it is frequently the case that whenever two propositions are in fact related semantically, there exists a shared argument. Obviously, this is neither a sufficient nor necessary condition for semantic relatedness, but it works reasonably well in a statistical sense, and it is easily computed and does not require uncertain subjective judgments. Some-times, however, argument overlap provides too crude an approximation, and we need a more powerful analysis (e.g., the role of causal connections in story understanding as discussed later).

Comprehension, then, consists of the construction of some sort of propositional network in our model. In the following, we introduce a special set of construction rules that take advantage of syntactic cues that signal the importance of the various meaning elements that have been constructed.

There are, however, several further considerations that cannot be neglected. First, listening as well as reading is sequential. The capacity limitations of working memory make it impossible to maintain in an active state all of the previous information in a discourse. Hence, processing must be cyclical. Depending on the level of analysis desired, comprehension may be analyzed word by word (e.g., if we are interested in the speed-accuracy trade-off in sentence recognition, as in Kintsch, Welsch, Schmalhofer, & Zimny [1990]), or, more usually, sentence by sentence (as in Kintsch & van Dijk, [1978]), or even paragraph by paragraph, if we are only concerned with the macrostructure of a long text (e.g., the campaign speeches analyzed in Kintsch & Vipond, 1979). In any case, we need a memory buffer to form a bridge between cycles. Therefore we assume that a few propositions from the current processing cycles, which are considered to be the most important ones, are retained in the buffer to form a connection between the previous text and the current input. If there is no connection between the contents of the buffer and the new input, extra processing is required from the reader to make the textbase cohere. This may either involve a search of previous text that is no longer actively available in working memory, resulting in the reinstatement of a connecting proposition, or it may require a knowledge-based inference to form a connection when it is not explicitly expressed in the text (e.g., Kintsch & Vipond, 1979).

A second consideration concerns the way in which a text activates the reader's relevant knowledge, and how this knowledge becomes integrated with the current text. Kintsch (1988) has argued that the activation process is quite unselective and driven mostly by local associations, rather than controlled by some sort of schema that filters out anything but the contextually appropriate knowledge. In this way, a lot of irrelevant knowledge is activated, but a spreading activation process can then select those portions of the activated knowledge that actually fit into the given context. Thus, if activation is spread around the network consisting of the text propositions as well as the associatively activated knowledge elements, it will tend to collect in those portions of the network that are most strongly interconnected, and isolated elements or elements connected with inhibitory links will tend to become deactivated. Thus, the end effect is the same as in a schema theory: only contextually appropriate knowledge remains, but this effect is produced in a psychologically more plausible and computationally more flexible way.

Van Dijk and Kintsch (1983) have distinguished between the construction of a mental representation of the text itself (termed a *textbase*) and a representation of the situation described by the text and integrated into the reader's previous knowledge (which we have termed the *situation model*). The textbase includes a representation of both the microstructure as well as the macrostructure of the text, reflecting its local and global organization, respectively. The structure of the situation model is not necessarily the same as the macrostructure of the text. It is independent of the rhetorical organization of the text, and reflects primarily the structure of the situation described by the text. It is a domain structure rather than a text structure.

Knowledge about the world, the situation in question, is therefore needed to form situation models. But situation models are not mere knowledge structures. They are the product of the combination of information provided by the text and already existing world knowledge. To "really understand" a text, say a story, a great deal of specific world knowledge is often required, as well as a great deal of analysis: exactly what leads to what, and why—inferences about goals, motivations, psychological states, causal relations, and implications. On the other hand, we can understand, though maybe not "really understand" a story from a different culture where we are not sure about people's goals and reactions, or we can understand a story without thinking very deeply about it, without fully analyzing its implications. There are strong, powerful methods for building situation models that require a certain amount of effort and resource commitments, but there also seem to be weaker, more general but easier methods, which we can use when we lack precise knowledge or are unwilling to take the trouble. Syntax, together with some weak, general semantic principles, allows readers to generate situation models that, although not as accurate and complete as models based upon full knowledge and deep analyses, can be quite adequate for many purposes, or may even serve as stepping stones towards a more sophisticated model.

Syntactic cues in the text signal to the reader what is likely to be important for the construction of a situation model, and some rather general semantic rules allow the reader to put these elements together into a weak or sloppy situation model. Givón (1989) has shown how the grammar provides processing instructions for the formation of a referentially coherent mental representation of a text. The grammar tells the reader quite precisely where to look for what in a text. I cannot summarize here Givón's important work, but use only two of his examples in the analyses to reported: cues for topicality, such as the indefinite "this," and the signaling of importance via subject-verb-object constructions. In the latter case the syntactic signals must be filtered semantically because it makes a difference for the construction of a situation model in story understanding whether the verb is an action verb, or a verb of saying or believing.

Picking only a few examples like this from the wealth of material described by Givón may seem arbitrary, but I am concerned here with a principle. If we can show that in the cases analyzed here, syntactic cues can indeed function as mental processing instructions, we would have established an important point, and a wider range of syntactic phenomena could be examined later. First, we examine how syntactic signaling via an indefinite "this" can be built into the construction–integration model.

Grammar as Mental Processing Instructions:
Givón (1989) and a Fragment Completion Experiment
by Gernsbacher & Shroyer (1989)

Gernsbacher and Shroyer (1989) performed an experiment in which subjects received discourse fragments with or without an indefinite "this." Subjects were asked to complete these fragments. Following Givón, Gernsbacher and Shroyer hypothesized that more completions would involve nouns emphasized by an indefinite "this" than nouns without this emphasis. This prediction was confirmed in their experiment. My goal here is to explore how these phenomena can be dealt with in the construction–integration model.

The following is a sample fragment from Gernsbacher & Shroyer:

1. I went to the coast last weekend with Sally.
    We had checked the tide schedules
    and planned to arrive at low tide,
    because I just love beachcombing.
    Right off, I found three whole sand dollars.
    Sally found *an/this* egg.............

We assume that when subjects complete a discourse fragment, they tend to talk about topics that are highly activated in the memory representation they have created. Thus, the model needs to produce a noticeably higher activation for "egg" in the "find this egg" text than in the "find an egg" text.

Suppose the text in the example is processed in six cycles, one for each of its lines. For present purposes, I completely neglect one major aspect of the model, namely knowledge activation and integration: in many situations that is a crucial aspect of comprehension, but here it would be merely a needless complication. Thus, we obtain for the first processing cycle (the first line of text in the example) the following network of concepts and propositions (columns are labeled by the first letter of each proposition):

2.

	I	S	A	G	C	L	T	activation
I	1	0	1	0	0	0	0	.08
SALLY	0	1	1	0	0	0	0	.08
AND[I, SALLY]	1	1	1	1	0	0	0	.20
GO[AND[. .], COAST]	0	0	1	2	1	0	1	.30
COAST	0	0	0	1	1	0	0	.12
LAST-WEEKEND	0	0	0	0	0	1	1	.07
TIME[GO[. .],L-W]	0	0	0	1	0	1	1	.15

The default rule of argument repetition has been used in the second example to construct the propositional network: whenever two propositions share an argument they are connected by a 1, and 0 otherwise.[2] Each proposition is assumed to be connected to itself, hence the diagonals are 1. In one case, however, we have used Givón's syntactic signals to emphasize a proposition by increasing its self-connection strengths from a 1 to 2: the GO[..] proposition because it corresponds to the syntactic core of the sentence (subject-verb-object). What this means is that in the first sentence of the first example, the writer has signaled, by purely syntactic means, that this element should be considered as a potential discourse topic.

The seven propositions constructed from the first sentence are initially equally activated, but once we start spreading activation around the network defined by the second example, activation will collect in the more central nodes in the network. The reader can check this quite easily by typing the matrix (second example) into a spreadsheet and postmultiplying it by a column vector of seven ⅟₇s. The resulting column vector is normalized so that the total activation always sums to 1, and is then used again as a multiplier for the second example, until a stable vector is obtained. The last column of the second example shows this asymptotic activation vector.

The model's memory for the sentence, at this point, has three components: a list of propositions, a connectivity matrix that connects these propositions, and their activation values. It is often convenient to combine the last two components in a way that parallels more closely connectionist practice, so that the process of encoding a text in memory modifies not merely the activation value of the nodes, but the actual interconnections among the nodes. It has been shown (Kintsch & Welsch, in press) that if $c(i,j)$ is the original connection strength of nodes i and j, and $a(i)$ is the activation value of node i and $b(j)$ is the activation value of node j, a modified long-term memory network can be obtained with connection strength of element $l(i,j)$ is given by $l(i,j) = a(i)*b(j)*c(i,j)$. Figure 11.1 shows the network obtained after the first processing cycle, and illustrates the computation of the connection strengths in this network for the connections between the GO[..] proposition and its neighbors. Strength values are shown only for the links emanating from GO: the first number is the original value in the coherence matrix; it is multiplied by the product of the activation values of the two nodes being linked. For example, GO and AND are linked by a 1 in the second example, and their activation values are .28 and .20, respectively, yielding a memory strength of .056.

We now continue processing the next three lines of the first example in the same way, except that we have to decide how many and which propositions from the first processing cycle to keep in the buffer to connect this cycle with what is yet to come. Buffer estimates in previous work have ranged from 1 to 4 propositions, averaging about 2, which I use for these calculations. This means that the

---

[2]Because we are only interested in the qualitative patterns, there is no need to estimate precise parameter values. Simple illustrative numbers are used instead.

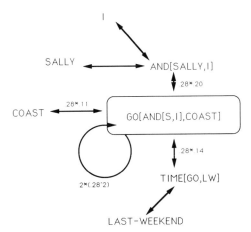

FIG. 11.1 Long-term memory strength values for GO and its neighbors.

two most highly activated propositions are carried over into the second processing cycle where they are reprocessed together with the new text.

For Cycle 2, another coherence matrix is constructed with AND[..] and GO[..]. as buffer contents, and CHECK[AND[..],TIDESCHED] and TIDESCHEDULE as the new input. The CHECK[..] proposition is derived from the main verb of the sentence, hence it is is emphasized.

In the third cycle, the syntax suggests PLAN[..] as another candidate for the situation model. However, we do not consider psychological and verbal processes (verbs of saying, thinking, feeling, reacting, and perceiving) for emphasis because the situation model of a story should be built around actions rather than psychological states. Thus, in the fourth cycle, "love" receives no emphasis in our analysis. In the fifth and sixth cycles we have syntactic emphases on FIND[I,SANDDOLLAR] and FIND[SALLY,EGG]. In addition, for the "this-egg" version of the text, EGG is emphasized. As a result, the activation values for this cycle differ for the focused and nonfocused version of the text:

	Focused	Non-Focused
Buffer: AND[I, SALLY]	.24	.27
GO[AND[. .], COAST]	.13	.15
Input: FIND[I, EGG]		
EGG	.37	.39
	.26	.18

EGG is more highly activated when it is emphasized by an indefinite "this" than when it is not. At the same time, the other propositions in the sentence are somewhat less strongly activated in the focused condition than in the nonfocused condition (a consequence of normalizing the activation vector). This observation agrees well with a recent report by Gernsbacher that concepts marked by indefinite "this" and spoken stress suppress the activation of other (potentially competing) topics (Gernsbacher & Jescheniak, in press).

Thus, we have achieved our first goal: We have shown how the construction–integration model can account for the findings of Gernsbacher and Shroyer (1989).

One of Gernsbacher and Shroyer's subjects continued the version with the focus on egg in the following way:

3. It looked like it came from a lizard.
   We couldn't tell whether it had hatched,
   so we put it back where we found it in case it was still alive.

We have simulated the way the model would process the combined texts in the first and third examples, both the version with "an egg" and "this egg." Note that the texts are exactly the same, the only difference is the little word "this" that replaces an "an" in the nonfocused version. Nevertheless, the resulting memory representation is strikingly different, especially for the portion of the network corresponding to the third example, for which the correlation between the memory strength values calculated for the two versions is only $r = .62$.

However, the memory trace for this story consists not only of the strength values of its elements, but also of their pattern of interrelations. This is quite different for the focused and nonfocused versions for the portion of the text corresponding to the third example. In the focused version, EGG is clearly the central node for the second half of the story; EGG clearly has subtopic status, in that everything else is related to it, which is not the case in the nonfocused version of the text. The grammar—a single verbal signal in this case—has determined what sort of situation model was constructed: a linear sequence of Going-to-the-Coast episodes, versus a topic/subtopic structure in the other.

Other syntactic means of indicating the discourse function of particular concepts or propositions (see Givón, 1989) can be handled within the construction–integration theory. For instance, particle movement provides another example of syntactic emphasis: In *He picked up a friend*, the *friend* is likely to persist longer as a discourse object than in *He picked a friend up* (Chen, 1986), and is more strongly activated psychologically (Clifford, 1990)—findings that are readily incorporated within the framework already proposed.

Causal Reasoning in Story Understanding: Trabasso and van den Broek (1985)

Conventional stories are about people, about some problem in which the hero gets involved, and about how this problem gets resolved. The domain knowledge the reader needs to understand these stories is about people, their motivations, goals, social relations, and so on. This is the same knowledge we need to interact with others in our daily lives. Even very young children already know a lot about such matters (and learn more from the stories they are told). Much of this knowledge takes the form of causal relations: a goal causes an action, a mental state causes a goal, and so on. (The term "causal" is used here in the broad sense of an enabling relation.) A situation model for a story, therefore, consists primarily of the specification of the causal relations among the various events and actions in the story (in addition there is some setting information). Trabasso and his colleagues (e.g., Trabasso & van den Broek, 1985) have extensively explored the role of these causal relations in story understanding.

There are at least three different aspects of a story that could, in principle, contribute to the formation of a coherent memory representation: causal relations, as claimed by Trabasso and van den Broek, but also the pattern of argument overlap among the story propositions, as well as the syntactic signals, as in the example previously analyzed.

In the following, a story used by Trabasso and van den Broek (1985) (see also Omanson, 1982) is analyzed in the same way as the "Going-to-the-Coast" story. How different will the resulting structure be from the causal structure of the story, as determined by Trabasso and van den Broek? Furthermore, what will happen if, in addition to the default structure generated by argument repetition, we build into our network the causal relations identified by Trabasso and van den Broek?

The story is as follows:

4. One day Mark and Sally were sailing their sailboat in the pond. / Suddenly, the sailboat began to sink. Mark was surprised. He lifted the boat up with a stick / and found a turtle on top of it. The turtle became frightened and tried to crawl off the boat. The turtle put Mark in a playful mood. / Mark thought the turtle was hurt. Mark had always wanted Sally to see a turtle, so he waded out to the turtle and brought it back to her. / Sally thought Mark was going to hurt the turtle. Sally felt sorry for Mark. Sally tried to touch the turtle, but the turtle bit her. / Sally didn't like this and threw the turtle into the pond. The turtle crashed into the sailboat. Sally knew she had made a mistake.

Comprehension of this story has been simulated by means of the construction-integration model with the following parameters:

1. Input cycles: sentence or phrase boundaries, so that cycles consist of no more than 6 propositions, if possible; this scheme results in 6 processing cycles, which are indicated by slashes in the example.
2. Buffer: the two most strongly activated propositions from the previous cycle.

3. Coherence matrix: a 1 if two propositions are related by argument overlap, and 0 otherwise; self-connections are 1, except for propositions that are emphasized syntactically, which are assigned a value of 2.

4. Syntactic emphasis: propositions corresponding to the main verb and subject in a sentence are emphasized, except for verbs of psychological processes or verbal action. This use of syntactic processing signals falls far short of Givón's proposals, but my intent here is merely to explore the potential of this kind of an approach.

Note that these parameters are in no way "best" estimates, but rather a priori guesses, based on previous experience with the model and/or general expectations of what would be reasonable values, as in the case of buffer size and input size, or just simplicity, as in choosing values of 0, 1, and 2 for the coherence matrix. I have chosen this informal approach to parameter estimation because I am not primarily interested in fitting data quantitatively, but in demonstrating some robust principles about comprehension.

Figure 11.2 illustrates the construction of the coherence matrix for the second processing cycle. The propositions held over in the buffer from the first processing cycle, as well as the input propositions of the current cycle, are shown. The buffer consists of AND[...] and SAIL[...]. Propositions that are syntactically emphasized are boxed. Links among propositions indicate argument overlap. (The bold arrows are causal links and will be discussed later.) Among the current input propositions, SINK[..] and LIFT[..] are emphasized as they are derived from the main verbs of sentences, but SURPRISE[..] is not, because it is a "psychological" verb. Figure 11.3 shows the pattern of activation after the integration is completed.

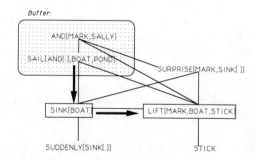

FIG. 11.2. Buffer and input propositions for the second processing cycle. Plain lines indicate argument overlap, bold arrows causal relations. Boxes enclose syntactically emphasized propositions.

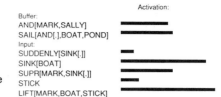

Activation:

Buffer:
AND[MARK,SALLY]
SAIL[AND[.],BOAT,POND]
Input:
SUDDENLY[SINK[.]]
SINK[BOAT]
SUPR[MARK,SINK[.]]
STICK
LIFT[MARK,BOAT,STICK]

FIG. 11.3.   Activation after the second processing cycle.

After completing the simulation through all six cycles, a long-term memory matrix can be calculated as in Fig. 11.1. This long-term memory matrix can be used to predict recall data by assuming that the likelihood of recall of an item is monotonically related to its memory strength as calculated. Indeed, recall data collected by Omanson (1982) on 20 subjects correlate reasonably well with these predictions, Spearman rho = .76. A nonparametric measure of correlation had to be used, because the relationship between recall likelihood and predicted memory strength is highly nonlinear (regression on a fourth order polynomial gives equally high correlations). Because Omanson's data were not scored in terms of propositional units but in terms of slightly more global idea units, appropriate propositions were combined to match his analysis.

Omanson (1982) was interested in a story grammar analysis, for which purposes he categorized all statements in the fourth example as belonging to one of the categories Setting, Initiating Event, Internal Response, Attempt, Consequence, and Reaction (after Stein & Glenn, 1979). His main point was that statements belonging to a certain story grammar category are recalled/judged differently than statements in some other category. This was taken as evidence for the psychological validity of the story grammar analysis. Because we have predicted memory strength values for all statements, the average memory strength of statements in each story grammar category can be calculated. These memory strength values derived from the construction-integration model correlate (Spearman's rho) .80 with the averages of the measures Omanson had collected (importance judgments, summaries, immediate recall, delayed recall). It is interesting that we thus can account for Omanson's finding that story grammar category affects the way statements in a story are processed, although our analysis makes no use whatever of the concepts of story grammar. The story grammar results simply fall out as consequences of normal discourse processing; story grammar appears to be an analytic scheme imposed by the theorist, not something that actually guides the reader's processing of a story. This question deserves further scrutiny, but, if the results reported previously are confirmed, we may conclude that general principles of discourse comprehension may be sufficient to account for the phenomena described by story grammars.

But let us return to the role of causal relations in story understanding. So far, our network does not take into account causal relations; it is based entirely on the default-semantics of argument overlap, together with the emphasis on situation-model relevant propositions cued by the syntax. So far, the situation model used has been a very weak one: The syntax signals mostly topics and subtopics as well as the main actors and action components. Now suppose we assume that subjects develop a "strong" situation model by figuring out all the causal networks determined by Trabasso and van den Broek (1985; their Fig. 1). It is a simple matter to add these causal relations to our coherence matrices. What is involved is shown in Fig. 11.2 by the bold arrows: there is a causal path from SAIL to SINK, and from SINK to LIFT. Note that these relations are asymmetric. We can therefore obtain a new coherence matrix which is identical with the previous one, except that for each causal relation among propositions a value of 1 is added in the appropriate cell of the matrix. Recalculating activation values based on the new coherence matrices containing causal links yields a new pattern of memory strengths. Surprisingly, this new pattern correlates with the one obtained without the causal links r = .98. Whether or not we include the causal links makes almost no difference at all!

What is going on can be glimpsed from Fig. 11.2: The syntactic cues we have used overlap to such an extent with the causal links that they make them redundant. In other words, a "weak" situation model, as was described, will do just as well for present purposes as a "strong," causal one. What does this mean psychologically? It means that whether or not subjects actually infer causal relations during reading, more or less the same recall pattern is predicted. At least for recall, readers do *not* have to infer causal links in a story; they can do just as well with weak, general strategies, based on syntactic and semantic relations as reflected by argument overlap. We show in the next section, however, that this is not so when it comes to forming higher-order macrostructures: the model must have access to causal information in this case.

We now have two models, a complete model that defines coherence in terms of causal links (CAUS) plus syntactic emphasis (SYN) plus argument overlap (AROV), and a weaker model that defines coherence in terms of the latter two relations only.[3] Consider two more models, one that is obtained by defining coherence in terms of argument overlap only (this is the model of Kintsch & van Dijk, 1978), and one that relies only on the causal relations of Trabasso and van den Broek (1985, their Fig. 1). For each of these models a memory strength matrix was calculated as described. The interrelations among these models, as well as the correlations between the various models and the Omanson data are as follows:

---

[3]Although Trabasso & van den Broek (1985) have shown the importance of causal inferences for story understanding, they did not actually explore whether argument repetition is also a factor; they merely demonstrated that a coherence measure based on the identity of words in the text is irrelevant.

	ASC[1]	AS[1]	A[1]	C[1]	DATA[2]
AROV + SYN + CAUS	—	.98	.90	.40	.79
AROV + SYN		—	.84	.49	.76
AROV			—	.16	.55
CAUS				—	.61

[1] Pearson r, n = 36
[2] Spearman rho, n = 20

Note that the correlations between the various versions of the model and the data merely present a lower bound for the theory. These correlations were obtained not by adjusting the parameters of a model to maximize goodness of fit, but by simply postulating a certain set of (plausible) parameter values, that is, by giving equal weight to argument overlap, causal relations, and syntactic cues. (The other parameters of the model, input and buffer size, are at least historically motivated through estimates obtained in other studies.)[4] Thus, whereas the model has a potentially large number of parameters, it does appear to be reasonably robust.

Obviously, very similar predictions are obtained whether or not causal relations are included in the coherence matrix, and these predictions fit the data about equally well. The argument-overlap-only model correlates fairly well with the complete model, but does not predict the data as well. The cause-only model is more different from the complete model, and has a very low correlation with the argument-overlap-only model. Argument overlap and causal analysis make quite different contributions to the coherence matrix, and syntactic emphasis and causal analysis appear to be redundant.

Macrostructures and Summaries: Kintsch (1976)

In general, the macrostructure of a text cannot be obtained merely by deleting all the unimportant propositions of the microstructure. Constructive processes involving generalization and construction rules are usually involved (van Dijk, 1980). However, there are special cases where the deletion of macro-irrelevant proposition suffices to obtain a good macrostructure. One such case that has been reported before is the (first part) of the Boccaccio story analyzed in Kintsch

---

[4] The choice of input size makes a difference in the model: If sentences are used as input units irrespective of length, the resulting pattern of memory strengths correlates only r = .73 with the values based on input units of at least seven propositions.

(1976). In the following, I show how the construction–integration model predicts summarization data for this text. To create a macrostructure, some *ad hoc* rules had to be used in Kintsch (1976). Will the extension of the construction–integration model previously introduced generate the same macrostructure as had been obtained earlier, without the ad hoc assumptions?

Thus, I analyze the Boccaccio story discussed in Kintsch (1976) in the same way as the Going-to-the-Coast and the Mark-Sally-and-Turtle stories, indeed, with the same parameters. The Boccaccio story is about a merchant named Landolfo, who is involved in a risky venture, goes bankrupt, becomes a successful pirate, is shipwrecked and loses it all again, is saved, finds a chest of jewels, and finally returns home happily. The first part, the one analyzed here, is presented in detail in Table 5.4 in the original paper. It breaks down into four processing cycles. The coherence matrix for each cycle is obtained by adding three separate components: one based on argument overlap, one based on syntactic cues, and one based on the causal relations in the story. A long-term memory matrix is obtained for this story in exactly the same way as has already been described.

Given the long-term memory strengths predicted by the model, what sort of retrieval processes should we assume to generate a macrostructure from this memory representation? Consider how we could obtain a model summary. Suppose the subject has some means of entering the memory representation for the story at the beginning, and picks the strongest proposition of the first processing cycle. From that proposition, the strongest link will be followed to another proposition, which will be included in the summary if its strength is above some threshold value. This link following-plus-editing process is continued until the end of the story is reached. The propositions traversed in this process will be the modal summary. If at any point the strongest link leads to a below-threshold proposition, the next strongest link is tried. If no link can be found to an above-threshold proposition, the process backtracks and tries to find another path from the previously selected proposition. There are two comments to be made about this retrieval model. First, the restriction to following the strongest link is merely a simplification. In general, choices could be probabilistic, so that the model would generate a whole family of summaries, differing in their likelihood, rather than just a single model summary. Second, the same process, minus the response threshold, could be used to derive recall predictions from the model, instead of the simplified assumptions previously used. Thus, each prediction would involve a whole recall path. Averaging many such recall paths, we would probably generate predictions close to those obtained from the mere response strengths of each separate item, as was done for the Sall-Mark-and-Turtle story.

Figure 11.4 shows what happens for the Landolfo story: We start out with *Landolfo is a merchant,* which leads to *He purchases a ship,* which leads to *He loads the ship with cargo,* which leads to *He sails to Cyprus,* which leads to *He discovers other ships,* which leads to *Which are docked in Cyprus,* which does

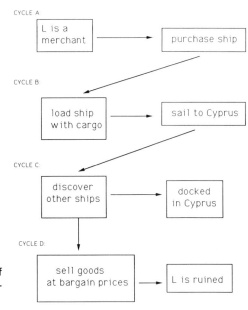

FIG. 11.4. The construction of a summary for the Landolfo story.

not have link to a strong enough proposition; backing up one step, we find another link to *He sells his goods at bargain prices,* which leads to *Landolfo is ruined.*

The Kintsch (1976) summary includes all the statements listed, plus three other, redundant ones: *He pays for the goods he bought, He arrives in Cyprus,* and *He gives away his goods.* Clearly, we have done, if anything, better—and without ad hoc assumptions. If we model the construction of a situation model, based upon general syntactic cues and some general semantic constraints, the macrostructure will be implied (excepting construction and generalization processes).

As before, the memory strength values for the propositions of the Landolfo story are almost the same whether or not causal links are or are not included in the coherence matrices. Specifically, exactly the same summary results as shown in Fig. 11.4 if causal links are deleted. Hence, the conclusion reached is supported such that if we take into account syntactic signals, precise causal inferences are not necessary to predict either recall or summarization.

However, Kintsch (1976) reports not only a first-order summary, as described, but also a second order summary, where the whole first part of the Landolfo-story gets summarized as *The merchant Landolfo was ruined.* This second-order summary is well motivated, both empirically and theoretically (macrostructures have always been thought of as hierarchical). Can the construction–integration model

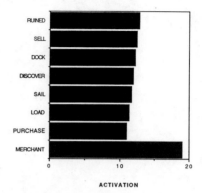

FIG. 11.5.   Activation clues for macropropositions.

ACTIVATION

produce this second-order summary, too? It can, but only if it is given the causal link information. Figure 11.5 shows the pattern of activation that is obtained when the eight summary propositions of Fig. 11.4 are integrated. The same values are entered into the coherence matrix for the summary as were used for the microstructure analysis. The strongest proposition turns out to be *Landolfo is a merchant,* and it is linked most strongly to *Landolfo is ruined*—exactly what is needed for the second-order summary. *Landolfo is ruined* wins out over its competitors, because it is at the end of a long causal chain: one event enables the next, and ruin is the end result. Activation flows from cause to effect, and hence favors the end result. Without the causal links this does not happen, and for the given summary matrix, all events would be equally activated.

This is an interesting result because it indicates that causal inferences are necessary for story understanding. They are not really needed for comprehension, recall, or the generation of a first-order summary, in the sense that we get essentially the same memory trace with or without causal inferences, because the situation model emphasizes the same propositions that play a role in the causal network. Thus, the causal inference does not add much to other information already gleaned from the text. Generating a second-order summary, however, is another matter: all the model has to work with now is a list of propositions; the syntactic information from the text has already been used up in selecting this particular list from the original input. Now the only way to structure the macrostructure further hierarchically is to rely on the causal network.

Conclusions

It has often been said that "comprehension is problem solving." The construction–integration model sets the accent differently. It emphasizes the bottom-up, perception-like aspects of comprehension, as distinct from the controlled, conscious problem-solving processes. Perfetti (1989) has made a similar point:

Without denying the importance of knowledge-based strategies in comprehension, he finds compelling evidence that general reading strategies and abilities also play a significant role in comprehension.

Our model describes normal comprehension as a highly data-driven process based upon constraint satisfaction, more like perception, but it does not deny that as comprehension difficulties arise, more controlled, problem-solving type behavior plays a role. Indeed, we have just seen an example of how comprehension shades into higher-level processes: just to read and retell a story, we may or may not infer causal links; weaker, more general operations will suffice. But to reach a higher understanding of a story, we can't do without a causal analysis.

Indeed, syntax-guided processing may play a significant role in the actual process of generating causal inferences by selecting from the multitude of propositions in a text those propositions that are most important and that, in a story, are likely to be relevant causally. Thus, it is not necessary to test for the presence or absence of causal relations among all the numerous pairs of propositions in a story, but only for those propositions that, on other grounds, have already been determined to be important.

This chapter is an exploration of the linguistic richness of texts that so far has not been considered sufficiently in psychological processing models of texts. Of course we must simplify, even radically, if we want to understand language processes. As a first approximation, it makes sense to study comprehension as the integration of a network of propositions, but we also need to look more closely at the language itself to refine our model of language comprehension. Givón (1989) has suggested viewing syntax as a set of processing instructions. Realizing this suggestion within the construction–integration model of text comprehension has yielded a rich payoff: If we attend to the processing instructions the syntax gives us, our model of language comprehension will be much more powerful and capable of dealing with a range of phenomena that were previously out of its reach.

We have finally found a use for syntax in a psychological processing model. It provides the comprehender with "weak" but general methods for comprehension, to be complemented by "strong" knowledge-based and domain specific methods. As in problem solving, weak and strong methods have their respective advantages and uses, and the complete comprehender would not forego either.

ACKNOWLEDGMENTS

This research was supported by Grant MH 15872 from the National Institute of Mental Health. I thank Paul van den Broek for making his data available to me, and Paul van den Broek, Susanna Cumming, Stephanie Doane, Alice Healy, Eileen Kintsch, and Valerie Reyna for their comments on this work.

REFERENCES

Chen, P. (1986). Discourse and particle movement in English. *Studies in Language, 10,* 79–96.

Clifford, J. (1990). Grammar and activation of referents in working memory: The case of particle movement. Unpublished manuscript, University of Colorado.

Gernsbacher, M. A., & Jescheniak, J. (in press). Cataphoric devices in spoken discourse. *Cognitive Psychology.*

Gernsbacher, M. A., & Shroyer, S. (1989). The cataphoric use of the indefinite this in spoken narratives. *Memory & Cognition, 17,* 536–540.

Givón, T. (1989). *Mind, code and context: Essays in pragmatics.* Hillsdale, NJ: Lawrence Erlbaum Associates.

Kintsch, W. (1976). Memory for prose. In C. N. Cofer (Ed.), *The structure of human memory* (pp. 90–113). San Francisco: Freeman.

Kintsch, W. (1988). The use of knowledge in discourse processing: A construction–integration model. *Psychological Review, 95,* 163–182.

Kintsch, W., & van Dijk, T. A. (1978). Towards a model of text comprehension and production. *Psychological Review, 85,* 363–394.

Kintsch, W., & Vipond, D. (1979). Reading comprehension and readability in educational practice and psychological theory. In L. G. Nilsson (Ed.), *Perspectives of memory research* (pp. 325–366). Hillsdale, NJ: Lawrence Erlbaum Associates.

Kintsch, W., & Welsch, D. (in press). The construction-integration model: A framework for studying memory for text. In W. E. Hockley, & S. Lewandowsky (Eds.), *Relating theory and data: Essays on human memory.* Hillsdale, NJ: Lawrence Erlbaum Associates.

Kintsch, W., Welsch, D., Schmalhofer, F., & Zimny, S. (1990). Sentence memory: A theoretical analysis. *Journal of Memory and Language, 29,* 133–159.

Omanson, R. C. (1982). The relation between centrality and story category variation. *Journal of Verbal Learning and Verbal Behavior, 21,* 326–337.

Perfetti, C. A. (1989). There are generalized learning abilities and one of them is reading. In L. B. Resnick (Ed.) *Knowing, learning, and instruction.* (pp. 307–336). Hillsdale, NJ: Lawrence Erlbaum Associates.

Stein, N. L., & Glenn, C. G. (1979). An analysis of story comprehension in elementary school children. In R. O. Freedle (Ed.), *New directions in discourse processing* (pp. 53–120). Hillsdale, NJ: Lawrence Erlbaum Associates.

Trabasso, T., & van den Broek, P. (1985). Causal thinking and the representation of narrative events. *Journal of Memory and Language, 24,* 616–630.

van Dijk, T. A. (1980). *Macrostructures.* The Hague: Mouton.

van Dijk, T. A., & Kintsch, W. (1983). *Strategies of discourse comprehension.* New York: Academic Press.

12

Culture and Cognitive Development: From Cross-Cultural Comparisons to Model Systems of Cultural Mediation

Michael Cole
University of California, San Diego

Although Bill Estes is best known for his mathematical models of adult learning and memory, at least since the mid1960s he has also thought about and conducted research on the development of mental abilities. Our shared belief that developmental research is relevant to the more general enterprise of understanding intelligent behavior can serve as a useful touchstone linking our work over the past 25 years, despite marked differences in style and content.

The specific starting point for this discussion is a remark that Bill wrote at a conference on intelligence held in 1974, emphasizing the potential role of comparative, developmental research in promoting our understanding of behavior:

> Studies of mental retardation from the standpoint of learning theory (Estes, 1970) and studies of the development of discriminative and mnemonic abilities in different cultural settings (Cole, Gay, Glick, & Sharp, 1971; Cole & Scribner, 1974; Goodnow, Chapter 9) point to the overwhelming importance of the occurrence and proper sequencing of relevant experiences as a prerequisite to efficient intellectual performance. We cannot, however, assume that major advances in this area will come automatically as a function simply of increased industry on the part of empirical investigators. Rather, they may wait upon innovations at a theoretical level comparable to those attendant upon the application of computer simulation models to human problem solving. (Estes, 1976, p. 300)

Because my own work has been concentrated on the role of culture in regulating the occurrence and sequencing of experience during ontogeny, I have chosen this topic as my focus. I begin by discussing the benefits and shortcomings of using a cross-cultural, experimental research strategy for this purpose. My conclusion is that despite its surface attractiveness and important lessons that can be

279

learned from it, there are difficulties inherent in the cross-cultural enterprise that limit its usefulness for specifying culture's role in learning and development. Turning from cross-cultural to a "cultural–mediational" approach, I next attempt to offer some theoretical ideas and methodological innovations that, although perhaps not as well developed as the application of computer simulation models to human problem solving, nevertheless represent one form of artificial intelligence and show promise of contributing to psychological understanding in useful ways. In this second line of work, I follow a second strategy suggested by Bill in his writing on cognition and intelligence: analyze intellectual performance for the purpose of "creating more effective educational settings for the development of intelligent behavior" (Estes, 1976, p. 302).

The Cross-Cultural Approach to Development and its Limitations

In the 1970s, when the passages cited from Bill's work were written, my colleagues and I were deeply immersed in empirical studies of the development of memory, problem solving, and categorization among tribal peoples living in remote rural areas of Liberia, West Africa. Two phenomena we observed indicate the force of Bill's remarks about the importance of developmental theory in shaping commonalities and differences in intellectual performance.

From our own experience in the field, as well as from the anthropological literature, we knew that when urban-educated Americans and Europeans go to rural Africa, they often experience difficulty learning to distinguish various plants that are well-known to the local population, including the children. So severe can these difficulties be that native peoples respond with incredulity when European visitors display their woeful lack of discriminative powers (for a particularly vivid example, see Bowen, 1954, p. 15–16). We decided to investigate this problem in a formal experiment (see Cole et al., 1971, for details).

Our subjects were 30 American and Canadian college students and Peace Corps volunteers living at or near the small college that was our base of operations, and 30 nonliterate rice farmers who were residents of the local area. Our materials were 14 leaves, seven from vines, seven from trees, that were indigenous to the area. Subjects from each of the two population groups were assigned haphazardly to one of three experimental conditions. In the first condition the subjects were told that they would be shown leaves that were either from trees or vines and they should say which leaves came from which source. In the second condition they were presented exactly the same set of leaves dichotomized in the same way but they were told that some of the leaves belonged to Sumo and some to Togba (two common local names) and they were to say to which person the leaves belonged. In the third condition, their instructions were the same as in the second condition, except that the leaves were assigned at random to names, so that the local categorization of leaves was irrelevant to the solution of the problem.

TABLE 12.1
Number of Complete Presentations Required to Complete One Correct Identification of All Leaves

	Experimental Condition		
	Tree-Vine Rule	Sumo-Togba Rule	Sumo-Togba Random
Liberians	1.1	7.3	6.8
Amer./Canad.	8.9	9.8	9.0

The data are shown in Table 12.1. Two results stand out. First, on the average, the American/Canadian students required about nine presentations of the set to be able to identify all of the leaves correctly, regardless of the conditions of learning. Second, the rice farmers generally learned more rapidly, but the conditions of learning made an enormous difference. If they were told to identify leaves according to the categories of tree and vine, they performed almost errorlessly from the beginning. However, when asked to identify which items belonged to Sumo or Togba, they performed no better in the case where all the tree leaves belonged to Sumo and all the vine leaves to Togba than when the leaves were assigned at random with respect to category names (although they still performed somewhat better than the American/Canadian group). They completely failed to use a categorical distinction that they certainly knew. (In a follow-up to this study, we actually found cases where American college students were so focused on discovering categories in paired associate lists that they were greatly impeded in learning lists where obvious category members were not paired; whereas, again, the rice farmers were indifferent to latent category structure and hence learned such scrambled lists faster than the American students.)

The second example concerns reasoning about logical syllogisms. In recent years, considerable evidence has been amassed to demonstrate that American college students fail to solve logical syllogisms unless they already possess rich knowledge of the content domain of the problem (D'Andrade, 1990). Still, the typical response of college students (or second graders, as shown by Orasanu & Scribner, 1982) is quite different from that of nonliterate farmers in Liberia, Mexico (Sharp, Cole, & Lave, 1979), or Uzbekistan (Luria, 1976). The following example is typical of data we collected in many locales on many occasions.

Experimenter: . . . Spider and black deer always eat together. Spider is eating. Is black deer eating?
Subject: Were they in the bush?
Experimenter: Yes.
Subject: They were eating together?
Experimenter: Spider and black deer always eat together. Spider is eating. Is black dear eating?
Subject: But I was not there. How can I answer such a question? (Cole et. al, 1971, p. 187)

Several attempts have been made in the past 20 years to understand precisely how the differing developmental histories of the nonliterate farmers produce these very different outcomes (see Laboratory of Comparative Human Cognition, 1983; Segall, Berry, Dasen, & Poortinga, 1990, for relevant reviews). Whereas much has been learned in the course of this empirical work, definitive explanations for such cultural differences remain elusive. Ironically, it is the fact that the subjects in this research have different developmental histories that makes it difficult to reach firm conclusions from the data of cross-cultural research!

This problem is especially clear with respect to a number of studies in which we found that increases in sophistication of cognitive performances as a function of age occurred only if the subjects had attended school. The obvious conclusion is that there is something about schooling that promotes developmental, cognitive change. However, there are at least three reasons to be very cautious about making such causal attributions. First, as with any experiment involving naturally occurring groups, there is the possibility that selection factors are responsible for differential performance. Thus, for example, it might be argued that when schooling is taken as the independent variable differentiating different groups of Liberians from small farming communities, the initially brighter children went to school or stayed in school longer. Such selective effects can be assessed by proper pretesting and on balance the evidence seems to indicate that it really is schooling, and not some selection factor, that leads to improved cognitive performance on a variety of learning tasks; however, in many cases some degree of selection cannot be ruled out (see Rogoff, 1981, and Sharp, Cole, & Lave, 1979, for a discussion of this issue).

Second, as is often the case in cross-cultural work, replications of school/nonschool comparisons in different societies are not completely consistent. Although it is usually found that formal schooling involving the acquisition of literacy and the mastery of large amounts of esoteric information seems to play a major role in improving performance on such syllogistic reasoning problems as children grow older, in some locales, nonliterate people seem to perform similarly to those who have attended school (Das, 1988).

Third, even in cases where schooling does bring about a marked change in performance, there is deep uncertainty about the generality of the mental changes wrought. First, when researchers have varied the contents and procedures of the particular tasks they use, it has often been found that presumably absent or underdeveloped skills reveal themselves (See LCHC, 1983, for a review). Even in cases where modifications of experimental procedures fail to evoke a particular kind of performance (as has generally been the case in syllogistic reasoning studies[1]), the failure of the rice farmers to use categorical structure or expected

---

[1]An exception is to be found in studies of syllogistic reasoning by Scribner and Cole, 1981, where it was shown that by first using problems with fantastical content, nonliterate subjects treated problems involving familiar content in a more theoretical manner.

forms of deductive reasoning almost certainly does not indicate a generalized failure to use categories or deduction as a part of their everyday remembering and problem solving; analysis of such everyday activities virtually demands the conclusion that such processes are in use (a point made with particular clarity by Jahoda, 1982).

The general difficulty in relying on the results derived from experimental paradigms routinely used by psychologists in industrialized countries is that insofar as the learning and problem-solving tasks used to assess cognitive processing derive from the structure and content of schooling, they are really mute with respect to cognitive processes in systems of activity organized for different purposes. The historical linkages between the structure of psychological tests and experimental procedures on the one hand and schooling on the other makes it logically indefensible to use such tasks as the basis of **general** comparisons on the relationship between different life histories and different patterns of intellectual development.

To be sure, we can study the organization of classroom practices to determine how their structure might induce children to accept the premises of a syllogism or to seek out potential categorical structure in an array of stimuli presented for remembering. In such work, the fact that there are fairly detailed models of the processing that generates various patterns of performance is very useful. However interesting and valid, this narrowed focus has the unfortunate property of restricting our analysis of the relationship between developmental history and thinking, the topic we were presumably interested in addressing.

Realization of the limitations of empirical cross-cultural research based on the cognitive–psychological paradigms that I learned to use during and immediately after my graduate career led me and my colleagues to explore a number of alternative ways to get more deeply into the culture–cognition relationship. In addition to increased attempts to ground our experimental work in local practices, we engaged in methodological investigations of the experimental method itself, that, although not without interest, failed to get as deeply into the question of the cultural mechanisms of developmental change as we hoped they would (Cole, Hood, & McDermott, 1979). As a consequence, in the past decade we have shifted our strategy; instead of focusing on cross-cultural variations in the products of developmental history, my colleagues and I began to seek an understanding of the role of culture in the process of developmental change.

This shift from the study of products to processes has led to a substantial change in research strategy. In particular, instead of engaging in cross-cultural research, in which culture is treated as an independent variable in the classic sense, we have sought to understand general mechanisms by means of which culture as a medium constitutes both human learning and development. This approach has led us to focus on children in our own society and on the creation of special learning environments within which to study the processes of change. Following this line of approach led us to another of Bill's prescriptions for progress in the study of intelligent behavior: instead of starting from the study of "differences in performance manifest at a particular time by individuals with varied and unknown learning histories" (1976, p. 303), concentrate on understanding how efficient, intellectual performance can be produced. It has also forced us to consider more deeply what it is we mean by culture, the issue to which I now turn.

Needed: A Psychologically Relevant Conception of Culture

The task of specifying the mechanisms through which culture enters into the process of human development is seriously hampered both because currently dominant theories of development do not consider culture fundamental to the process and because there are severe conceptual disagreements about the nature of culture even among anthropologists, for whom the concept is central. As Super (1987) has noted, these definitions seem to vacillate between two poles. At one end of the spectrum are omnibus characterizations such as E. B. Tylor's early definition of culture as a complex "which includes knowledge, belief, art, morals, law, custom, and any other capabilities and habits acquired by man as a member of society" (1871, p. 1). At the other end of the spectrum are such presumably narrower notions, like "culture is a society's system of shared meanings" (Geertz, 1973). Psychologists who seek "the" correct definition within this set are certain to be disappointed. A well-known monograph by Kroeber and Kluckhohn (1952), for example, offered more than 250 definitions of culture—and the number has certainly grown considerably since that time!

Because appeal to a "generally accepted" (let alone "the correct") definition of culture is almost certainly a hopeless enterprise, I take the alternative tack of adopting a conception of culture that can be considered respectable, if not universally adopted by modern anthropologists, and that affords deeper understanding of the relationship between culture, learning, and development that I am seeking (see Shweder & LeVine, 1984, for an extensive discussion of this issue by anthropologists of varying persuasions, and Lave, 1988, for an anthropologist's view of the shortcomings of both anthropological and psychological approaches to the study of the relation between culture and psychological processes). Moreover, I seek a conception that will allow me to make empirical observations relevant to traditional topics of psychological research. The case in point to be taken up later in this chapter is the topic of reading instruction.

Culture and Artifact Mediation.   For many years, my ideas about the role of culture in development have been influenced by the writings of Soviet psychologists associated with the cultural–historical school of L. S. Vygotsky, A. R. Luria, and A. N. Leontiev (see Cole, 1988, for a summary of my interpretation of this line of thought in relation to earlier cross-cultural work by myself and my colleagues). Central to their formulations (and a good deal of anthropological theorizing) is the notion that human beings are distinct from other creatures in that they live in an environment transformed by the artifacts of prior generations, extending back to the beginning of the species (Ilyenkov, 1977; Geertz, 1973; Sahlins, 1976; Wartofsky, 1979). The basic function of these artifacts is to coordinate human beings with the physical world and each other.[2]

Cultural artifacts are simultaneously ideal (conceptual) and material. They are ideal in that they contain in coded form the interactions of which they were previously a part and that they mediate in the present. They are material in that they exist only insofar as they are embodied in material artifacts. This principle applies with equal force whether one is considering language/speech or the more usually noted forms of artifacts that constitute material culture. Thus, when one first hears someone speak a foreign language, the material aspect of language is easily experienced, but the ideal aspect, the meanings being conveyed, are inaccessible; what gives the artifacts called words their ideality is the shared histories of interaction that they have mediated in the past.

The American anthropologist, Leslie White, expressed this relationship between the ideal and material aspects of artifacts as follows:

> An axe has a subjective component; it would be meaningless without a concept and an attitude. On the other hand, a concept or attitude would be meaningless without overt expression, in behavior or speech (which is a form of behavior). Every cultural element, every cultural trait, therefore, has a subjective and an objective aspect. (1959, p. 236)

The special characteristics of human mental life are precisely those characteristics of an organism that can inhabit, transform, and recreate an artifact-mediated world. As Soviet philosopher Evald Ilyenkov put it, "the world of things created by man for man, and therefore, things whose forms are reified forms of human activity . . . is the condition for the existence of human consciousness" (1977, p. 94). The special nature of this consciousness follows from the dual material/ideal nature of the systems of artifacts that constitute the cultural environment—human beings live in a "double world," simultaneously "natural" and "artificial" (see Luria, 1981, for an exploration of further implications of this view).

The characteristics of human psychological processes that accompany the view that human nature is created in culture-as-historically-accumulated-systems-of-artifacts was described in particularly powerful language by White, who wrote:

> Man differs from the apes, and indeed all other living creatures so far as we know, in that he is capable of symbolic behavior. With words man creates a new world, a

---

[2]Recently Donald Norman has elaborated on the notion of artifacts with a special emphasis on those deliberately created to amplify cognitive functions (Norman, in press).

FIG. 12.1. The basic mediational triangle in which subject
and object are seen not only as
"directly" connected, but simultaneously "indirectly" connected through a medium constituted of artifacts.

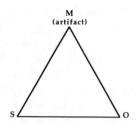

world of ideas and philosophies. In this world man lives just as truly as in the physical world of his senses. . . . This world comes to have a continuity and a permanence that the external world of the senses can never have. It is not made up of the present only but of a past and a future as well. Temporally, it is not a succession of disconnected episodes, but a continuum extending to infinity in both directions, from eternity to eternity. (1942, p. 372)[3]

Several characteristics of human cognition associated with their formation in systems of artifacts that White highlights in this passage are important to the way in which we currently approach the issue of culture and cognition. Most promi-nent, perhaps, is the "dual worlds" implication of symbolic mediation. Less obvious at first, but just as important, is the change in subjective temporality. Both properties will be important in the pages to follow.

Mediation and Indirectness.   The notion that artifact mediation and human symbolic capacities are the source of specifically human forms of cognition is often represented as a triangle, in which the vertex is a mediating artifact and the remaining points are subject and object (see Fig. 12.1). (For an early statement of this perspective containing such a triangle, see Vygotsky, 1929.) In such a representation, the "first" world is conceived of as the "direct" link between subject and object, and the "second" world is given by the indirect pathway through the mediator, the structure of which is continuously being modified by its participation in the patterns forms of activity embodied in culture.[4] Note, as the Soviet cultural–historical theorists emphasized, that mediators (artifacts) enter into the organization of behavior in two ways arising from their concep-

---

[3]Although it would be an error, in view of recent decades of work on protocultural features among primates (Goodall, 1986; Kawamura, 1963; Premack & Premack, 1983; Tomasello, 1989), to over-state the discontinuities between Homo sapiens and other species, I concur with Robert Hinde (1987) in believing that these phenomena do not imply culture in the way in which human beings have culture.

[4]Common usage of the term *mediation* tends to disguise its etymological link to the notion of indirectness. The underlying semantic relations are revealed by noting that a synonym for *direct* is *immediate; indirect* is an antonym for *direct;* the antonym for *immediate* is *mediated.* Hence, the notion of indirectness is inherent in the concept of mediation.

FIG. 12.2. The closed system of Figure 1 is replaced by an open system in which the state of the subject-object relation at time n ($S_n \rightarrow O_n$) must be coordinated with the information in the S_n-M-O_{sm} link of the triangle, out of which emerges the state of the organism at time n + 1 (S_{n+1}).

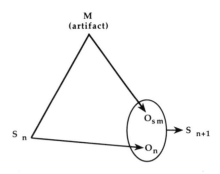

tual/material nature. They act simultaneously as tool and constraint; in coming to master aspects of the world, children come to master themselves (Luria, 1932; Vygotsky, 1978).

Although the static image of a triangle providing both direct and indirect sources of knowledge represents the dual sources of knowledge, it underrepresents the fact that it is only at rare moments that the "culturally" given and the "directly" given coincide completely to determine the "behaviorally taken." Hence, my colleagues and I like to draw the basic mediational triangle, as in Fig. 12.2. This figure emphasizes both the dual nature of culturally mediated activity and the ineluctable discrepancies that exist between competing sources of knowledge requiring a constant, active process of synthesis out of which a new state of knowledge emerges.

Culture as Medium.   This basic triangular schema, although useful as a specification of minimal structural constraints on adult cognition, needs to be supplemented in several ways in elaborating the cultural constitution of development. First of all, it represents adult consciousness, not that of a newborn, and hence we have to understand how it develops. Second, whereas artifact creation and artifact mediation are central to culture, culture is not a random assemblage of such artifacts. As Geertz (1973) put the matter, "It is through culture patterns, ordered clusters of significant symbols, that man makes sense of the events through which he lives" (p. 363).

Hence it is essential to say something about the matter of the structuring of artifacts if one is to elaborate a cultural theory of development. For this purpose, it is helpful to draw upon a notion of culture that is embedded deeply in our own cultural heritage.

As Raymond Williams has remarked, culture is one of the most complex concepts in the English language. Its roots can be traced back through old English to Latin. The core features that coalesce in modern conceptions of culture refer to the process of helping things to grow. "Culture," Williams wrote, "in all of its early uses was a noun of process: the tending of, something, basically crops or animals" (1973, p. 87). Sometime around the 16th century, culture began to refer to the tending of human children, in addition to crops and animals.

From the beginning, the core idea of culture as a process of helping things to grow was combined with a general theory for how to promote growth: create an artificial environment where young organisms could be provided optimal conditions for growth. Such tending required tools, of course, and it is somehow provocative to learn that one of the early meanings of culture was "plowshare."

Although it would be foolish to overinterpret the metaphorical parallels between the theory and practice of growing next generations of crops and next generations of children, the exercise, I argue, has considerable heuristic value. Broadly speaking, gardeners must attend simultaneously to two classes of concerns: what transpires inside the garden and what transpires around it. These issues often seem to be addressable independently of each other, but in reality are interdependent. Inside the garden, for every kind of plant, one must consider the quality of the soil, the best way to till the soil, the kinds of nutrients to use, the right amount of moisture, as well as the best time to plant and nurture the seeds, and the need to protect the growing plants against predators, disease, and so on. Each of these tasks has its own material needs, associated tools, and knowledge. The theory and practice of development at this level focuses on finding exactly the right combination of factors to promote life within the garden walls.

Gardens do not, obviously, exist independently of the larger ecological system within which they are embedded. Although it is possible to raise any plant anywhere in the world, given the opportunity first to arrange the appropriate set of conditions, it is not always possible to create the right conditions, even for a short while. And if what one is interested in is more than a short run demonstration of the possibility of creating a development-promoting system, but rather the creation of conditions that sustain the needed properties of the artificial environment without unsustainable additional labor, then it is as important to attend to the system in which the garden is embedded as the properties of the "garden itself."

Applying the Concept of Culture.   The utility of thinking about culture as a medium constituted of historically cumulated artifacts that are organized to accomplish the maintenance and development of human life must be established by its ability to help us understand the processes of learning and development that occur in our daily lives and form the core of professional concerns among psychologists. In the sections that follow, I offer two examples of the way that I apply this way of thinking about culture and development, one derived from observations made by an eminent pediatrician and one from my own work. The first is selected from a natural observation of a baby being born; I have chosen it because it illustrates the special temporaral properties of culture-as-medium (one of its least understood aspects), in a particularly clear way. The second example is an application of the idea of culture-as-medium to a familiar practical problem in human mediated activity, reading.

Bringing the Future into the Present

One of the great puzzles in the study of development is what controls the sequences of forms and functions that characterize the growing organism over time. As the cells in the zygote begin to multiply, they also begin to take on a variety of forms; we explain the fact that certain cells become bone while others become nervous tissue by invoking the notion that interactions between the cells and their prenatal environment (including other cells) is constrained by a genetic code. Crudely speaking, future forms are (at least potentially) present at birth in the genetic material contained in the zygote (Lewontin, 1982).

An analogous process works at the level of the behavior of whole human organisms, whose behavior is mediated by cultural constraints. Culture is able to "bring the future into the present" because the conceptual/material artifacts that mediate human interactions with the environment enable human beings to project prior successful adaptations into the (imagined) future and then embody them as material constraints in the present. This uniquely human form of development is beautifully illustrated by the work of pediatrician Aiden Macfarlane (1977), who published several transcripts of the reactions of parents when they first catch sight of their newborn child and discover its sex. Typical examples include such comments as "I shall be worried to death when she's 18" or "It can't play rugby" (said of another girl). In each of these examples, the adults interpret the biological characteristics of the child in terms of their own past (cultural) experience. In the experience of English men and women living in the mid20th century it could be considered "common knowledge" that girls do not play rugby and that when they enter adolescence they will be the object of boys' sexual attention, putting them at various kinds of risk. Using this information derived from their cultural past and assuming that the world will be very much for their daughter as it has been for them, they project a probable future for the child (recall White's notion of culture providing continuity from "infinity to infinity"): She will be sought after by males as a sexual partner causing them anxiety; she will not participate in a form of activity (rugby) requiring strength and agility that is the special preserve of males, and so on.

Of crucial importance to understanding the contribution of culture in constituting development is the fact that the parents' projection of their children's future becomes a fundamentally important cultural constraint organizing the child's life experiences **in the present,** because, as copious research has demonstrated, even adults totally ignorant of the real gender of a newborn will treat it quite differently depending upon its symbolic/cultural "gender." Adults confronted with babies in blue or pink diapers (assigned at random with respect to sex) literally create different material forms of interaction based on conceptions of the world

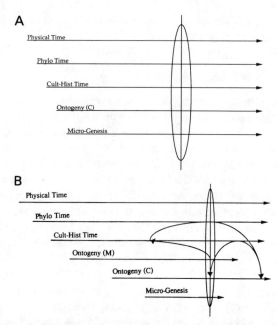

FIG. 12.3. (a) Different time scales simultaneously operative in the organization of human development. The ellipse indicates the context of the birth of a child. (b) Different time scales with ontogeny of the mother added and arrows indicating the cultural origins and social organization of the child's context at birth. The entire cycle from past to future and back to the present is needed to understand cultural constraints on development.

provided by their cultural experience. For example, they bounce "boy" infants (those wearing blue diapers) and attribute "manly" virtues to them, while they treat "girl" infants (those wearing pink diapers) in a gentle manner and attribute "feminine" attributes to them (Rubin, Provezano, & Luria, 1974).

Macfarlane's simple example also demonstrates an important distinction between the social and the cultural, which are conflated in traditional theories of development. It also motivates the special emphasis placed on the social origins of higher psychological functions by cultural psychologists (Cole, 1988; Rogoff, 1989; Vygotsky, 1978; Wertsch, 1985). These points are best illustrated by referring to Figs. 12.3a and 12.3b.

Figure 12.3a presents five time lines, the bottom four of which correspond to the three "developmental domains" (Wertsch, 1985) that, according to the cultural framework espoused here, simultaneously serve as major constraints for human development. At the top of the figure is what might be called "physical time," or the history of the universe that long precedes the appearance of life on earth. The second line represents phylogenetic time, the history of life on earth.

The third represents cultural–historical time, which co-evolved with phylogenetic time. The fourth line represents ontogeny, the history of a single human being, and the fifth line represents the moment-to-moment time of lived human experience. The ellipse transecting these lines represents the events surrounding the baby in Macfarlane's observations. Four kinds of genesis: phylogenesis, culturogenesis, ontogenesis, and microgenesis, each "lower" level embedded in the level "above it." What Macfarlane's example forces upon is the need to keep in mind that not one but **two** ontogenies must be represented in place of the single ontogeny in Fig. 12.3a. That is, at a minimum one needs a mother and a child for the process of birth to occur and for development to proceed. These two ontogenies are coordinated in time by the simultaneous structuration provided by phylogeny and culture (Fig. 12.3b).

As Macfarlane's transcripts clearly demonstrate, human nature is social in a sense different from the sociability of other species because only a culture-using human being can "reach into" the cultural past, project that remembered past imaginatively into the future, and then "carry" that (purely conceptual) future "back" into the present in the shape of beliefs, which then constrain and organize the present sociocultural environment of the newcomer.

Remediating Reading Failure[5]

It is a very large jump indeed from the birth of a baby to the initiation of a process called "learning to read." However, I suggest that many of the same mechanisms involved when parents create a future in the present for the newborn can be invoked as a way of understanding and guiding the process of learning to read. For example, the adults who arrange the environments of reading, like the mother with her newborn, arrange the current circumstances of the child in terms of expectations about the child's future. They also, of course, draw on their own culturally organized prior experience in deciding how to behave.

In moving from observation of an event organized by medical practices to an experimental intervention organized specifically to promote a particular kind of cognitive development, we are adopting the strategy of creating change, which was one of Bill's prescriptions for making progress in the understanding of intellectual development in his 1976 paper. In doing so, I self-consciously emphasize the way in which we make use of the garden metaphor in arranging the environment for growth of the children's reading ability, and I also make the (perhaps outrageous) suggestion, that our procedures are a form of artificial intelligence. The relevance of the garden metaphor becomes clearer as the exposition proceeds. But a few words are in order about the notion of artificial.

---

[5]Owing to a variety of circumstances, a full report of this work has only appeared in Russian. It appears in *A Socio-Historical Approach to Learning and Instruction,* Moscow: Pedadogika Publishers, 1989, in the article by Peg Griffin, Esteban Diaz, Catherine King, and Michael Cole entitled, "Remediating learning difficulties."

In his classic discussion of sciences of the artificial, Herbert Simon (1969) gives four criteria that distinguish the artificial from the natural, providing boundaries on the sciences of the artificial:

1. Artificial things are synthesized.
2. Artificial things may imitate appearances in natural things while lacking, in one or many respects, the reality of the latter.
3. Artificial things can be characterized in terms of functions, goals adaptation.
4. Artificial things are often discussed, particularly when they are being designed, in terms of imperatives as well as descriptives. (p. 5–6)

In the work to be described here, the artificial thing in question is a somewhat unusual form of group reading activity called "Question Asking Reading." It is synthesized out of a variety of elements, it involves imitation of mature forms of reading by children who are often lacking aspects of the behavior it is modeled on, it is clearly intended to be goal oriented in several respects, and there are strong imperatives associated with it. The subjects are children for whom the usual instructional process (guided by theories of learning and development that are not consistent with the notion of culture that I have been promoting) has failed. They have been attending school for 3 or more years and have failed to learn to read, although most of them have developed some skill at providing oral versions of written words. This failure is sufficient to have them classified as learning or reading disabled and to induce their teachers to send them to our special afterschool activities in the hopes that we can remedy a situation they see as bad for the child.

Theories of Reading Acquisition

There is broad agreement that reading is "a complex skill requiring the coordination of a number of interrelated sources of information" (Anderson, Hiebert, Scott, & Wilkinson, 1985), and a great deal is known about the processes involved for those who have acquired some degree of skill. But despite intensive research efforts throughout this century, and especially over the past two decades, the process of acquisition remains disputed (see Foorman & Siegel, 1986, for a juxtaposition of conflicting views). The problem is an important one because at present a great many children of normal intelligence fail to acquire reading skills deemed adequate for productive participation in modern societies (Miller, 1988).

Despite significant differences among them, modern approaches to reading have distinguished two, presumably distinct, major components of the reading process: Decoding (the process by which letters of the alphabet are associated with corresponding acoustic patterns) and comprehension (the process by which meaning is assigned to resulting visual/acoustic representation). Within this seemingly obvious dichotomy, theorists differ on the question of how to sequence instruction (code emphasis first vs. meaning emphasis first) and how best to help children "break the code" (by teaching phonetic analysis or by teaching whole words) (Chall, 1967).

An example of the "code emphasis first" approach can be found in the work of Jean Chall (1983) who proposes the following stage theory of reading development (I concentrate here on the early stages).

Stage 0: Prereading. Children at this stage may pretend to read and know some letter names.

Stage 1: Decoding. The basic task of Stage 1 is to learn the arbitrary set of letters in the alphabet and to decode their correspondence to the sounds of spoken language.

Stage 2: Confirmation, fluency, ungluing from print. New readers confirm and solidify the gains of the previous stage. To avoid confusion, they are given familiar texts that do not demand much mental effort to comprehend.

Stage 3: Reading for learning something new. Instead of relating print to speech, children now are asked to relate print to ideas. It is only at this stage, writes Chall, that "reading begins to compete with other means of knowing." (p. 21)

In the two remaining stages, children elaborate their comprehension skills, learning to juxtapose facts and theories, and to construct complex ideas with the help of print.

Goodman and Goodman (1979) start from the assumption that children living in a literate society arrive at school with the rudiments of reading-as-comprehending-the-world-through-print already in their repertoires; for example, children can read various road signs, pick out the MacDonald's sign, and perhaps recognize their own names in print. Their model of acquisition is nondevelopmental in the sense that acquisition does not entail the emergence of any new process or the reorganization of old ones. All they need to do from the beginning is to expand the repertoire of functions that they can accomplish with the aid of print. This expansion process occurs naturally with the accretion of experiences in comprehending the world through print. Consequently, mastery of the code goes hand in hand with expanding the functions to which reading is put.

A Cultural-Mediational Model

Like Chall, we believe that reading is a developmental process and that the goal of reading instruction is to provide means for children to reorganize their interpretive activity using print. Like the Goodmans, we believe that reading text is an elaboration of the preexisting ability to "read the world" using signs of various kinds. Our own approach is distinctive in its simultaneous emphasis on three, interrelated points. First, we believe that reading instruction must emphasize both decoding and comprehension in a single, integrated activity (an assumption that can be interpreted in terms of the idea that reading requires the coordination of "bottom up" (feature → letter → word → phrase → ....) and "top down" (knowledge-based, comprehension-driven processes out of which new schemas emerge [McClelland & Rumelhart, 1981]).

Second, we believe that under ordinary circumstances, adults play an essential role in coordinating children's activity such that the development of reading becomes possible. Third, we believe that successful adult efforts depend crucially on their organizing a "cultural medium for reading" that has the properties of culture that I have been emphasizing here: It must use artifacts (most notably, but not only, the text) and orchestrated social relations to coordinate the child with the to-be-acquired system of mediation in just the right way to make possible the desired developmental achievement.

As a starting point for our analysis, we begin by modifying slightly the common sense definition of reading. Reading, in a cultural–psychological perspective, is the process of expanding the ability to mediate one's interactions with the environment by interpreting print. There are two significant aspects of this definition. First, learning to read and proficient reading are both subsumed in the same definition. What one learns to do is expand; what one does, having learned, is to continue expanding (see Engeström, 1987, for a general discussion of "learning by expanding"). Second, there is no dichotomy between decoding and comprehension as comprehension is understood as the process of mediating one's interactions with the environment, including text processing (interpreting letter groups) as a condition.

Figure 12.4, which repeats the structure of Fig. 12.1, but with Text substituted for artifact, reminds us that reading, in the broadest sense, requires the coordination of information from "two routes." Any reader must "see" the world as refracted through a text; but in order to do so, the reader's more direct access to the world, topicalized by the text, must be simultaneously engaged. As was true in the case of the general discussion of mediation earlier in this chapter, the mediational process depicted in Fig. 12.4 is a timeless ideal. Even among skilled readers, the act of coordinating the two routes may require adjustments in the representation of the "worlds" arrived at by either route to permit a new repre-

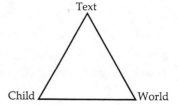

FIG. 12.4.   Figure 1 with "text" substituted for "artifact."

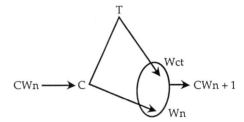

FIG. 12.5. Figure 2 with "text"
substituted for "artifact."

sentation (expanded understanding) to emerge. The slight discoordination depicted in Fig. 12.5 (a specialized version of Fig. 12.2) more accurately reflects the dynamic process that we have in mind.

With this minimal structural apparatus in hand, we can now turn to the crucial question: Assuming that children do not enter school already able to read, that is, expand their ability to comprehend by reading alphabetic text, how can we arrange for them to develop this ability? In attempting to answer this question, we simultaneously tackle the crucial question of how it is possible to acquire a more powerful cognitive structure unless, in some sense, it is already present to begin with. This question, called the "paradox of development" by Fodor (1983) and the "learning paradox" by Bereiter (1985), calls into doubt any developmental account of reading that fails to specify the preexisting constraints that make development possible. Bringing the endpoint "forward" to the beginning is not less relevant in developing the ability to read than in any other developmental process.

From our perspective, developmental theories of reading such as Chall's are vulnerable to the learning paradox. Because we share with her a belief that the acquisition of reading is a developmental process requiring a qualitative reorganization of behavior, we must begin by showing in what sense the endpoint of development, the ability to mediate one's comprehension of the world through print, could in principle be shown to be present in embryonic form at the outset of instruction. The solution to this problem, following the principles of cultural psychology, is to invoke Vygotsky's (1978) "general genetic law of cultural development": functions that initially appear on the interpsychological plane shared between people can then become intrapsychological functions of the individual. In this case, what we seek is the structural endpoint of mature reading in the interaction between child and adult as a precondition for this new structure of activity to appear as an individual psychological function in the child.

Figure 12.6 displays in graphic form the fact that at the beginning of instruction there are two preexisting mediational systems that can be used as resources for creating the necessary structural constraints to permit the development of reading in the child. At the far left of the figure we represent the common sense fact that children enter reading instruction with years of experience mediating their interactions through the world via adults. In the center we represent the

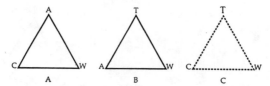

FIG. 12.6.   Three systems of mediation present at the start of instruction. (a) The child already knows how to mediate interaction with the world through an adult. (b) The adult already knows how to mediate interaction with the world through text. (c) The to-be-constructed system of mediation.

equally common sense fact that literate adults routinely mediate their interactions through text. Finally, on the far right of the figure is the to-be-developed system of mediation that is our target.

Figure 12.7 shows the next stage in the analytic/instructional strategy: The given and to-be-developed systems of child mediations are juxtaposed and the given adult system is then superimposed, to show or reveal the skeletal structure of an "interpsychological" system of mediation that, indirectly, establishes dual system of mediation for the child, which permits the coordination of text-based and prior-world-knowledge-based information of the kind involved in the whole act of reading.

Creating the Medium

The instructional/developmental task is now better specified: We must somehow create a system of interpersonal interaction such that the combined child–adult system at the right of Fig. 12.7 can coordinate the child's act of reading before the child can accomplish this activity for him/herself. Our strategy for accomplishing this goal was a modification of the reciprocal teaching procedure of Palinscar and Brown (1984), in which teacher and student silently read a passage

FIG. 12.7.   Juxtaposing the already-existing and to-be-constructed systems of mediation. (a) The child-text-world (to be constructed) system is juxtaposed with the already-existing child-adult-world system. (b) The adult-text-world system is added, to put in juxtaposition all three systems in need of coordination.

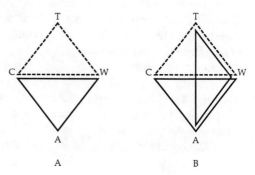

of text and then engage in a dialogue about it that includes summarizing the text, clarifying comprehension problems that arise, asking a question about the main idea, and predicting the next part of the text. For a number of reasons (see LCHC, 1982, for additional details), our modification of reciprocal teaching was instantiated as a small group reading activity with third to sixth grade children identified by their teachers as experiencing extraordinary difficulties learning to read.

The core elements of the procedure is a set of roles, each corresponding to a different hypothetical part of the whole act of reading, and each printed on 3 × 5 index cards. Every participant is responsible for fulfilling at least one role in the full activity of Question-Asking-Reading. These cards specify the following roles:

- The person who asks about words that are hard to say.
- The person who asks about words that are hard to understand.
- The person who picks the person to answer questions asked by others.
- The person who asks a question about the main idea.
- The person who asks about what is going to happen next.

All participants including the instructor had a copy of the text to read, paper and pencil to jot down words, phrases or notes (in order to answer questions implicit in the roles), and the card to remind them of their role. In light of the general principles of cultural psychology, we consider the role cards and the script within which they were sequenced to be cultural artifacts that could be used by the adults to create a structured medium for the development of reading. In order to move from the script to an appropriate medium of development, the procedural script was embedded in a more complex activity structure designed to make salient both the short-term and long-term goals of reading and to provide a means of coordinating around the script. It is in this embedding process that we make the transition from a focus on the structural model of reading depicted in Figs. 12.5 to 12.7 to focus on the necessary transformation of the mediational structure of the child's interactions with print.

Recognizing the need to create a medium rich in goals that could be resources for organizing the transition from reading as a guided activity to independent, voluntary reading, we saturated the environment with talk and activities about growing up and the role of reading in a grown-up's life. This entire activity was conducted after school in a global activity structure we called "Field Growing Up College" (it took place in the auditorium of the Field Elementary School). As part of their application to participate in Field College, of which Question-Asking-Reading was a major activity, the children filled out applications that emphasized the relationship between reading and growing up. They got involved with us in discussions about the difference between growing older and growing up as well as how our activities related to their goal of growing up.

As shown in Fig. 12.8, Question-Asking-Reading began each session with

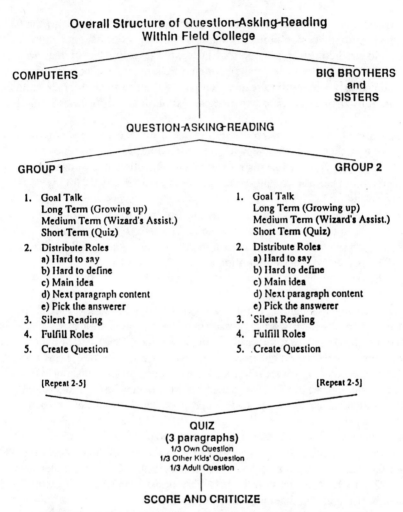

FIG. 12.8. The overall structure of Question-Asking-Reading within the afterschool activity called Field College. (The Computer and Big Brother and Sister elements are not further specified here.) The sequence of activities for the two reading groups is further described in the text.

such "goal talk," discussion about the various reasons that children might have for wanting to learn to read. These included such poorly understood reasons (from the children's point of view) as the need to read in order to obtain an attractive job such as becoming an astronaut, intermediate-level goals such as graduating from Question-Asking-Reading to assist adults with computer-based instruction, to quite proximate goals—the desirability of getting correct answers on the quiz that came at the end of each reading session.

Joint work with the text began with a group discussion of the title or headline of the story to be read that day. Then, following the script outline written in Fig. 12.8, which was written on the blackboard, the role-bearing cards and the first paragraph of the text were passed around. A good deal of discussion usually ensued about who had gotten what roles; "pick the answerer" was an obvious favorite, whereas the card implicating the main idea was avoided like the plague. Once the role cards were distributed, the text for the day (usually taken from local newspapers with content that related to matters of potential interest to the children) was distributed, one paragraph at a time. The participants (including the instructor and one competent reader, usually a University of California, San Diego undergraduate, and the children) then bent over their passages to engage in silent reading.

These and other procedural arrangements constituted our attempt to organize a medium that would repeatedly create moments when the three mediational triangles depicted in Fig. 12.7 would be coordinated to create the conditions for "re"-mediating the children's entering systems of mediation.

The Data

Our evidence for the way in which this procedure worked is derived from several sources: videotaped recordings of the instructional sessions, the children's written work on the quizzes that completed each session, and various test results. Here we concentrate on the **in situ** process of coordination and discoordination around the scripted activity as a key source of evidence about individual children's ability to internalize the scripted roles and the points where internalization fails, resulting in selective discoordinations of the ongoing activity structure. In this example, two children, both of whom are failing in their reading classes, differentially discoordinate with the publicly available scripted activity, permitting differential diagnosis of their specific difficulties.

In the transcripts that follow, the two boys, Billy and Armandito, are starting to read the second paragraph of the day. Katie is their teacher and Larry is an additional competent reader.

Evidence for internalization of the scripted activity is provided by instances in which the children's talk and actions presuppose a next step in the procedure with no overt provocation from the adults. For example:

1. Katie: OK, lets go on to the second paragraph then.
2. Billy: How did they find them?
3. Armandito: The Eskimos.
4. Katie: I think it was an accident (as she says this, she begins to pass out the role cards, face down).
5 Billy: (Taking a card from the stack). How come, what kind of accident?
6. Billy: (looking at his card). That's the same card again.

In (2), Billy's question is an internalized version of the "what's going to happen next" role in the script that no one specifically stimulated. He takes the card handed to him, asks a relevant question about the text, and comments on the relationship between his role in the previous segment of interaction and its relationship to what he is about to do. Armandito's participation is of a different order. His comment ("The Eskimos") is relevant to the topic at hand, but opaque. He does not take one of the role cards and has to be stimulated by Katie while Billy continues to show evidence of coordination:

6. Katie: Armandito! (He looks up and takes a card)
7. Billy: We each get another one (referring to the cards; there are only four participants and Katie has not taken one, so someone will get an extra).

In a number of places in the transcript we see Armandito discoordinating within the activity that the other three participants maintain, permitting him to recoordinate from time to time. These discoordinations are of several types. The most obvious are such actions as drawing a picture instead of reading, or feigning abandonment of the activity altogether. But repeatedly, Armandito presupposes the scripted activity sufficiently to motivate quite specific analyses of his difficulties. The next example illustrates his aversion to the question about the main idea and provides information (corroborated in many examples) of his core difficulty.

8. Larry: (He has the card which says to pick the answerer.) Armandito. What's the main idea?
9. Armandito: I want to ask mine. I want to ask what happens next.
10. Larry: No. I know what you want, but I am asking. I pick the answerer.
11. Armandito: The main idea is . . . how these guys live.

Armandito is both accepting the joint task of Question-Asking-Reading ("I want to ask mine") and attempting to avoid the role that is at the heart of his problem (figuring out the main idea) by skipping that part of the scripted sequence. When Armandito accepts his role (11) and attempts to state the main idea, his answer ("The main idea is . . . how these guys live") is not only vague, it is about the **previous** paragraph.

Through an accumulation of many such examples over several sessions, we were able to obtain a consistent pattern. This pattern showed that Billy experienced great difficulty in coming "unglued" from the letter–sound correspondences when he attempted to arrive at the main idea. When asked about the main idea, he repeatedly returned to the text and sought a "copy match" in which some word from the question appeared in the text. He then read the relevant sentence aloud, and puzzled over meaning. Armandito's problem was of a quite different order: he continually lost track of the relevant context, importing information from his classroom activities that day or previous reading passages that had no relevance.

The first conclusion that we draw from this exercise is that we were in fact successful in creating a structured medium of activity that allowed diagnostically useful information about which part of the structure depicted in Fig. 12.7 was deficient in the children with whom we worked. However, we also wanted to establish that the Question-Asking-Reading procedure is an effective procedure for the acquisition of reading. Both Billy and Armandito did in fact improve their reading abilities and Armandito's general behavior in the classroom changed so markedly that he won an award from the school recognizing his unusual progress. However, such individual change could not be attributed to question asking reading, both because it was part of the larger activity system of Field College and because we had no proper control group.

To remedy these shortcomings, King (1988) replicated the small group reading procedures in a follow-up experiment that included appropriate control conditions, more stringently quantified pre- and post-test measures, and was conducted as the sole activity in a school prior to the start of regular classes.

In addition to testing the effectiveness of Question-Asking-Reading against a no-treatment control group, King included a group of children who were provided the kind of structured intervention that Scardamalia and Bereiter (1985) call "procedural facilitation" to assess whether the dynamic, dialogic characteristics of Question-Asking-Reading were any more effective than workbook exercises in which children completed each of the tasks corresponding to the role cards individually in written form. The children in this experiment, like those in the original work illustrated in the transcript fragment, were selected from the upper elementary grades owing to their difficulties in learning to read.

King found that both Question-Asking-Reading and her version of the procedural facilitation technique boosted children's reading performance. However, children in the Question-Asking-Reading group retained significantly more material from the training passages than did the students in the Procedural Facilitation group. The students in the Question-Asking-Reading group also spent more total time actively engaged with the task and demonstrated a greater interest in the content of the readings, indicating an intimate link between the motivational, social-interactional, and cognitive aspects of activity-in-context.

These results, although sketchily presented here owing to limitations on space, provide support for the approach to reading we have developed in this chapter. Reading, we can conclude, is an emergent process of meaning making that occurs when information topicalized by the text is synthesized with prior knowledge as part of a general process of mediated interaction with the world. Moreover, it is useful to conceive of the process of acquisition as developmental in nature. Where this process differs from other developmental approaches to reading acquisition is in its emphasis on the special role of the teacher in arranging the medium that coordinates preexisting systems of mediation in a single system of activity subordinated to the goal of comprehension.

Some Concluding Remarks

In this chapter I have attempted to sketch the evolution of a research program that was linked at its outset to Bill Estes' suggestion that attention be paid to the way that the occurrence and sequencing of various experiences in ontogeny operate as prerequisites to the development of intellectual performance. Starting out with theoretical tools and methods derived from mid20th-century American learning theories, it was not long before we discovered the truth of Bill's admonition that simple hard work applying existing theories and methods might well prove inadequate to promoting continued progress of scientific understanding. The very fact that Liberian rice farmers undergo such a different course of experience than (say) American office workers, offers very serious methodological barriers to the use of the familiar apparatus of American experimental psychology.

Turning to a second strategy recommended by Bill, I then described a mode of research that begins with a conceptual examination of the phenomenon called *culture* and focuses directly on promoting the development of desired forms of behavior. This new strategy highlights a property of cultural mediation that is generally absent from the models of learning that dominated my thinking in the 1960s and 1970s: cultural mediation is a mechanism through which potential future child experiences (such as a newborn playing rugby 18 years hence) are embodied in the present, converting what appear to be purely ideal/conceptual beliefs into material/interactional constraints that shape development in ways appropriate to that "imagined" future.

The practical significance of this property of cultural mediation was then explored in a study of how to organize for children who have failed to learn how to read to acquire this ability so important to life in modern American society. The crux of the methodology I proposed was to create a system of "artificial intelligence" structured so that the to-be-acquired form of mediation, "reading with comprehension," existed as a coordinated group activity that nonreading children could participate in before they were competent to read on their own. In learning to coordinate within this artificial system, the children both revealed unique patterns of misunderstanding to the their adult teachers and were placed in circumstances where they could reinvent the desired, new system of mediation.

Perhaps some day my colleagues who are simulating such complex processes as reading for comprehension using such notions as back propagation and the interaction of parallel distributed processing systems will advance to the point where they can model in mathematical form the complex interactions that have come to be the focus of my attention in recent years. Until such a time, I continue to hope that there will be sufficient interaction among researchers pursuing different strategies to provide a rich environment for the promotion of progress on the scientific problems that have occupied Bill Estes during his long and distinguished career in science.

ACKNOWLEDGMENTS

This manuscript was completed while the author was a Fellow at the Center for Advanced Study in the Behavioral Sciences, Stanford, California. Support for my stay at the Center from the Spencer Foundation is gratefully acknowledged.

REFERENCES

Anderson, R. C., Hiebert, E. H., Scott, J. A., & Wilkonson, I. A. G. (1985). *Becoming a nation of readers*. Washington, DC: National Institute of Education.

Bereiter, C. (1985). Toward a solution of the learning paradox. *Review of Educational Research, 55*(2), 201–226.

Bowen, E. (1954). *Return to laughter*. New York: Doubleday.

Chall, J. S. (1979). The great debate: Ten years later, with a modest proposal for reading stages. In L. B. Resnick & P. A. Weaver, *Theory and practice of early reading* (pp. 29–56). Hillsdale, NJ: Lawrence Erlbaum Associates.

Chall, J. S. (1983). *Stages of reading development* (p. 21). New York: McGraw-Hill.

Cole, M. (1988). Cross-cultural research in the socio-historical tradition. *Human Development, 31*, 137–157.

Cole, M. (1990). Cultural psychology: A once and future discipline? In J. Berman (Ed.), Nebraska symposium on motivation: cross-cultural perspectives. Lincoln: University of Nebraska Press.

Cole, M., & Cole, S. R. (1989). The development of children. New York: Scientific American Books.

Cole, M., Hood, L., & McDermott, R. P. (1978). Concepts of ecological validity: Their differing implications for comparative cognitive research. *The Quarterly Newsletter of the Laboratory of Comparative Human Cognition, 2*(2), 34–37.

Cole, M., Gay, J., Glick, J. A., & Sharp, D. W. (1971). *The cultural context of learning and thinking*. New York: Basic Books.

Cole, M., & Scribner, S. (1974). *Culture and thought*. New York: Wiley.

D'Andrade, R. (1990). Culture and cognition. In J. W. Stigler, R. A. Shweder, & G. Herdt (Eds.), *Cultural psychology: Essays on comparative human development* (pp. 65–129). New York: Cambridge University Press.

Das, J. P. (1988). Coding, attention, and planning: A cap for every head. In J. W. Berry, S. H. Irvine, & E. B. Hunt (Eds.), *Indigenous cognition: Functioning in cultural context* (pp. 39–56). Dordrecht: Martinus Nijhoff.

Engeström, Y. (1987). *Learning by expanding*. Helsinki: Orienta-Konsulttit Oy.

Estes, W. K. (1970). *Learning theory and mental development*. New York: Academic Press.

Estes, W. K. (1976). Intelligence and cognitive psychology. In L. B. Resnick (Ed.), *The nature of intelligence* (pp. 295–306). Hillsdale, NJ: Lawrence Earlbaum Associates.

Fodor, J. (1983). *The modularity of mind*. Cambridge, MA: MIT Press.

Foorman, B. R., & Siegel, A. W. (Eds.). (1986). *Acquisition of reading skills: Cultural constraints and cognitive universals*. Hillsdale, NJ: Lawrence Erlbaum Associates.

Geertz, C. (1973). *The interpretation of culture*. New York. Basic Books.

Goodall, J. (1986). *The chimpanzees of Gombe: Patterns of behavior*. Cambridge: Harvard University Press.

Goodman, K. S., & Goodman, Y. M. (1979). Learning to read is natural. In L. B. Resnick & P. A. Weaver (Eds.), *The theory and practice of early reading* (pp. 137–154). (Vol. 1). Hillsdale, NJ: Lawrence Earlbaum Associates.

Goodnow, J. (1976). The nature of intelligent behavior: Questions raised by cross cultural study. In L. Resnick (Ed.), *The nature of intelligence* (pp. 167–188). Hillsdale,

Hinde, R. (1987). *Individuals, relationships, and culture.* Cambridge: Cambridge University Press.

Ilyenkov, E. V. (1977). The concept of the ideal. *Philosophy in the USSR: Problems of dialectical materialism.* Moscow: Progress.

Jahoda, G. (1982). *Psychology and anthropology.* London: Academic Press.

Kawamura, S. (1963). The process of sub-culture propagation among Japanese macaques. In C. H. Southwick (Ed.), *Primate social behavior* (pp. 82–90). New York: Van Nostrand.

King, C. (1988). *The social facilitation of reading comprehension.* Unpublished doctoral dissertation, University of California, San Diego.

Kroeber, A. L., & C. Kluckhohn. (1952). *Culture: A critical review of concepts and definitions. Papers of the Peabody Museum of American Archeology and Ethnology* (Vol. 47, No. 1). Cambridge, MA: Harvard University.

Laboratory of Comparative Human Cognition, (LCHC). A model system for the study of learning difficulties. *The Quarterly Newsletter of the Laboratory of Comparative Human Cognition, 4*(3), 39–66, (Special Issue).

Laboratory of Comparative Human Cognition, (LCHC). (1983). Culture and cognitive development. In P. H. Mussen, (Ed.), W. Kessen (Vol. Ed.), *Handbook of child development, Vol. 1,* pp. 295–356. New York: Wiley.

Lave, J. (1988). *Cognition in practice.* New York: Cambridge University Press.

Lewontin, R. (1982). *Human diversity.* New York: Scientific American Books.

Luria, A. R. (1932). *The nature of human conflicts.* New York: Liveright.

Luria, A. R. (1976). *Cognitive development.* Cambridge, MA: Harvard University Press.

Luria, A. R. (1981). *Language and cognition,* J. V. Wertsch (Ed.). New York: Wiley.

Macfarlane, A. (1977). *The psychology of childbirth.* Cambridge: Harvard University Press.

McClelland, J. L., & Rumelhart, D. E. (1981). An interactive activation model of context effects in letter perception: Part 1. An account of basic findings. *Psychological Review, 88*(5), 375–407.

Miller, G. A. (1988). The challenge of universal literacy. *Science, 241,* 1293–1298.

Norman, D. (in press). Cognitive artifacts. In J. Carroll (Ed.). *Designing instruction: Psychology at the human-computer interface.* New York: Cambridge University Press.

Orasanu, J., & Scribner, S. (1982). The development of verbal reasoning: Pragmatic, schematic, and operational aspects. In W. Frawley (Ed.), *Linguistics and literacy* (pp. 285–313) New York: Plenum.

Palinscar, A. S., & Brown, A. L. (1984). Reciprocal teaching of comprehension-fostering and monitoring activities. *Cognition and Instruction, 1,* 117–175.

Premack, D., & Premack, A. J. (1983). *The mind of an ape.* New York: Norton.

Rogoff, B. (1981). Schooling and the development of cognitive skills. In H. C. Triandis & A. Heron (Eds.), *Handbook of cross-cultural psychology* (Vol. 4, pp. 233–294). Boston: Allyn & Bacon.

Rogoff, B. (1989). *Apprenticeship in learning.* New York: Cambridge University Press.

Rubin, J. Z., Provezano, F. J., & Luria, Z. (1974). The eye of the beholder: Parents' view on sex of newborns. *American Journal of Orthopsychiatry, 44,* 512–519.

Sahlins, M. (1976). *Culture and practical reason.* Chicago: University of Chicago Press.

Scribner, S., & Cole, M. (1981). *The psychology of literacy.* Cambridge, MA: Harvard University Press.

Segall, M. H., Dasen, P. R., Berry, J. W., & Poorting, Y. (1990). *Human behavior in global perspective: An introduction to cross-cultural psychology.* Pergamon General Psychology Series, 160. New York: Pergamon Press.

Sharp, D. W., Cole, M., & Lave, J. (1979). Education and cognitive development: The evidence from experimental research. *Monographs of the Society for Research in Child Development, 44* (1–2, Serial No. 178).

Shweder, R. A., & LeVine, R. A. (1984). *Culture theory: Essays on mind, self, and emotion*. New York: Cambridge University Press.

Simon, H. (1969). *The sciences of the artificial*. Cambridge, MA: MIT Press.

Super, C. M. (Ed.). (1987). *The role of culture in developmental disorder*. New York: Academic Press.

Tomasello, M. (1989, Winter). Chimpanzee culture. *SRCD Newsletter*, pp. 1–3.

Tylor, E. B. (1871). *Primitive culture: Researches into the development of mythology, philosophy, religion, art, and customs* (2 vols.). London: John Murray.

Vygtosky, L. S. (1929). The problem of the cultural development of the child, II. *Journal of Genetic Psychology, 36*, 414–434.

Vygotsky, L. S. (1978). *Mind in society*. Cambridge, MA: Harvard University Press.

Wartofsky, M. (1979). *Models: Representation and scientific understanding*. Dordrecht: D. Reidel.

Wertsch, J. (1985). *The social formation of mind*. Cambridge MA: Harvard University Press.

White, L. (1942). On the use of tools by primates. *Journal of Comparative Psychology, 34*, 369–374.

Williams, R. (1973). *Keywords*. New York: Oxford University Press.

Author Index

Subject Index